EXPRESSION IN POP-ROCK MUSIC

CRITICAL AND ANALYTICAL ESSAYS

SECOND EDITION

EDITED BY
WALTER EVERETT
University of Michigan

Routledge
Taylor & Francis Group
New York London

Routledge
Taylor & Francis Group
270 Madison Avenue
New York, NY 10016

Routledge
Taylor & Francis Group
2 Park Square
Milton Park, Abingdon
Oxon OX14 4RN

Routledge is an imprint of Taylor & Francis Group, an Informa business

Printed in the United States of America on acid-free paper
10 9 8 7 6 5 4 3 2 1

International Standard Book Number-13: 978-0-415-97959-7 (Softcover) 978-0-415-97958-0 (0)

Library of Congress Cataloging-in-Publication Data

Expression in pop-rock music : critical and analytical essays / edited by Walter Everett.
-- 2nd ed.
p. cm.
ISBN 978-0-415-97958-0 -- ISBN 978-0-415-97959-7
1. Rock music--History and criticism. 2. Rock music--Analysis, appreciation. 3. Musical criticism. 4. Musical analysis. I. Everett, Walter, 1954-

ML3534.E985 2008
781.66--dc22 2007015175

Visit the Taylor & Francis Web site at
http://www.taylorandfrancis.com

and the Routledge Web site at
http://www.routledge.com

Contents

Preface

Collected here are thirteen essays by leading scholars in pop and rock music, including three new chapters written for this expanded edition, all devoted to an understanding of how the most popular music of the second half of the twentieth century expresses itself, whether its central thrust be social, political, cultural, stylistic, or personal. We have sought to bring to the table a multiplicity of issues, a mix of various techniques and perspectives, and (as affirmed by a glance through the index) the representation of a great variety of styles from all periods of pop-rock history. The authors relate to various interests of the reader in different and complementary ways. Some combine a number of analytical and/or historiographical methods in the process of understanding how a single piece works, while others draw from a larger number of examples from the repertoire to illustrate how a given technique might be useful. Some concentrate on drawing out the listener's imagination, while others appeal more directly to the listener's sense of craft. Some focus on the new presentation of original methodology, while others address an existing dialogue that has been rapidly growing through new branches of musicology and music theory. But one common thread weaves through all of the book's discussions about compositional intent and results, pitch structure and thematic development, poetic themes and text-music relations, performance practice and stage presentation, style consciousness and marketing decisions, and listening skills and audience reception. That is our interest in the multitude of manners through which rock music expresses itself on a number of levels that are primarily musical and then secondarily sociological in nature, and the variety of processes an intelligent well-rounded listener/consumer can employ in participating in that expression.

Two chapters, those by Nadine Hubbs and Walter Everett, serve as exhortations for the listener, analyst, and critic, in an overtly prescriptive effort to encourage the development of both imaginative and technical apparatus. Hubbs sets the book's main goal by arguing (in the wake of Edward T. Cone and Joseph Kerman) that the analyst must follow the suggestions of the piece under consideration to get to its aesthetic heart of value and meaning, and that the critic should reflect the artistry of the object-work in the formulation of a response. While similarly guided by Cone, Everett (who has updated his essay with a new section treating the tonal milieu of hip-hop) adapts Schenkerian technique to argue that, no matter how expressively rich are matters of form and design, tone color, or rhythm and tempo, relationships among pitches lie at the core of musical expression. By combining the procedures of Hubbs and

Everett, it is hoped that the reader will develop rich and rewarding listening strategies.

Three chapters deal head-on but in very different ways with political and social issues of the 1970s, 1980s, and 1990s. Tim Hughes considers the racial tension underlying Stevie Wonder's "Living for the City" as he explores the work's mesh of cyclic groove-based repetition at multiple levels as a representation of cultural memory, and spontaneous flexibility as a means of propulsion, intensification, and immediacy. Susan Fast considers the central role of music as part of a larger, theatrical *Gesammtkunstwerk* that emerged out of the post-prog aesthetic; her thoughts could be applied to similarly staged presentations ranging from Elvis' gyrations or Motown choreography to the films of David Byrne, where a large part of the story is told visually. She decodes the cultural commentary and roles of idealism and irony embedded in the musical relations, rhetorical tone, and visual imagery of a number of U2 presentations. Ellie M. Hisama chooses a controversial Cure song, "Killing an Arab," that portrays and subtly criticizes racial dominance through a mix of musico-cultural references, and in so doing combines approaches to musical representation and reception history.

Two essays focus on combinations of style markers in the progressive rock literature of the 1970s. Mark Spicer takes the reader through the last of this book's five extended discussions of a single piece. In this case, it is "Supper's Ready," the 23-minute series of connected tableaux by the early Genesis. Spicer traces the work's unifying harmonic and thematic motivic elements through an array of contrasting textures, tonal languages, and historical style markers with many references to related procedures of the classical tradition. John Covach compares elements of jazz-rock fusion and progressive rock, and the intersections of these worlds, in the works of two American bands, Happy the Man and the Dixie Dregs. This investigation supports his study of the nature of stylistic crossover, a phenomenon he distinguishes from the sort of crossover that is much more often discussed: the market-driven crossover from one chart to another.

Albin Zak considers large-conception works of the 1970s that do not come from the prog-rock camp, but rather from various other styles, their expansive natures due more to the emergence of the LP as art form and the rise of a freer-format FM radio as rock music's progressive outlet than to an adoption of classical pretensions. Led Zeppelin's "In the Light," David Bowie's "Station to Station," and Bruce Springsteen's "Incident on 57th Street" are among many songs explored here to demonstrate how very different rock epics could be.

We present two different takes on Frank Zappa's recompositions of his own work over a quarter century. Both James Borders and Jonathan W. Bernard address the recompositions of rock's most earnest taunter, Frank Zappa. Borders chooses a single rock-oriented piece, "The Black Page," for an extended discussion of the personnel-related differences between a single work's manifestations in various notated versions, live performances, and recordings. Bernard lays out a large number of pieces (with a few—"Dupree's Paradise," "A Pound for a Brown (on the Bus)," and "Sinister Footwear"—given closer attention) for a broad view of the considerations that balance Zappa's straddling of the classical/rock divide, and the sorts of ensembles particular to each. Both authors show that there is much more than simple rearrangement at stake.

The notion of stylistic crossover, explored by both Covach (jazz-rock) and Bernard (classical-rock), is the focus of Jocelyn R. Neal's chapter, which displays the infiltration of pop markers into country music (or is it vice versa?) in working through many musical aspects of the collaborations of singer Shania Twain and her producer, husband, and co-composer, Mutt Lange. While her argument might be conceived as stemming from a central totem, Twain's *Up!*—an album by which the same vocal tracks were released with instrumental backings arranged differently for the pop, country, and international markets—Neal contextualizes much of Twain's work within the contentious history of pop-vs.-country audience reception from the 1980s into the twenty-first century.

Two writers offer views on the expressive relations between modal and tonal behaviors in the work of two important singer-songwriters of the 1990s. Lori Burns and Timothy Koozin examine modal colorings and languages in rock music in their investigations of voice leading in the work of the two composers. Burns offers her detailed hearing of Tori Amos's "Crucify" in support of her procedure for comprehending the tonal characteristics of melody, harmony, and counterpoint in a framework reflective of idiomatic behaviors within modal scales. Although she borrows heavily from Schenker, Burns does not permit this song a background-level reduction, one that would devalue its defining modal technique. Koozin chooses four songs by Sarah McLachlan ("Building a Mystery," "Ben's Song," "Elsewhere," and "Circle") to demonstrate how modal inflections and harmonic and voice-leading tendencies can serve the larger goals of expressing introspective aspects of deeply personal narratives.

Having arrived at the half-century mark of rock 'n' roll's beginnings, it is refreshing to consider both how still-new are the post-journalistic efforts of music scholars to find meaning in this music, and how vast and wide-open is the terrain still unexplored to any significant extent. It is our hope that this book's readers will share that perspective and, in time, add to the development of attitude and technique that will enrich our understanding of a powerfully expressive medium.

I would like to express my deep gratitude to Richard Carlin, who suggested not only a second edition of this book in an affordable paperback printing, but power—or anyone else whose own creative output reflects the melding of such disparate influences as extensively or convincingly.

Part of what made Zappa (b. 1940) such a special case is his musical education, or rather the lack thereof in any conventional sense. His early musical experiences instilled few if any aesthetic preconceptions, something that can be said of many who are self-taught; but what made Zappa's development as autodidact unusual was that it took place in a virtual vacuum. The fact that as a teenager he had even heard of Varèse or Stravinsky can be attributed mostly to rumor and a few LPs filtering into the cultural wasteland that was suburban/small-town southern California in the 1950s. Yet things were not altogether as bad as they might have seemed. What Zappa's background lacked in quantity of musical stimuli it made up for in diversity: he did not grow up exposed to just one variety of music, only subsequently and gradually to discover the possibilities that lay beyond it. Unschooled but highly intelligent and curious, Zappa proved able in the long run to turn the apparent deprivations of his environment to his advantage. In fact, they helped him find his utterly distinctive voice.

From very early on, Zappa fairly burned with ambition, of which he made no secret, to write music—especially, if possible, exciting, gratifyingly noisy and dissonant "modern music"—that ensembles of formally trained musicians, such as symphony orchestras, could play. This in itself was not unusual; any number of musically inclined adolescents growing up in post-World War II America must have harbored similar fantasies at one time or another. Zappa's story departed from the usual plot, though, when his aspirations failed to wither away for lack of nourishment or in the face of more practical considerations. Nor did he pursue a formal compositional training, go to graduate school, earn his doctorate, submit his work to competitions, take a university teaching job, join the American Society of University Composers, learn to express effusive thanks when marginally competent readings of his music were done, patronizingly, by second- and third-rate orchestras ... or, in general, settle into the somewhat cultish existence of the typical contemporary American art-music composer.

Instead, he joined an R&B band. And in doing this, it must be emphasized, Zappa was not simply settling for what he could get. No doubt he would have preferred to work with more accomplished musicians than the Soul Giants of 1964, whose name he changed (not the most important of his many modifications) to the Mothers the following year. Still, the standard rock band and the standard symphony orchestra both had their own peculiar strengths; the point for Zappa was to adjust his compositional aims to whatever performing forces were available at the time. He learned how to be flexible, how to exploit most effectively what was at his disposal, right from the start. Naturally, this experience, especially early on when his options were still quite limited, also taught him that if he ever planned to get anywhere as a composer, he would always have to be pushing the envelope, maintaining a constant tension between what was and what could be. The musicians in his bands had to get used to stretching themselves, to being challenged to break out of their previous experience—and this stretching went on in both directions across the division between art and pop. An R&B drummer would find himself playing the role of avant-garde percussionist; a classically trained mallets player would learn to find her bearings in a rock or fusion context.

Having wrestled for some years with the difficulties involved in getting his own musicians, whatever their backgrounds, to do what he wanted, Zappa turned his attention to the challenge of making music with "foreign" ensembles, i.e., groups with which he was forced to communicate mainly through score and parts, since the culture of these ensembles gibed only fitfully with that of his own band. And it is safe to say that, starting with the semi-debacle of his collaboration with Zubin Mehta and the Los Angeles Philharmonic in 1970, he found the institutional obstacles to departure from his habitual orbit to be more than mere annoyances (Tullius 1971). For this reason, among others, the recorded legacy of Zappa's orchestral ventures is somewhat uneven, and for the most part lacks the vividness and surefooted musicality of his live and studio recordings with his own bands from the late 1960s on.[1] But despite the problems and frustrations that arose in the process of getting these works played, for Zappa the pieces he wrote or arranged for mostly or completely acoustic concert ensembles (from here on called ACEs for short) had an importance to him that extended beyond even their potential for establishing his credentials as a "real" composer in the musical world at large, beyond their potential to prove that he did not subscribe to the Neanderthal sensibilities that (in his view) dominated most of rock and roll, and beyond the rather small proportion of his total oeuvre that they represent. In particular, the ACE works that also, in some form, were brought to performance by Zappa's studio or touring rock bands all engage, to greater or lesser degrees, issues of intersection, interaction, and even conflict between the realms of "art" music and the more "popular" (that is, commercially successful) musics such as rock and jazz. These works, which might be called Zappa's brand of crossover, stand at the very heart of his identity as a composer, and for that reason are probably the most indispensable to its study. (Given John Covach's distinction expressed in this book between "chart" crossover and "stylistic" crossover, Zappa's work falls squarely in the latter category, although much of his later work, perhaps most of all the *Yellow Shark* material, had broad sales among twentieth-century "classical" audiences.) They are paradoxical creations that both affirm the common ground on which Zappa always said that all of his music stood and, at the same time, play off the expectations of stylistic difference raised in the listener by the sharp contrast in performing forces. Contemplating this paradox, one is impelled to ask certain questions. To what extent are these pieces changed by being thrust into a different performance medium? Are

> after that I had a request for an arrangement of it for the Netherlands Wind Ensemble, which was twenty-some pieces. It was cut down and re-orchestrated for the size and shape of the group. This [1992] version was re-orchestrated from the 1983 ensemble version by Ali Askin.[6]

Of course, as Zappa also made clear, the original components of this medley go back even further, specifically to the album *Uncle Meat* (recorded 1967–1968, released 1969). Here they were titled "The Dog Breath Variations" and "Uncle Meat (Main Theme)," and appeared at the end and the beginning of Side 1, respectively. Example 1.1 displays the beginnings of both tunes.[7] (Elsewhere on Side 1 was "Dog Breath, in the Year of the Plague," on which the variations were ostensibly based but which played no direct role in the eventual medley.) Even before the 1975 Royce Hall date, Zappa was already performing these two pieces as a medley with his touring bands. A concert in Helsinki in September 1974 begins "The Dog Breath Variations" with an intro very much like the one used for slightly earlier concert versions of "Dog Breath"[8] (see Example 1.2), but then the "Variations" as heard on *Uncle Meat* (only a good deal faster) are played straight through.[9] The match between concert and studio recordings is nearly exact, with only slight alterations made in some of the more intricate melodic figuration; rhythmically everything remains the same, too. What is quite patently *not* the same is the musical affect, which in the original version was markedly introspective: a quiet moment on the album, as a reprise sometimes is in a Broadway-style musical.[10]

At the downbeat of the last chord of the "Variations," the concert recording segues into "Uncle Meat (Main Theme)." Here, too, the music of the earlier album is faithfully transcribed; the big difference in the treatment of this tune is that it is considerably extended in the concert version. Instead of breaking off the *da capo* restatement, as is done in the studio version, after the first six bars and proceeding directly to a slower coda in which the principal motive (initial five notes) of the theme is dwelt upon, Zappa in concert opts for a full reprise of the theme (0:59).[11] In the reprise, one short segment is played at half speed (1:33), corresponding to measures 27–33 of the complete, forty-three-bar theme; measures 34–43 then return to tempo (1:51), after which (2:03) a short coda—newly composed, although embedding the principal motive once in long notes—concludes the performance.

The score for wind ensemble entitled "The Dog Breath Variations," encompassing the same two-tune medley, was apparently put in its definitive form sometime between the mid-1970s and early 1980s. It really is an arrangement: compared to the 1974 rendition, as a chart the medley has hardly changed at all. Owing to the much enlarged instrumental forces and the slower tempo, there are many changes of detail, particularly in transitions between phrases where bridging runs are often added, and in previously simple homophonic textures where a melodic line is built up with additional voicings. Zappa has

Example 1.1a The Mothers of Invention, "The Dog Breath Variations" (Frank Zappa), *Uncle Meat* (1969): opening. © 1968 Frank Zappa Music, BMI.

Example 1.1b The Mothers of Invention, "Uncle Meat (Main Theme)" (Frank Zappa), *Uncle Meat* (1969): opening. © 1968 Frank Zappa Music, BMI.

Whether with words or not, whether for orchestra or for stage band, "Strictly Genteel" remained, in all its essential aspects—harmony, melody, rhythm, form—the same piece, and in all versions is practically the same bar-for-bar as well. The revisions it underwent in its seventeen-year history as documented on recordings are quite minor, consisting principally of the insertion of twenty-four new bars in the interlude (after m. 120: 3:58) in 1975 and a further new, immediately succeeding eight bars in the 1981 version (4:07).[13] In other words, when Zappa had a new idea about "Strictly Genteel," he apparently worked mainly with reference to the immediately previous version, whatever it was; there weren't separate, parallel courses for orchestra and stage band. All thirty-two new bars are retained in the 1983 LSO version; four bars near the end (corresponding to mm. 181–184 in the 1981 version, 5:05) were cut, which, however, remain intact in the 1988 stage-band version (4:50), in agreement with all three versions before 1983. Conceivably, these were taken out to compensate for the generally slower tempo and additional thirty-two bars in the LSO version by comparison to *200 Motels*; in any case, their absence is hardly noticeable. From the start, "Strictly Genteel" never fit either side of the orchestral/rock dichotomy perfectly, causing corresponding difficulties in dealing with it as a real crossover piece. Nevertheless, in this case it is clear that the differences of performance medium were only incidental to the makeup of the musical material.[14]

"Dupree's Paradise"

For Zappa, using his compositions to bridge the gap between seemingly quite disparate performance media was not always simply a matter of cranking out an arrangement for acoustic concert ensemble of something originally composed for rock instrumentation, or vice versa. Sometimes, evidently, making the transformation proved more of a challenge, and required more drastic changes than were needed in any of the pieces discussed so far. Three of Zappa's works in particular are especially interesting in this regard, and they will receive extensive attention in the pages that follow.

"Dupree's Paradise" is one Zappa composition that is neither entirely an ACE work nor an arrangement of something preexisting. Its difference derives from the fact that, although it originated as a band number in the early 1970s, it was in large part recomposed for the score that was recorded by Pierre Boulez and the Ensemble InterContemporain in 1984. It is thus in no sense a "typical" Zappa work. But it is precisely because of its unique position that it deserves scrutiny, for it affords the opportunity to see what happened when a Zappa work crossed over from a pop context to an ACE context—and then crossed back to pop.

The student of "Dupree's Paradise" has four recorded and commercially available performances to work with: the aforementioned Boulez-directed studio recording, plus three live-band performances, two from before 1984 and one after (see Appendix). The earliest of these (1973) is also the least satisfactory from a technical standpoint, having been recorded illegally, apparently off Swedish television. The recording on *Piquantique* fades out less than four minutes into the piece proper, in the middle of Jean-Luc Ponty's violin solo. However, there does exist a videotape of this television broadcast, in which "Dupree's Paradise" can be heard complete.[15] This and the 1974 version are quite similar, with one important divergence at the end to be discussed.

In keeping with its basic jazz inflection, this opening section of the piece has much of the character of a head, as it will be referred to henceforth, and in quick succession presents several motives or themes (or riffs). In the first group, **A** (see Example 1.5), a basic chord (7:38) establishes the "harmonic climate" over a characteristic rhythm; this is followed (7:46) by a brief, somewhat angular pentatonic melody based on the descending fourth F♯–C♯ then a more elaborate, extended form of the melody.[16] **B** (7:59) is essentially a "pyramided" arpeggiation with two different terminal chords alternating in its repetitions. **C** (8:09; see top line of Example 1.6b) is the most elaborate of the three, melodically speaking, and the least complicated metrically. Note the motivic connection to **B** embedded in **C** (marked with a bracket in Example 1.6b).

Once the head has been fully stated, the rhythmic impulse of the opening **A** material is consistently maintained by means of the metrically compound 2/4-plus-6/8 of that opening. In the 1973 version, the solos are taken by violin, trombone, and guitar in that order, ending with an abbreviated reprise (**A**, **B**,

Example 1.5 The Mothers, "Dupree's Paradise" (Frank Zappa), 1974 tour version: harmonic and thematic material in head. © 1974 Munchkin Music, ASCAP.

and **C** truncated after its first six bars). The 1974 solos begin in almost jazz-cliché fashion with the flute, proceed to bass (in trade-off with the drums), then to keyboard. Then a very long drum solo gives way to odd synthesizer effects and duck calls, followed by a segue into the next piece on the program. What is most notable here for our purposes is that there is no reprise of the head. This "open-ended" kind of design is familiar enough from some of Zappa's other jazz-inflected work, such as the long, improvisation-oriented "King Kong." Judging from the 1973 and 1974 performances, it would seem that the reprise in "Dupree's Paradise" was an optional component, the inclusion or exclusion of which depended on the placement of the piece in the playlist on a particular occasion.

We must now jump ahead ten years, to January 1984, the date of Boulez's recording. In preparing the chamber-ensemble score for this recording, Zappa apparently decided to remake the piece in a fashion appropriate for ACE performance; thus he used just about everything (presumably) that had been written down for the band version—that is, nothing much more than the head—transforming it slightly but significantly. He then wrote a good deal of new material, interspersed with enough recurrences of the opening 2/4-plus-6/8 rhythm to maintain a thread of thematic continuity. Finally, the head is reprised at the end, incompletely; only the **A** material is heard.[17]

Apart from deletion of the lead-in, not much is different in the head of the ACE version until the **C** material at measure 30 (0:37). Before that point, Zappa inserts some "fills" between the riffs of the **A** material, adjusting the meter to do so (see Example 1.6a). Example 1.6b shows how the tune of **C** has been altered, with some parts transposed exactly by various intervals, and other parts revised but with the rhythm remaining essentially the same. This change, together with a radical reharmonization, disrupts rather markedly the tonal characteristics of the original material; notice, among other things, that the melodic connection with the **B** material, noted in the 1974 version, has disappeared. There is now much greater contrast with the preceding **A** and **B** material, in a much more "modern-music"-like idiom. Finally, the

Example 1.6a "Dupree's Paradise" (Frank Zappa), 1984 score: fills in **A**.

Example 1.6b The Mothers, "Dupree's Paradise" (Frank Zappa): comparison of **C** melodies, 1974 (band) and 1984 (ACE) versions.

last change in the head is an addition: a repeat of **A** (0:57), at measure 46 initially with just the descending-fourth motive, then with the complete theme up a semitone.

As the rest of the chamber-ensemble version of "Dupree's Paradise" unfolds, one question that might occur to a listener is: Has this now become, actually, a whole new piece? Certainly, beyond the head, the surface wears a very different aspect in the ACE version. But, curiously, the mode of listening required of us has changed very little, which may be owing to Zappa's basically episodic method in composing this score. There is a great wealth of melodic and harmonic invention that can easily at first come across as almost a surfeit; but apart from the 2/4-plus-6/8 thread of continuity mentioned earlier, what lends an overall coherence is the repetition of textures and instrumental groups. There is something about the entire score between the head and its reprise—most of its length—that has the character of an improvisation. There are even

Example 1.7 "Dupree's Paradise" (Frank Zappa), 1984 score: mm. 195–200. © 1982, 1984 Frank Zappa/Munchkin Music. All rights reserved.

tradings-off between groups of instruments that could be taken to emulate the kind of complementary riff-trading that sometimes happens in more spontaneous settings (Example 1.7, mm. 195–200: 4:33). The real difference here, of course, is that Zappa is doing all the improvising himself: improving his degree of control over the result, in other words, much in the same way as he eventually sought to do in his Synclavier pieces.

It is also worth noticing that this process of improvisation (or re-improvisation) involves moving things around, taking chunks of material from their former accustomed locations, and inserting them into the design elsewhere. Two such chunks occur early in the 1973 and 1974 versions: the previously mentioned lead-in, and something named, for the purposes of this discussion, the "flurry," a single 4/4 measure of very rapid figuration that immediately precedes the tune proper of **A**. In the chamber-ensemble version, the lead-in becomes the basis for a much longer, contrasting section for two pianos and accompanying low instruments; the clearest relation comes in the passage excerpted in Example 1.8 (mm. 175–80: 3:56). As for the flurry, it is not much changed at all, but occurs in the reprise of the head instead of the opening (see Example 1.10b, m. 280: 7:05).

Example 1.9 *(Continued)*

recordings on for quoting (especially from Stravinsky), and knowing also of his distinct and professed fondness for "Agon."[18]

Returning to the main subject, let us consider "Dupree's Paradise" in, presumably, its final manifestation (or a representative sample thereof), as played by the 1988 touring band. This was an appreciably larger band than the one Zappa brought on tour to Helsinki in 1974 (twelve members as opposed to the sextet of that earlier date), and the full exploitation of horn resources in particular gives Zappa's new version a markedly big-band sound of the sort

Example 1.8 "Dupree's Paradise" (Frank Zappa), 1984 score: mm. 175–180, pianos.

As mentioned earlier, the addition of a reprise bears some notable resemblance to the conventions of jazz. It may also be that Zappa hit upon this compositional stratagem as a way of imposing a kind of closure that was not available in the previous, open-ended design. After all, this piece had to have a definite ending and not segue into whatever was next on the evening's playlist, as the band version could do. Further—and this may be regarded as pure speculation on my part—Zappa may actually have had a definite model in mind from modern art music when he made this revision: a specific piece, that is, from which he drew very general characteristics. The piece is, I believe, Stravinsky's "Agon," which has the following overall scenario:

- It starts with some diatonic music in which there is an alternation between rhythmic complexity (involving repeated notes), in two distinct textures, and relative simplicity;
- it becomes quite chromatic, dissonant, and nontonal in the middle; and
- then, after a quiet, nontonal passage of dovetailed parts that for the most part follows a straightforward beat, suddenly the opening diatonic music (not heard since the beginning) emerges again and ends the piece.

Now, granted, this is not a very profound analysis of "Agon," but in this connection such an analysis wouldn't be particularly useful to us anyway. For Zappa has not ripped off Stravinsky, he has not imitated or really even emulated his ballet; all he has done is appropriate a very general idea of design.

Example 1.9 displays the opening music of "Agon." In this putative correspondence to "Dupree's Paradise," measures 1–6 are reflected in Zappa's **A** material, measures 7–9 in **B**, and measures 10–13 in **C**. In Example 1.10, the transition into the coda and the first few measures of that coda in

"Agon" (Example 1.10a, mm. 551–567) are juxtaposed with the formally corresponding measures of "Dupree's Paradise" (Example 1.10b, mm. 269–283; 6:52). Notice how the rhythmic shape of the characteristic motive in both pieces (without its melodic component) is foreshadowed in the transitional music before emerging full-blown in the coda or restatement of the head (mm. 553–557 in "Agon"; mm. 272–277 [6:58] in "Dupree's Paradise"). All this "proves" nothing, of course. But the possibility of an intentional resemblance here is fascinating—knowing, as we do, Zappa's penchant from his earliest

Example 1.9 "Agon" (Igor Stravinsky): mm. 1–19. © 1957 by Hawkes & Son (London) Ltd. Copyright renewed. Reprinted by permission of Boosey & Hawkes, Inc.

generically familiar, at least, from the style known as fusion. The rendition of this piece by the crack ensemble assembled by Zappa for his final tour sounds positively turbo-charged by comparison even to that of the remarkably proficient 1974 band. Figure 1.1 presents a kind of schematic diagram of the effects of crossover on this piece—a double effect, for in going back to the live-band realm, this piece has taken several features of its experience as an ACE work. These are marked by left-to-right arrows. Compared to the 1973 and 1974 versions, the most striking contrasts, which evidently are directly owing to the

Example 1.10a "Agon" (Igor Stravinsky): mm. 551–567. © 1957 by Hawkes & Son (London) Ltd. Copyright renewed. Reprinted by permission of Boosey & Hawkes, Inc.

Example 1.10a *(Continued)*

1984 scoring, are marked by the lower three solid arrows. First, the repetition of **A** material in the head up a semitone; second, a much greater degree of variation in texture and tempo in the middle, i.e., between head and reprise. A third contrast is the character of the reprise, now more extensive than in either the 1973 or 1984 versions and clearly marked by the character of the 1984 head. In 1988, this reprise has now achieved a solidity of definition that suggests it is no longer optional—again, as if the fully written-out score of 1984 had established it.

Three other, smaller yet still significant points are marked by the upper solid arrows: the deletion of the lead-in music and the 4/4 measure of "flurry," both of which (as discussed) are played in 1973 and 1974 but disappear from the head in 1984; and the replacement of the vamp on the initial chord (1973, 1974) by an intro (1984). Other traces of Zappa's ACE experience with this piece seem to have affected, in particular, the 1988 bass part, which plays fills

Example 1.10b "Dupree's Paradise" (Frank Zappa), 1984 score: mm. 269–283.

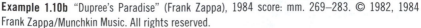

Example 1.10b *(Continued)*

between the motives of **A** that sound *almost* "composed," like the ones that were actually composed for the 1984 score. Also (see Example 1.11), there is the ostinato played by the bass under the first solo (trumpet) of the 1988 version (1:13), which very definitely stresses the descending fourth of the **A** material of the head. It even occurs as F#-C# when first heard. Again, these latter features cannot be directly attributed to the 1984 score, but their presence in 1988 strongly suggests the effects on Zappa of having put "Dupree's Paradise" into a fully written-out compositional shape, with the kinds of definite attributes that such shapes customarily have.

Figure 1.1 "Dupree's Paradise" (Frank Zappa): comparative chart of three versions.

1973, 1974	1984		1988
Lead-in (1 or 2 solo instruments)	No lead-in	⟶	No lead-in
Vamp on initial chord; "flurry" preceding **A** material	Vamp replaced by intro	⟶	Intro retained from 1984
	No flurry here	⟶	No flurry
A B C	**A** with composed fills between riffs	-------->	Active bass part functions analogously to composed fills
	C segmentally transposed and otherwise modified, re-harmonized, "detonalized"		**C** returns to 1973/74 form
A not repeated in head	**A** repeated in head, semitone higher	⟶	**A** repeated in head, semitone higher
		-------->	Bass under first solo takes "motivic" role
Solos	(Notated) "ensemble solos" of considerable variety	-------->	Solos marked by big contrasts in tempo, texture, affect
(1973) Reprise (**A**, **B**, abbrev. **C**) *or*	Reprise (abbrev. **A** only)	⟶	More extended reprise (**A**, **B**, **C**) but no repeat of **A**
(1974) No reprise	(preceded by resumption of 2/4 + 6/8 meter)	⟶	(preceded by resumption of 2/4 + 6/8 meter)

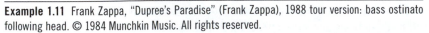

Example 1.11 Frank Zappa, "Dupree's Paradise" (Frank Zappa), 1988 tour version: bass ostinato following head.

"A Pound for a Brown (on the Bus)"

"Dupree's Paradise," having endured long enough in Zappa's active playlist to cross over twice, is unique among his compositions. But there is one other crossover composition in his oeuvre that, owing in part to its even greater longevity, presents a history that is also quite intricate and at least as interesting. "A Pound for a Brown (on the Bus)" entered the Mothers' repertory early in 1968 and, as Zappa recalled toward the end of his life, was "played by just about every one of the touring bands, in one version or another" (Zappa 1993). Zappa made this observation in the liner notes accompanying the Ensemble Modern's release of a number of his works on a CD drawn from their September 1992 Hamburg concerts, for which Zappa had arranged several pieces, including "A Pound for a Brown." As what could be called a basic chart, over that nearly twenty-five-year period, this piece changed hardly at all. Yet during the same time, its form, as defined in large part by its context, underwent considerable revision—a process that, for Zappa, was at least as significant to his activity as a composer as were revisions in the usual sense of that term, i.e., actual rewriting of the score (Bernard 2000).

Actually, in a way, "A Pound for a Brown" did cross over more than once. Although there is no record of its public performance by Zappa and his musicians before 1968, the composition reputedly dates in its earliest version from 1957–1958, when Zappa was still in high school. It was originally conceived as a string quartet and had at least one other following movement or section. This additional music, later known as "Sleeping in a Jar," remained part of "A Pound for a Brown" in live performance until at least 1971. Judging from the fact that as late as November 1968 Zappa was still announcing this two-part "suite" of tunes from the stage as "The String Quartet," the title by which the first of these became eventually and definitively known was attached only shortly before its first recorded release, on *Uncle Meat* (1969).[19] (More about "Sleeping in a Jar" later.)

Among the complete list of recordings of "A Pound for a Brown," comprising both Zappa's "legitimate" releases and legally reissued bootlegs, *Uncle Meat* is the one studio issue. Although it was released only in April 1969, more than a year after the earliest live recording was made, it appears first in the chronological listing in the Appendix because the basic tracks for *Uncle Meat* were laid down at Apostolic Studios in New York between October 1967 and February 1968. (During March and April, Zappa did some overdubbing and further assembly of material on his own in Los Angeles.) In the two versions of "A Pound for a Brown" included here (one of them titled "The Legend of the Golden Arches"), we can already see Zappa's crossover aspirations being put into action. Neither version bears more than a remote resemblance to the pop or rock music of the time. The instrumentation does not even include the guitar, much less emphasize it, and consists basically of wind instruments with a backing rhythm section. The work seems to be a *concert* piece, with its parts all fully written out and with no opportunity taken for improvisation. Significantly, neither version is heard in the "key" in which the live versions invariably appear. The first, slower version ("The Legend of the Golden Arches") is "in B" and has the character of a mock-solemn fanfare or prelude (see Example 1.12); the second version, in B♭, is much faster and has a cartoonish, synthetic quality that clearly derives from the speeding up of most of the constituent tracks. (Originally, these tracks may have been

Example 1.12 The Mothers of Invention, "The Legend of the Golden Arches" (Frank Zappa), *Uncle Meat* (1969): mm. 1–16. © 1968 Frank Zappa Music, BMI.

Example 1.12 *(Continued)*

recorded in F, the key of all the live versions, although the evidence on this point is ambiguous.)[20]

Compared to many of the other cuts on *Uncle Meat*, both versions are relatively brief (the second extremely so). Both, however, are also effectively extended by their contexts, as if to make up for the absence of "Sleeping in a Jar," which on *Uncle Meat* has been given words, slowed down and abridged, and placed elsewhere in the order of cuts. "The Legend of the Golden Arches" is broken off as Zappa splices in some sardonic laughter; the music that immediately follows, as if in segue only momentarily delayed, is a kind of reprise variation on "Uncle Meat (Main Theme)," the cut that opens the album—music that is actually longer than "Arches" itself. "A Pound for a Brown," on the other hand, leads directly into a monologue by Ian Underwood, recounting how he came to join Zappa's band, followed immediately by a lengthy live-performance excerpt, featuring Underwood as soloist and entitled "Ian Underwood Whips It Out," which concludes Side 2 of the original four-side LP set. Both kinds of extension—segue to a new, obviously "composed" work and segue into a long solo or series of solos—play important roles in the subsequent history of "A Pound for a Brown," as we shall see.

Already in the earliest live recordings, some differences from the *Uncle Meat* versions are obvious. It seems as though Zappa, from the start, saw the

Example 1.13 The Mothers of Invention, "A Pound for a Brown (on the Bus)" (Frank Zappa), *Uncle Meat* (1969): mm. 14–16 (compare Example 12). © 1968 Frank Zappa Music, BMI.

necessity of making certain minor adjustments in the basic chart for the piece to fit the conditions of live performance. The three from 1968 are all very similar to one another. The tempo is a kind of compromise between the two studio versions; the **A** section is always heard through the first time with the melody played solo (by guitar or electric piano, or both) against the ostinato bass, then joined by accompanying winds (soprano sax and clarinet) at the repeat. The melody of measures 14–16, as shown in Example 1.13, is slightly altered to close this first section. Changes are more noticeable in the **B** section: the ostinato bass in ascending/descending fifths is dispensed with in favor of periodic punctuation by unison keyboard/bass/drums; the melody is also simplified at its most complicated moments, and some minimal counterpoint is added in a lower treble part. (In Examples 1.14 and 1.15, for the purposes of easier comparison, the "Golden Arches" version is transposed down a tritone to match the pitch level of the concert version of "A Pound for a Brown.")

Example 1.14 The Mothers of Invention, "A Pound for a Brown (on the Bus)" (Frank Zappa): comparison of (a) studio [*Uncle Meat* (1969)] and (b) live **B** sections, mm. 29–34. © 1968 Frank Zappa Music, BMI.

Example 1.15 The Mothers of Invention, "A Pound for a Brown (on the Bus)" (Frank Zappa): comparison of (a) studio [*Uncle Meat* (1969)] and (b) live **B** sections, mm. 39–41. © 1968 Frank Zappa Music, BMI.

More telling, perhaps, than these small revisions are the differences in form (see Figure 1.2). In all three of the 1968 recordings, immediately succeeding the **B** section and preceding the *da capo* reprise of the **A** material, there is inserted several minutes of a kind of free-style avant-garde noodling, a twittering texture initiated by the winds and gradually spreading to the rest of the ensemble. This, along with a moderately lengthy improvised solo after the reprise, had the effect of considerably extending the basic chart—as does also, of course, the segue of the solo into "Sleeping in a Jar." It would seem, then, that Zappa undertook these revisions mainly to allow "A Pound for a Brown" to stand on its own in a live concert setting—a rather different context from that of a painstakingly produced studio album with serious aspirations as contemporary, composed music. (As for the noodling insertion, one can guess that Zappa meant to remind his audience that they were not, after all, attending a typical rock concert.)

Figure 1.2 "A Pound for a Brown (on the Bus)" (Frank Zappa): five basic versions.

1967–68 (studio)	**1968 (live band)**	**1971 (live band)**	**1976–82 (live band)**	**1992 (ACE)**
intro 7/8, 4 bars	intro 7/8, 4 bars	intro 7/8, 4 bars	[vamp] on 7/8	intro 7/8, 4 bars
A mm. 5–28	**A** mm. 5–28	**A** mm. 5–28	**A** mm. 1–24	**A** mm. 5–28
(All versions include repeat with first and second endings)				
B mm. 29–45	**B** mm. 29–46 "twittering" interlude	**B** mm. 29–46	**B** mm. 25–42	**B** mm. 29–46
Coda:shortened **A** mm. 46–54 or mm. 46–56	brief reprise of **A** mm. 47–58	brief reprise of **A** mm. 47–58	brief reprise of **A** mm. 47–58	Coda: short **A** mm. 47–58 (approx.)
segue to: ("Gold. Arches": "Uncle Meat" Reprise)	segue to: guitar solo	segue to: guitar solo	segue to: multiple solos	segue to: new trans. (mm. 59–72 approx.)
	segue to:	segue to:		
OR ("Pound for a Brown": Ian Underwood monologue)	"Sleeping in a Jar"	"Sleeping in a Jar"		segue to: "Exercise #4"

The so-called Mark II Mothers of Invention, which took its definitive form in 1970 and remained together until the very end of 1971, was a far more virtuosic group than its predecessor, with a stripped-down sound emphasizing solo roles for guitar and keyboards underlaid by a rhythm section. Zappa's desire to play "A Pound for a Brown" faster than could his original Mothers, a situation possibly implied by the artificially sped-up version on *Uncle Meat*, is effectively realized in the two 1971 recordings. Also realized clearly for the first time is the polymetric relationship between the bass ostinato, which continues in the 7/8 established in the introduction, and the alternating 4/4 and 3/4 of the upper parts. This was always implicit in the chart, as the transcription in Example 1.12 shows, but was more or less effaced by the plodding tempos of the 1968 versions and, undoubtedly, the limitations of the Mothers' rhythm section at that time. In 1971, with the choir of winds no longer present, the voicings of the **A** and **B** sections sound somewhat different, though substantively the music has not been altered at all. The improvised twittering has disappeared, however. In part this can be explained by the change in band instrumentation, but it must also be attributed to Zappa's changing tastes and his tendency, more and more evident as the 1970s wore on, to discard as musically amateurish the sort of experimentalism that was so much in vogue during the 1960s and to concentrate on large, impressive projects using the best musicians he could find to work with him, whether in the realm of "serious art" music or in pop/jazz/rock.

The two 1971 performances also show that Zappa, as he developed into a virtuoso musician in his own right, became much more interested in playing long solos varied in texture, rhythm, and tempo. The sudden slowing of tempo at the onset of the solo passage in both performances suggests strongly that something quite new is beginning at this point. This, together with the deletion of the interlude of twittering and the greatly accelerated tempo of the tune itself, has begun to shift the focus of performances of this piece toward the solo work, as if the musicians were in a great hurry to get through the "head" and on to the main event. "Sleeping in a Jar," finally, remains in place at the end in both performances, where it hurtles along at breakneck speed. The Fillmore East version showed that this tune had even grown a new limb, some previously unheard music allowing for a third and final rendering of the *subito adagio* chorus.[21]

The later recordings of "A Pound for a Brown," beginning with late 1976 in New York, bring further changes. Deletion of the introductory four bars of 7/8 and making old bars 5–6 a vamp in their place has the effect of further streamlining the head; the tempo has also picked up even more, allowing the band to get through the entire head in less than a minute and a half (hardly more than a minute, actually, if one discounts the opening vamp). Seemingly in response, the soloists' section has also increased in intensity, with much more virtuosic combinations and tradeoffs than ever conceived of or, perhaps, ever possible before. This sometimes has the effect of making the solo section quite short, as in the 1976 performance. At other times, notably in the Saarbrücken version of 1978, with big contributions from vibraphone, synthesizer, and guitar (in that order), and with major shifts in tempo, style, and affect between them, the solo section seems to have become a separate, even if improvised, composition. Zappa apparently was thinking along those lines when, in 1991, he detached the solos from an October 1979 performance of the piece and presented them on an album as a self-sufficient entity: "Pound for a Brown—Solos 1978." Perhaps because these solos became such a hard act to follow, "Sleeping in a Jar" no longer follows them from 1976 on. The 1982 European tour recording, the last of the band performances issued to date, more or less completes the process of burlesquing the tune itself, reducing it almost to the status of prelude to the *real* music.

Under the circumstances, the reappearance in 1992 of "A Pound for a Brown," arranged for an ACE (though possibly not by Zappa himself),[22] represents both a resurrection and a restoration of the work to its original art-music medium. But although many features of the dual version on *Uncle Meat* have indeed been restored, some aspects of the new version are marked by Zappa's experience of the work in live performance. The introductory four bars of 7/8 are back, as are the original melody and voicing of measures 14–16 of the **A** section. By contrast, the melody of the **A** section is given unaccompanied the first time through (except in mm. 14–16), in a form essentially identical to its customary presentation live. The melody of the **B** section remains in the form it assumed for live performance from 1968 on; the key of the whole piece is F major. And the tempo is closest to that of the earliest live versions—in other words, ironically, probably closest to that of its original string-quartet conception.

As for the coda, it sounds much as it did on *Uncle Meat*—and it is there that Zappa, perhaps in collaboration with his arranger, builds a new context for "A Pound for a Brown" that also effectively reconnects the work to its original album presentation. In this new ACE arrangement, "Sleeping in a Jar" has not been restored from the (putatively) original form of "The String Quartet," and, especially in the absence of a large solo section, the composer clearly felt that something more was needed. This is supplied by a new transitional passage, beginning as shown in Example 1.16, segueing into a piece called "Exercise #4" and recognizable as the music placed at the beginning of "The Uncle Meat Variations" on *Uncle Meat*, in a much faster, more fluid and extended form.[23]

Example 1.16 Frank Zappa, "A Pound for a Brown (on the Bus)" (Frank Zappa), 1992 version: beginning of transition to "Exercise #4."

In a sense, "A Pound for a Brown" moved along a trajectory in mirror image to that of "Dupree's Paradise." The longer and more richly exemplified history of the former reveals also a more extensive struggle with the compositional setting of a work that evidently never seemed quite long enough by itself and always needed something further to balance it—whether it be the complex latticework of studio album design, or a competing, different tune, or a dazzling solo performance.

"Sinister Footwear"

The third work of Zappa's singled out in this essay for special consideration has the shortest story to tell—and, because it is not well known, it is perhaps the most enigmatic. "Sinister Footwear" was originally (it appears) composed as a three-movement ballet for large orchestra sometime in the late 1970s or early 1980s but was never legally recorded or released in this form.[24] Zappa listeners, if they have heard it at all, are likely to know it only through recordings of rock-ensemble versions of the second and third movements (hereafter referred to, in whatever version, as "Sinister II" and "Sinister III"). The complete ballet, however, was performed at least once. Comparison of a bootleg recording of that (orchestral) performance with the rock-ensemble performances (two of "Sinister II," one of "Sinister III") reveals that while Zappa has carried over "Sinister III" essentially intact in his own band performance, he has drastically revised "Sinister II," cutting about half of the orchestral version and inserting some new material into what remains. (See Figure 1.3.)[25]

In both the orchestral and rock-ensemble versions, "Sinister II" begins with a very regularly shaped sixteen bars, as sketched in Example 1.17. After some transitional material, there follows—at 1:28 in the orchestral performance and 1:15 in the two rock-ensemble performances—a recitative-like passage in four large phrases, which again in all essential aspects is exactly the same in all versions. As Figure 1.3 shows, however, at about 1:45 the rock version diverges radically from the orchestral score, with material such as ostinato bass patterns specifically designed to highlight various solo instruments. Somewhat later—at 6:19 on *Them or Us* and 4:06 on *Make a Jazz Noise Here*—the rock version rejoins the orchestral score, corresponding to 2:11 in the recording of the latter. From here to their final bars, both rock performances follow the orchestral score closely in the convolutions of what is essentially one long melody, of considerable intervallic and rhythmic intricacy (see Example 1.18), with a lightly scored accompaniment. By contrast, from 5:26 to its own ending more than six minutes later, the orchestral version consists of material not heard in the rock version at all, with the possible exception of a certain fleeting resemblance between the string parts at about 6:05 and the "looping" synthesizer lines at 2:20 (taken up by the marimba at 2:42) in the *Them or Us* performance.

Figure 1.3 "Sinister Footwear" (Frank Zappa), Second Movement: comparison of orchestral and rock versions.

Orchestral:		**Rock:**		
		Them or Us		*Make a Jazz Noise Here*
16 bars: Theme I transition			16 bars: Theme I transition	
"recitative" in four phrases	1:28	1:15	"recitative" in four phrases	1:15
		1:45	First bass ostinato	1:47
		2:20	looping synthesizer lines or trumpet solo	2:25
		2:42	Second bass ostinato under solo(s)	2:45
		5:44	repeat of first bass ostinato	3:30
long melody underlaid by Theme I-type accompaniment	2:11	6:19	long melody underlaid by Theme I-type accompaniment	4:06
coda	5:06	8:29	coda	6:27
faster section (strings pizzicato)	5:26	8:39	(end)	6:39
slower (strings arco)	6:29			
marcato (pizzicato again)	7:36			
brief Theme I recap; percussion to the fore	8:18			
more allusions to opening; percussion continues to dominate	10:05			
(end)	11:47			

Example 1.17 "Sinister Footwear" (Frank Zappa), Second Movement: mm. 1–16.

Example 1.18 "Sinister Footwear" (Frank Zappa), Second Movement: long melody: beginning.

There is less to say about "Sinister III." The rock version on *You Are What You Is*, billed as "Theme from …," more or less matches the orchestral score measure for measure.[26] Zappa's performance is basically a guitar solo accompanied by a very busy rhythm section. In truth, the orchestral version does not appear to consist of much more, and in fact Zappa gives the orchestral percussion less to do than he requires of his own drummer. Melodically speaking, however, the two versions are to all intents and purposes the same, which, of course, raises the interesting question as to what the "original" version of this movement really is. Much of Zappa's music, undoubtedly, was written "at the guitar," in the same sense as the music of many another composer (Stravinsky, for instance) was written at the piano. Is "Sinister III" therefore in some sense *originally* for guitar, even if it was not first explicitly realized on paper in that medium? Certainly, in Zappa's adept hands, it sounds quite idiomatic for the guitar—a quality that is also reflected in Steve Vai's painstaking transcription, excerpted in Example 1.19 (Zappa 1982).[27]

To varying degrees, this question is also of relevance to "Sinister II," and indeed to all of Zappa's other crossover music. Although in the case of "Sinister II" we are probably on safe ground in claiming that the orchestral version came first, it requires no great stretch of the imagination to hear the recitative-like phrases and the long melody discussed earlier (for example) as originating on Zappa's own instrument. But unlike "Dupree's Paradise," none of the movements of "Sinister Footwear" has any recorded history of performance before its creation as an orchestral score. Also unlike "Dupree's," "Sinister II," in the details of its rock version, really does seem to be a revision of the orchestral version, rather than the other way around. Of course, there is no way of proving finally that either came first without access to documentary evidence, assuming that there even is any remaining to be uncovered at this point.

Since both rock-band performances of "Sinister II" date from after the orchestral performance of June 1984, one cannot ask, as one could with "Dupree's," whether the experience of this performance led to changes in the rock version compared to earlier rock performances. However, it is interesting to note that in the 1988 performance much more is made of the bass "fills" in bars 2, 4, 6, and so on, of the opening music than in the 1984 recording, perhaps in emulation of the orchestral bass parts in the corresponding bars.

For Zappa, it should now be clear, crossover was not simply a matter of arrangement of an old piece for new performing forces. Sometimes, of course, arrangement was pretty much the whole story. But more often we see Zappa's desire to make something substantially new in the process, whether by actually recomposing the piece in question (in the traditional sense) or by revising its setting (on an album, in a medley, or in a concert suite that is customarily performed in a certain order) in some fundamentally important way.

Example 1.19 "Sinister Footwear" (Frank Zappa), Third Movement: rock version: beginning.

Arranging per se was probably not Zappa's forte—as it is not, incidentally, that of most pop composers, even those who normally work in genres such as Broadway musicals. This may explain why he effectively hired out, to someone with real professional training in this area, most of the work involved in preparing some of the scores for the Ensemble Modern's *Yellow Shark* concerts. But if the ACE versions of "The Duke of Prunes" and "The Dog Breath Variations" or the stage-band version of "Strictly Genteel" are relatively uninteresting, this has more to do with the more modest goals Zappa set himself in these cases than with the lack of a specialized skill. Quite different are pieces like "Envelopes" and "Sinister Footwear" (the second movement, at least), which were first heard in rock-band versions, not just as a strange sort of stunt, but because Zappa had put a lot into composing them in their original orchestral form and saw that they would rarely—if ever, as it must have seemed at one point in the early 1980s—get played in those versions.[28] I would submit that one important reason why these pieces come across so vibrantly at the hands of Zappa's own bands is that they are more than arrangements. Zappa saw an opportunity to make changes that would play to the particular strengths of rock instrumentation and modes of performance. Often, these changes entail what Zappa called "putting the eyebrows on it": making certain alterations in style, sometimes very slight, that translate into major differences in the final result (Zappa 1989). At least as important are, for one, the seemingly minor changes in proportions—deleting eight bars here, inserting a solo there—that by turns tighten up and air out the form in ways that almost always reveal a keen musical judgment at work; and, for another, revisions of a sort that could be called musical reframing, as in the case of "A Pound for a Brown," which have the effect of placing a basically untouched chart in an entirely new light.

The same is true of "Dupree's Paradise," rethought from its jazz-flavored origins into a work for conventional forces that absorbs the jazziness into the instrumentation in ways that are analogous to the methods of many neoclassical American composers earlier in the twentieth century—while mixing a good deal else into the bargain. The labor involved in redesigning this piece, in a sense composing out an elaborate set of ensemble solos to replace the formerly improvised material, must have been considerable, which probably explains why there are no other works of this sort in Zappa's oeuvre. In other words, if the desired outcome was an ACE composition, and mere arrangement was not an option, it was probably easier to start from scratch. Finally, "A Pound for a Brown" shows how artificial in many respects the distinction is for Zappa between his endeavors in "serious art" music and rock "entertainment." In which of these categories are the two versions on *Uncle Meat* to be classified? As for the ever-faster live versions from the 1970s and 1980s, for all that they may have given over much more time to the solos than to the tune itself, in bringing this polymetric vehicle to liftoff velocity did they not also lend it a furious and remarkable vigor that it lacked in Zappa's earlier realizations?

Collectively, all of these pieces reveal a breadth to Zappa the musician that cannot be assessed simply by listing the idioms he had mastered. It is true that Zappa was keenly aware of the stylistic pigeonholes into which our culture insists on sorting its music—and he often took advantage of the audience's usual overreliance on stylistic distinctions to define its tastes, keeping his listeners off balance by engaging in lightning-fast transitions from one style to another, parodying these styles in the process while also poking fun at the conventions of a typical rock or orchestral concert. But for Zappa, on the most important level, music was really one big continuum, on which "anything, any time, anywhere—for no reason at all" could happen (Zappa 1989). The so-called worlds of rock, jazz, and classical music deserved, so far as he was concerned, to be treated as fictions: convenient ones sometimes, it was true, but mainly to be overridden or ignored in the interests of greater freedom of expression. In the ideal musical universe, there would be no need for crossover, for everything would be available, all the time, to everyone. These are the pieces that reveal the most clearly how Zappa attempted to realize his dreams.

Appendix

Discography for Zappa's crossover pieces, listed in the order discussed (Table 1.2). All issues listed are the most recently available. (The entire Rykodisc catalog remains in print; I make no guarantees about other items.) All recordings are single CDs, unless otherwise indicated.

Table 1.2 Discography for Frank Zappa's Crossover Pieces.

Date	Location	Album Particulars
I. "The Duke of Prunes" (including "Amnesia Vivace" and "The Duke Regains His Chops")		
11/1966	Los Angeles (studio)	*Absolutely Free* (1967/88) Rykodisc 10502
9/17–18/1975	Los Angeles	*Orchestral Favorites* (1979) Rykodisc 10529
II. "Envelopes"		
4/1982	Los Angeles (studio)	*Ship Arriving Too Late to Save a Drowning Witch* (1982) Rykodisc 10539
1/12–14/1983	London (studio)	*London Symphony Orchestra, Vols. 1 and 2* (1983, 1987; 1995) Rykodisc 10540/41 (two CDs)
5/30–31/1992	Cincinnati	*Songs and Dances* (The Cincinnati College-Conservatory of Music Wind Symphony, cond. Eugene Corporon) (1992) Mark MCD-1116
III. "The Dog Breath Variations" (a.k.a. "Dog/Meat")		
10/1967–4/1968	New York (studio tracks); Los Angeles (overdubs)	*Uncle Meat* (1969/1988) Rykodisc 10506/07 (two CDs)
9/22/1974	Helsinki	*You Can't Do That on Stage Anymore, Vol. 2* (1988) Rykodisc 10563/64 (two CDs)
5/30–31/1992	Cincinnati	*Songs and Dances* (see above)

(*Continued*)

Table 1.2 Discography for Frank Zappa's Crossove Pieces (*Continued*)

Date	Location	Album Particulars
IV. "Strictly Genteel"		
2–5/1971	London; L. A. (overdubs)	*200 Motels* (1971/1997) Rykodisc 10513/14 (two CDs)
9/17–18/1975	Los Angeles	*Orchestral Favorites* (see above)
10/31/1981	New York	*You Can't Do That on Stage Anymore, Vol. 6* (1992) Rykodisc 10571/72 (two CDs)
1/12–14/1983	London	*London Symphony Orchestra* (see above)
5/15/1988	Seville	*Make a Jazz Noise Here* (1991) Rykodisc 10555/56 (two CDs)
V. "Dupree's Paradise"		
8/21/1973	Stockholm	*Piquantique* (1991)* Rhino Foo-eee R2-70544
9/22/1974	Helsinki	*You Can't Do That on Stage Anymore, Vol. 2* (see above)
1/10–11/1984	Paris	*The Perfect Stranger* (1984) Rykodisc 10542
5/25/1988	Mannheim	*Make a Jazz Noise Here* (see above)
VI. "A Pound for a Brown (on the Bus)"		
10/1967–4/1968	New York and Los Angeles (studios)	*Uncle Meat* (see above)
2/1968	The Family Dog, Denver	*Electric Aunt Jemima* (1992)* Rhino Foo-eee R4-71019 (cassette)
10/28/1968	Royal Albert Hall, London	*Ahead of Their Time* (1993) Rykodisc 10559
11/8/1968	Fullerton, Calif.	*Our Man in Nirvana* (1992)* Rhino Foo-eee R4-71022 (cassette)
6/6/1971	Fillmore East, New York	*Tengo Na Minchia Tanta* (1992)* Rhino Foo-eee R4-71018 (cassette)
12/4/1971	The Casino, Montreux (Switzerland)	*Swiss Cheese/Fire!* (1992)* Rhino Foo-eee R4-71021 (cassette)
10 or 12/1976	New York	*Zappa in New York* (1978/91) Rykodisc 10524/25 (two CDs)
7/1/1978	Circus-Krone, Munich	*At the Circus* (1992)* Rhino Foo-eee R4-71020 (cassette)
9/3/1978	Ludwigsparksta-dion, Saarbrücken	*Saarbrücken 1978* (1991)* Rhino Foo-eee R2-70543

**Legally reissued bootlegs.*

(*Continued*)

Table 1.2 Discography for Frank Zappa's Crossover Pieces (*Continued*)

Date	Location	Album Particulars
10/31/1979	The Palladium, New York	*You Can't Do That on Stage Anymore, Vol. 4* (1991) Rykodisc 10567/68 (two CDs)
5–7/1982	1982 European Tour	*You Can't Do That on Stage Anymore, Vol. 5* (1992) Rykodisc 10569/70 (two CDs)
9/17&19/1992	Alte Oper, Frankfurt	*The Yellow Shark* (1993) Rykodisc 10560
VII. "Sinister Footwear"		
7–8/1980	studio (III)	*You Are What You Is* (1981) Rykodisc 10536
6/15/1984	Berkeley, Calif. (I, II, III)	Berkeley Symphony Orchestra, cond. Kent Nagano; *Apocrypha* (1994) Great Dane Records GDR-9405/ABCD [Italian bootleg]
1984	studio (II)	*Them or Us* (1984) Rykodisc 10543
8/11/1984	Madison, Wisc. (III, titled Variations on Sinister #3)	*Guitar* (1988) Rykodisc 10550/51 (two CDs)
3/19/1988	Allentown, Pa. (II)	*Make a Jazz Noise Here* (see above)

Notes

This essay represents a substantial expansion of a paper I read at the "Cross(over) Relations" conference, held at the Eastman School of Music, Rochester, New York, in September 1996. My heartfelt thanks to Arved Ashby, my session-mate at that conference, for his perceptive reading of a draft of this essay, for providing me with copies of certain recordings and other information essential to my research, and for sharing his own work and his insights into many of the issues engaged here.

1. There were exceptions to this pattern, of course. Pierre Boulez's recordings on *The Perfect Stranger*, in 1984, far outshone any previous realizations of Zappa's orchestral or chamber music in their technical competence. The very successful collaborations with Joel Thome and his Orchestra of Our Time (1991) and with the Ensemble Modern (1992) would certainly have been followed by others, had Zappa lived longer.
2. Partly to keep this project to the relatively modest dimensions of a single essay and partly to facilitate the reader's access to relevant material, I have worked almost exclusively with legitimately released recordings: the commercial LPs and CDs brought out by Zappa during his lifetime, together with a few by his heirs after his death, and the legal reissues of recordings originally marketed

as bootlegs (see Appendix). There is a vast underground catalog of hundreds, perhaps thousands, of recordings of widely varying quality currently in illegal distribution, transmitting the content of Zappa's many, many concerts over a quarter century in largely unedited form. The evidence afforded by such recordings would undoubtedly be of value in refining, particularizing, and extending the conclusions reached here. However, I find it difficult to imagine that it would substantially alter them.

3. Some ambiguities in this regard arise with the pieces included on the Ensemble Modern's Zappa disc, *The Yellow Shark* (1993). See discussion below, and note 22. After some thought, I decided to omit "Bogus Pomp" from consideration, since as an actual, single work under that title it exists only in two orchestral versions. Some of its ancestors can be heard as a kind of incidental music to the playlet "Progress?" from the live concert of October 1968 in London recorded on *Ahead of Their Time* (1993); and, in a form more closely related to the orchestral version, in the score of *200 Motels* (1971). Also not included in Table 1.1 are the arrangements of "King Kong," "The Idiot Bastard Son," "Twenty Small Cigars," and "America Drinks and Goes Home," done by Zappa for jazz violinist Jean-Luc Ponty's 1970 album *King Kong*. These are in some sense crossover efforts, but into jazz rather than the ACE art-music world. At that time, Zappa had no firm standing yet among jazz musicians, but thanks to his *Hot Rats* album (1969) he already had the makings of a reputation there. And Zappa's own "regular" charts for the Mothers of 1966–1969, which featured winds as well as keyboards and a rhythm section, were not radically different in instrumentation from those he wrote for Ponty.
4. See Bernard 2000. The version on *Orchestral Favorites* was reissued on *Läther* (Rykodisc 10574/76, three CDs, 1996), where it bears the title "The Duke of Orchestral Prunes."
5. This history is not entirely as straightforward as it might at first seem from the details recounted here. According to available playlists, Zappa began to play some version of "Envelopes" in concert as early as fall 1977. An illicit tape from a concert in early 1978 reveals this piece to be, if not quite in finished form, at least in possession of its basic shape by that time (it also had some rather filthy lyrics, later expunged). Thus it is possible that the rock version actually predates any ACE version, or that the two were somehow written in parallel—although in the absence of certain knowledge of the exact date(s) of composition for the ACE scores, it is impossible to resolve such questions once and for all. Arved Ashby makes a cogent case for the rock version's precedence, arguing not just on the basis of extrinsic evidence but on intrinsic as well: that the wind parts of the opening section transparently emulate the idiomatically guitar-like phrasing in which the work was originally conceived (Ashby 1999). One informative source of Zappa playlists can be found at http://www.wins.uva.nl/~heederik/zappa/faq/text/fzshows.txt.
6. Zappa 1993. In his statement, Zappa does not mention the wind-ensemble score available (at least at one time) from his publisher, Munchkin Music/Barfko-Swill, which bears a copyright date of 1970. However, either this date is an error or the score in question existed in some form at that time but actually received some final revisions a good while later, since the instrumentation includes a Syndrum and a CS-80 (a type of keyboard synthesizer), neither of which was in manufacture by 1970. (I am grateful to my colleague Tom Collier at the

University of Washington School of Music for supplying this information.) Perhaps this arrangement is actually the one done for the Netherlands Wind Ensemble, even though it requires at least thirty-two musicians (not "twenty-some") if all parts are properly doubled.

7. In Example 1.1, the excerpt from "The Dog Breath Variations" is my transcription from the 1969 recording. "Uncle Meat (Main Theme)" is taken from a reproduction of Zappa's manuscript chart for this work, included in the booklet insert with the original two-LP release of *Uncle Meat* (Bizarre/Reprise 2MS-2024, 1969).
8. This shortened title of "Dog Breath, in the Year of the Plague" was adopted, for instance, for the version included on the 1972 Mothers' album, *Just Another Band from L.A.* (Rykodisc 10515).
9. The link forged here between "Dog Breath" and its variations works well because the first two phrases of "The Dog Breath Variations," as played in its original version on *Uncle Meat*, are, in melodic terms, simply a rhythmic variation of the first two phrases of "Dog Breath."
10. For some comments on the reprise in Zappa's music, and on its stylistic debts, see Bernard 2000.
11. This timing and the others cited in this paragraph are taken from the recording on *You Can't Do That on Stage Anymore, Vol. 2*, Disc 2, Track 6 (see Appendix).
12. This voice appears on Mothers of Invention recordings after the departure of Ray Collins from the band. Zappa was not happy with his natural singing voice and had little confidence in it; in the meantime, lacking a replacement for Collins, he adopted the cartoon-voice stratagem so that his albums would not have to consist entirely of instrumental cuts. See Zappa's self-deprecating remarks in the liner notes to *Uncle Meat* and *Cruising with Ruben and the Jets* (1968), as well as "My Splendid Voice" (Zappa 1989, 182).
13. My numbering of bars and calculation of the duration of sections in number of bars have been done without reference to any printed score. A steady meter of 3/4 is assumed throughout. The only two places where rhythmic intricacies or tempo fluctuation (or, possibly in one case, a fermata) create any uncertainty as to exact number of beats or bars occur (in all versions) at mm. 40–41 and (in all but the *200 Motels* version, and assuming that my count at the earlier spot is correct) mm. 73–76.
14. As Ashby has pointed out, "Strictly Genteel" in its original form is a parody of Broadway musical-style finales, and for that reason is not really akin to the "high art" of modernist orchestral music (Ashby 1999).
15. Many thanks to Andy Hollinden for providing me with a copy of this videotape.
16. Timings for this earliest version of "Dupree's Paradise" are taken from the 1974 recording, on *You Can't Do That on Stage Anymore, Vol. 2*, Disc 2, Track 3. "Dupree's Paradise" proper is preceded in this performance by a long, partly played and partly spoken introduction (until 7:26).
17. One wonders, not altogether idly, whether Zappa's and Boulez's mutual attraction might have been a reflection of their similar willingness to engage in continual revision and re-revision of their pieces—something for which Boulez is thought to be somewhat unusual among contemporary Western art-music composers.

18. Zappa referred to "Agon" as "a beautiful thing" and as one of his two most highly recommended works by Stravinsky in "My Favorite Records" (1967; reprinted in Chevalier 1986, 108). Zappa is known to have included an arrangement of "Agon"'s opening in at least one of his band concerts (May 11, 1970, at the Fillmore East in New York). See http://www.wins.uva.nl/~heederik/zappa/faq/text/fzshows.txt. Other influences are also at work in this ACE remake of "Dupree's Paradise." Particularly obvious is the "American neoclassic" flavor of the opening **A** material, with its doubling of a vaguely folksy melody by xylophone and marimba. That this might in some sense have been a conscious homage is suggested by Zappa's response to an interviewer's question about Aaron Copland, holding him responsible for listeners' tendency to register the typical sound of an American symphonic work as "it's a hoedown tune and there's a xylophone doubling the melody on top"—a typically left-handed compliment (Diliberto and Haas 1981).
19. The evidence attesting to this practice is found on the legally reissued bootleg *Our Man in Nirvana* (see Appendix).
20. In his liner notes to *Uncle Meat*, Zappa reports that "things that sound like trumpets are actually clarinets played through an electric device made by Maestro with a setting labeled 'Oboe D'Amore' and sped up a minor third with a V.S.O. (variable speed oscillator)" (Zappa 1969). However, other production facts related here, as well as the resultant sounds on the album, suggest that many additional techniques were used to modify the natural sounds of acoustic and electric instruments.
21. In the Montreux performance, the presence of "Sleeping in a Jar" is registered mainly by implication, since the anonymous bootlegger saw fit to fade out the recording just as the introductory bars of that tune were coming to an end.
22. The liner notes to *The Yellow Shark* are self-contradictory on this point. The list of contents credits the arrangement of six of the eighteen works on this CD, *not* including "A Pound for a Brown," to Ali N. Askin. However, in the accompanying prose, Askin is credited with having done this arrangement. It must be kept in mind that by mid-1992 Zappa was already quite ill with terminal prostate cancer, forcing him to adjust to considerably reduced energies in ways that no doubt seemed less than ideal. Given the fact that Askin, on all his arrangements (whichever ones these actually are), worked from Zappa's own Synclavier printouts, perhaps these versions of works on *The Yellow Shark* are best regarded as collaborations.
23. The opening music to "The Uncle Meat Variations" is distinctly different from the "Uncle Meat" theme proper; the treatment of that theme begins about one minute into the cut. In the liner notes to *The Yellow Shark*, Zappa identifies "Exercise #4" as a composition of his dating from about 1962.
24. The full score of "Sinister Footwear" is apparently still available from Zappa's publisher, Munchkin Music/Barfko-Swill (now owned and operated by the Zappa Family Trust), at the rather steep price of $500. According to Zappa, most of his ACE scores (with the obvious exception of his work in *200 Motels*) were written in the "late '70s, early '80s" (Birchall 1984).
25. The track entitled "Variations on Sinister #3" included in the Appendix could be regarded as a kind of trope upon the third movement. It is based on the same E-Lydian scale (with E pedal) but is appreciably longer than the "Theme from the

Third Movement of Sinister Footwear" found on *You Are What You Is* (5′15″ vs. 3′31″). Further, the melodic material is quite different, even if some of the figures are notably reminiscent of those of the original piece. In other words, it behaves very much like an improvised guitar solo, in which one would never expect exactly the same music from one occasion to another. This spun-off version, perhaps, provides the most accurate indication of the origins of "Sinister III."

26. The form of that title, however, does leave open the possibility that in 1981 or even later the third movement of the orchestral score was longer than it ended up being in performance in 1984. Or the third movement could simply have been truncated in performance for practical reasons, such as technical difficulties and lack of adequate rehearsal time.
27. Again, as in the case of "Envelopes," resolution of such questions is hampered by lack of certainty as to actual dates of composition for the ACE score. It is entirely possible, if Vai's transcription came early enough, that Zappa used it as the basis for the third movement of his ballet. The chronology is clouded further by reports that the transcription published in Zappa 1982 is not Vai's *original* transcription. The "original version," as Vai calls it, of this music was called "Persona Non Grata" and dates, most likely, from a concert at the Palladium in New York City around Halloween 1978. For more details, see Watson 1995, 390–391. Ashby's insightful reading of these details, as well as his hearing of the orchestral version as mimicking the feedback, string-scraping, and other characteristic noises of Zappa's guitar technique, leads him to believe that the rock version of this movement was composed first (Ashby 1999).
28. Chapter 8 ("All about Music"), in Zappa 1989 (also see notes 5 and 27).

References

Ashby, Arved. 1999. Frank Zappa and the Anti-Fetishist Orchestra. *The Musical Quarterly* 83, 557–606.

Bernard, Jonathan W. 2000. Listening to Zappa. *Contemporary Music Review* 18/4, 63–104.

Birchall, Steve. 1984. Modern Music Is a Sick Puppy. *Digital Audio Magazine* 1/2 (October), 43–49; 1/3 (November), 44–47.

Chevalier, Dominique. 1986. *Viva! Zappa*. New York: St. Martin's Press.

Diliberto, John, and Haas, Kimberly. 1981. Frank Zappa on Edgar Varèse. *Down Beat* 48/11 (November), 21–23, 64.

Grier, James. 2001. The Mothers of Invention and *Uncle Meat*: Alienation, Anachronism, and a Double Variation. *Acta Musicologica* 73, 77–95.

Tullius, F. P. 1971. Zubin and the Mothers. *Playboy* (April), 149+.

Watson, Ben. 1995. *The Negative Dialectics of Poodle Play*. New York: St. Martin's Press.

Zappa, Frank. 1968. Liner-note credits to *Cruising with Ruben and the Jets*. Verve V6 5055-X; currently available as Rykodisc 10505.

———. 1969. Liner notes to *Uncle Meat*. Bizarre-Reprise Records 2MS-2024 (two LPs); currently available as Rykodisc 10506/07 (two CDs).

———. 1982. *The Frank Zappa Guitar Book*. North Hollywood: Munchkin Music.

———. 1989. *The Real Frank Zappa Book*. With Peter Ochiogrosso. New York: Poseidon Press.

———. 1993. Conversation with Peter Rundel. In liner notes to *The Yellow Shark*. Rykodisc RCD-10560.

2

Frank Zappa's "The Black Page"

A Case of Musical "Conceptual Continuity"

JAMES BORDERS

The release of preliminary versions of well-known rock songs—the Beatles' *Anthology* volumes and *The Pet Sounds Sessions* come immediately to mind—presents listeners with the rare opportunity to eavesdrop on the development of their favorite songs. For those who study the processes of composition and production in rock more closely, these newly available recordings also pose some new and interesting questions. How do earlier versions of songs differ from final releases? What musical factors played into decisions to change an arrangement, a timbre, or a tempo? What other contingencies were involved? When is a song truly finished? Evaluating the choices made, the ideas accepted, rejected, or transformed, holds the promise of illuminating what ultimately took shape and why.

To be sure, the use of recordings in analysis taxes one's aural acuity and patience, but may strain the memory and imagination even more. This is because of the need to compare musical events (generally un-notated and otherwise undocumented) that have unfolded over time and in layers of activity undertaken by numerous persons with different roles in the production process. Moreover, to fill gaps in a song's chronology, as many versions as can be found (including recordings of live performances) must be put into proper order and compared. The results of such efforts would be the beginnings of an analytic approach to rock that could be considered analogous to the comparison of a composer's sketches and drafts with the finished work. They are analogous because the processes and products in rock are categorically different from those in Western concert music of the classical tradition.

There is no longer any excuse for making this comparison naïvely, thanks to a recent book by Theodore Gracyk, *Rhythm and Noise* (1996). Using terms appropriated from philosophy and aesthetics, Gracyk argues that an important difference between classical and rock music has to do with the properties of sound, particularly recorded sound. While he would describe most classical music as ontologically thin, i.e., identifiable in terms of the written score irrespective of instrumentation or approach to performance, rock songs or albums are by comparison ontologically thick. This means that their identity depends not on notation or even instrumentation, but on aural factors that are not easily reduced to writing, such as timbre, the amount of echo, and the mix of the recording. The line of investigation I will take up here will extend Gracyk's approach to another aspect of recordings: how repeated listening to recorded performances bears upon the perception of form in rock.

This essay concerns the music of Frank Zappa which, as is so often the case, does not fit neatly into categories or submit to theories, even those as carefully formed as Gracyk's. True, some of Zappa's recordings could be called (to use Gracyk's terminology) ontologically thick. "I'm The Slime" and "Montana" from *Over-nite Sensation*, for example, are relatively well fixed in many listeners' memories. Zappa himself recognized this instinctively; live performances of these numbers (as documented on subsequent releases and other recordings) recreated the tempos, grooves, and even the timbres of the originals. Rather than being the rule, however, the popularity of these songs makes these live performances distinctive.[1] Generally speaking, Zappa changed arrangements of the same song considerably from one release to the next.

Many listeners know that the catalog of Zappa's recordings is immense. There are nearly eighty official releases plus countless bootlegs, unauthorized and authorized.[2] Not all of these, however, feature completely new music, and many songs can be found on two or more albums. There are, in addition, numerous reissues and repackagings as well as apparent re-releases that contain new overdubbed material. The most famous (or infamous) such case involves the Mothers of Invention's *We're Only in It For the Money*, originally released in January 1968. For its first Ryko CD reissue, Zappa substituted new bass and drum parts for those he claimed had degenerated on the master tapes. The bassist on the session, Arthur Barrow, offers a different interpretation, suggesting that Zappa simply no longer liked them (Slaven 1996, 264–265). Adding insult to injury, so to speak, Zappa instructed Barrow to incorporate a riff from "My Sharona" on "Flower Punk," despite the fact that the Knack's hit (1979) postdated Zappa's caustic ode to hippies by some twelve years. At least the lyrics censored on the original release were restored.

More pertinent than reissues to the kind of analysis I have in mind would be comparisons of songs recorded live with prior studio releases. These fall into two categories. In some cases, such as the live versions of "Inca Roads," "Zoot Allures," and "Black Napkins," Zappa's touring bands reproduced almost flawlessly (overdubs aside) the most difficult studio releases.[3] In most other cases, though, the differences between studio and live work involved changes in timbre, tempo, and groove, often in an effort to update an old song. "Trouble Every Day," for example, written in reaction to the 1965 Watts riots and released on the first Mothers of Invention album, *Freak Out!* (July 1966), combines a blues-guitar riff with the trebly timbres popular with West Coast bands at the time. As originally released, the song can be heard as an exaggeratedly extended blues progression—Zappa may have taken his cue from Bob Dylan, whose "Subterranean Homesick Blues" stretches the limits of a different, though no less commonplace, chord progression to similar effect.[4] As reworked on Zappa's 1984 tour and heard on *Does Humor Belong in Music?* (January 1986), "Trouble Every Day" became an up-tempo number complete with horns, drum fills, a new blues hook, and guitar solo. This funky reincarnation has more in common with Earth, Wind, and Fire than with the 1960s group Paul Revere and the Raiders, whose sound the early Mothers sometimes mimicked.[5] Almost completely absent in the later, more complex arrangement is the sense of formal extension in the original release.

"Orange County Lumber Truck" is another case in point. First heard on the Mothers' *Weasels Ripped My Flesh* (August 1970), it is arguably the best groove this particular incarnation of the Mothers ever managed.[6] The abbreviated version heard on *Make a Jazz Noise Here* (June 1991) completely transforms this rhythmic feel. Played by a very different kind of band, "Orange County Lumber Truck" here becomes a quick, ironic circus march that matches Zappa's interpretation of a movement from Igor Stravinsky's *l'Histoire du soldat* suite, which he likewise recorded for the same CD. It too is played unusually fast.

As important as such updatings were to an artist with as long a career as Zappa's, there are instances in which a song was reworked for different reasons. For example, the meter of "You Didn't Try To Call Me" was changed from 4/4 to 3/4 in the transition from *Freak Out!* to *Cruising with Ruben and the Jets* (November 1968), probably because the grand pauses and over-the-top Phil Spector-like sound of the 1966 recording did not fit the 1950s parody theme of *Ruben*.[7] A similar triple-meter rendition can be heard in live performance on *You Can't Do That On Stage Anymore, Vol. 1.*

A song transformed under a still different set of circumstances is "The Black Page," an instrumental that Zappa realized in three notated versions: a drum solo and two instrumental arrangements identified as "The Black Page #1" and "The Black Page #2." (A score for the first and lead sheets for the other two have been published by Munchkin Music and made available through Barfko-Swill, Zappa's mail-order company. "The Black Page #1" was also printed in the February 1987 issue of *Keyboard* magazine. I shall refer to that widely available score in this essay.) All three versions were presented live for the first time in late December 1976 and later released on the double LP, *Zappa in New York (ZINY)*, in March 1978. (Following Zappa's own practice, it is customary to abbreviate the titles of his releases with acronyms. Zappa also observed his own rules for capitalizing the titles of songs and albums.) Besides this record, there are another four official releases of "The Black Page #2," making it one of the most frequently re-recorded instrumentals in the Zappa catalog (see Table 2.1). It is also found on at least thirteen known bootlegs, some of which were included in this study despite their relative obscurity (see Table 2.2). Even were these not consulted, the long list of bootleg recordings suggests how frequently Zappa's bands performed "The Black Page #2" in the late 1970s and 1980s.

Table 2.1 "The Black Page" (Frank Zappa): authorized releases.

Song Title	Album Title	Date of Recording	Timing
1. "The Black Page Drum Solo" and			
2. "The Black Page #1"	*Zappa in New York*	December 26, 1976	3'51"
3. "The Black Page #2"	*Zappa in New York*	December 26, 1976	5'36"
4. "The Black Page #1"	*Läther*	December 26, 1976	1'57"
5. "The Black Page #2"	*Baby Snakes*	October 31, 1977	2'51"
6. "The Black Page #2"*	*YCDTOSA #5*	Summer 1982	9'57"
7. "The Black Page #2"	*YCDTOSA #4*	November 1984	5'15"
8. "The Black Page #1"	*Keyboard*	February 1987	2'02"
9. "The Black Page (new-age version)" [#2]	*MAJNH*	1988 Tour	6'45"

* *The last part of the solo (from* 6:09) has been released as "Which One Is It?" on *Shut Up 'n Play Your Guitar*. The *YCDTOSA #5* track probably comes from the Munich performance, since this is where "Which One Is It?" was recorded, according to the *Guitar* liner notes. At 2:51, in the right channel, the distinctive (and arguably annoying) guitar riff from "Ya Hozna" (*Them Or Us*) is heard; it continues through the rest of the cut.

Table 2.2 "The Black Page #2" (Frank Zappa): known bootleg releases.

Album Title	Place	Date
*Zurkon Music**	New York	October 31, 1977
Wax Flags	Los Angeles	December 31, 1977
Punky's Whips Shown on Stage	Los Angeles	December 31, 1977
Live am Rhein	Düsseldorf	February 1, 1978
Berlin [Part 2] (CD)	Berlin	February 15, 1978
Apocrypha	Poughkeepse, NY	September 12, 1978
Peepers Parts 2 & 3	Poughkeepse, NY	September 21, 1978
As An Am	Cologne	May 21, 1982
Dweezil Has Messed My Mind Up	Vienna	June 28, 1982
Underground Record	Bolzano, Italy	July 3, 1982
Autographe '82	Italy?	July 1982
Carousel	Berlin	September 11, 1984
Raffle	Barcelona	May 17, 1988

* Subsequently reissued under different titles, including *Tiny Nightmares* (two LPs), *Donna U Wanna* (CD), *Invocations* (CD), *and The History & Collected Improvisations of Frank Zappa & the Mothers of Invention* (LP no. 9).

The point of this essay is to trace the transformation of "The Black Page" over successive notated versions, live performances, and recordings. It will also show how the instrumentation and competencies of Zappa's bands over the years influenced the decision to program and record the piece, as well as how and in what contexts it was played. Ultimately this examination will support two observations about the song's development: first, that "The Black Page #1" was never truly finished, and second, that "The Black Page #2" did become a viable instrumental number, but only after a usable form had emerged from a series of performance-based drafts. In the last of these, I will argue, structural coherence depends not so much on what was actually heard on stage as listeners' familiarity with earlier performances, especially those available on recordings.

"The Black Page": Three Identities

From the beginning, "The Black Page" was a piece that needed an explanation. In a monologue recorded for *ZINY*, Zappa tells his audience that it was first conceived as a solo for drummer Terry Bozzio. To this Zappa added a melody and chord progression, which he refers to as "The Black Page, Part 1, the Hard Version":

> All right, now watch this. Let me tell you about this song. This song was originally constructed as a drum solo. That's right. Now, after Terry learned how to play "The Black Page" on the drum set, I figured, well, maybe it would be good for other instruments. So I wrote a melody that went along with the drum solo. And that turned into "The Black Page, Part 1, the Hard Version"....

Then, allegedly for altruistic reasons in consideration of his listeners (though Zappa's characteristic irony is palpable on the recording), he reworked "Part 1" using the same melody and harmonic structure, but simplified some of the complex rhythms to fit a rock groove. This became "The Black Page, Part 2, the Easy Teenage New York Version":

> Then I said, well, what about the other people in the world, who might enjoy the melody of "The Black Page" but couldn't really approach its statistical density in its basic form. So I went to work and constructed a little ditty which is now being set up for you with this little disco-type vamp. This is "The Black Page, Part 2, the Easy Teenage New York Version." Get down with your bad self, so to speak, to "The Black Page, Part 2."

Side 2 of the *ZINY* LP presents the three versions of "The Black Page" in the order of their reported genesis as a series of movements in a suite. (The *ZINY* CD reissue has a different order, with the unrelated early single "Big Leg Emma" and the more recent "Sofa" interpolated between "#1" and "#2.") Zappa was of course familiar with the normally understood concept of the suite at the time (whereas other rock artists have shown misunderstandings in this regard).

He sometimes used the term in describing his own music, and clearly knew well suites by composers like Ravel, Stravinsky, and Holst.

The three versions of "The Black Page" could hardly have come into being in a way other than what Zappa described, but the sequence of music on the *ZINY* LP—drum solo–Part 1–Part 2—is an *ex post facto* restructuring, the product of studio editing not unlike the overdubs alluded to in the album's liner notes. According to set lists for the December 26–29, 1976, New York Palladium shows, the dates on which material for *ZINY* was recorded, "The Black Page #2" was always heard before the drum solo and "#1" with no fewer than six songs intervening.[8] Moreover, the same set lists indicate that Bozzio's solo and "The Black Page #1" were seamlessly and anonymously worked into another Zappa instrumental, "A Pound For A Brown (on The Bus)," a song that is covered extensively by Jonathan Bernard in Chapter 1. Perhaps the most attentive audience members would have caught the musical relationship between "The Black Page #2" and its varied reprise at the end of the familiar Zappa classic from *Uncle Meat*, played some time later. But they certainly did not hear "The Black Page" as a series of movements proceeding logically from the drum solo to the "Easy" version.

Thus we may draw two preliminary conclusions based on what we have learned so far. First, both on stage and in the production studio "The Black Page" was very much a work in progress in 1976–1977. When editing *ZINY* for its LP release, Zappa spliced the successive versions into a single unit. What held this together was not musical form in the traditional sense, however, but the tale of the work's emergence, which itself became an integral and self-conscious part of the recording. Yes, it was a pragmatic solution to the problem of organizing material on a record, but it was not an approach Zappa ever adopted in live performance. The three versions of "The Black Page" were never heard this way on stage, in New York or anywhere else.

The second preliminary conclusion is that the drum solo and "The Black Page #1" were already receding into the background even before the Palladium shows, probably because Zappa was unhappy with the level of performance. Why else would he call "The Black Page #2" the "Easy Teenage New York Version" in a pinched tone of voice that would have been readily associated with Johnny Carson's skits on "The Tonight Show"? The simplified arrangement—a compromise to his band's capabilities—was obviously written and rehearsed before the New York shows. Our initial suspicions about Zappa's dissatisfaction are all but confirmed once we note that neither the drum solo nor "The Black Page, Part 1" survived the 1976–1977 world tour. Zappa's sarcastic tone of voice clues us in to the main problem his sidemen had with the "Hard" version, namely a degree of rhythmic complexity matched only by the most difficult post-1945 avant-garde compositions.[9]

Although "The Black Page #1" is regular in its 4/4 meter, its syncopation and rhythmic subdivisions made it challenging even for Zappa's elite

1976–1977 group. Two levels of rhythmic subdivision can be identified, which will be referred to here as first- and second-generation complexities. This distinction is based on whether a tuplet (i. e., triplets, quintuplets, and so on) divides a regular metric unit (thwarting the pulse, and thus signifying level-one complexity) or is itself part of a larger-level tuplet (neutralizing the pulse still further, and thus signifying level-two complexity). A good example of the first generation can be seen in measure 4 (Example 2.1), where groups of seven notes are placed on the third and fourth beats. Here performers must feel the quarter-note pulse while placing the sixteenth-note groupings. The second beat of the same measure also falls into the first-generation category, since the triplet and quintuplet fall within the space of a quarter note, though performers must place three sixteenth notes in the first half of the beat and five thirty-second notes in the second. Gestures like these are difficult for an ensemble to execute in unison—as Zappa's does—but the placement of these rhythms in relation to the basic pulse at least makes them easier than those we call second-generation rhythmic complexities.

One such second-generation complexity may be seen in measure 5, beats three and four (Example 2.2). This gesture, which comprises two groupings of five equal note values plus one of six, is placed within a higher-level quarter-note triplet. The performer must not only feel the quarter note as the basic pulse, but must also sense the first-generation quarter-note triplet, simultaneously placing five notes within the first and second triplets, and six within the third. Another example of a second-generation complexity can be seen in measure 15 (Example 2.3), where the irregular tuplets divide quarter-note triplets.

On *ZINY* we hear a performance of "The Black Page #1" that is anything but sloppy, but it seems not to have completely satisfied Zappa, whose desire to hear his music played accurately was widely reported (for instance, in

Example 2.1 Frank Zappa, "The Black Page #1" (Frank Zappa), *Zappa In New York* (1978): level-one rhythmic complexity.

Example 2.2 Frank Zappa, "The Black Page #1" (Frank Zappa), *Zappa In New York* (1978): level-two rhythmic complexity.

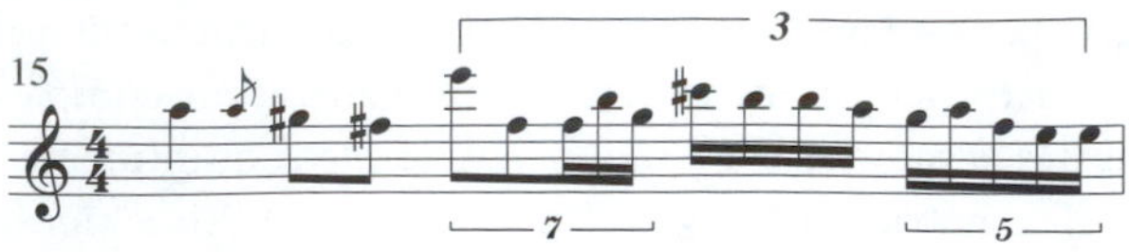

Example 2.3 Frank Zappa, "The Black Page #1" (Frank Zappa), *Zappa In New York* (1978): level-two rhythmic complexity.

Zappa and Occiogrosso 1989, 155–156 and 173–176). This record was the only commercial release of the piece, that is, until the posthumous re-release of one of the 1976 New York performances (probably December 26) on the triple CD *Läther* (September 1996). Zappa continued to attempt an accurate rendition of the rhythmically difficult "#1," as indicated by his programming of it for the Synclavier. But the fact that he authorized the distribution of this realization on a flexible vinyl "Soundpage" accompanying the February 1987 issue of *Keyboard* rather than on *Frank Zappa Meets the Mothers of Prevention* (November 1985) or *Jazz From Hell* (November 1986), both of which featured Synclavier music and which were produced about the same time as the *Keyboard* feature, strongly suggests that Zappa had relegated "The Black Page #1" to "freebie" status. This was, in all likelihood, an attempt to introduce a new audience of music-tech types to his music.[10] A further speculation as to why Zappa set "#1" aside will be explored at the end of this essay, but for now let's look at "The Black Page #2," which stood alone as the version he thought appropriate for his touring bands from 1977 on.

The beginnings of the development of "The Black Page #2" must be traced back to *ZINY,* and here similarities with "The Black Page #1" tell us almost as much as the differences. The shapes of the melodies, for instance, are nearly identical apart from some variations and extensions in "#2." Both oscillate between A major and A minor until a decisive move to A♭ major at the end. Like other Zappa tunes, this one involves unexpected shifts between stepwise motion and leaps as large as a major ninth, although perfect fourths and fifths are more common (see Example 2.2). Melodies like this tend to support Zappa's long-standing claim of being a composer who happened to play the guitar, since gaps like these were more idiomatic to that instrument than, say, a keyboard (Rosen 1997, 102). Other rock instrumentals in the Zappa catalog with the same characteristic are "Uncle Meat" and "Big Swifty" (*Waka/Jawaka).*

The strings of suspended-second chords that underlie the two versions give them both the same bitonal edge. The progression involves metrically predictable alternations between two chords a minor third apart (G^2 to $B\flat^2$) cadencing on D^2 ("#1": mm. 1–8/9–16; "#2": mm. 1–32/33–51), followed by the same alternating G^2 to $B\flat^2$ chords cadencing on C ("#1": mm. 19–23/24–28; "#2": mm. 56–75/76–88). "The Black Page #1" closes $C\sharp^2$–B^2–$A\flat^2$ (mm. 29–30), the first of these chords simultaneously "splitting the difference" between the dominant (D) and subdominant (C), and serving as the dominant (enharmonically, D♭) of an unexpected G♭² chord ("#1": mm. 17–18) that follows the dominant. "The Black Page #2" ends similarly, except that the last phrase is heard three times in varied repetition; it closes G♯²–B²–E/F. This difference aside, the basic chord structure of both versions, clearly out of place in rock of the late 1970s, illustrates two features common to other Zappa progressions (including some used for his most famous guitar solos): a preference for two-chord ostinatos and unpredictable root motion, in this case first to the dominant then to the subdominant, a kind of reverse and perverse "Louie Louie."[11]

As for the differences between the *ZINY* instrumentals, the most obvious one is rhythm. The ratio of total measures, "Hard" to "Easy" versions, is approximately 1:3, the number of measures increasing from 30 in "#1" to 102 in "#2." (Keep in mind, though, that the repeated phrase at the end of "#2" adds an extra eight measures.) This gross comparison of events as notated suggests that Zappa simply multiplied the rhythmic values of "The Black Page #1" in creating "#2," which he sometimes did. For instance, sixteenth-note sextuplets (such as those in "#1," mm. 5 and 8) became pairs of quarter-note triplets. Other rhythms were simplified in their notation if not also in actual performance: sixteenth-note quintuplets in "#1" became, in "#2," two eighths plus quarter-note triplet or quarter-note triplet plus dotted quarter plus eighth note. The most important change in the rhythmic vocabulary, however, was the elimination of all second-generation complexities from "The Black Page #2," which presumably led Zappa to label this version "Easy." (Retained at the end of "#2" were the difficult elevens, but these are level-one complexities.)

A second difference between the versions involves the bass and drum parts. The derivation of the "Black Page" melody from the original solo is made plain in "#1" by the drummer's doubling of the xylophone and synthesizer; the hi-hat marks the beat both here and in the preceding drum solo. The bass, for its part, plays mainly long notes along with some fragments of the melody. This approach reinforces the slow-moving changes and avoids any competition with the complex rhythms. In "#2," by contrast, the bass propels the piece rhythmically by maintaining the disco groove; the drum set continues to play the melody, but Bozzio's fills on sustained notes obviously do much more than merely provide a clue as to where the beat is.

The instrumentations of the two *ZINY* instrumentals also differ. "The Black Page #1" features primarily drums, bass, xylophone, and synthesizer. Guitar, winds (saxophones, trumpet, trombone), and overdubbed harp play a secondary role consistent with the placement of these instruments far back in the mix. In "#2," rhythm guitar and electric piano play more prominent accompanimental roles; horns are not used in the arrangement until the close, which is capped off by Randy Brecker's camp plunger-mute trumpet solo. Zappa

Table 2.3 "The Black Page #1" (Frank Zappa), *ZINY*: sectional form.

Sections:	**A**	**Transition**	**A'**	**Codetta**
No. of measures:	11	4	11	4
Measures:	1–11	12–15	16–26	27–30

himself wrote of this version in the *ZINY* liner notes: "And, once again, our theme re-orchestrated, rhythmically modified, and set to a cheap little disco vamp, against which the polyrhythmic anomalies become yet more enchanting."

Despite the obvious importance of changes in rhythm, arrangement, and instrumentation in distinguishing the two *ZINY* versions, the most significant difference from the standpoint of the song's later development involves formal structure. "The Black Page #1" is a two-part form with an **A** section plus transition, followed by an **A'** section plus codetta (see Table 2.3). The form is articulated by repetitions of rhythm and melody: Compare measures 1–3 and 16–18 (rhythm only), and measures 5–8 and 19–23 (rhythm and melody), noting that in **A'** the latter part of the melody is played a whole step lower than in **A** (compare mm. 9–11 and 24–26).

In reworking the piece as "The Black Page #2," Zappa changed the rhythm and melody precisely at the point that would otherwise have been the opening of section **A'**. Example 2.4 compares "#2," measures 1–13 and 50–56, with "#1," measures 1–3 (**A**, beginning) and 16–18 (**A'**, beginning). Because the connection between the rhythms at these points of "#2" is lacking, the repeat of melody in measures 56–75 takes on increased prominence as a form-giving device. Therefore, I would argue that as a result of this change one hears "The Black Page #2" as a variation rondo (**A–B–C–B'–D**). This was Zappa's favorite classically oriented form for untexted music and one that he used repeatedly in recordings from *Lumpy Gravy* (1968) through *Chunga's Revenge* (1970) (see Borders 2001). Note further (in Table 2.4) that four of the five sections (**B–C–B'–D**) can be heard as comprising three smaller subunits each (**t u v | w x y | t u' v' | z z' z"** respectively), due largely to metrical expansion. As we shall see, this new formal scheme was an important, though intermediary, step in the song's evolution.

Later Versions of "The Black Page"

As noted earlier, "The Black Page" was dropped from the set lists of the *ZINY* group immediately after the New York dates. This may have been because percussionist Ruth Underwood and the musicians in the horn section were engaged only for those shows. According to the website FZShows v. 6.0,[12] there were no performances of "The Black Page" during the European leg of this band's tour, completed in March 1977. Indeed, "The Black Page #1" was never again played live. "The Black Page #2," on the other hand, reappeared on set

Example 2.4 Frank Zappa, "The Black Page" (Frank Zappa), *Zappa In New York* (1978): comparisons of a) "#2" (mm. 1–12) and b) "#1" (1–3), and of c) "#2" (mm. 50–55), and d) "#1" (16–18).

lists less than a year after the *ZINY* dates. This version can be heard on *Baby Snakes*, a live album recorded on October 31, 1977 (see Table 1.1). Featuring *ZINY* veterans Bozzio and Patrick O'Hearn (bass), along with Ed Mann on mallet percussion, this recording has a disco groove similar to that heard on *ZINY*, but without the horn and synthesizer breaks and variations in tempo. (Following the practice of other writers I shall refer to the band that recorded *Baby Snakes* as "Zappa 2," numbering succeeding bands in sequential order.) The form of the *Baby Snakes* version is practically identical to that on *ZINY* except for the closing chord, which segues into "Jones Crusher Love."

Zappa seems to have closely connected the *Baby Snakes* lineup with "The Black Page #2." Not only did Zappa 2 perform it often, but the number was all but shelved after this group disbanded in the spring of 1978. True, Zappa's next band (Zappa 3), which included Vinnie Colaiuta (drums) and Arthur Barrow (bass) along with the veteran Mann, attempted "The Black Page #2," but their efforts bore no fruit—Zappa never officially released any of their

Table 2.4 "The Black Page #2" (Frank Zappa), *ZINY*: sectional and subsectional form.

Sections:	A		B			C			B'			D	
No. of meas.:	[12]		[29]			[14]			[29]			[18]	
Measures:	1-12		13-41			42-55			56-84			85-102	
Sub-sections:		t	u	v	w	x	y	t	u'	v'	z	z'	z"
No. of meas.:		[8	16	5]	[5	5	4]	[8	16	5]	[10	4	4]
Measures:		13–20	21–36	37–41	42–46	47–51	52–55	56–63	64–79	80–84	85–94	95–98	99–102

performances of it. Perhaps the placement of the number in the shows was wrong. Zappa tried three different ones between September 17 and October 27, 1978:

Sept. 17	... "Mo 'n Herb's Vacation," "The Black Page #2," "Uncle Meat" ...
Sept. 21	... [Same as Sept. 17]
Oct. 11	... "Titties And Beer," "The Black Page #2," "Black Napkins" ...
Oct. 27	... "Conehead," "The Black Page #2," "Little House I Used To Live In" ...

Legend also has it that the band rehearsed a samba version of "The Black Page #2" in early August before the tour.

Maybe he didn't like the sparse instrumentation of Zappa 3 (as can be heard on the bootleg, *Apocrypha*), which would perhaps have been more appropriate for "The Black Page #1" than "#2." It may also have been that he found the straight-ahead rock beat or individual performances unsatisfactory. Colaiuta's playing, in particular, is competent but much less driving than Bozzio's. Whatever the reason, after a short period of experimentation in 1978, Zappa set "The Black Page #2" aside for nearly three years. Zappa 5 and 6, bands that did not include mallet percussionists, never played it.

"The Black Page #2" surfaced again some years later for Zappa's last three tours in 1981–1982, 1984, and 1988. Recordings by Zappa 7, 8, and 9—bands whose lineups all included the same bassist, drummer, and percussionist, Scott Thunes, Chad Wackerman, and Ed Mann, respectively—demonstrate a significant change in the song's function. It had become, and would remain, the setting for an extended guitar solo. A more subtle change compared with the *ZINY* and *Baby Snakes* versions, however, is the form, which was reworked again to draw greater attention to the connection between measures 13–20 and 56–63 (the two subsections "t" in Table 2.4). To accommodate the piece to its new purpose, Zappa divided the melody into two unbalanced sections: the opening 64 measures followed (after the guitar solo) by the last 23 (mm. 80–102)—fifteen measures of music, 65–79, were cut. The reprise of music in what now had become the head suggests a jazz- rather than rock-oriented form: **A** (Introduction) + **B C B** (truncated). The form of the complete arrangement may be diagrammed as follows:

A **B** **C** **B** **B'** **D**

|**t u v** |**w x y** |**t**| guitar solo |**v'** |**z z' z"**

This formal reorganization rendered somewhat tenuous the connection between the head and the music played after the guitar solo, the relationship apparently hinging on the varied repetition of a single phrase (**v'**). Rather than actually hearing the form unfold onstage, however, let me suggest that coherence depends on listeners' familiarity with either the *ZINY* or *Baby Snakes* version of the song. With one or the other of these renditions in the mind's ear, the guitar solo seems like an insertion into a complete and coherent instrumental number. Anyone familiar with the earlier recordings, in other words, would not have truly missed the missing fifteen bars (65–79), a passage that contained a varied repeat of music (**u'**) that would have been heard before the solo, but which was cut because of the new contingency of use. Given Zappa's devoted cult following, and his penchant at the time for using musical sound bytes from popular recordings for their associative connections, an explanation of formal coherence based on listeners' long-term memories does not seem particularly far-fetched.[13]

If the recordings by these later bands present us with the final, if discursively complex, solution to the form of "The Black Page #2," they also illustrate that other aspects continued to change. Zappa 7 played the number as a reggae, Zappa 8 as a polka (!), and Zappa 9 as a driving rock number with syncopated rhythm-guitar chords, perhaps a variation on the reggae theme. The last version in this chronology, which can be heard on *Make a Jazz Noise Here* (Zappa 9), opens with a slow, jazz-like rendition of the first twenty bars in a style reminiscent of "Outside Now" from Zappa's *Broadway the Hard Way* (October 1988). From a critical standpoint, the *MAJNH* version is arguably the most successful since the bass riff underlying the guitar solo, derived from a new bass part for instrumental, affords greater tonal variety than the two previous ones, in which Zappa played above a single chord. As illustrated in Example 2.5, the solo unfolds over an ostinato that oscillates between F and E. Besides style, Zappa continued to experiment—particularly during the tours of Zappa 7 and 8—with different placements of the song in sets, which were performed (as always) in continuous fashion. This kind of experimentation had begun with the *Baby Snakes* lineup in 1977. Finally, as regards performance style, it should be noted that these three last bands each played "The Black Page #2" in a consistent way, i.e., as rehearsed.[14] Regardless of what was said and written about the practice, Zappa apparently did not use hand signals to cue the instant transformation of the piece, perhaps on account of its rhythmic difficulty.[15]

Example 2.5 Frank Zappa, "The Black Page #2" (Frank Zappa), *Make a Jazz Noise Here* (1991): bass ostinato.

In this essay I have argued that the 1988 performance of "The Black Page #2" on *Make a Jazz Noise Here*, which one might call the final draft, was the product of two transformations of the song's form that occurred under very different circumstances. The first came about, you might say, the old-fashioned way: on paper, as an act of compositional intentionality. It was the result of Zappa's reworking the rhythmically challenging "#1" during rehearsals before the New York shows late in 1976. A second form emerged much more slowly and quite differently: as the collective by-product of the song's redeployment as the introduction and postlude to a guitar solo. Yet the formal coherence of this later version depended to a great extent on listeners' memories of the prior arrangement, memories that were enhanced by repeated listening to recordings. In this way "The Black Page #2" reached closure—a closed loop, really—by 1988. In trying to explain what was happening, one could apply Zappa's term "Conceptual Continuity," which he used to describe the self-referential quality of lyrics or visual allusions on album covers (Watson 1993, 229). This was Conceptual Continuity for the musically inclined.

But was the book really closed on "The Black Page #2"? Given the radical changes in performance style between 1981 and 1988, how can it be said that "The Black Page #2" was finished except as a result of its composer's untimely death?

As for "The Black Page #1," it is of course impossible to determine exactly why Zappa made no progress on it after 1976. Perhaps he considered its difficult rhythmic vocabulary more appropriate for the nontonal music that he called "Serious." Although not a work Zappa would himself have put in this category (because of the media of performance, among other reasons), its level-two complexities place it closer to his atonal "The Girl in the Magnesium Dress" or "Mo 'n Herb's Vacation" than to "A Pound for A Brown (on the Bus)." Zappa himself wrote that the piece's rhythmic patterns sounded "like the missing link between 'Uncle Meat' and 'The Be-Bop Tango.'"[16] Yet recalling that he tried unsuccessfully to revive "#1" in 1985 or 1986 leads one to wonder whether the same thing wasn't wrong with this realization of "The Black Page" as with the *Baby Snakes* version. Perhaps, in other words, the problem was form.

Zappa's most successful Synclavier releases in the tonal idiom, like "G-Spot Tornado" (*Jazz from Hell*), employ the verse-chorus structure of pop and rock music. By this measure "The Black Page #1" was incomplete, comprising only two verses (**A** and **A'**) without a chorus containing different music. One might reasonably speculate that it may have been the lack of a contrasting section of music, which was apparently never composed, that kept the piece a fragment. Being a practical and inventive musician, composer, and bandleader, though, Zappa along with his talented sidemen and devoted listeners were together able to transform "The Black Page" into something useful and rich in possibilities.

Notes

The ideas presented in this essay began taking shape in a class I taught in the 1990s called "Frank Zappa and American Pop." Because this course was designed to appeal to many different kinds of students, the musical competencies of the sixty-some class members ranged from little to professional-level. Among the latter group was a then-doctoral student, Anthony DeSanza, whom I encouraged to examine, in a preliminary way, the different versions of "The Black Page." An outstanding percussionist and assistant director of the University of Michigan's Percussion Ensemble at the time, DeSanza had directed rehearsals and performances of the piece—experience that proved invaluable to his work that term. Although my approach to, and conclusions about, "The Black Page" are different from his, I have adopted one particularly useful aspect of his presentation in describing the foreground rhythms in terms of two levels of complexity. I am also indebted to DeSanza's insights as a conductor in understanding how performers should think about or feel certain rhythmically challenging passages. I would thus like to express my sincere thanks to him and the other members of that memorable group of students, and also to my research assistant, Alex Ruthmann, who worked long hours to locate many of the sources to which this essay refers.

1. *Over-nite Sensation* was among Zappa's most commercially successful albums (Gray 1994, 155), appearing on *Billboard* album charts for fifty weeks and peaking at #32. (Zappa's next offering, *Apostrophe*, squeaked into the Top Ten, the composer's only such achievement.) Live versions of "I'm the Slime" can be found on *Zappa in New York* and *You Can't Do That On Stage Anymore, Vol. 1*; "Montana" can be found on *You Can't Do That On Stage Anymore, Vol. 2* and *Vol. 4*.
2. A list of albums up through the early 1990s can be found in Gray 1994, 244–248.
3. Compare the studio release of "Inca Roads" on *One Size Fits All* (June 1975) with *You Can't Do That On Stage Anymore, Vol. 2; The Best Band You Never Heard in Your Life*; and *The Lost Episodes*. "Zoot Allures," on the studio album of the same name (October 1976), should be compared with live recordings on *Make a Jazz Noise Here, The Best Band,* and *Does Humor Belong in Music?* The "Black Napkins" on *Zoot Allures* is the studio version; compare this with *Make a Jazz Noise Here; You Can't Do That On Stage Anymore, Vol. 3*; and *Does Humor Belong in Music?*
4. It may not be coincidental that the producer of the Mothers' album, Tom Wilson, had also produced Dylan's first electric album, *Bringing It All Back Home* (1965), which included this song. For background, see Gray 1994, 61, 64.

5. For basic information on Paul Revere and the Raiders, see Marsh 1993, 89–101. As for Zappa's sending up this Portland band, compare the end of "Motherly Love" (*Freak Out!*) with the Raiders' hit, "Steppin' Out" (1965).
6. In a 1970 interview with Richard Green (excerpted in Slaven 1996, 129), Zappa criticized the earlier band for being "too static." He continued, "In order to synchronize both drummers, they had to be limited in the types of things they could play so that the beat stayed pretty monotonous."
7. For the connection between Phil Spector's "Wall of Sound" records and Zappa, see Borders 2001.
8. The order of songs between versions of "The Black Page" for these five shows was consistent: "The Black Page #2," "Punky's Whips," "I Promise Not to Come in Your Mouth," "Honey Don't You Want a Man Like Me?" "Illinois Enema Bandit," "Sofa #2," "I'm the Slime," "A Pound For a Brown (on the Bus)" (including "The Black Page" drum solo and "#1"), and "Big Leg Emma." My thanks go to Jon Naurin for maintaining these set lists (http://www.frontiernet.net/~prem/fzshows/htm).
9. One could, for example, compare the rhythmic subdivision of "The Black Page #1" with Karlheinz Stockhausen's *Klavierstücke I-IV* (1952–1953), with which Zappa was likely familiar. For a brief discussion of the extraordinary demands that Stockhausen's approach to rhythm made on contemporary performers, see Watkins 1988, 518.
10. The "Soundpage" accompanied a three-paragraph introduction by Jim Aikin, "Pervasive Polyrhythms in Zappa's 'The Black Page'," *Keyboard* (February 1987), 66–67. The "Soundpage" carries a 1986 copyright date (Pumpko Industries Ltd.); the lead sheet of "The Black Page #1" is copyrighted 1977.
11. I have suggested elsewhere (Borders 2001) that "Louie, Louie" remained an *idée fixe* for Zappa throughout his career, even more than such reworkings as "Plastic People" and "Ruthie Ruthie" would suggest. The song is used, for example, as a marker in a number of extended pieces, including *Lumpy Gravy* and *Uncle Meat*.
12. Refer to http://home.swipnet.se/fzshows/76b77a.html.
13. For an example of borrowed snippets of music from popular recordings being used for their associative connections, see "Rhymin' Man," *Broadway the Hard Way*.
14. On the intensity of Zappa's rehearsals, see Slaven 1996, 219–220.
15. Much has been made of these hand signals in the writings about Zappa. See, for example, Chevalier 1986, 14–15.
16. See the liner notes for *ZINY*. "The Girl in the Magnesium Dress" is found on *The Perfect Stranger* and *Yellow Shark*; "Mo 'n Herb's Vacation" is found on *The London Symphony Orchestra, Vol. 1*.

References

Borders, James. 2001. Form and the Concept Album: Progressive Rock, Modernism, and the Avant-Garde in Frank Zappa's Early Releases. *Perspectives of New Music* 39/1 (Winter), 118–160.

Chevalier, Dominique. 1986. *Viva! Zappa*. Rev. ed. New York: St. Martin's Press.

Gracyk, Theodore. 1996. *Rhythm and Noise: An Aesthetics of Rock*. Durham, NC: Duke University Press.

Gray, Michael. 1994. *Mother! The Frank Zappa Story*. Rev. ed. London: Plexus.

Marsh, Dave. 1993. *Louie Louie*. New York: Hyperion.

Rosen, Steve. 1997. Frank Zappa: Guitarist. Reprinted in Richard Kostelanetz, ed., *The Frank Zappa Companion: Four Decades of Commentary*. New York: Schirmer Books.

Slaven, Neil. 1996. *Electric Don Quixote: The Story of Frank Zappa*. London: Omnibus Press.

Watkins, Glenn. 1988. *Soundings: Music in the Twentieth Century*. New York: Schirmer Books.

Watson, Ben. 1993. *Frank Zappa: The Negative Dialectics of Poodle Play*. New York: St. Martin's Press.

Zappa, Frank, and Peter Occiogrosso. 1989. *The Real Frank Zappa Book*. New York: Poseidon Press.

3

Analytic Methodologies for Rock Music

Harmonic and Voice-Leading Strategies in Tori Amos's "Crucify"

LORI BURNS

In the fields of musicology and music theory, there is little agreement on our analytic methodologies for rock music. Theoretical approaches range from basic letter-name chord labels to detailed Schenkerian analysis[1]. Regardless of the chosen approach, every analyst ought to be aware of the difficulties of analyzing popular music using the theoretical systems devised for common-practice tonal music. The potential exists in any theoretical system for bias, false judgment, or the ascription of privilege, but when the system was admittedly intended for a different application, the interpretive problems abound. A song such as Tori Amos's "Crucify," chosen to represent here an application of my analytic method, introduces aspects of voice leading and harmony not common in the literature addressed by Schenker. I'll precede examination of the song itself with a general consideration of a central issue it poses, that being the interpretation of modal and tonal languages when used in combination.

Before going further, it is important to assert that there are stylistic connections between "classical" and popular musics. Indeed, such relations have been explored by several authors (Brackett 1992; Covach 1997a, 1997b; Middleton 1990; Walser 1992). Invoking harmony as an important part of the classical/popular relationship, Allan Moore writes that "part of the heritage of rock lies within common-practice tonality. This should alert us to the expectation that we will find both parallels and more distant relationships between cadences in the two practices" (Moore 1995, 191). It is significant here that Moore focuses on common cadential patterns. His emphasis illustrates the interpretive value attached to the harmonic gestures at phrase endings: the goal of directed musical motion. Common cadential patterns between classical and popular music lead to the comfortable analysis of well-known idioms, such as dominant-tonic cadential resolutions. But theoretical and interpretive problems arise when the cadential pattern does not derive from common-practice tonal harmony. Rock music frequently uses modal scales, harmonic patterns, and cadences. It is then very common for analytic descriptions of modal harmonic patterning to reveal an implicit tonal bias. In other words, the modal pattern is evaluated using the tools of common-practice theory and therefore is judged to be lacking something. For instance, Alf Björnberg describes harmony in the Aeolian mode as "static" or "less tense," i.e., as nondirectional, incapable of creating expectations or a sense of tension and repose (Björnberg 1985).[2]

Is such music truly nondirectional, or does our analytic system (that is, Roman numerals and linear analysis) simply fail us? After all, analysis is not just the act of hearing, but the act of applying a theoretical model. Roman numerals and linear analysis were both conceived to chart the relationships of tonal music. I would argue that there is an implicit tonal bias when we analyze any harmonically conceived music. When we identify a chord as "I" or "tonic," this evokes a host of associations of tonic as the generator of harmonic activity, the goal of directed motion, and the source of unity. These functions of tonic depend on the presence of another harmony: "V" or "dominant." If we cannot locate dominant-tonic patterns, we are likely to assert that the music is static, nondirectional, or unconventional.

To illustrate some of these interpretive problems, I will examine a passage from Robert Walser's analysis of a Bon Jovi song, "Livin' on a Prayer," in a 1993 article entitled "Forging Masculinity: Heavy-Metal Sounds and Images of Gender." I should point out that Walser's analytic goal is not to develop a theory of harmonic practice. However, his discussion of harmony is offered in the context of his attempt to explore meaning, and *harmonic* meaning is privileged at one point in the discussion. Walser identifies the chorus (in the verse/pre-chorus/chorus formal design) as a moment of "romantic transcendence" in the song, thus identifying it as a moment of great affective change, from the gloomy mood of the opening to the sense of liberation and excitement offered by the chorus. Walser relies on harmonic analysis to illustrate this affective shift in the music. He identifies the modulation scheme and the actual harmonic progression as the means by which the affective shift is represented. I will quote extensively from his analysis in order to maintain the integrity of Walser's language and emphasis:

> First, and simplest, it is at this moment that the piece moves out of its minor key and into its relative major. Such a key change accomplishes a tremendous affective change, moving from what is conventionally perceived as the negativity or oppression of the minor key to the release and affirmation of the major. Experientially, we escape the murk that has contained us since the beginning of the song. Second, this moment in the chorus offers an escape from the C–D–E pattern that has been the only chord progression the song has used until this point, and which thus has seemed natural and inevitable, however cheerless. "Livin' on a prayer" breaks out of its gloomy treadmill at this point of transcendence, moving from C to D to G, not E. By breaking free of its oppressive minor tonality,

> and by doing so through a brand-new progression, the song leaps into an exciting new tonal area and constructs a transcended context for Tommy and Gina, and for the song's audience (Walser 1993, 165).

With this analysis, Walser invokes the binary opposition of minor/major, calling on the tradition (stemming from the early Baroque) of interpreting minor as the darker side of the tonal system. I do not take umbrage with the notion that we have been conditioned to make particular affective associations with the minor mode. I would caution, however, that certain phrases in Walser's commentary suggest that the minor/major duality is something absolute and fixed. For instance, the evaluation of the opening harmonic progression as the "oppressive minor tonality." This is an absolutist and thereby simplistic assertion. The binary opposition, the "either/or" approach to analysis, is too limiting. The minor/major duality is not an accurate way of representing harmonic practice in rock, in which there exist more than just minor or major scale forms.

When Walser identifies the harmonic progressions, C–D–E for the earlier sections of the song and C–D–G for the movement into the chorus, he avoids the Roman numeral analysis and key identification that would represent these progressions. I will take the liberty of inferring his functional analysis to be VI–VII–I in E Aeolian and IV–V–I in G major. With his analytic commentary, he does not explore the potential of the progression C–D–E (on its own terms) to create a sense of tension or directionality. It is simply understood in relation to the later harmonic event: the C–D–G progression. That is, the major-mode dominant-tonic resolution "corrects" the earlier minor-mode (or Aeolian) stepwise ascending progression. The modal passage is valued for its ability to offer contrast to the "real" progression that happens in the major key. One of the implicit judgments in Walser's commentary, as with Björnberg's judgment, is that modal progressions are nondirectional and static.

I linger over Walser's commentary here, in order to alert the reader to the pitfalls of a tonal bias. I do not mean to say that Walser's interpretation is incorrect. I am convinced enough by his analysis that "Livin' on a Prayer" has a moment of significant affective change and that the harmonic strategies contribute in large part to the shift in expression. I am simply identifying the need for greater precision in and sensitivity to our theoretical/analytical methodologies. To what extent does a strict tonal analysis impose an unfair system of evaluation and therefore lead to false judgments of the music? How ought we interpret a song whose harmony is at times modal, at times tonal, at times a conflation of the two? How do we evaluate such different discursive strategies? How do we define harmonic expectations in the context of a pluralistic system? What features of line, harmony, and counterpoint contribute to the creation of tension and resolution, as well as to the constrasting strategies of directionality and stasis?

A purely harmonic analysis is an extremely limited form of analysis for exploring affective or expressive meaning in music. It necessarily fixes music as a series of verticals, and does not accommodate linear or voice-leading content. The harmonic labels can be useful, but I would argue that an analysis that purports to explore the meaning and discursive significance of harmony must also consider the specific voice leading of that harmony. Thus, one of my goals with this study is to develop a method for the analysis of harmony and voice leading in a popular song. The method I will propose is reductive and admittedly influenced by Schenkerian analysis. However, I will address the very serious and legitimate problems associated with strict Schenkerian analysis of popular music. Indeed, what I propose is a revision of Schenkerian techniques in order to respond to these problems.

What I am suggesting requires the careful distinction of modal versus tonal harmony and voice leading. I do not intend this essay to be an exhaustive study of rock harmony. However, the song I have chosen to analyze—Tori Amos's "Crucify" (1992)—illustrates a variety of strategies, both modal and tonal, and thus affords the opportunity to reflect on the analytical issues I have raised.[3] I will present the problematic aspects of interpreting harmony and voice leading so as not to privilege the common-practice tonal events above all else. Before I begin my analysis, I must explain my reductive technique.

Reductive Method

The application of reductive analysis, specifically Schenkerian analysis, to popular music is the subject of much debate. In order to continue the dialogue on this issue, I will review some of these criticisms and respond. Used strictly, Schenkerian analysis is not entirely effective for the analysis of many popular songs. But in modified form, reductive analysis can yield important analytic results. It is a valuable tool for illustrating the voice-leading and harmonic features of a particular song, as well as the unique manipulations of harmonic convention that might be peculiar to the narrative of the individual song or to the stylistic practices of the artist.

I will begin with a criticism that is launched at Schenker quite frequently, regardless of the musical repertoire in question: Schenkerian analysis does not adequately represent rhythmic features of the music. For instance, Richard Middleton analyzes a Gershwin melody that features syncopations across the bar line; he demonstrates that a Schenkerian sketch ignores the importance of this rhythmic device (Middleton 1990, 193). To be fair, I should first argue that systems of "tonal" analysis are not usually intended to reveal rhythmic/metric features. Second, when one compares a reduction (which normalizes rhythmic features) with the actual music, one can understand the true nature of the rhythmic features as well as the contrapuntal treatment of dissonance within a metric framework. Yet despite my defense of the reductive method, I believe that Middleton does raise an important issue here for the analysis of popular song. I would go so far as to say that the specific way in which a vocal line is staggered contrapuntally with the bass is a very important feature of popular music performance and one that contributes in large part to the distinctive sound of a given song or artist. It is possible to include such details in a reductive sketch, and to allow rhythmic features to emerge prominently in the analysis. In my reductive method, I graph each musical phrase or section of the song using bar lines to indicate metric emphasis; I also have developed a notation for indicating melodic syncopations. The specific rhythmic subdivisions do not lend themselves well to reductive analysis, so I do not attempt to indicate those.

A potentially more serious criticism is that strict Schenkerian analysis does not accommodate modal harmony.[4] Schenker's paradigmatic progressions are all derived from common-practice tonal syntax of the eighteenth and nineteenth centuries. A modal pattern such as I–♮VII–I in the Aeolian or Mixolydian mode does not fit with any of Schenker's paradigms, and thus would pose interpretive difficulties.[5] A strict Schenkerian theorist would be tempted to analyze the ♮VII chord as a substitute for the dominant, thereby adjusting the actual pattern to fit the theoretical paradigm. By evaluating ♮VII as a mere substitute, one robs the pattern and therefore the song in which the pattern occurs of its unique modal identity. The particulars of the composition are "recomposed" to uphold the theory.

This may seem to be an insurmountable problem, but I believe there are solutions. As Middleton suggests, "if we rewrite the V–I bias in terms of a principle of tonicity—the prolongation of a tonic chord through structures of harmonic difference, which may take many other forms than V—a method which is more flexible but which retains the concept of hierarchy emerges" (Middleton 1990, 196). But here we must be careful to formulate what constitutes those "structures of harmonic difference." Moore worries that the "Othering" of harmonic structures that are not dominant-tonic based would lead to the identification of modal harmonies as aberrants, or departures from the norm: "Such an argument leads inevitably to the model of rock as a deformed offspring of classical tonality" (Moore 1995, 186). Moore also worries that Other progressions, such as ♮VII–I, would be viewed merely as substitutes for the norm of V–I. However, I would posit that these *unique* (not "aberrant" and not "substitute") modal progressions might themselves be elevated theoretically to the level of paradigm or norm. This would result in a pluralistic system, one that would admit many possibilities, not just I–V–I. I have explored this possibility elsewhere for a repertoire that is based on the modes, the modal chorales of J. S. Bach (Burns 1995). My solution there was to identify those progressions that are common to each individual mode and to integrate the modal patterns into the reductive sketch. This might be considered overly formalistic; however, I would argue that a knowledge of modal idioms comparable to our knowledge of tonal idioms is valuable as one attempts to analyze popular music. The temptation to dismiss all modal progressions as "static" would not be so strong. Modal progressions can be static (just as tonal chord successions can be), but they can also be directional, depending on the context.

One of the most serious difficulties in adapting the Schenkerian method to modal harmony is how to handle interpretive decisions at the most abstract level of Schenkerian analysis: the *Ursatz*. In conventional Schenkerian theory, the harmonic progression that is ascribed the privileged role of background structure is always I–V–I. But it is possible for a popular song to avoid that progression entirely. For instance, Moore gives an example of a song (Supertramp's "Crime of the Century") that elaborates "middleground" IV–I Aeolian cadences in the verse statements and a VI–I cadence in an extended coda (Moore 1995, 187). In such a case, one must decide either to allow a structural plagal arpeggiation in the *Ursatz*, or to eschew the notion of the background.

Middleton raises the point that the Schenkerian bias towards a I–V–I fundamental structure is also a problem for songs that might articulate a I–V–I cadence, but which emphasize modal progressions elsewhere, in other sections of the song. Middleton is concerned here with an important feature of popular songs, which is that they are formally organized into different sections—verse, chorus, bridge, and so on—and that these individual sections can have very different harmonic identities. A Schenker graph would privilege the section of the work that articulates the tonal structure and all other sections would be viewed as prolongational, i.e., as subservient. Thus, a Schenker graph, which seeks to create a unified view for the harmony and voice leading of the entire piece of music, would fail to illustrate an important feature of the song. Indeed, as Middleton states, in certain songs "sections of riff-based circularity are *set against* sections with cadential closure" (Middleton 1990, 195).

I believe that Middleton's sensitivity to the sectional design of this music is worth serious consideration. Indeed, this will be an important point in my analysis of "Crucify." Simply put, each section of the song explores a different harmonic idiom (at times tonal, at other times modal) and also a different harmonic strategy (at times goal-directed, at other times static). To reduce this music to the level of *Ursatz* would mean to privilege a progression located within only one of the song's sections. My solution to this problem is to avoid an ultimate *Ursatz* interpretation.[6] If I eschew that aspect of the reductive technique and if I work instead closer to the surface of the music, it is possible to allow each individual section of the song to maintain its integrity and harmonic identity. This is a deliberate resistance to the level of abstraction that is at the very heart of Schenkerian analysis, so it is a serious modification. It is a rejection of the notion of organicism. Rather than taking an organic view of the music, I will attempt instead to illustrate not only the continuities (the organic connections) within the harmonic and voice-leading narrative of the song, but also the discontinuities, contrasts, and contradictions.

Another critical issue raised by Middleton is the structure of the melodic line (for Schenker, the *Urlinie*). As Middleton demonstrates, popular songs explore many different kinds of melodic motions, not all of which involve stepwise, descending resolutions. I will not review his discussion in detail, but will identify some of his melodic categories that avoid descent: chant (melodies that do not leave a repeated note), axial (melodies that circle around a central note), oscillating (melodies that move back and forth between two structural notes), and terrace (melodies in which the oscillation is applied to a whole unit) (Middleton 1990, 201). As I have already stated, different sections of a song can explore different melodic strategies. One might explore an oscillating pattern, while another might descend in *Urlinie* fashion. If a strict Schenkerian analysis is applied, the descending line will be immediately valued as the overriding gesture of the entire composition. Once again, my solution to this will be to avoid representing the many sections of the song with a single progression. Each musical section will be graphed on its own terms, so that different strategies can be appreciated for what they convey. For each section, it will be possible to identify an overriding harmonic and melodic structure, thus a background or deep middleground for that musical unit. But a reduction further, to identify a contrapuntal structure for the song as a whole, will not be made. That is not to say that I will avoid making connections from one section to the next. On the contrary, the reductive analysis will reveal certain relationships that are worth careful interpretation. It is possible, without moving to the level of *Ursatz*, to describe certain narrative processes that emerge over the course of the song as we move from one section to another, each based on its own particular strategies.

In my proposed method of reduction, I work with three different graphs or representations of the music: the "normative progression," the "voice-leading graph," and the "reduction." Each of these serves a different analytic purpose. First I must establish my intent to illustrate the formal organization of the song by dealing with each section (verse, refrain, etc.) individually. I must also establish my assumption that each phrase or musical section is based on a clear harmonic progression within a particular key or mode. It is likely to be varied or elaborated in different phrase statements, due to the strophic nature of the song form; but despite the variations, its identity will be apparent. The actual musical performance is much more complex than this basic set of "changes"; nevertheless, the governing harmonic progression is an important part of the musical expression. I refer to this graph as the *normative progression* in order to indicate its function as a straightforward voice-leading structure. The *voice-leading graph* is closer to the surface of the music. It indicates the actual contrapuntal relations between bass and vocalist as they articulate this basic progression, including elaborative pitches and unique voice-leading events. I do not intend the normative progression to be understood as a reduction of the voice-leading graph. Rather, it is intended as a point of reference, comparable to a listing of the chord changes, but it is written out in pitch notation for ease of reference to the analytic sketch. My decision to offer both the normative progression and the voice-leading graph is a response to what I perceive to be an important aspect of the music; that is, while a basic chord progression underlies the musical phrase or section, in the actual performance the harmony is manipulated and developed to create a unique musical expression.

I offer a third analytic sketch as the *reduction* of the *voice-leading graph*. In general, the reduction illustrates the principal voice-leading connections and harmonic prolongations for each section of the song. The "reduction" differs from the "normative progression" by being a hierarchical interpretation of the voice-leading graph. The "reduction" is implicitly Schenkerian in its efforts to reduce the greater details of the voice-leading sketch to a prolongational structure, including a thorough characterization of the contrapuntal relationship between the underlying structure of the vocal line and the bass. However, it accommodates modal progressions and eschews the requisite Schenkerian *Ursatz*. This level of reduction—at the level of each phrase or section of music—is as far as I wish to go with the reductive process. As I have already stated, I will respect the formal divisions of the song by not attempting to locate an overriding progression that would dismiss some sections as "nothing but" a prolongation and assert other sections as containing the "real" movement of the song. Until I begin to analyze Tori Amos's "Crucify," the differences between and the analytical advantages to the *normative progression* and the *reduction* may not be clear. I will comment on those later. For now, the following explains some of my notation:

Normative progression. Harmonic progression that governs the given phrase or section of music.

Voice-leading graph. Analysis of the actual contrapuntal relations between vocal line and bass support as these structural outer voices articulate the *normative progression*, including elaborative pitches and unique voice-leading events.

Reduction. Reductive representation of the principal voice-leading connections and harmonic prolongations evident in the *voice-leading graph.*

Bar lines. Note values used do not represent actual rhythmic events, but the bar lines make it possible to determine approximate metric emphasis.

Dotted bar lines. Dotted bar lines in the *reduction* and the *normative progression* indicate phrase divisions.

Stemmed notes and note heads. In the *voice-leading graph,* stemmed notes indicate pitches that belong to the prevailing harmony for that metric unit (measure or part of the measure). Unstemmed note heads are elaborative pitches.

Solid slurs. Solid slurs are analytic slurs that connect elaborative pitches to structural pitches, group notes into a linear progression, or outline an arpeggiation.

Dotted ties. The structural attack, i.e., the moment when the bass and voice are in harmonic agreement, is notated as a stemmed note. Suspensions or anticipations are notated as note heads. A dotted tie connects the structural "attack" to the suspension or anticipation.

Open note heads. These indicate the prolongational structure for any given section of the work (i.e., for each section of the song, open note heads will illustrate harmonic or voice-leading emphasis).

In order to discuss in greater detail the analytic and methodological issues relevant to this kind of reductive analysis, I will illustrate my analytic technique using only one song.[7] A single example will also allow me to develop a complete analysis of the harmonic and voice-leading events of the song. I have purposely selected a song that uses a variety of harmonic and voice-leading strategies: "Crucify," from Tori Amos's album *Little Earthquakes* (1992).[8] The song is sketched in Examples 1 through 4, which provide for each section of the music (verse, pre-chorus, chorus, and bridge) the three graphs discussed earlier: normative progression, voice-leading graph, and reduction. The upper line throughout the analytic reduction is based on the vocal line; the lower line is based on the bass guitar. These two voices, which articulate the outer-voice contrapuntal framework, are very prominent throughout the song. (The song's full instrumentation is as follows: acoustic piano [Amos], bass, mandolin, ukulele, drums, and percussion.)

In my analysis, I will attempt to separate my commentary on each individual formal section from commentary on the narrative connections across the entire song. Each section requires individual attention in order to explore phrase design as well as harmonic and voice-leading content. Each section also raises different interpretive issues and thus provides an opportunity for reflection on the analytic methodology. Once each section has been discussed, I'll then explore how the whole comes together in a narrative of voice leading and harmony.

Since the purpose of this essay is to illustrate a methodology for the interpretation of harmony and voice leading, I will not engage the song lyrics to a great extent. Although I believe that the poetic text is significant for an ultimate interpretation of the song, I will make only general references to its content. For the reader's ease of reference, the lyrics of "Crucify" are transcribed here:[9]

Verse 1	Every finger in the room is pointing at me I wanna spit in their faces then I get afraid of what that could bring I got a bowling ball in my stomach, I got a desert in my mouth Figures that my courage would choose to sell out now
Pre-chorus	I've been looking for a savior in these dirty streets Looking for a savior beneath these dirty sheets I've been raising up my hands, drive another nail in Just what God needs, one more victim
Chorus	Why do we crucify ourselves every day I crucify myself Nothing I do is good enough for you I crucify myself everyday I crucify myself My heart is sick of being I said my heart is sick of being in chains oh oh chains, oh oh
Verse 2	Got a kick for a dog beggin' for love I gotta have my suffering so I can have my cross I know a cat named Easter he says "Will you ever learn" You're just an empty cage girl if you kill the bird
Pre-chorus	I've been looking for a savior in these dirty streets Looking for a savior beneath these dirty sheets I've been raising up my hands, drive another nail in Got enough guilt to start my own religion
Chorus	
Bridge	Please be. Save me. I cry. Aha aha.
Pre-chorus	Looking for a savior in these dirty streets, looking for a savior beneath these dirty sheets. I've been raising up my hands, drive another nail in. Where're those angels when you need them
Chorus and Coda	

Tori Amos

Before I begin my analysis, I will provide a brief background on Amos. Born in 1962 and raised in the Baltimore area, she studied piano on full scholarship at the Peabody Conservatory from 1968 to 1974. Her musical interests as a pianist went beyond her classical training to include influences such as Jimi Hendrix, the Beatles, and Led Zeppelin. Such influences occasionally led her to "reinterpret" the classics, sometimes at important moments in her Peabody career, and eventually her interests and those of the Institute were no longer compatible (Rogers 1996, 11–14). She went on to begin her performing career as a piano player/singer/entertainer, working in various bars and hotels (always chaperoned by her Methodist minister father) and building a solid reputation. Her songwriting career also began before the age of twenty, with her first single "Baltimore" (co-written with brother Mike) in 1980. With the efforts of her supportive parents, Amos was eventually taken seriously by producer Narada Michael Walden in 1983. She moved to Los Angeles and began a long search for a strong band. In 1987, Atlantic Records offered her a record deal. The rock album *Y Kant Tori Read* was released in 1988, and was evaluated by *Billboard* as "bimbo music" (Rogers 1996, 37). Recognizing its failure, and her own need to return to the piano, Amos worked in 1989–1991 on a new album of her own material, which she recorded at home and in the studio. The result, *Little Earthquakes*, featuring the hit single "Crucify," was released by Atlantic in 1992. The success of the album launched her singer-songwriter career and a highly successful international tour, followed by subsequent Atlantic albums *Under the Pink* (1994), which sold over a million copies; *The Bee Sides* (1995); *Boys for Pele* (1996), which also went platinum; *From the Choirgirl Hotel* (1998); *To Venus and Back* (1999); and a collection of cover songs, *Strange Little Girls* (2001). Amos moved to Epic for her most recent albums, *Scarlet's Walk* (2002), *The Beekeeper* (2005), and *American Doll Posse* (2007).

"Crucify": Verse

In the text of verse 1, the protagonist explores a profound tension between subject and object. She feels herself to be the object of scrutiny in a room with other people. Although she would like to react to the oppressive social force, she feels powerless to do so and is angry as a result. The musical setting evokes her alienation: the vocal amplification is very dry and the instrumental texture is sparse. We hear open fifths in the bass (an unusual effect), accompanied by a strong attack on beats two and four in the bass drum. The phrase design and voice-leading structure contribute in large part to the mood and message of the text.

The phrase design and harmonic patterning of the verse are repetitive, but carefully manipulated to create a sense of contrapuntal tension. As is indicated in the voice-leading sketch of Example 3.1, the form of the verse

Example 3.1 Tori Amos, "Crucify" (Tori Amos), *Little Earthquakes* (1992): verse.

comprises four phrases, two of which repeat with some minor modifications. The harmonic pattern that recurs is a kind of neighboring construction that circles around the modal tonic, G♯ Dorian.[10] This pattern is most easily seen in the graph labeled "normative progression." The harmonic pattern derives its tension from a motion away from tonic, up to II, then down to ♮VII, before returning to tonic. The bass guitar and voice present the progression in a very simple parallel-fifth voice-leading. In the first phrase the harmonic motion is complete or closed, in the second it is incomplete or open, ending on ♮VII. The harmonic effect of the stop on ♮VII is comparable to a half cadence; it is a dissonance that requires resolution. These two phrases form a closed-then-open design, the opposite of a typical period structure.[11] The third and fourth phrases move through the same "reverse" closed-then-open patterning.

The graph labeled "reduction" represents the prolongational structure for each phrase of the verse. The first phrase is a closed harmonic motion that begins and ends on G♯, with $\hat{5}$ in the melody. The reduction represents this phrase as a prolongation of G♯. The second phrase takes the same harmonic pattern but avoids the final resolution; thus, it is interpreted as an open harmonic motion from G♯ to F♯. The reduction indicates this motion, with parallel fifths working at the deepest level. Phrases three and four repeat the content of phrases one and two.

The voice-leading graph illustrates the vocalist's foreground interaction with the bass progression. As with most popular-music vocal performance, Amos's pitches do not always line up with the vertical harmonies to which they belong. That is, she uses various devices to offset the melody and harmony. For instance, she might anticipate her next vocal pitch before its harmony has arrived in the other instruments, or she might suspend a pitch from the previous harmony, resolving only after the new harmony has arrived. One might argue that this offsetting technique is simply a feature of the performance style, and that this is done without much thought or intent of purpose. I would argue, however, that the musical results of this performance practice are worthy of careful consideration. Indeed, intuitive or not, I would suggest that there are moments when the offsetting of voice with harmony creates deliberate dissonance, or contrapuntal tension.[12] The dissonance is quite apparent since at the same time that the voice is syncopating the upper part of the parallel-fifth progression, the bass guitar is actually articulating the parallel fifths. (The upper fifth in the guitar progression, essentially a doubling rather than an independent voice, is not shown in the graph.)

The offsetting of the voice with the bass yields several noteworthy moments of contrapuntal tension. For instance, the fifth between E♯ in the voice and A♯ in the bass is subjected to interesting treatment. In the first two phrases, the E♯ is articulated in time with the bass, moving through a passing D♯ to C♯ (heard first as the third of the triad and then as the next note in the parallel-fifth structure, the fifth against the bass F♯). In the third and fourth phrases, Amos displaces the arrival of E♯. In phrase three, it is heard before the A♯ arrives in the bass. By the time the bass does arrive, the E♯ has moved on to what was heard before as a passing note, D♯. E♯ returns at the end of the measure. The graph of phrase three illustrates the contrapuntal tension that is created by this manipulation. When we first hear E♯, it is articulated as a neighbor to D♯, but as the neighbor returns, the D♯ is then dissonant as a fourth against the bass. The fourth phrase also distorts the arrival of E♯ such that it is never heard within the same metric unit as its bass support, A♯.

The normative progression simplifies the matter and we know from the first two phrases what the harmonic reference really is, but the voice-leading graph is useful to convey the tension that Amos can develop out of a simple structure. Another noteworthy dissonance occurs at the end of phrase two. The stop on ♮VII is articulated by the bass, F♯. The voice takes its C♯ above, but moves away at the phrase ending, to conclude on D♯, just as the first phrase ended. However, here the vocal D♯ is not given its G♯ bass support, so it creates a contextual dissonance against the F♯ in the bass. As stated before, the text for the first verse speaks of a tension created by a situation in which the protagonist feels she is being watched in a room filled with people. The manipulation of the counterpoint contributes to the tension.[13]

Based on this analysis, how can we describe or classify the harmonic and contrapuntal strategies of the verse? It is modal and repetitive, but what do we mean by those classifications? Modality and repetition do not necessarily add up to a sense of stasis, or lack of directionality. Although repetitive, the pattern is manipulated within the phrase design such that we hear the stops on ♮VII as incomplete or unstable, thus harmonically and contrapuntally filled with tension. Even the normative progression and the reduction make that evident. And the voice-leading graph illustrates in detail how tension is developed out of the basic progression. Yet although the pattern is manipulated to create dissonance and resolution, thereby implicitly creating directionality, I remain tempted to classify the verse as static, or contained, especially when this music sets the textual theme of oppression or self-containment. The cyclic nature of the referential harmonic pattern (motion away from the tonic to the harmony a step above, followed by the motion to the harmony a step below, followed by the return, all of which is mirrored a fifth above in the voice) might fairly be classified as stationary. That this pattern provides the basis for four entire phrases contributes further to the sense that movement is being contained. Thus, the *specific handling* of harmony and voice leading within the context of cyclic repetition and phrase design justifies this description of the harmonic idiom, and also justifies the association of that description with an affect and thereby ultimately with the textual message of the song. The mode of the passage and the progression in and of themselves do not warrant a label such as "static" or "oppressive."

The verse leads directly into the pre-chorus such that we hear a harmonic link or liaison between the two sections. This connection will be explored in greater detail later when I discuss the overall narrative of the song. For now, I will simply say that the stop on F♯ at the end of the verse is followed by what is to become a B-major tonic triad at the beginning of the pre-chorus. It is possible and very likely that a listener would hear the F♯–B harmonic succession as V–I in B. But this is not an unproblematic assertion, as I will explore later on. For now, I shall leave it at that and analyze the pre-chorus as an independent section of the song.

"Crucify": Pre-Chorus

The pre-chorus is heard in striking contrast to the verse for a number of reasons. Textually, the context shifts from the subjective perception of alienation and oppression in the verse to a broader context in which the protagonist invokes a possible identity for the oppressive social force—that of organized religion—as well as her own resistance. The remark "drive another nail in" and the final ironic jab demonstrate the futility of her efforts to resist, but the act of ironic commentary is in itself an indication of her resistance and power. Musically, as the textual shift occurs, we hear a mode shift from G♯ Dorian to B major (or Ionian). The voice's D♯ is reinterpreted, its function shifting from the stark fifth above G♯ to the softer tenth above B. At the same time, the dry vocal amplification of the verse is replaced by a warm reverberation, the texture expands to include a very active piano part, the guitar articulates a more melodic bass line, and the phrase structure is based on a conventional formal design. Through Amos's manipulation of the latter, she conveys her attempts to resist the social forces.

As I pointed out in my analysis of the verse, there were moments of deviation from the strict parallel-fifth relation between the bass guitar and voice, but the voice worked essentially within that pattern. Now, in the pre-chorus, the vocal line does not depend on the bass for its line; instead, its contrapuntal (intervallic) relation to the bass is more varied and changes constantly.[14] In addition, whereas the verse melody was predictable because of its repeated neighbor-note construction, the pre-chorus melody is not locked into a pattern of repetition. The pre-chorus melody works with the notion of linear and harmonic expectations, thus in a sense with tonal "predictability." However, these expectations result from Amos's manipulation of a phrase design that requires a longer span of time (the full eight measures in a four-plus-four relationship), and a studied manipulation of harmonic and voice-leading conventions, as well as a contrapuntally complex relationship between voice and bass.

The pre-chorus is sketched in Example 3.2. The normative progression for phrase one of the pre-chorus features the harmonic motion from tonic to dominant, with a half cadence. The I–V motion happens immediately and then the harmony hovers around the dominant of B, F♯, with the bass line moving to its upper and lower neighbors, G♯ and E (harmonies VI and IV), before cadencing on F♯ (V). Phrase two begins similarly, suggesting the parallel period structure and implying a continuation that will be closed this time. In other words, after the V–VI–IV–V progression of the antecedent, one would expect a clear tonic resolution in the consequent, thus diffusing the tension created by the antecedent's dominant prolongation. However, the harmony takes a sudden shift when the bass moves to the chromatic E♯, the leading tone to the dominant, harmonized by an applied dominant function (VII^{ø7} of V). This chord is first heard as a chromatic intensification of

Example 3.2 Tori Amos, "Crucify" (Tori Amos), *Little Earthquakes* (1992): pre-chorus.

the earlier progression; instead of the antecedent's diatonic V–VI–IV–V, one might expect the progression now to be V–VI–VII^{ø7}/V–V, before finally moving on to I. It is not an unusual tactic for an antecedent phrase to "raise the stakes" like this, i.e., to intensify the motion to V. However, the E♯ does not resolve to F♯ as expected, but rather continues down to E♮ and the harmony of IV, where the phrase closes. There is neither a return to V nor an ultimate resolution of V to I.

The voice has an important role in the creation of expectations in the antecedent and the denial of these expectations in the consequent. The antecedent establishes the conventional melodic progression that descends from $\hat{3}$ to $\hat{2}$ (D♯ to C♯), suggesting an implied continuation to $\hat{1}$ (B). This descent occurs immediately at the beginning of the phrase, but with the wrong bass support, i.e., the B in the voice is supported by the deceptive G♯ (VI). The bass has avoided the expected continuation, so now the voice has to set up the potential progression for another attempt. The ensuing melodic motion is therefore concerned with the linear descent from $\hat{3}$ to $\hat{2}$. The antecedent phrase occupies itself so much with the $\hat{3}$–$\hat{2}$ motion in the voice that it creates an expectation that this descent will be answered eventually by a complete linear progression $\hat{3}$–$\hat{2}$–$\hat{1}$, harmonized by I–V–I.

However, the consequent phrase denies these expectations. The phrase begins with the same $\hat{3}$–$\hat{2}$–$\hat{1}$ descent over the deceptive bass progression I–V–VI. But this time when the harmony digresses, the melodic line gives up its efforts to create closure and similarly digresses. In response to the bass's deceptive turn to VI, the voice outlines a G♯-minor triad, precisely at a moment of ironic self-reflection in the text: "just what God needs," which continues "one more victim." The bass supports this G♯-minor arpeggiation with the chromatic E♯ discussed earlier. As the harmony cadences on the surprising harmony of E major, the voice comes to rest on B, but then leaps down to a dissonant and unresolved F♯.

This consequent phrase creates in musical terms an ironic expression that matches the ironic commentary in the text. The musical irony is created by a number of details that combine to disrupt the expected or conventional narrative of harmony and voice leading. I have already commented on the harmonic turn to IV, which avoids the resolution of the chromatic E♯ and supplants the expected authentic cadential progression. In addition, the vocal B for the cadence is the B we were expecting at the conclusion of the phrase, but certainly not with this particular harmonization (E major), and not with this particular approach: a G♯-minor arpeggiation as opposed to a clear $\hat{3}$–$\hat{2}$–$\hat{1}$ descent. Our surprise at the cadence is not just based on immediate musical events from one measure into another; rather, we hear the disruption at a larger level. As I have pointed out, our expectations for a particular harmonic or voice-leading event are based on the antecedent/consequent phrase design. In addition, we hear the disruption at the level of the relationship between the verse and pre-chorus. Out of the repetitive neighbor progression in G♯ Dorian emerges a long-breathed melodic line that in its teleological design will surely offer us a satisfying resolution. However, these expectations dissolve (textually and musically) into ironic reflection at the end of the pre-chorus. In making these comparative remarks about the verse and pre-chorus, I must caution that I am doing so in order to identify different discursive strategies. I am deliberately attempting to avoid a corrective view of these approaches.

"Crucify": Chorus

The chorus uses yet another set of harmonic and voice-leading strategies, which contribute to the sense of sectional division within the song. Indeed, the chorus itself divides into two—and perhaps even three—distinct units. In order to discuss these easily, I will refer to the poetic text. In the first section of the chorus (beginning at 0:46), the protagonist asks, "Why do we crucify ourselves?" addressing a generalized problem and invoking a sense of shared experience or community through the reference "we." The second section (1:08+) breaks from the repetition of the "crucify" section and repeats its own text "my heart is sick of being," which is self-reflective and resistant. Although the text thought is not yet complete, I make a musical subdivision here, based on the musical pattern, that suddenly shifts before the text has been completed. The third section (1:14+) completes the thought with "in chains."

Throughout the chorus the voice and bass line are repetitive, repeating a particular pattern for a few measures and then going on to another pattern. There is an absence of phrase structure in the conventional sense. The chorus asks the listener to focus on individual events as opposed to broader goals and connections. Throughout, we hear repetitive articulation in the percussion with a relatively strong accent on beats one and three, a bass drum kick on beats two and four, and a constant shaking of maracas. The piano part is now restricted to a very narrow range, essentially functioning as simple "chording." After a repetition of music and text for the "crucify" section, the voice initiates a change with "my heart is sick of being." A new vocal pattern sets this text, which is then repeated. The instruments announce the shift by holding back: the maracas drop out, and the bass guitar avoids the earlier repetitive pattern and changes chords only once per bar. This announcement leads into the setting of "in chains," for which the voice assumes the greatest melodic range and level of activity thus far in the song. (This phrase also represents the song's only articulation of the pentatonic scale, one that admits of no dissonance such as that suggested by the harsh Dorian E♯ of the verse, as if to imply that the singer's chains work against dreams of freedom.) The singer is accompanied by piano, mandolin, and ukulele, as well as bass guitar. There remains, however, a repetitiveness to the expression as the voice repeats the "chains" material and the bass runs through a repeated two-bar harmonic pattern.

Now to my interpretation of the harmony and voice leading for the chorus. My reduction is provided in Example 3.3. First, I would point out a similarity between this language and that of the verse. Although the specific mode is now G♯ Aeolian (as opposed to the Dorian patterning of the verse), the voice-leading progression is essentially a motion from the open fifth on G♯ to the open fifth on F♯ (I to ♮VII). In the verse, that progression was articulated in such a way as to contribute to a clear phrase structure. The functions of

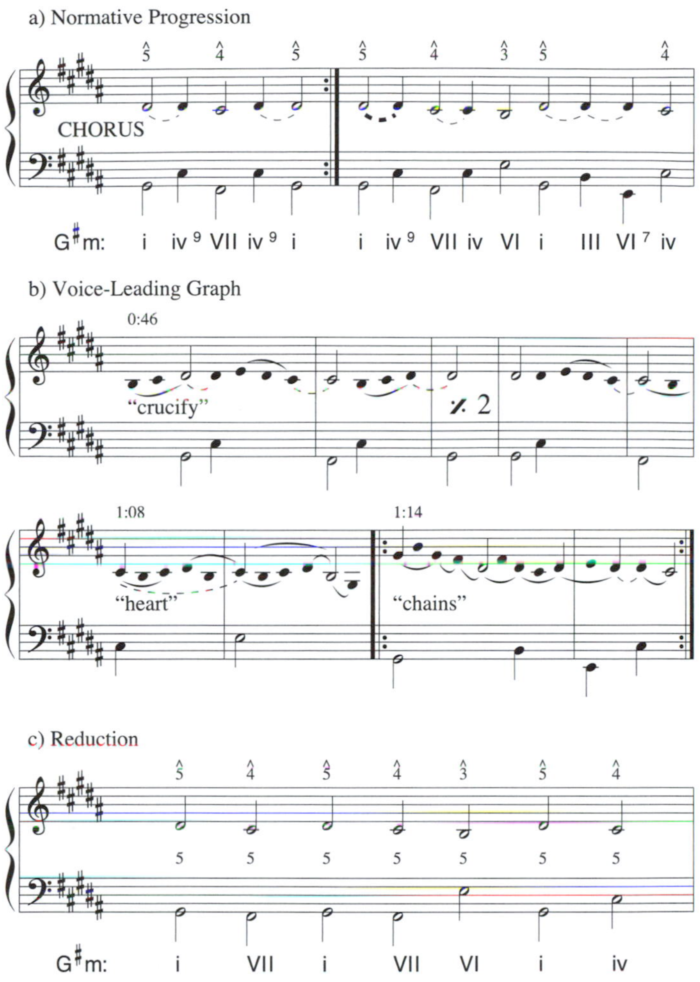

Example 3.3 Tori Amos, "Crucify" (Tori Amos), *Little Earthquakes* (1992): chorus.

G♯ and F♯ were also well defined, as I and ♮VII. In the chorus, however, the melodic and bass patterning are organized so as to confuse form and function. Each of the harmonic progressions from I to ♮VII, then ♮VII to I, is mediated by C♯ (IV). In keeping with the bass repetition, the vocal line reiterates the motion from D♯ to C♯ and back to D♯. The harmonic progression seems simple, yet an interpretive problem arises from this scenario: it is very difficult to sort out the phrase structure given the cyclical nature of the pattern repetition. That is, one statement of the pattern runs into the next. The pattern begins on "Why do we" harmonized by G♯; "crucify ourselves" is heard to the progression C♯^{9}–F♯, the falling fifth perhaps creating a kind of resolution into F♯. However, the text "every day" is set to a progression from C♯ to G♯, returning us to the place where we started. From that G♯, which may sound like an ending, we really do begin again, as the whole pattern repeats. There are three complete statements of this material, during which we are lost in the repetition of IV–♮VII, IV–I, IV–♮VII, IV–I, and so on, not knowing whether F♯ (♮VII) or G♯ (I) represents the harmonic goal. Indeed, it is not possible to identify a phrase ending, i.e., a cadence, throughout this entire passage. The voice does not help matters, as it just repeats the motion between D♯ and C♯. As the "heart" section announces a change, the harmony breaks the pattern; we hear the progression I–IV–♮VII–IV as before, but it stops on IV for an entire measure for the announcement "my heart is sick of being" and moves on to the new harmony of VI for a repetition of that text. Over each of these harmonies, the voice shifts from C♯ to B. (I will comment on this contrapuntal structure later.)

The most significant change in the "chains" section is the pentatonic liberation of the vocal line from its previous emphasis throughout the song on the pitches D♯ and C♯. The musical irony here is evident as the voice is liberated at the same time that the protagonist is decrying the "chains" that hold her, suggestive of those underlying dreams of freedom. The voice is now in a higher register (G♯4 and B4) and the line is more elaborate. The harmony also breaks free from its oscillation between G♯ and F♯. The bass is still repetitive, but now the progression features mediant relationships in G♯: I–III–VI – IV, repeated. The rise from I to III, especially in the context of the liberated vocal line, contributes to the sense of musical freedom at this point in the chorus. The references to III and VI require careful evaluation, in relation to the broader implications of the harmony and the overall narratives of the song. (I will also discuss these later.)

A reduction of the chorus is difficult to create, a problem that speaks to the nature of the music. Because of the lack of a clear phrase structure, as well as the repetition of cyclic progressions, it is difficult to determine the prolongational structure. That is, for the "crucify" section of the chorus, the harmony oscillates between G♯ and F♯, without an obvious tonal emphasis. Thus my reduction includes both harmonies, with the result that the oscillation itself becomes a significant aspect of the structure. In other words, it is important at this level of reduction that I avoid the inclination to "correct" the pattern into a higher-level prolongation of G♯. On the contrary, I am allowing the ambiguity felt at the surface of the music to figure prominently in the sketch. I did not feel so inclined in my analysis of the verse, thus I am making a distinction between the two harmonic strategies. In the verse, although the progression was also based on G♯ and F♯, the phrase design and the harmonic/voice-leading strategies contributed to the definition of G♯ as a prolonged harmony.

The "heart" section of the chorus is also difficult to reduce. Its text announces or leads to the "chains" section, and its music contributes to the effect of the textual shift. Following the very active "crucify" section, the harmonic rhythm slows to one chord per measure. It begins on the C♯ harmony and moves to E. Over each of these chords, the voice descends from C♯ to B, thus breaking away from the oscillation between D♯ and C♯ of the "crucify" section. The melodic descent from C♯ to B "sounds" as if it should be an appoggiatura gesture, a dissonance resolving to a consonance. However, over the harmony of C♯, the goal of the melodic motion, B, is actually dissonant. In the second statement, over the harmony of E, the B is consonant, in keeping with expectations. Because of its treatment as the voice-leading goal, in my reduction I have chosen E major as the prolonged harmony for the section. The C♯ harmony is treated as a subsidiary chord, on its way to E, much as it was treated during the "crucify" section where it mediated between G♯ and F♯.

The "chains" section is also based on a cyclic chord progression: a harmonically open-ended two-bar pattern, I–III–VI–IV, that is immediately repeated. The primary melodic motion is from D♯ to C♯, and the supporting harmony can be reduced to the initial G♯ moving to C♯. Thus the pattern's internal harmonies of III and VI are eliminated from the "reduction" graph.

I linger over the interpretive difficulties of the chorus reduction in order to illustrate an important aspect of the music as well as to suggest how my proposed reductive method can represent different musical strategies. In the context of the preceding verse and pre-chorus, which did not pose such reductive problems, the chorus stands out. Its subdivision into three sections, the cyclic repetition of each section, and the lack of conventional goal-directed phrase structure are important aspects of the chorus's harmonic and voice-leading strategies. That these strategies are resistant to reductive notation is not something that I wish to cover up for the sake of a theoretical system. Indeed, I believe that the tension between the actual music and the theoretical system is significant. I'm not saying that the reduction is impossible or unwarranted. After careful consideration, I believe that the voice-leading pattern I have brought out in the reduction can be theoretically supported as the deeper structure of the passage. The fact that it does not conform to traditional voice-leading models and does not appear to project a tonally unified harmonic structure is not something to shy away from, but rather to illuminate. The limitations of the reduction are also not to be dismissed in the interest of a theoretical stance. Indeed, I purposely work with three different graphs in the interest of achieving different results with each one. The merits and limitations of each are to be equally recognized.

"Crucify": Bridge

The song moves through two complete statements of verse, pre-chorus, and chorus; after that is a single statement of a bridge passage, which leads into the final statements of pre-chorus and chorus, followed by a coda. The bridge is textually and musically unique. The utterance is a simple prayer-like declamation ("Please be. Save me. I cry.") that represents a marked shift in poetic style. Musically, we are also brought into a different sound world. Here Amos sings an elaborate, melismatic line, accompanied by the backing vocals. The "prayer" is thus illuminated by a rich vocal sound, an effective use of a devotional style of singing. The voice leading of this passage is significant because of the way it relates to the earlier sections of the song. Later I will explore these connections carefully. For now, to the extent that it is possible, I will analyze the bridge on its own terms.

The bridge is graphed in Example 3.4. As illustrated in the normative progression for the bridge, the bass line repeats the pattern G♯–A♯–B–F♯, which sets up an interesting interpretive problem. The pattern begins on G♯, and thus ascribes to it a referential function. However, as the pattern is repeated, we hear the overlapping succession F♯–G♯–A♯–B (starting with the last note of the pattern, F♯, and continuing to the B), a pattern that invokes a V–I progression in B major. The vocal part has a critical role in defining the tonal focus, i.e., in projecting the governing harmony for this progression. The voice and the backing vocals emphasize B♯; as is indicated in the voice-leading graph, the voice moves through a repetition of the pattern B♯–D♯–C♯ against the bass G♯–B–F♯. It is not possible to interpret this contrapuntal structure as a prolongation of B; the cross-relation of B♯ in the voice against B in the bass disrupts any effort to hear B as stable. In addition, as the pattern is repeated, a linear progression develops in the vocal part. In other words, the vocal pattern itself is based on a B♯–D♯–C♯ gesture, but as the pattern begins to repeat, the C♯ continues down to B♯, creating the linear third progression D♯–C♯–B♯. Thus, the specific voice leading within the cyclic repetition of the pattern creates the effect of an elision: the end of one statement is directed into the beginning of the next statement. My harmonic interpretation of the pattern is indicated in the normative progression as I–III–♮VII, which then returns to I as the pattern repeats.

The interpretation of pattern repetition has been important elsewhere in the song, and is something that I believe to be critical for popular-music analysis. A common criticism launched against popular music is that its repetition patterns usually yield a "simple" harmonic language. I would argue on the contrary that such repetition can yield complex voice-leading structures that require and deserve careful interpretation. It is noteworthy that the progression is not interpreted as an open-ended motion from I to ♮VII, which was the case with the second and fourth phrases of the verse, and which was also the case in the "crucify" section of the chorus. It is important to consider these sections individually, to consider the subtle manipulation of phrase design in order to justify the different analytic treatment. In the verse, the first phrase sets up a phrase structure that moves from I to ♮VII and then back to I, while the voice also articulates a closed neighboring pattern around D♯. Therefore, when the second phrase repeats the pattern but makes ♮VII rather than the

a) Normative Progression

b) Voice-Leading Graph

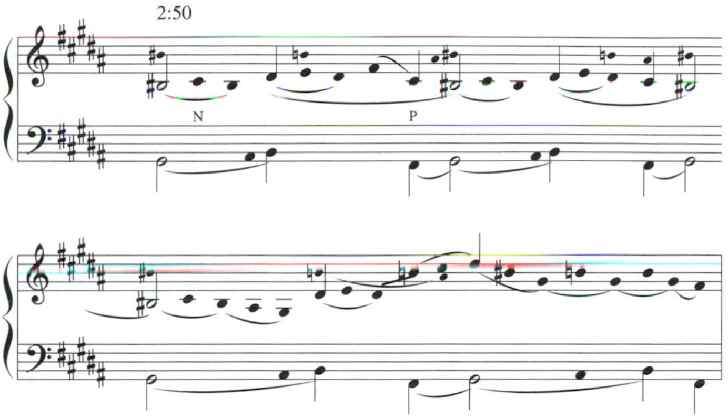

c) Reduction

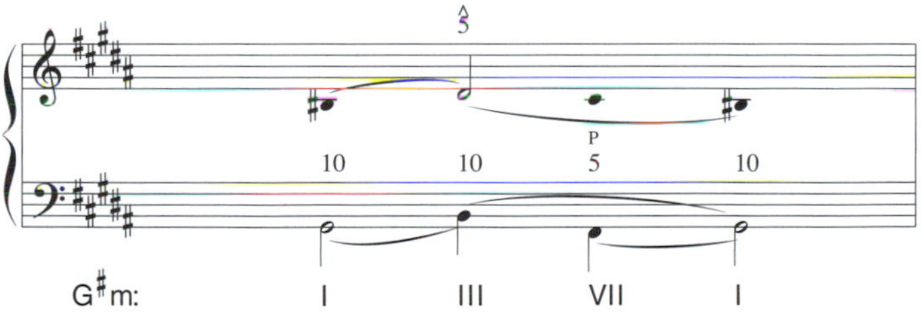

Example 3.4 Tori Amos, "Crucify" (Tori Amos), *Little Earthquakes* (1992): bridge.

closed I the cadence point, it is heard as an open harmonic progression. In the chorus, the G♯ and F♯ chords switch back and forth without any particular goal. Now in the bridge, one statement of the pattern elides into the next because of a linear progression in the voice. That is, the C♯, supported by F♯, descends into the B♯, which is supported by G♯. The linear progression is so influential that it governs the way I interpret the cyclic repetition pattern.

The analytic significance I attribute to the linear progression in the voice is worthy of further reflection. The linear descent into the B♯ is simultaneous with the bass arrival on G♯; I assert that the linear directionality of the melodic progression contributes to the definition of the harmonic goal. I am aware of the value that I attribute to a descending linear progression. I am also aware that this is an overlay of tonal (perhaps Schenkerian) hearing, but this linear progression is strategically used to create the very effect that I am experiencing, i.e., to recognize this moment in the song as a unique musical expression. At times Amos uses particular voice-leading constructs that invoke common-practice idioms. In the instance of the pre-chorus, her manipulation of the antecedent/consequent phrase design plays on formal conventions. Here, the linear progression and the harmonic conflict between G♯ and B invoke the teleological voice leading of common-practice tonality.

It is very difficult to create a "reduction" graph of the bridge section. As I've mentioned, the repeated pattern prolongs the harmony of G♯; we hear the progression I–III–♮VII repeated such that the ♮VII returns to I. How does one create a voice-leading reduction for this kind of cyclic repetition? Should the entire section be reduced to a single statement of the pattern? Or should the section be reduced to its governing harmony? If I choose the former, I am not really creating a reduction. If I choose the latter, I am claiming that the section contains no real motion. This is a remarkable analytic result, given that I find it to be one of the few moments in the song where a linear progression actually does occur. In part, the problem of reduction exists in the use of repetition, but it is also problematic to represent the contrasting material at the end of the bridge. There, the pattern changes in the voice, moving up into the higher register. A reduction of the bridge that would comprise only the repetition pattern would not be a fair representation of what occurs in the music. It is also important to consider how the bridge section connects to the following section, a return to the pre-chorus. In other words, the final statement of the bridge pattern in the bass (G♯, A♯, B, F♯) is immediately followed by the B-major tonic of the pre-chorus, and so the pattern resolves into itself, into the harmony of G♯, but at the end it continues on to B, the contrasting harmony in the song's tonal design. This theoretical difficulty indicates something here about the musical style and content. It speaks to the way in which this style of expression resists reductive analysis, and thus resists a form of simplification or basic representation. We cycle through a riff, but then move on to another gesture such that the opposing techniques of repetition and change yield interpretive challenges.

"Crucify": Overall Musical Narrative

Up till this point I have attempted to analyze each section of music individually, only occasionally indicating connections between and among the sections. Now I'll explore such relationships in greater detail. For this discussion I will continue to refer to the three different graphs of each section in Examples 1 through 4. I am deliberately not redrawing the "reduction" graphs as a single new example. I don't wish for the reduction graphs to be read apart from the context of the other two graphs, as an abstract formulation, but I'd like to reflect on the overall narrative of "Crucify." What are the connections and conflicts that occur over the course of this song? How does this narrative contribute to an ultimate interpretation of the song as a whole?

Before revisiting the sketches, I would also like to comment on why I avoid the final reductive step into the background: the *Ursatz* level. The song uses both tonal and modal conventions, applying different discursive strategies in the different sections. Each of the verse, pre-chorus, chorus, and bridge sections explores thematic harmonic and voice-leading structures in its own way. If one attempts a reductive analysis based on Schenkerian techniques, the unique features of certain sections would be lost for the sake of "organicism" or, at the very least, for the sake of linear continuity. The passages that are not based on paradigmatic tonal constructs would be "rewritten" so as to "fit" the system. Linear progressions and harmonic resolutions that do not exist would be "implied." Harmonic tensions or polarities would have to be resolved in favor of one or the other. As I stated in the introduction to this essay, I am not taking a corrective stance on this music. I believe that Amos is deliberately manipulating mode, voice-leading, and harmony to explore the potential for continuity and discontinuity in the overall musical narrative.

As I consider the totality of the sketches in Examples 1 through 4, for the purpose of examining the degree to which these disparate sections interconnect, I am struck by three features of the harmony and voice leading. The first is a conflict between the key or modal areas of G♯ and B. The second feature is the way in which the harmony of F♯ major is implicated in this conflict—specifically how it functions within each of the two opposing keys or modes. The third feature is the vocal line's treatment of D♯ as a point of descent, either to C♯ or to B (or B♯). I am the first to admit that my choice of these three features—a tonal conflict, a question of harmonic function, and a melodic linear progression—derives from a Schenkerian orientation. However, it is not my intention to develop from these features a picture of resolved tonal conflicts.

The tonal focus for each of the four main sections can be represented as follows:

Verse	Pre-chorus	Chorus	Bridge
G♯	B	G♯	G♯
Dorian	major	Aeolian	major/minor

The diagram is not organized to show the ordering of sections, which occur as verse 1, pre-chorus, chorus, verse 2, pre-chorus, chorus, bridge, pre-chorus, chorus, and coda (= modified chorus). The diagram is also incapable of illustrating the relative weight of the tonic within each section. I am willing to assert the tonal focus for each section, but with qualifications that have to do with the remaining two thematic features identified earlier: the harmonic conflict concerning the function of F♯ and the treatment of the linear progressions from D♯.

In the verse, the harmony of F♯ functions clearly as ♮VII in the mode of G♯. The two harmonies of G♯ and F♯ are presented as the primary source of harmonic tension, and are therefore elevated to a level of structural significance. In the pre-chorus, the harmony of F♯ shifts its function from ♮VII in G♯ to V in B. Indeed, the final harmony of the verse is an F♯-major chord, which immediately begs the question of its function. (In my discussion of the individual sections, I had mentioned that the connection between verse and pre-chorus posed an interpretive problem.) Once we are well launched into the pre-chorus, there is no doubt that the key is B major and that F♯ is the dominant. However, the harmony of G♯ has not been completely displaced. The voice-leading graph for the pre-chorus illustrates how G♯ acts as a neighbor harmony to the dominant. In addition, the voice outlines G♯ minor at the end of the pre-chorus at the moment when that dominant ought to resolve to B major. The chorus brings us back to G♯, and back to a progression that directly opposes G♯ and F♯. This time, the functions of these two chords are less clear, because of the lack of both phrase articulation and clear harmonic focus. The reduction asserts G♯ as the tonic for this section, but that is a decision supported by the larger context and not by the immediate details of voice leading and harmony. At the end of the chorus, the tonal focus on G♯ is much clearer, and at this point the harmony of F♯ is not involved in the cyclic patterning. So the tension between G♯ and F♯ is no longer immediately apparent. The bridge is once again interpreted in G♯, but the key of B is subtly invoked through the bass patterning, which outlines the contour from F♯ to B.

The melodic emphasis on D♯ is constant throughout all sections of the song. The reduction of the verse illustrates the motion between D♯ and C♯ as $\hat{5}$ and $\hat{4}$ in G♯. The verse ends with an unresolved melodic descent to C♯. It is interesting to consider the implications of this descending pattern. Does the C♯ ultimately imply a continuation down to B? In the closed form of the harmonic pattern that is repeated in the verse, C♯ does not continue to B, but rather returns up to D♯. Based on that context, then, does the verse's final gesture down to C♯ suggest a potential resolution upward, to D♯? Given the context of the rest of the song, the question of continuation is pertinent. There are descents to B (and B♯) later in the song that provide a context for the D♯–C♯ progression, and such a context cannot be ignored. But this truly raises the issue of "corrective" analysis. By making the connection between an event in one section and an event in another section (handled differently), am I necessarily asserting a corrective stance? I hope not. As much as it is possible, I would prefer to understand the two events as intentional conflicts, as a refusal to conform to a single standard.

The pre-chorus melodic line explicitly invokes the linear descent from D♯ through C♯ to B, although now in the contrasting key of B major and with an unusual harmonic support for the final descent to B (E major). The chorus then returns to the D♯–C♯ oscillation, for which only the "heart" section offers relief when the pattern shifts to a C♯–B oscillation. (The reduction for the chorus indicates the melodic descent from D♯ to B, but I would not go so far as to interpret this as a linear third-progression.) The final gesture of the chorus returns to the stepwise D♯–C♯ melodic progression.

The bridge offers a clear third-progression from D♯ to B♯ in which the goal of the melodic motion (B♯) is given tonic support in G♯ for the first time in the song. It is tempting to attach a great deal of significance to this linear progression and therefore to view the bridge as a moment of clarity in the harmonic and voice-leading narrative of the song. However, the bridge is not the final section of music. It is followed by statements of the pre-chorus and chorus as well as a coda; these sections send us back into the tonal conflicts inherent in their harmonic and voice-leading organization. (The coda repeats the material heard at the end of the chorus, with a final melodic gesture D♯ to C♯ over the harmony of G♯.) But more than that, it is not a productive analytic goal to search for a final resolution or an ultimate erasure of all previous conflicts.

With this study of Amos's "Crucify," my analytic goal has been to explore harmony and voice leading with an overt sensitivity to different strategies, and to manipulations of convention with particular caution with regard to the theoretical tools used in the interpretive process. Each of the three analytic graphs offers valuable information about the unique content of each musical section. The normative progression allows us to consider the harmonic progressions in a simple format (a basic pattern); the voice-leading graph can be read as a path through the actual counterpoint, including the specific handling of consonance and dissonance; and the reduction allows the analyst to consider the implications of this contrapuntal framework at a deeper structural level. A potential criticism of this (for lack of a better word) pluralistic approach to linear analysis is that one is not left with the image of a final solution or ultimate representation of the song's music, which is so often the case with reductive analysis. I have deliberately attempted not to identify and attach significance to a *single* moment in the song when all conflicts are resolved. Tonal theorists (especially Schenkerian theorists) have been trained to tie up the loose ends so that music is heard as ultimately unified. But I am arguing here that this is not an appropriate stance for the evaluation of this popular song and, I would venture to generalize, for the vast majority of popular songs. Perhaps it is simply a matter of musical style, perhaps a reflection of textual content. Indeed, in "Crucify," the overall message is one of non-resolution. Amos's text can be read as a resistance against patriarchal constructs and institutions, but she does not attain (or even explicitly define) an ultimate goal of knocking down those barriers. She simply illustrates in her text and in her musical language a degree of resistance to the systems and structures she invokes.

Notes

1. Heinrich Schenker (1868-1935) developed a system that recognized the role of the relationship between voice leading (passing and neighbor tones) and harmony (chords and the ways they relate to each other) in shaping tonal events at music's surface and in underlying levels.
2. Unfortunately I have not been able to locate this paper. My comments here are based on Richard Middleton's discussion of the article (Middleton 1990, 200).
3. Some valuable references for the study of rock harmony include Bobbitt 1976; Moore 1992, 2001; and Winkler 1978.
4. See, for instance, Middleton 1990, 195.
5. Allan Moore explores this problem in Moore 1995.
6. In my work with modal chorales (Burns 1995), my decision there was to follow through to the final reductive stage of *Ursatz* determination. I was willing, for that repertoire, to assert that a single progression could express and reflect the surface levels of structure. I still believe this to be a defensible position. For many popular songs, however, I believe the *Ursatz* level is inappropriate. The two compositional styles (chorale versus popular song) yield completely different harmonic/formal profiles, and my (seemingly inconsistent) theoretical positions are based on these compositional distinctions.
7. Although I will only use one example in this essay, the interested reader can refer to two additional essays for further consideration of my analytic method (Burns 2001–2002, 2005).
8. My analysis is based on a careful transcription of the song version that was released on the CD *Little Earthquakes* (Atlantic). An analysis of another performance would yield different analytic details and possibly even different analytic conclusions. This is a common problem in popular music analysis, given that it necessarily becomes an interpretation of a particular musical performance. Peter Winkler explores some methodological problems of transcription and interpretation (Winkler 1997).
9. "Crucify" (Tori Amos); Music and Lyrics: Sword and Stone Pub., Inc. I have written elsewhere on the text and video of "Crucify" (Burns and Lafrance 2002).
10. The choice of mode for the song does not remain fixed. The verse is in G♯ Dorian, the pre-chorus in B major, the chorus in G♯ Aeolian, and the bridge in G♯ with a major/minor ambiguity. My examples 1 through 4 use the key signature of five sharps, which does not adequately reflect the modal shifting that occurs; however, this is the key signature that is used for the printed score (Amos 1992). Incidentally, Amos's choice of key here (with five sharps) is not that uncommon in her work. Perhaps because of her classical training, she quite frequently plays in keys that would require five or six flats or sharps.
11. Allan Moore discusses rock-music period structure. He identifies the open/closed pattern, or period design, as the normative rock position. He explores the different possible combinations of open and closed phrases, commenting that he is "unaware of any songs using closed/open pairings" (Moore 2001, 58).
12. The contrapuntal combinations described here refer to the first verse. The second verse takes the same material and handles it slightly differently so that other tensions emerge.
13. I have written elsewhere on the meaning of this contrapuntal division of work (Burns and Lafrance 2002). In that paper, I suggested that the tension apparent

between subject and object perspectives in the text and video is represented musically through this tension between the voice and bass.

14. The contrast between parallel-fifth structure and a varied intervallic structure contributes a great deal to the sense that we shift from stasis to directionality. Oswald Jonas provides some valuable comments in this regard on the stasis of the open fifth: "The fifth is the boundary interval of the triad. It underscores most emphatically the root-potential of the lowest tone and therefore contributes significantly to its quality of immobility." He then continues with the effects of parallel fifths: "When the ear, having extricated itself only with effort from an intervallic situation of this kind, is immediately placed in an identical situation in relation to another tone, it is unable to find adequate orientation with respect to the intended tonal environment. . . . As a consequence of its stationary quality, the fifth applies a brake that arrests motion." Thus, Jonas establishes the stationary quality of the fifth, a quality that he then contrasts with that of the imperfect consonances: "The characteristic element of motion is the sixth, because it does not rest at peace in itself, but, in a sense, always moves on in search of the root. Thus the sixth—and in counterpoint of three or more voices, the $^{6}_{3}$ chord—becomes the soul of voice leading." Jonas's comments are particularly interesting in light of the verse/pre-chorus contrast that I attempt to define here (Jonas 1982, 111).

References

Amos, Tori. 1992. *Little Earthquakes.* Sword and Stone Publishing Company, Amsco Publications, a division of Music Sales Corporation.

Björnberg, Alf. 1985. On Aeolian Harmony in Contemporary Popular Music. IASPM Nordic Branch Working Paper No. 1.

Bobbitt, R. 1976. *Harmonic Technique in the Rock Idiom: The Theory and Practice of Rock Harmony.* Belmont, CA: Wadsworth Publishing Company.

Brackett, David. 1992. James Brown's "Superbad" and the Double-Voiced Utterance. *Popular Music* 11/3, 309–324.

Burns, Lori. 1995. *Bach's Modal Chorales.* New York: Pendragon Press.

———. 1997. "Joanie" Get Angry; k.d. lang's Feminist Revision. In *Understanding Rock: Essays in Musical Analysis.* Edited by John Covach and Graeme M. Boone, 93–112. New York: Oxford University Press.

———. 1999–2000. Genre, Gender, and Convention Revisited: k.d. lang's Cover of Cole Porter's "So in Love." *repercussions* 7–8, 299–325.

———. 2000–2001. Sarah McLachlan's "Possession" (1993): Representations of Dominance and Subordination in Lyrics, Music, and Images. *Studies in Music at the University of Western Ontario* 19–20.

———. 2005. Meaning in a Popular Song: The Representation of Masochistic Desire in Sarah McLachlan's "Ice." In *Engaging Music: Essays in Musical Analysis.* Edited by Deborah Stein, 136–148. New York: Oxford University Press.

Burns, Lori and Mélisse Lafrance. 2002. *Disruptive Divas: Feminism, Identity, and Popular Music.* New York: Routledge.

Burns, Gary. 1987. A Typology of Hooks. *Popular Music* 6/1, 1–20.

Covach, John. 1997a. Progressive Rock, "Close to the Edge," and the Boundaries of Style. In *Understanding Rock: Essays in Musical Analysis.* Edited by John Covach and Graeme M. Boone, 3–32. New York: Oxford University Press.

———. 1997b. We Won't Get Fooled Again: Rock Music and Musical Analysis. In *Keeping Score: Music, Disciplinarity, Culture*. Edited by David Schwarz, Anahid Kassabian, and Lawrence Siegel, 75–89. Charlottesville: University Press of Virginia.

Everett, Walter. 1985. Text-Painting in the Foreground and Middleground of Paul McCartney's Beatle Song "She's Leaving Home": A Musical Study of Psychological Conflict. *In Theory Only* 9, 5–13.

———. 1992. Voice Leading and Harmony as Expressive Devices in the Early Music of the Beatles: "She Loves You." *College Music Symposium* 32/1, 19–35.

Forte, Allen. 1993. Secrets of Melody: Line and Design in the Songs of Cole Porter. *The Musical Quarterly* 77/4, 625–647.

———. 1995. *The American Popular Ballad of the Golden Era, 1924–50*. Princeton: Princeton University Press.

Hawkins, Stan. 1992. Prince: Harmonic Analysis of "Anna Stesia." *Popular Music* 11/3, 325–336.

Jonas, Oswald. 1982. *Introduction to the Theory of Heinrich Schenker*. Translated and edited by John Rothgeb. New York: Longman.

Middleton, Richard. 1990. *Studying Popular Music*. Buckingham: Open University Press.

———. 1993. Popular Music Analysis and Musicology: Bridging the Gap. *Popular Music* 12/2, 177–188.

Moore, Allan F. 1992. Patterns of Harmony. *Popular Music* 11/1, 73–106.

———. 1995. The So-called "Flattened Seventh" in Rock. *Popular Music* 14/2, 185–201.

———. 1997. *The Beatles: Sgt. Pepper's Lonely Hearts Club Band*. Cambridge: Cambridge University Press.

———. 2001. *Rock: The Primary Text, second edition* [1993]. Aldershot and Burlingame: Ashgate.

Rogers, Kalen. 1996. *Tori Amos. All These Years*. London: Omnibus Press.

Tagg, Philip. 1982. Analysing Popular Music: Theory, Method, and Practice. *Popular Music* 2, 37–67.

Walser, Robert. 1992. "Eruptions: Heavy Metal Appropriations of Classical Virtuosity." *Popular Music* 11/3, 263–308.

———. 1993. Forging Masculinity: Heavy-Metal Sounds and Images of Gender. In *Sound and Vision: The Music Video Reader*. Edited by Simon Frith and Lawrence Grossberg, 153–181. London: Routledge.

Winkler, Peter. 1978. Toward a Theory of Popular Harmony. *In Theory Only* 4/2, 3–26.

———. 1997. Writing Ghost Notes: The Poetics and Politics of Transcription. In *Keeping Score: Music, Disciplinarity, Culture*. Edited by David Schwarz, Anahid Kassabian, and Lawrence Siegel, 169–203. Charlottesville: University Press of Virginia.

4

Jazz-Rock? Rock-Jazz? Stylistic Crossover in Late-1970s American Progressive Rock

JOHN COVACH

Introduction: Crossing Over

The term "crossover" arises frequently in writing about post-World War II popular music. It is perhaps most familiar from discussions of the early years of rock and roll, in which crossover is an important phenomenon that helps account for the rise of rock and roll in the 1950s out of a combination of R&B, C&W, and mainstream pop elements. In this common usage, crossover refers to the marketing of recordings as reflected by charts published in music-industry trade magazines, especially *Billboard*.[1] These charts (*Billboard*'s "Hot 100," for instance) rank hit records and were originally designed to help businesspeople at record labels, radio stations, record stores, and distribution centers assess current trends with an eye toward anticipating future opportunity and demand. The charts thus attempted to represent which songs were popular while providing a rough sense of the kind of listener to which a record appealed. For this second purpose, listeners were—and to some extent continue to be—divided along economic, geographic, and racial lines for marketing purposes. Pop charts tracked records directed at a generally middle-class white audience, while the R&B charts followed records intended for urban black audiences, and C&W charts followed those made for rural white listeners. Whenever a record appears on more than one of these charts—on both the pop and R&B charts, for example—it "crosses over." This is, strictly speaking, only a fact in regard to the consumption aspect of the music in question (as much as charts ever reflect facts, that is). A crossover hit may be assumed to appeal to two distinguishable listening audiences. Chart crossover is not necessarily a reliable indicator in matters of musical style, however; a record can certainly cross over on the charts while remaining absolutely true to a single style. The earliest R&B crossovers in the mid 1950s are a good example of this. Little Richard, for one, did not straddle a stylistic border between R&B and pop with tunes like "Tutti Frutti" and "Lucille"; he did, however, cross audience borders when his songs appealed to both black (R&B) and middle-class white (pop) audiences.

Therefore, it makes sense to distinguish between crossover in the domain of marketing ("chart crossover") and crossover in the domain of musical style ("stylistic crossover"). Crossover hits *can* work to change the style into which they cross over—as did Richard's hits—but they need not always cross over in a stylistic sense. In fact, here lies an important distinction between a cover version and a crossover: the cover version (a song that is re-recorded by another artist) *does* tend to be more likely to feature stylistic crossover, since the idea of a cover is often to assimilate a song from one style into another. As much sport as there may be in picking on Pat Boone's covers of Little Richard and Fats Domino songs, his versions do blend R&B into the mainstream pop style of the 1950s. Boone's covers clearly straddle the two styles far more than Richard's or Domino's originals do, effecting stylistic crossover where no real chart crossover was present (since Boone's records were always targeted at a pop audience).

This study focuses on the second kind of crossover discussed earlier, stylistic crossover, and explores how pieces can refer simultaneously to at least two styles that are usually thought to be distinct from one another—a situation that often makes stylistic identification a slippery but at the same time fascinating task. The two styles that I'll be especially concerned with here are 1970s progressive rock ("prog") and 1970s jazz-rock (or "fusion"). After providing a brief summary of these two styles, I will focus on the music of two late-1970s American groups, Happy the Man and the Dixie Dregs. I will argue that the music of each group is a stylistic hybrid. Happy the Man is easier to situate stylistically (their music is progressive rock with pronounced fusion characteristics), while the Dregs' music is such an eclectic blend that it defies easy categorization ("progressive-fusion-country-chamber rock"?). Both groups emerge out of a distinctively American scene in the mid-1970s that celebrates instrumental prowess and virtuosity, and it is this characteristic that allows for a blending of jazz-rock with progressive rock. In this sense, then, I will argue that the music of both groups can be seen as crossing over stylistically.[2]

Progressive Rock and Jazz-Rock

Before examining the music of these two American bands, let's first briefly consider the history of progressive rock and jazz-fusion. Progressive rock, sometimes called "art rock" or "classical rock," was developed mostly by British groups in the late 1960s and early-to-mid 1970s—groups like Yes, Genesis, King Crimson, Emerson, Lake & Palmer, Jethro Tull, and Gentle Giant.[3] This music is characterized by a pronounced attempt to blend European classical music with rock. (A related stylistic crossover from classical to rock is examined in this book by Jonathan Bernard and Mark Spicer.) Emerging out of the music of the late Beatles, and their *Sgt. Pepper's Lonely Hearts Club Band* (1967) especially, progressive rock celebrated virtuosity, musical complexity, and an engagement with big philosophical, spiritual, and religious ideas as topics for ambitious concept albums like Yes's *Tales from Topographic Oceans* (1973), Jethro Tull's *Thick as a Brick* (1972), Emerson, Lake & Palmer's *Brain Salad Surgery* (1973), and Genesis' *The Lamb Lies Down on Broadway* (1974). In fact, it is this very kind of musical and poetic ambition that both attracted young musicians to the style and caused certain critics to hate it with a passion. Rock critic Lester Bangs, for instance, once called for Emerson, Lake & Palmer to be tried as war criminals (Macan 1997, 167). Prog musicians Steve Howe and Robert Fripp on guitar, Keith Emerson, Rick Wakeman, and Patrick Moraz on keyboards, Chris Squire on bass, and Phil Collins and Bill Bruford on drums enjoyed tremendous respect among a slightly younger generation of budding rock instrumentalists, especially in the United States. This is borne out by readers' polls in various magazines such as *Guitar Player*, for example, in which Yes's Steve Howe won in the Best Overall Guitarist category five years in a row (1977–1981); he was then retired to the magazine's Gallery of Greats in 1981, where his name currently resides along with those of Andrés Segovia, Chet Atkins, Eric Clapton, and others of such legendary stature.[4]

For many young musicians in the early 1970s, prog rock was viewed as a style that encouraged a player to become as accomplished an instrumentalist as possible. An important characteristic of most prog was at least some focus on singing, and vocal arrangements at times could be very elaborate; this music was, after all, often modeled on post-Beatles-type rock songs. For musicians who were not particularly concerned with the vocal aspect of music, jazz-rock offered a style that was exclusively dedicated to instrumental playing itself; there were no backup vocal harmonies to worry about and no temperamental lead singers writing lyrics about starship hobbits from the south side of the sky. It is, in fact, hardly coincidental that as prog was emerging out of the psychedelic haze of the late 1960s, Miles Davis was developing a fusion of rock and jazz. Miles's *In a Silent Way* (1969) and *Bitches Brew* (1970) LPs launched the jazz-rock fusion style, as Miles band members like John McLaughlin, Chick Corea, Joe Zawinul, and Tony Williams went on to form the most influential fusion ensembles of the decade: the Mahavishnu Orchestra, Return to Forever, Weather Report, and Lifetime, respectively.[5] And parallel to the progressive-rock musicians, fusion guitarists John McLaughlin, Larry Coryell, and Al Di Meola; keyboardists Chick Corea and Jan Hammer; bassists Stanley Clarke and Jaco Pastorius; and drummer Billy Cobham were celebrated in the jazz categories of the same magazines that featured the progressive-rock musicians. Like Steve Howe, for instance, Al Di Meola was voted into *Guitar Player*'s Gallery of Greats in 1981 after winning first place in the Best Jazz Guitarist category five years in a row.[6] And like the progressive rockers, the fusion musicians endured attacks from hostile critics who thought that these musicians had sold out a basic tenet of their style. If the progressive rockers were accused of selling out the visceral thrill of good ol' rock and roll, the fusion players were accused of not swinging—after all, what were all those odd meters and straight eighths doing in jazz anyway?[7]

So while progressive rock and fusion are often discussed in isolation from one another, the two styles shared many of the same aspirations as well as endured similar criticism.[8] However, these parallels generally had a greater effect on the younger generation of musicians who modeled themselves on the principal figures of the two styles than it did on the founders themselves. While it is unlikely that John McLaughlin would have wanted to replace Steve Howe in Yes and even more unlikely that Howe would have played in the Mahavishnu Orchestra or Return to Forever, it was fairly common for young players to emulate both Howe and McLaughlin, or say, emulate both Chick Corea and Keith Emerson.[9] There were, of course, many players who did not cross party lines from jazz to rock, but still, there was plenty of common ground among their respective listeners.[10] It is also important to acknowledge that there were in fact significant differences between the two styles, lest anyone get the idea that 1970s prog and jazz-rock were pretty much the same music—one with vocals and one without. In terms of stylistic crossover, it is indeed essential that there be clear distinguishing characteristics between the two styles; for if the styles cannot be distinguished from each other, it is impossible for any single passage or piece to cross between them. Perhaps we might imagine fusion and prog stylistically as two circles that intersect (in the manner of a Venn diagram). It is in the area of intersection that crossover occurs, and in any consideration of stylistic crossover, it is important to determine both the characteristics of each circle as well as those at the point of intersection. It is to those moments of stylistic intersection that we will now turn.

Return to Forever, the Mahavishnu Orchestra, and Yes

The general stylistic similarities between jazz-rock and progressive rock are reinforced when certain specific passages, pieces, or entire albums from the leading groups in both prog rock and fusion seem to cross over. A good example of this is "Medieval Overture," the opening track on the 1976 Return to Forever LP, *Romantic Warrior*, which finds jazz-rockers Chick Corea, Stanley Clarke, Al Di Meola, and Lenny White crossing over into progressive rock in a marked manner.[11] The piece is composed by Corea and built up from a number of strongly contrasting sections that create an episodic formal structure. The first of these sections (0:00–0:49; see Table 4.1) features a brisk ostinato pattern established by Corea on the synthesizer that might be notated metrically as two measures of 10/8 (2 + 2 + 3 + 3) followed by a measure of 16/8 (2 + 2 + 3 + 3 + 3 + 3). After twice through this pattern, the electric guitar, bass, and drums enter, with the guitar and bass playing a series of riffs that are rhythmically aligned yet melodically contrasting against Corea's ostinato, all establishing the key of A minor. Corea then initiates a brief transition on synthesizer (0:50–1:01)—four bars in 4/4 time based in part on a stepwise whole-tone descent

Table 4.1 Return to Forever, "Medieval Overture" (Chick Corea), *Romantic Warrior* (1976): formal design.

0:00–0:49	**A** section	ostinato in keyboard; riffs in guitar/bass	A minor
0:50–1:12	transition	whole-tone keyboard then drums	B♭ whole-tone
1:12–1:36	**B** section	keyboard, guitar, bass riffs vs. drums	A minor
1:36–2:01	transition	"church organ" and synthesizer	Am to E minor
2:02–2:30	**C** section	chromatic guitar and bass in counterpoint	E, chromatic
2:30–4:16	**D** section	theme and bass solo	A Mixolydian
4:17–4:49	**A'** section	ostinato in keyboard; riffs in guitar/bass	A minor
4:49–5:10	Codetta	features reprise of first transition	A minor/major

(in thirds) from B♭ to D (much more a jazz trait than a rock one) followed by an ascending return to B♭ and played twice. This passage contrasts strongly with the material that has preceded it, as well as with the next important section that begins at 1:12; White provides eight bars of 4/4 on the drums to drive toward this arrival point (1:01–1:12.). The new section (1:12–1:36) features a return to A minor with melodic riffs played by the keyboards, guitar, and bass that are answered by drum fills in a call-and-response manner.

Already in the first ninety-six seconds of this track, then, Return to Forever has presented the listener with three contrasting and carefully arranged sections in rapid-fire succession. Following on the heels of this comes yet a fourth section (1:36–2:01), this one featuring Corea playing a soaring, angular melody on the synthesizer to the accompaniment of a synthetic organ patch, modulating from A minor to E minor while employing a rubato feel and creating an eerie effect that makes an unmistakable reference to classical organ music (though perhaps the reference is more to a Phantom-of-the-Opera-like caricature of "spooky" organ music). The section that follows (2:02–2:30) features Di Meola's fuzz-box guitar meandering chromatically in a Bartókian manner to the accompaniment of a creeping bass line by Clarke. The rest of the piece does not continue to present new music as quickly as in the first two-and-a-half minutes; there is a Stanley Clarke bass solo over a theme that is first introduced melodically at 2:30 and this section extends to 4:16. At 4:17 the group brings back the first section in a revised form, and this and a brief coda bring the track to an end at 5:10.[12]

While the references to classical music—and especially to a vague sense of orchestral grandeur—might be enough in themselves to make for stylistic crossover, the juxtaposition of complex, "composed" sections is the key ingredient that pushes "Medieval Overture" to the stylistic boundary that might be thought to separate jazz-rock and progressive rock. Except for Clarke's bass solo, the piece is tightly arranged with the musicians playing fixed parts that are not likely to change from performance to performance. This highly arranged aspect of the music is drawn from prog, where almost any passage from Yes, Gentle Giant, King Crimson, and many others could be brought forward as an example. In fact, Stuart Nicholson (1998, 202) views much of

Return to Forever's music from the mid-1970s as influenced by progressive rock, citing features such as "pompous themes, a preoccupation with speed and execution for its own sake, a reliance on the latest electronic equipment, and a shared spiritual and/or cosmic preoccupation." He even suggests that *Romantic Warrior* as a whole is "a riposte to Rick Wakeman's *Myths and Legends of King Arthur and the Knights of the Round Table* of 1975" (202).[13] The album does employ the concept-album approach by keeping with the medieval theme (in which the album art—picturing a knight in armor on horseback—also participates). Subsequent tracks are titled "Sorceress," "Romantic Warrior," "Majestic Dance," "The Magician," and "Duel of the Jester and the Tyrant." Despite such obvious similarities between the two records, Nicholson may overstate his case somewhat. Stylistically speaking, there is an abundance of passages on *Romantic Warrior* that would never be mistaken for prog (including most of the two tracks that immediately follow "Medieval Overture"), making the album a fusion LP that at times crosses over into prog.

The music of the Mahavishnu Orchestra is also central to the 1970s fusion scene. As a guitarist, John McLaughlin was known for his great speed and agility in soloing, often employing pentatonic scales that fit comfortably under the hand within single-position fingerings. As a composer, the McLaughlin of the 1970s worked at integrating materials drawn from Indian music into jazz, as well as building up pieces from synthetic scales. The result is a kind of Ravi Shankar-meets-John Coltrane hybrid, and the 1971 track "Dance of Maya" is a representative example of this approach. The piece is built up from a lengthy arpeggiated chord progression; the sonorities found in this progression are based on a simpler two-chord model that features two tritones a half step apart (see Example 4.1a). These two tritones can be seen as implying V^7-type chords with roots in descending fifths, with a G pedal tone that is not a chord member in the first sonority but is a chordal seventh in the second. This two-chord succession is then sequenced in continuing descending-fifth root motions (assuming the functions of E–A–D–G beneath the slurred chords of the sequence in Example 4.1b) to create a kind of creeping chromaticism in the bass and upper voice. This passage is set in a meter of 10/8, and McLaughlin uses distortion and wah-wah pedal on the electric guitar in a way that is more likely to conjure up images of Jimi Hendrix or Eric Clapton than of Tal Farlow or Barney Kessel. It is interesting to note that in his published full-score version of this piece, McLaughlin describes "Dance of Maya" as being based on super-Locrian and octatonic scales based on E. The use of the octatonic scale is especially noteworthy here, since this symmetrical scale crosses many stylistic boundaries in twentieth-century music.

Unlike the music of Return to Forever discussed earlier, the music of McLaughlin's Mahavishnu Orchestra does not really cross over into prog in a marked fashion. It is, rather, a strong influence on certain prog musicians and helps to account for many moments when prog crosses over into fusion.

Example 4.1 Mahavishnu Orchestra with John McLaughlin, "Dance of Maya" (John McLaughlin), *The Inner Mounting Flame* (1971): (a) two-chord model; (b) the first six chords of the sequence.

An example of this can be found in a number of passages from the 1974 Yes album, *Relayer*, especially the track entitled "Sound Chaser." At 3:01, for instance, guitarist Steve Howe tears into an aggressive and angular electric-guitar cadenza, employing the symmetrical character of the octatonic scale to create a nontonal musical environment that is not very far removed from the one created by John McLaughlin on "Dance of Maya" or on similar tracks such as "Meeting of the Spirits." While Howe's solo is ultimately a kind of psychedelic, post-tonal, Flamenco hybrid stylistically, the general harmonic and melodic language he employs creates a similar musical effect to the one created frequently by McLaughlin through his use of synthetic and exotic scales.[14]

A Patrick Moraz Moog synthesizer solo at 7:46 seems to draw heavily on Jan Hammer's MiniMoog style, and perhaps to a certain extent on that of Chick Corea. Moraz plays a quick succession of fast runs, "bending" and modulating the pitch of certain held notes to emulate an electric guitar's string bend and vibrato. It is noteworthy how stylistically different this Moraz solo is from anything Rick Wakeman ever played with Yes, or even anything that came from Genesis' Tony Banks. This marked departure from the progressive-rock norm further underscores the stylistic crossover present here. In fact, the opening moments of this track prominently feature Moraz playing a series of fast runs and dramatic chords on his Fender Rhodes: the electric piano of choice for almost all fusion keyboardists at the time but an instrument almost completely absent from most progressive rock.

In this discussion, there is perhaps a danger in exaggerating the similarities between fusion and prog. It would certainly be possible, for example, to present another collection of excerpts from *Romantic Warrior*, *The Inner Mounting Flame*, and *Relayer* that would emphasize the clear differences between the two styles. (That such examples could be readily produced explains to some degree why many writers have not thought to link the two styles more than they have to date.) The main purpose in highlighting these particular examples, however, is to suggest how young musicians listening to both kinds of records could have imagined a style that crosses over more thoroughly than these models do—a style that is more securely poised between prog and fusion. In fact, the members of Happy the Man and the

Dixie Dregs were just such musicians. These were a younger group of players who did not see any need to choose between the two styles, and their music reflects this.

Happy the Man and the Dixie Dregs

The Washington, D.C.-based Happy the Man released two albums during their time together (see Table 4.2).[15] The first, *Happy the Man*, appeared in 1977 and the second, *Crafty Hands*, was released in 1978. After being dropped by their label (Arista), the group recorded a final demo LP in late 1979, which was released as *Happy the Man 3rd, "Better Late . . ."* in 1983 on a label (Azimuth) run by Kit Watkins, the group's keyboardist. The beginnings of the Happy the Man story go back to the early 1970s.[16] Guitarist Stanley Whitaker and bassist Rick Kennell met on a U.S. Army base in West Germany in 1972. Whitaker, then a high-school student and member of the group Shady Grove, had developed an interest in the European prog groups. There, Whitaker was exposed not only to the music of Genesis, Yes, and ELP, but also to groups that were not very well known in the States at the time, among them Gentle Giant, Van der Graaf Generator, and Gong. Whitaker graduated high school and entered James Madison University in Virginia in the fall of 1972. Soon Kennell relocated to Harrisonburg, Virginia, and he, Whitaker, and keyboardist David Bach joined forces with drummer Mike Beck and singer Cliff Fortney. By January 1973, Bach had decided to leave the newly formed group to focus on his music studies, and keyboardists Kit Watkins and Frank Wyatt joined the group. With this latest personnel adjustment, the first Happy the Man lineup was in place. Fortney would leave the group before the making of the

Table 4.2 Happy the Man albums, tapes, and personnel.

Albums:	*Happy the Man*. Arista AL 4120 (1977). (Michael Beck, drums)
	Crafty Hands. Arista AB 4191 (1978). (Ron Riddle, drums)
	Happy the Man 3rd: "Better Late . . ." Azimuth AZ 1003 (1983). (Coco Roussel, drums)
Tapes:	*Beginnings*. Cuneiform Records 55003 (1990). (Demo tapes from 1974–1975)
	Live. Linden Music LM 2021 (1994). (Live tape from 1978 using third lineup)
	Death's Crown [1974]. Cuneiform Records 55015 (1999). (Live tape of a multimedia piece featuring *Happy the Man* lineup with Dan Owen but without Stanley Whitaker)
Personnel:	Group formed in Harrisonburg, Virginia, in 1972; disbanded in 1979. Rick Kennel (bass), Kit Watkins (keyboards), Stanley Whitaker (guitar), Frank Wyatt (keyboards, sax); drummers indicated above in parentheses.

first Arista LP, to be replaced by Dan Owen, who would likewise depart before the group's first commercial release.

Tapes of the early versions of Happy the Man reveal that the group was very much influenced by the British progressive-rock groups; there are many moments that could even pass for Genesis outtakes. It is interesting in this regard that Happy the Man auditioned as Peter Gabriel's backup band in the period after Gabriel left Genesis, but, according to guitarist Whitaker, the overall sound was a little too close to that of Genesis for everybody's comfort.[17] By the time the group recorded their first LP, they had decided against having a singer front the group, concentrating instead on instrumental music. Whitaker was subsequently drafted as the group's singer during the recording of the first album, but only on a couple of tracks. (The hope was that vocals might get the band a little more radio play.) The group's music is thus mostly instrumental, and in this regard more like fusion than prog.

Three members of Happy the Man wrote material for the group: guitarist Whitaker, keyboardist Watkins, and keyboardist and sax player Frank Wyatt. "Steaming Pipes," from the group's second LP, provides a representative example of Stanley Whitaker's compositional style. The piece is in 11/8, the beats falling in a 4 + 3 + 4 pattern. The rhythmic feel of the 11/8 in this section is contrasted by a second section in 6/8. Particularly notable on this track is the way Kit Watkins' characteristic MiniMoog lines play off Whitaker's angular and Mahavishnu-styled arpeggios on the guitar, doubled by electric harpsichord. Example 4.2 shows the chords that form the basis for the 11/8 section. Note that the tritone, noted earlier in "Dance of Maya," is present in the upper two voices of Whitaker's chord progression. Whereas in McLaughlin's two-chord model the tritone moves downward by half step, here the tritone descends by whole step. The bass alternates between the tritone A–D♯ in the first chord, an ascending perfect fourth in the second, and a descending perfect fifth in the third, creating a much less chromatic bass than can be found in "Dance of Maya." The band's arrangement of "Steaming Pipes," like much progressive rock, is highly structured. While both Whitaker and Watkins solo over both the 11/8 and 6/8 sections, the accompanying parts are set and unlikely to change from performance to performance. I will return later to a consideration of how live versions of this and other Happy the Man

Example 4.2 Happy the Man, "Steaming Pipes" (Stanley Whitaker), *Crafty Hands* (1978): basic chords from the 11/8 section.

works help mark an important distinction between the band and their fusion mentors, the Mahavishnu Orchestra. For now it is enough to note a blending of stylistic characteristics often associated with both fusion and prog.

"Morning Sun" (also from the group's second album) is a beautiful and haunting Kit Watkins number that provides a representative example of his compositional tendencies. Since I have discussed the technical particulars of this piece elsewhere (Covach 1999, 29–31), I will only briefly touch on the aspects of crossover in regard to this track. The most obvious reference to fusion in this case is the prominence of the arpeggios in the Fender Rhodes piano (doubled by the guitar). The sustained synthetic orchestral-string backdrop creates a delicate atmosphere that highlights the music's reference to Debussy's music, especially in the use of augmented triads throughout the song and in the free use of diatonic combinations. The arrangement of "Morning Sun" consists mostly of layered keyboards, with Watkins soloing over repeated iterations of the basic song structure, although there is also a section (2:31–3:00) in which Whitaker plays an acoustic steel-string guitar solo against the orchestral keyboard textures. As the guitar solo comes to a close, the drums make a dramatic entrance and the song moves toward its close in a very measured, almost stately manner. Here again, fusion elements are drawn into a prog context to create a marked instance of stylistic crossover.

In regard to the form of the Whitaker and Watkins tracks, these pieces follow a common fusion practice: after the principal sections of the pieces are performed once or twice through, the remainder of the track consists of soloing over these sections, sometimes with a return to the "head" to conclude. In Happy the Man's music, there may be composed transitions as well as endings that take the place of the standard return to the head at the end of the tune, but it is still often the case that the tunes are vehicles for soloing. The music of the third composer in the group, Frank Wyatt, is less often structured this way; Wyatt tended to write longer and more complicated multi-sectional works. Although there is some soloing in these pieces, the parts are almost entirely worked out to be performed the same way in each performance. Wyatt's harmonic and melodic practice owes much to fusion, but he is perhaps the group composer most indebted to progressive rock in his "composerly" attitude toward his arrangements.

Let's now look at the music of the Dixie Dregs, who offer a nice comparison to Happy the Man in a number of ways. Whereas Happy the Man were initially modeled on the British progressive rock groups, the Dregs were from the start modeled on the Mahavishnu Orchestra. The instrumentation betrays this: like McLaughlin's band, the Dregs employ guitar, bass, drums, keyboards, and electric violin. The group actually began as a rock combo in the University of Miami's jazz program in 1973. According to drummer Rod Morgenstein, "I was just living and breathing the Mahavishnu Orchestra, and here I found Steve Morse, who was actually writing in that style."[18] Morse wrote most of the

Table 4.3 The Dixie Dregs albums, tapes, and personnel.

Albums:	
	The Great Spectacular. Dregs Records DRG 0197 (1975). (Frank Josephs, electric piano)
	Free Fall. Capricorn Records CPN 0189 (1977). (Steve Davidowski, keyboards)
	What If. Capricorn Records CPN 0203 (1978). (Mark Parrish, keyboards)
	Night of the Living Dregs. Capricorn Records CPN 0216 (1979). (Mark Parrish, keyboards)
	Dregs of the Earth. Arista AL 9528 (1980). (T Lavitz, keyboards)
	Unsung Heroes. Arista AL 9548 (1981). (T Lavitz, keyboards)
	Industry Standard. Arista AL 9588 (1982). (T Lavitz, keyboards; Mark O'Connor, violin)
	Bring 'Em Back Alive. Capricorn Records 9 42005-2 (1992). (Dave LaRue, bass; T Lavitz, keyboards; Allen Sloan, violin)
	Full Circle. Capricorn Records 2-42021 (1994). (Jerry Goodman, violin; Dave LaRue, bass; T Lavitz, keyboards)
	California Screamin'. Zebra Records ZD 44021-2 (2000). (Jerry Goodman, violin; Dave LaRue, bass; T Lavitz, keyboards)
Tapes:	
	Dixie Dregs. King Biscuit Flower Hour Records 70710-88031-2 (1997). (Live broadcast recorded June 17, 1979; T Lavitz, keyboards; Allen Sloan, violin)
Personnel:	
	Group formed in Miami, Florida, in 1973; disbanded in 1982, and reformed in 1992. Rod Morgenstein (drums), Steve Morse (guitar), Allen Sloan (electric violin), Andy West (bass); all deviations from this line-up are indicated above in parentheses.

group's material through the 1970s and into the 1980s, and his debt to John McLaughlin can be heard clearly in a number of Dregs tracks. But Morse also admits to a deep admiration for the playing of Yes guitarist Steve Howe (who actually plays on a Dregs track, "Up in the Air," from *Industry Standard*), making Morse the very kind of crossover listener that was posited above.[19]

In the context of the present discussion, an important feature of Dixie Dregs music is that it blends together aspects of prog and fusion. It is also important to note that there are more than these two styles present in the band's music; the wide range of styles found on the group's 1978 release, *What If*, provides a representative example. The influence of both fusion and progressive rock can be heard in the album's second track, Morse's "Odyssey." The piece begins with a Mahavishnu-esque, chromatically weaving melody that employs striking chromatic third-related chord pairs: A major to F major and G major to E♭ major (0:00–0:34). This lyrical section gives way to a faster section in 13/8 (accented 7 + 6), driven by a perpetual-motion bass and guitar line that modulates constantly as a more sustained melodic line is layered above (0:35–1:28). At 1:29–3:54, a section is based on acoustic-guitar arpeggios that play on a harmonic shift from C♯m^7 to Am^9 (in the context of E major) and provide a repeated pattern over which an extended violin solo occurs. This solo is interrupted (2:56–3:11), however, with a strongly contrasting passage employing "composed" parts for the band, before giving way to a return to the more relaxed and improvisatory continuation of the violin solo. Though the piece lasts almost eight minutes, these opening four minutes already evince a close blending of prog and fusion elements; the "composed" sections contrast with the looser solo (in a way reminiscent of "Medieval Overture"), and the McLaughlin-esque angularity of the opening contrasts with the harder driving power chords found in the section that follows.

The influence of fusion is especially evident in the LP's title track, "What If." This piece directly adopts the Mahavishnu Orchestra sound, as it also approaches the lyrical, slow ballad according to a familiar jazz practice. After a brief introduction, the sixteen-bar melody is stated by the violin and guitar in unison, with the Rhodes, drums, and fretless electric bass accompanying (0:16–1:15). A four-bar transition leads to the return of the harmonic framework of the sixteen-bar tune, over which Morse solos (1:31–2:32). The third time through (2:48–3:49) features a synthesizer solo over the first eight bars, with the "head" returning for the last eight bars as the synth solo continues. After the four-bar transition, the head continues as the track fades out. By contrast, the album's first track, "Take It Off the Top," is an up-tempo rock number that would not likely have appeared on a John McLaughlin or Chick Corea record. With a complicated arrangement and sophisticated harmonic and rhythmic features, the track has more in common with Kansas—the American progressive-rock group with whom Morse played in the 1980s—than with most fusion of the 1970s. The band's connection to progressive rock is further reinforced by "Little Kids," which features Morse on two tracks of classical guitar together with Allen Sloan's electric violin. This short piece makes a clear reference to classical music—so much so that it seems more suited to a classical-guitar recital than to the rock stage. It is clearly indebted to the many classical-guitar passages found on Yes and Genesis albums from earlier in the 1970s (played by Steve Howe and Steve Hackett, respectively).

The music of the Dixie Dregs, like that of Happy the Man, often resides in that area of intersection between progressive rock and jazz-rock referred to earlier. Rather than being centered in one style and only venturing over to the other occasionally (as in the music of Return to Forever and Yes discussed previously), the music of both bands is more centered in this in-between ground. The situation in regard to the Dixie Dregs is more complicated than for Happy the Man, since the Dregs also cross over into country and funk at times (consider "Gina Lola Breakdown" and "Ice Cakes" from *What If* for examples of each).

The question of stylistic crossover is further complicated by the role of improvisation in the music of each group. Live tapes of the Mahavishnu Orchestra from the 1972–1974 period, for instance, reveal that album tracks were extended in performance and solos tend not to be duplicated, either from the record or from performance to performance. This is, of course, entirely consistent with jazz practice generally; no matter how arranged the tune is, the solos are always open to fresh interpretation. The practice in progressive rock is more constrained. Live versions of Yes tracks tend to keep close to the recorded versions; solos may change from performance to performance, but they sometimes also follow the album version fairly closely. For the most part, Genesis performances are even closer to the recorded version than those of Yes or Jethro Tull. In the case of Happy the Man, tapes from the late 1970s reveal that live versions of the album tracks were almost identical to their studio versions; even solos, however improvised they might sound on the record, are reproduced relatively faithfully. The Dixie Dregs are somewhat freer in their solos, although these tend not to be extended beyond the length of the studio versions. Broadly speaking, the contrasting relationship between studio and live versions of pieces in prog and fusion might be cast as follows: fusion musicians attempt to capture a live performance on the record, while prog musicians attempt to reproduce the record live. If this is the case, then both Happy the Man and the Dixie Dregs fall much more into the prog camp than into the fusion one.[20]

Stylistic Crossover

I have argued that crossover occurs in the music of Happy the Man and the Dixie Dregs because the members of these bands developed in a musical culture that privileged instrumental prowess and virtuosity. In the mid-1970s, a rock player had two stylistic options in following aspirations to the highest level of technical proficiency: progressive rock and jazz-rock fusion. There were, of course, other options as well; one could turn to classical music or to traditional jazz, for example. But for those who wanted to continue playing some form of rock music, the two choices were prog and fusion. In the mid-1970s, the British prog bands were at the peak of their popularity. Fusion artists were also enjoying commercial success. The Mahavishnu Orchestra's *Birds of Fire*, for example, rose as high as number 15 on *Billboard*'s "Top LP's & Tapes" chart in 1973. Considering the American reception of British progressive rock and American fusion, it is perhaps not so surprising that two American groups each developed a distinctive sound that straddled the stylistic boundary between jazz fusion and progressive rock.

But there were problems with the distinctiveness of the stylistic crossover in each case. Neither Happy the Man nor the Dixie Dregs experienced much commercial success, and this is certainly due in large part to the fact that each group was difficult to market. As instrumental bands, each was incompatible with late-1970s rock radio formats. As rock bands, each was also incompatible with most jazz formats, since even the fusion groups tended to be viewed with a certain disdain by the jazz purists. But the kind of aspiring musicians who had supported the original prog and fusion musicians in the 1970s came to embrace at least a few of this new generation. While the musicians in Happy the Man remained generally unknown, *Guitar Player* readers voted Steve Morse Best Overall five years in a row (beginning in 1982), and voted the Dregs' *Industry Standard* LP the Best Guitar Album of 1982.[21] Had more readers in these guitar, bass, percussion, and keyboard communities been aware of the Happy the Man LPs, it seems likely that these musicians would have been celebrated as well.

To conclude this study, let's return to the distinction that was made at the outset between chart crossover and stylistic crossover. It is clear that, in the case of most of the bands we have examined here, chart crossover has no real application. One could point to the Mahavishnu Orchestra crossing over into *Billboard*'s album chart as indicated earlier, but that's about all that the charts can tell us. Stylistic crossover is more helpful but at the same time a far more interpretive operation. Consider that we begin with two distinct styles that are themselves hybrids: progressive rock blends rock with classical music and fusion blends jazz with rock. Next we insert into this context music that might also be seen to be a stylistic hybrid, but in this case a hybrid of two hybrids. How is this second hybrid different from the first two? Can such distinctions ultimately be helpful?

The first step in understanding this situation is in seeing an important difference between prog and fusion on one hand and the music of Happy the Man and the Dixie Dregs on the other. We can think of both fusion and prog as distinguishable styles because there are many works that can be classified—if sometimes only roughly—under each stylistic label. There is, in short, a prog repertoire and a fusion repertoire. But aside from the albums under discussion, it would be difficult to produce a similar repertoire for American prog-fusion crossover music. So if we return to the Venn diagram suggested earlier, each of the intersecting circles is a collection of features derived from across some repertoire, while in the area of intersection are features shared by some pieces, but these pieces do not in themselves constitute a repertoire of comparable size and variety. When there are enough pieces that reside in this intersecting space, one can no longer speak profitably about crossover; instead, one may need to consider the possibility of a distinct hybrid style. Therefore, crossover always involves holding two repertoires simultaneously in view with the idea that the piece (or pieces) under scrutiny would not fit cleanly into a single repertoire. Such an operation is markedly interpretive in the sense that it is the music scholar who invokes the styles in force in any given case. And such an interpretive operation is relative in the sense that one could also construct a pair of Venn diagrams in which one circle represents jazz and the other rock, with fusion at the intersection, or a pair in which one circle represents rock and the other classical with prog in the middle. In this case, "crossover" might be applied in a much more general sense than the one used for the present analysis. Although this study has focused on the notion of stylistic crossover in 1970s progressive rock specifically, it seems clear that distinguishing the stylistic from the marketing aspects of crossover, as well as exploring the complex and sometimes intimate relationships between these two, is a potentially rich and worthwhile approach to a broad range of musical styles that might blend elements of popular and classical, western and nonwestern, and even current and past repertoires. The fascination of most crossover music is how it balances between two styles, refusing to be forced into a single stylistic category. Perhaps rather than attempting to resolve such conflicts, the analyst's job is to celebrate the tension.

Notes

1. Musicologist Charles Hamm (1983, 391–424) provides a clear explanation of the role played by crossover hits in the early years of rock and roll, as well as the role played by cover versions during this period. The classic study of the American popular-music business is Russell Sanjek's three-volume history, the third volume of which deals with the twentieth century and is reprinted and expanded as Sanjek 1996. For consideration of some of the political dimensions of crossover, see Perry 1988.
2. It should be admitted that, strictly speaking, the question of chart crossover never really arises in regard to the groups under consideration, since neither the Dixie Dregs nor Happy the Man ever had a Top-Forty album or single on any chart. As far as the eclectic blending of styles into 1970s rock is concerned, Frank Zappa's music is also fertile ground for the kinds of analytical discussions that follow. (Jonathan Bernard and James Borders explore the crossover nature of Zappa's music in Chapters 1 and 2, respectively.)
3. I offer condensed historical overviews of progressive rock in Covach 1997 and 1999. More detailed accounts of 1970s progressive rock can be found in Macan 1997 and Stump 1997. Martin 1997 also offers much detailed information on this music, but, owing to its informal and often idiosyncratic character, it must be consulted with caution.
4. Poll results for the 1977–1981 period can be found in the following issues of *Guitar Player*: 11/12 (December 1977), 30–31; 12/12 (December 1978), 40–41; 13/12 (December 1979), 72–73; 14/12 (December 1980), 24–25; and 15/12 (December 1981), 56–57. During these years in which Steve Howe won the Best Overall category, his bandmate Chris Squire took first place in the Bass category in 1980, and second place in the other four years. *Guitar Player* introduced a sister publication, *Contemporary Keyboard*, in September 1975. In the new magazine's first readers' poll (3/1 [January 1977], 24–25), Keith Emerson took first place in five categories: Best Overall, Rock Piano, Synthesizer, Rock Organ, and Multi-Keyboard. In 1978 he repeated this feat, adding Best Keyboard Album as his sixth honor (3/12 [December 1977], 20–21). In 1977, then Yes keyboardist Patrick Moraz won Best New Talent and Best Keyboard Album as well. In the first readers' poll conducted by *Modern Drummer* (3/3 [May/June 1979], 26–28), Carl Palmer and Bill Bruford placed second and third, respectively, behind Carmen Appice (ex-Vanilla Fudge and Cactus) in the Rock category.

5. Nicholson 1998 offers a detailed history of jazz-rock, with extended discussion of each of the groups mentioned here. Gridley 1997 (324–354) provides a briefer but more music-technical discussion, while Gioia 1997 (364–381) places jazz-rock within the context of other stylistic fusions in regard to jazz.
6. Before Di Meola's streak, John McLaughlin had placed first in the Jazz category of the *Guitar Player* readers' poll in three consecutive years (7/4 [May/June 1973], 42; 8/12 [December 1974], 22–23; and 9/12 [December 1975], 22–23). In the 1975–1979 polls, Stanley Clarke placed first in the Bass category, being retired to the Gallery of Greats in 1979. In the first *Contemporary Keyboard* poll (for 1976) in which Keith Emerson took first in five categories, Chick Corea placed first in Electric Piano, which he repeated along with Jazz Piano the next year. In the first *Modern Drummer* poll, Billy Cobham placed second in the Best Overall category behind Steve Gadd, while Tony Williams won in the Jazz category.
7. For an account of the attacks to which progressive rock has been subjected along these lines, see Macan 1997, 167–178. For an account of the parallel phenomenon in jazz-rock, see Nicholson 1998, xiii–xviii.
8. The separation of these styles continues even in some of the best recent scholarship. Nicholson 1998 only occasionally mentions progressive rock, and then mostly offers negative assessments. Macan 1997 devotes some attention to jazz-rock, but mostly in the context of the British Canterbury scene.
9. There was some crossing over of personnel among the big-name players in the two styles in the late 1970s. Genesis drummer Phil Collins played in the English fusion band Brand X in the late 1970s. As mentioned by Mark Spicer in Chapter 12, when Collins took over as lead vocalist from Peter Gabriel, American jazz-rocker Chester Thompson (drums) joined the band for all live performances, as did Daryl Stuermer (guitar/bass) after guitarist Steve Hackett's departure from the group. The late-1970s prog supergroup UK featured guitarist Allan Holdsworth, who subsequently became one of the most admired guitarists in jazz-rock. Some of this crossover is explained by the presence of a jazz-rock fusion in England within the Canterbury scene, of which 1970s Soft Machine is perhaps the best example. While most Canterbury music is not very well known in North America, its roots are in the same mid- to late-1960s scene that spawned the British prog bands. Pink Floyd, Soft Machine, and Tomorrow (featuring Steve Howe), for instance, were the most influential bands in the London psychedelic underground of the 1966–1969 period. Nicholson (1998, 14–28) provides a useful account of the late-1960s British scene with an eye toward the development of jazz-rock.
10. While this seems obvious from even a cursory perusal of periodicals from the 1970s directed at musicians (and these periodicals are cited throughout this study), I can attest that this was certainly consistent with my experience during this period as a young developing guitarist playing and teaching in the Detroit area.
11. The music-analytical descriptions that follow rely on CD timings to locate points of reference. The CD reissue used in each is listed in the chapter's references.
12. While this track's title refers to the overture in a classical-music sense, the ideas it presents do not prefigure those that follow on the album in any obviously thematic way.

13. For Nicholson, the influence of progressive rock on Chick Corea's music during the mid-1970s was unfortunate, and Nicholson's position on this point is indicative of aesthetic attitudes that continue to separate fans (and critics) of the two styles, even if these attitudes are not shared by the musicians themselves. Progressive rock bands are dismissed for their "empty virtuosity," with Corea as well "guilty of exploiting his technique at the expense of meaning," producing music that is ultimately "cute and pretentious" (1998, 202).
14. Howe's opening solo to the group's "Close to the Edge" (Yes 1972) seems also inspired in part by McLaughlin. Other Howe solos betray the influence of jazz on his playing as well, especially on *The Yes Album* (1971). Howe was something of an exception in the late 1960s and early 1970s in his use of a large-body Gibson ES-175 guitar—an instrument more often used by traditional jazzers.
15. I discuss Happy the Man in Covach 1999, where my principal concern is situating the band within the context of American progressive rock in the 1970s. They are considered there along with Kansas, Starcastle, and dozens of other groups. In that study I focused on demonstrating the ways in which the group's music integrates features drawn from classical music into a rock context (a basic feature of almost all progressive rock).
16. The following account of the band's history is drawn from the liner notes to the band's compilation CD, *Retrospective* (East Side Digital 80292 [1989]), many of the details of which were confirmed in a telephone conversation with Stanley Whitaker on November 8, 1995.
17. Telephone conversation, November 8, 1995.
18. Morgenstein's remarks are drawn from the liner notes to the live CD, *Dixie Dregs*, which also contains a band history. For additional accounts of the Dregs' history and influences, see Obrecht 1978 and 1982.
19. In 1982 Steve Morse was featured in *Guitar Player*'s "Essential Listening" column, in which well-known guitarists share the albums they consider most influential in the development of their playing. Of the nine guitarists Morse discusses, both McLaughlin and Howe rank very high. The feeling seems to be mutual, at least as far as Howe is concerned; in an interview with the author on June 25, 1998, the Yes guitarist mentioned that he and Morse are hoping to tour together in the near future.
20. This issue is not made any easier by considering the way the albums considered in this study were recorded. Tracks on Yes's *Relayer*, for instance, were composed by splicing together short stretches of recorded material; the group sometimes had to learn the tracks after they were recorded in order to perform them live. Mahavishnu Orchestra tracks seem to project a sense that they were done in real time as complete takes, although I don't know if this is the case or not. An important figure in all this might be engineer and producer Ken Scott, who worked on a number of records for a wide variety of artists, including the Beatles. He worked with the Mahavishnu Orchestra (as did Beatles producer George Martin) and produced albums for Happy the Man and the Dixie Dregs. The role of the recording process in this music is an area yet to be examined in any scholarly depth.
21. Poll results can be found in the following issues of *Guitar Player*: 16/12 (December 1982), 52–54; 18/1 (January 1984), 34–37; 19/1 (January 1985), 42–44; 19/12 (December 1985), 52–57; and 20/12 (December 1986), 64–65. Dregs bassist Andy West placed second in 1982 and third in 1983 and 1984.

References (see also Tables 2 and 3)

The Beatles. 1967. *Sgt. Pepper's Lonely Hearts Club Band.* Capitol 2653.

Covach, John. 1997. Progressive Rock, "Close to the Edge," and the Boundaries of Style. In *Understanding Rock: Essays in Musical Analysis*, ed. John Covach and Graeme M. Boone, 3–31. New York: Oxford University Press.

______. 1999. Echolyn and American Progressive Rock. In *American Rock and the Classical Music Tradition*, ed. John Covach and Walter Everett (special issue of Contemporary Review 18/4), 13–61.

Davis, Miles. 1969. *In a Silent Way.* Columbia 9875.

______. 1970. *Bitches Brew.* Columbia PG 26.

Emerson, Lake & Palmer. 1973. *Brain Salad Surgery.* Atlantic SD 19124.

Genesis. 1974. *The Lamb Lies Down on Broadway.* Atlantic SD2-401.

Gioia, Ted. 1997. *The History of Jazz.* New York: Oxford University Press.

Gridley, Mark. 1997. *Jazz Styles: History and Analysis*, sixth edition. Upper Saddle River, New Jersey: Prentice-Hall.

Hamm, Charles. 1983. *Yesterdays: Popular Song in America.* New York: W. W. Norton.

Jethro Tull. 1972. *Thick as a Brick.* Reprise MS 2072.

Macan, Edward. 1997. *Rockin' the Classics: English Progressive Rock and the Counterculture.* New York: Oxford University Press.

The Mahavishnu Orchestra. 1971. *The Inner Mounting Flame.* Columbia 31067.

Martin, Bill. 1997. *Listening to the Future: The Time of Progressive Rock, 1968–78.* Chicago and La Salle: Open Court.

Morse, Steve. 1982. Essential Listening. *Guitar Player* 16/6 (June), 58 ff.

Nicholson, Stuart. 1998. *Jazz Rock: A History.* New York: Schirmer.

Obrecht, Jas. 1978. Steve Morse and Andy West: Forging A New Southern Sound. *Guitar Player* 12/12 (December), 34 ff.

______. 1982. Steve Morse: Electric Guitar Master Class. *Guitar Player* 16/8 (August), 59 ff.

Perry, Steve. 1988. "Ain't No Mountain High Enough": The Politics of Crossover. In *Facing the Music*, ed. Simon Frith, 51–87. New York: Pantheon.

Return to Forever. 1976. *Romantic Warrior.* Columbia PC 34076. CD reissue: Columbia CK 46109.

Sanjek, Russell, with David Sanjek. 1996. *Pennies from Heaven: The American Popular Music Business in the Twentieth Century*, rev. and updated ed. New York: Da Capo.

Stump, Paul. 1997. *The Music's All That Matters: A History of Progressive Rock.* London: Quartet Books.

Yes. 1971. *The Yes Album.* Atlantic SD 19131.

______. 1972. *Close to the Edge.* Atlantic SD 19133.

______. 1973. *Tales from Topographic Oceans.* Atlantic SD2-908.

______. 1974. *Relayer.* Atlantic 18122.

5
Pitch Down the Middle

WALTER EVERETT

Whereas timbre, rhythm, and form are of undeniable interest, this essay argues that pitch relationships are of central importance, forming the core of the stucture, the identity, and even many of the expressive capabilities of pop-rock music.[1] Rhythm and form, while of great value in music, have similarly important roles in all temporal arts such as poetry, drama, prose, dance, and film. But whereas pitch may play a small part in most of these sister art forms, it is this quality alone that separates music from all other means of artistic expression.[2] It might be said that tone color as well is far more important in music than in these other forms, but this essay will argue that, as with the other musical parameters mentioned here, timbre must take a back seat to pitch in terms of core structure in all or nearly all of the music of the pop-rock literature.

Even though the technical ways that tones relate to one another along the pitch continuum are seldom appreciated by most rock performers and audience members alike, I believe that purely musical effects—nearly always connected in some way to matters of pitch relationships—contribute to any composer's or listener's appreciation, regardless of training or superficial awareness. If most listeners believe they are attracted only to rhythm or loud volume and "can't hear" the pitch or have no conscious understanding of functional tonal relations, I say they are merely unaware of why, for instance, they become more excited by expanded dominant-seventh retransitions enhanced by added uncontrolled dissonance than they do in the face of less tonally valent alternations of weak III and VI chords. (Where, musically, did the Beatles and their 1964 listeners shake their mop-tops and shriek most fervently? Follow the retransitional dominants![3])

Not only are pitch relationships at the core of pop-rock music, but they share many of the procedures of harmony and counterpoint by which tonal goals are identified, pursued, and frustrated in tonal musics of other styles. For this reason, many of the analytical systems devised over the past few centuries for the study of common-practice classical music are also applicable to our subject. Of course there are vast differences between the tonal processes and outcomes of centuries-old classical and modern rock musics, but differences can be just as vast between various rock styles, even those practiced by a single artist. The tonal-world distance is far greater between John Lennon's "If I Fell"

(1964) and his "I Found Out" (1970) than between Schubert's "Ständchen" (1828) and "If I Fell."

My aim is to illustrate that because rock musicians express their originality according to all significant musical parameters, a working understanding of all of these basic elements (whether nurtured by an expensive tuition through peer-reviewed programs in theory, analysis, and musicology, or developed by a bright independent performer with good ears) can be both appropriate and useful for a full appreciation of the literature's expressive import. I'll demonstrate expressive manipulations of formal construction, vocal and instrumental colorings, rhythmic relationships, melodic devices, and tonal systems, without once ever considering whether the composers, arrangers, artists, or engineers might have been fully conscious of how I might hear what they were doing. The only question of value to me is what might profit the imaginative *listener*'s consciousness. And such decisions will be guided by Edward T. Cone's advice of long ago: that the analyst ignore biases as fully as possible, and allow the piece at hand to reveal how it is to be most clearly understood ([1960], 54).

I will begin by addressing a small sampling of issues that fall under the headings of the basic parameters of musical construction ostensibly relating to matters other than pitch: form and design, vocal and instrumental color, and rhythm and tempo. Under these topics, analyses of performances by the Four Tops, Elvis Presley, the B-52's, and the Supremes will demonstrate that pitch relationships often have strong expressive implications for what are often thought to be extra-pitch subjects. These scattered observations are followed by an outline (illustrated with brief references to hundreds of well-known examples) of melodic, harmonic, and contrapuntal systems governing pitch structures in a wide array of pop-rock styles. Those wishing a still more comprehensive study of harmony in rock music are directed to Everett 2004b (and forthcoming).

Form and Design

Many elements of formal growth and contrast are readily acknowledged in pop-rock analysis. For epic works, such as progressive-rock movements (or any other non-blues-based pieces that go on for 4'30" or more), matters of formal construction are often of primary interest. But much more remains to be discovered, I think, in the design and structure of the non-expansive pop song. Following a summary of traditional formal conventions in the song of the pop-rock-era, and the presentation of a few examples of deviations from normal formal functions, I will proceed with a glimpse at some compositional emphases of design elements in examples by the Who and the Four Tops.

Conventional formal functions in the post-Tin Pan Alley pop song might be outlined as follows, with references to a few Beatles numbers. The pop song typically alternates verses (usually sung by a single lead, with different sets of lyrics for at least the first two occurrences, prolonging the tonic but possibly ending on a transitional V) and choruses (usually the source of the song's title as part of an unchanging set of lyrics for each hearing, sung in tonic with backing vocal counterpoint or harmonies). These will usually be balanced by one or two statements of a contrasting bridge (in early models, such as "From Me to You" [1963], beginning on the flat side with an emphasis on IV and leading to a thereby enhanced sharp side with a tonicized V, but nearly always with approaches to chromaticism and texture that contrast strongly with the song's other sections). An optional introduction presages motivic material of the song proper; it is usually instrumental, but chorus and/or lead vocal are possible, as in "Here, There and Everywhere" (1966). An improvisatory instrumental solo (usually based on the structure of the bridge or that of the verse, as in "Don't Bother Me," but sometimes on an unrelated twelve-bar model, as in "I Saw Her Standing There" [both 1963]) and coda (which may fade or end cold) are optional. As a refinement, sometimes the song title is sung unchanged as the final phrase of every verse; this would be referred to as a refrain. (In alternative rock, the song title is often not articulated at all.) If a refrain is present, sometimes a separate chorus is not necessary ("Yesterday" [1965]), but both can sometimes appear ("She Loves You" [1963]). Usually, the song's broad poetic theme will be outlined in the chorus, and successive verses will offer instances that enumerate its substantiations.

Against these conventions, variations are often of interest. For instance, an incipient form is suggested when the verse is very short in relation to its chorus, the opposite of a normal proportion. This might happen in very different contexts. One rationale might be folk-related, such as the Singing Nun's "Dominique" (1963), the stunted verse (four bars, as opposed to the chorus's eight) of which suggests an around-the-(Belgian?)-campfire volunteering of on-the-spot verses by rotating contributors (along the lines of "What do you do with a drunken sailor?"). But there seems to be no such social model for the oddly unbalanced weight of Steely Dan's "Through With Buzz" (1974), whose iconoclastic three-bar verses, eight-bar choruses, and ten-bar bridge defy time with rebellious interruptions.

Another example of a simple song that manages to confound structural norms is Friend and Lover's "Reach Out of the Darkness" (1968), which revises and reorders formal functions in unexpected ways as a celebration of social change. Following the bass/drums introduction, the formal role of the simple-as-a-chorus, unison-sung (by Jim and Cathy Post), repeated passage beginning at 0:08 ("I think it's so groovy now …") is made unclear by what follows, which is obviously the song's true chorus (its lyrics based on the repeated title, sung as a duet, beginning at 0:25). This precedes what seems like a verse ("I knew a man …," 0:44), which passage has a lone singer, Jim, present a very verse-like singular situation that falls under the theme umbrella of the chorus. But this music is never heard again, with either the same or different lyrics, and so acts more like a bridge than a verse, despite the fact that it simply prolongs tonic. A repeated chorus (1:11) is followed by the "groovy" section (1:29, reversing the order of these sections heard at 0:08–0:44, in the manner of an exuberant afterthought), which by now could perhaps be thought of as a motto as it is neither a chorus nor a refrain within a verse. A true bridge follows at 1:46 ("Don't be afraid …"), moving from the dominant's softer side (IV of V) to its more demanding V/V–V. The song concludes with another chorus, followed by the motto that repeats to fade. Thus, the song's design symbol would read **A** (intro/motto)–**B** (chorus)–**C** (would-be verse)–**B**–**A**–**D** (bridge)–**B**–**A**, a sort of rondo with offset arch, all befitting the song's downplay of communication problems as if they were an overcome thing of the past (as suggested by the defeated issue-raising verse) and its celebration of a new antiestablishment order of worldwide friendship.[4]

Another interesting deviation from formal norms obtains in various adaptations of the twelve-bar blues.[5] The verse of the Beatles' "Day Tripper" (1965) follows the first eight bars of a standard blues in E with a devious eight-bar explosion of chromatic harmony (featuring an augmented-sixth chord within a tonicized VI) that slowly finds its way back to the home key as John and Paul come to realize gradually ("it took me so long to find out") how they had been taken for a ride. James Brown's "Cold Sweat (Part 1)" (1967) is a masterpiece of tension that inflames a thirty-bar blues past its normal metric and harmonic boiling points. A nonchalant ("I don't care") sixteen bars of restrained D-major tonic (ornamenting $\hat{5}$ with its clean-boogie diatonic $\hat{6}$ upper neighbor in saxes, yet funkified as a $^{\sharp 9}_{7}$ sonority) give way to seduction in the next ten bars, which alternate single measures of ♮VII^9 and its own neighboring IV^7 five times before the now obviously sexual tension spills over in a remarkable four-bar ♮VII-expanding retransition (at 1:03 and 2:17; see Example 5.1), culminating in V^9 of the feverishly disoriented ♮VII, making the returning verse's I (instead of a logically expected ♮VII) sound suddenly composed. The three gestures (tonic stasis, departure involving [a transposed] IV–I motion, and

Example 5.1 James Brown, "Cold Sweat" (James Brown-Alfred Ellis) (1967): retransitional climax.

climax involving [an applied] V) all relate to the twelve-bar model, but with rhythmic and tonal exaggerations customary only for this godfather-figure.[6]

Terraced instrumentations often demarcate formal divisions in pop music. Jerry Wexler's expert management of textural growth in Aretha Franklin's "I Never Loved a Man (the Way I Love You)" (1967) is a case in point. Here, successive overlays help define formal sections with increasing intensity, by the additions of organ for the second verse (0:24) and punctuating brass for the chorus (0:40+). Such textural contrasts are effective carriers of emotions in Norman Whitfield's brilliant manipulation of pain in the imaginative vocal and instrumental arrangements in the Temptations' "I Wish It Would Rain" and Marvin Gaye's "I Heard It Through the Grapevine" (both 1968).[7] The texture of formal growth within Bruce Springsteen's "Born to Run" (1975) reflects the post-Jack Nitzschean *Übermensch*/Boss not in the homogenous stream of noisy energy found within the Palace—the great gaudy mansion of glory on the Asbury Park boardwalk—but in a formally worked-out rising undulation that springs the amusement park and its motorcycle and Stone Pony metaphors from the contextual cages of their restrained surroundings. Design can thus help establish formal divisions and events, usually to expressive ends. This section will conclude with more extensive comments on formal design functions in the Who's *Tommy* and the Four Tops' "Reach Out I'll Be There."

A full appreciation of works like *Tommy* (1969) could not ignore the sorts of musico-poetic text-painting issues that relate to the formal working-out of design that is so important there. Considering the monothematic—though catchy and compelling—nature of Shel Talmy's early Who productions ("I Can't Explain," "My Generation," both 1965), the contrast of ideas in *Tommy* is remarkable. (Under Kit Lambert, the group showed growth in their means of expression through subtle complexities; unexpected rhythmic contrasts betray the misanthropic character hidden within "Happy Jack" [1966], for example.) As for *Tommy*, little could be simpler than the texture of the rock "opera" (it's more of a cantata, if a classical model must be decided upon); Townshend's personal multitrack demos for the work are only marginally filled out by the four-man band's almost-live recording.[8] The materials are restricted, but freedom with and mastery of them are complete. What's more, formal demarcations attain an expressiveness that goes to the core of the story's subject matter. As the result of a severe psychological shock in early boyhood, Tommy has lost all sensate powers to learn from and communicate with his world; he is ultimately cured and becomes a cult idol with healing powers, literally a personified "Sensation" himself. Throughout the album, formal contrasts juxtapose the bold thoughts and the quiet dreams of the mute Tommy's troubled inner world. The contrast is introduced in the dynamic "Amazing Journey," which pits passages featuring pensive reversed guitar articulations (0:32–0:38) against Keith Moon's wild drumming (0:45–0:55+). In "Christmas," the singer tries to reach the mute boy amid surroundings of uncontrolled excitement. The latter is expressed in paradoxically precise backing-vocal outbursts of wordless rapid-fire sixteenth-note hockets (0:04–0:09), and defeated by interruptions of Tommy's unheard "see me, feel me" yearnings (2:28–3:02) that float timelessly in their contrast with the tempo and rhythm of the outside world. (The tempo change may remind the listener of the "Overture," which, like Lully's seventeenth-century French model, follows a pompous slow section with a fast one.) Rhythmic design underlines the differences between inner fantasy and outer reality, and between tyranny and freedom, in the unexpected change of perspective that accompanies the subtle but total transformation of piano/drum backbeat to downbeat (0:17) in "I'm Free." Finally, in "Pinball Wizard," the quiet tension of Tommy's inward stature, expressed in verses by the mock-Baroque grace of a descending sequence of 4-3 suspensions over the directional passacaglia-derived I–♭VII–♭VI–V bass steeled in acoustic tremolos (0:32–0:44), is answered by a jerky, outward-reaching, raucous, mean-pinball pentatonic-minor power-chord riff of a refrain (I–♭VII–♭III–IV [0:45–0:55]), aptly juxtaposing the poised care of clean-playing flipper-finger substitution (as played by offsetting guitar-finger substitution) against the full-tilt timbre-distorting power parallelisms. (4-3 sequences achieve the significance of motivic design in *Tommy*, playing roles over *chromatically* descending basslines in both the tortuous "Cousin Kevin" [ornamented through 0:16–0:50] and the emancipated "I'm Free" [presented plainly in 2:22–2:35], the latter thematically tied to the "Pinball" sequence.) While the designs and forms of *Tommy* would likely prove too basic for any extended analysis, still more remains to be said at another time about how those materials are manipulated for expressive ends.

Motown's writing-production partnership of Brian Holland-Lamont Dozier-Eddie Holland, the composers of all twenty-four major mid-1960s hits by the Supremes and the Four Tops, will be referred to several times in this essay, so pervasive is their domination over all musical parameters in so many pop masterpieces. The more interesting of the Tops' two biggest hits, "Reach Out I'll Be There" (1966), is instructive for its expressive form-defining contrasts of harmonic relationships. The confusion, illusion, fear, cold, and drifting that trouble the singer's love object in the verse turn to a raw paranoia in the chorus, and the withholding of harmonic support and clarity are the chief expressive factors. A spooky instrumental introduction, clearly a repeated I^{4-3}–V in E♭ minor, is shaken off by the verse, which begins (0:16) ("Now if you feel that you can't go on") on a major triad a half-step higher than the introductory V. This C♭ chord alternates with D♭ five times in an asymmetrical ten-bar pattern, the chords' goal as unclear as the hopeless woman's future until they resolve into the refrain's safety of G♭ (0:37), which seems at first like a well-prepared (IV–V–I) tonic, with the dissonant E♭-minor introduction (perhaps the ultimate source of the woman's troubles?) now seemingly part of the remote past. But the "Reach Out!" comfort offered in G♭ by a sincere lead-singing Levi Stubbs is undermined by the bass player, James Jamerson, who insists on playing the fifth of the chord for a full bar before moving to its root (at 0:39) ("Reach out!"). If that weren't unsettling enough, one lone bar of a true root-position G♭ is followed by a transitional bar of V^6_5 of E♭ (0:41), which then slides to a harsh $VII^{\circ 6}_5$ of E♭ (0:43) as the first tenor moves from B♭ to its dissonant upper neighbor, C♭ (mocking the once-stabilizing B♭-C♭ motion from the intro to the verse). The bass is wholly lost until it regains its footing on B♭ in a full-bar stop-time arpeggiated solo, setting up a return of the tonic in the chorus ("I'll be there with a love that will shelter you"). Apparently, E♭ minor is the home key after all, and the comforting G♭ of would-be rescuer Stubbs is merely a way-station (III within a large-scale minor-mode I–III–V–I arpeggiation outlining the intro–verse/refrain–transition–chorus sections, respectively) on the woman's hazardous and endless journey. In the chorus, Levi can sing strongly and with tonal exactitude, but his offer is lost in the mists of the woman's vague E♭-minor turmoil; although the chords attempt to alternate V–I, Jamerson is reluctant to give up the fifth scale degree (the woman can finally hear $\hat{1}$ in the bass only four beats after it should appear, at 0:51, at Levi's promise to "cherish" her). Not only is the tonic heard (again) in this highly unstable second inversion, but even though the texture is fairly thick with the house band plus flute and piccolo as well as three backing singers, the tonic chord has no third other than in Levi's stepwise vocal line. Normally an asylum, the home tonic chord when unstable and incomplete is instead an open, hollow, and ghostly emblem of difficulty, fear, and confusion. Try as he might, Levi cannot assure his object of his sincerity; his promise of shelter is not heard clearly because she continues to imagine a threat underneath his voice, whether the bass line is a hidden part of his true persona or merely an imagined horror of the unknown in her own mind. She never does take the helping hand, but drifts away to the hollow sound of thirdless promises. Jamerson's insistence on playing unstable bass tones will be seen below to have an expressive impact on the Supremes' "You Can't Hurry Love," and it might be noted that he also uses this unsettling technique in the same group's "You Keep Me Hangin' On." ("Reach Out" and both Supremes hits reached number 1, each for two-week stints, during a three-month period in the fall of 1966.) In a related story, Paul McCartney's attraction to Brian Wilson's strategic emphasis of chord fifths in the bass (note particularly how often the bass strays from roots, and sometimes even triad members, in Carol Kaye's and Ray Pohlman's bass playing throughout the Beach Boys' *Pet Sounds*) coincided with an expressive explosion of melodic craft in his own bass lines from the opening sonority of "Michelle" (1965) onward. The analyst must always keep one ear open to how it's being guided and persuaded by elements of form and design.

Vocal and Instrumental Color

Many rock listeners take refuge in the thought that tone color is the quality most consciously important to the artist as an expressive device. As with other domains, I believe that an awareness of the performer's manipulation of timbre, often involving factors encountered only in the academy (and often relating directly to more "abstract" tonal relationships), can enlighten the listener as to a rich musical meaning. We'll look at elements of tone production and ornamentation important in rock singing, even though few—aside from formally trained singers such as Linda Ronstadt or Eric Carmen, or perhaps even physiologists alone—would be fully aware of such issues. I'll then choose one specific instrumental timbre, the guitar harmonic, for brief discussion in terms of its expressive value.

A full study of vocal production techniques in rock could be quite lengthy, even without any coverage of filtering and compression; added reverb; flanging, artificial chorus, and other tape-speed manipulation; Leslie speaker; vocoder; or other studio effects both analog and digital. It would have to treat matters of

- range (Johnny Cash's or Melvin Franklin's bass rising through Elton John's wide-reaching tenor, which delivers some of rock's most interesting lyrics with some of its most distressed enunciation, to Art Garfunkel's guardian-angel boy-soprano clarity; and from Tracy Chapman's or Christine McVie's alto through Annie Lennox's or Joni Mitchell's contrasts of mezzo basis with falsetto heights to Minnie Riperton's, Debbie Harry's, or Mariah Carey's soprano, the high voices far outnumbering the low in chart success),
- degrees of diaphragm support (from none with Mick Jagger, Lou Reed, or Jerry Garcia to strong with Marilyn McCoo, Freddie Mercury, or Cyndi Lauper), and locus of greatest resonance (from the chest tones of Bill Medley and Huey Lewis through the head tones of Diana Ross and Madonna to the nasal sounds of James Taylor and Willie Nelson),
- timbral quality (David Bowie's light, supple, pure baritone as contrasted with the simple but expressive harmonics of Aretha Franklin's mezzo and with James Brown's rich tenor multiphonics, or all such approaches controlled in timbral modulation, as by Eddie Vedder),
- intonation (whether singing is right on pitch—as in the gorgeous sonorities of Roberta Flack, loosely or wildly out of tune—does Bob Dylan come to mind? or expressively "on top of" the note—as with Mary Wells or in the delicious thrown-away tones of the Shirelles),
- vibrato (whether absent—as with Paul Simon, Roger Daltrey, or Mark Knopfler; constant—as with Joan Baez, Meat Loaf, or Tiny Tim; or expressively applied in various speeds, widths, and structural placements—as by Ronnie Spector),
- the simple absence of pitch (at an extreme, the *Sprechstimme* rap technique goes back at least as far as Pigmeat Markham's version of "Here Come the Judge" [1968], and actually has a redneck heritage in Jimmy Dean's "Big Bad John" [1961], as well as individual phrases spoken "directly from the heart" to the listener for contrast in many literatures, including Elvis Presley's "Are You Lonesome Tonight?" [1960]),

- the constriction of the arytenoid muscles that cause vocal cord membranes to produce falsetto as opposed to "chest" voice, and other matters of register (witness Roy Orbison's $c\sharp^2$ in "Crying" [1961]; also note that registral expressivity is addressed by Susan Fast in this volume),
- timbrally matched choral blending (as with Carl and Jay Perkins or the Everly Brothers, or the double-tracked Neil Sedaka),
- tremolo (through which Aaron Neville's original master of "Tell It Like It Is" [1967] is nowhere near as affected as is the remake that replaced it decades later), and
- all sorts of approaches to articulation, phrasing, portamento, note bending and glissandi, dynamic shadings and other matters of stylistic ornamentation (with Janis Joplin unmatched for her variety of high-voltage techniques applied in multitudinous contextual relationships, exhibiting both talent and control that make Jim Morrison sound like Ringo Starr in comparison).

A singer's level of ease or tension is also palpable and an important conveyor of expression. Note, for instance, how David Byrne pushes beyond his limits to express exuberance in Talking Heads' "Happy Day" (1977). But instead of filling in such a comprehensive outline with further subtypes and examples, I'd like to take two unrelated approaches: (1) to address the role of singing methods in what made a single performer, Elvis Presley, once great but later second-rate; and (2) to examine the role of multiple simultaneous vocal qualities in the communication of an attitude in the B-52's.

For our purposes, Elvis's career will be understood according to three divisions: (1) those recordings made for Sun Records in Memphis (July 1954–July 1955), (2) the first Nashville and Hollywood/Culver City recordings for RCA (which signed him in November 1955), and (3) those made for RCA after the completion of his Army hitch (March 1958–March 1960).[9] Because they're much more physically involved with modulating the singing mechanism, Elvis's earlier recordings tend to be much more expressive than his later work. His Memphis output (not producing a single national hit outside of the country charts) represents a catalog of expressive singing techniques that, when applied to new recordings distributed by RCA, revolutionized the making of popular music. His was basically a baritone range, but he was capable of great dynamic shadings at the tenor end (as in "I Forgot to Remember to Forget" [1955]). Often, he would pit the low end versus the high with color contrasts: a limpid tenor contrasts with a richer, murky baritone in "I Don't Care if the Sun Don't Shine" (1954). Elvis would adjust the tonal focus for expressive value: in "Blue Moon of Kentucky" (1954), his chest tones bring an innocent, boyish Buddy Holly quality into an otherwise flippant, knowing baritone. Chest tones are often used for heartfelt sentiment, as in "I Love You Because" (1956), where a soft crooning resonates in the chest in both the tenor range and deeper pitches, symbolizing a direct, unimpeded flow from the heart to the ear. In the rationalizing "That's All Right (Mama)" (1954) and many others, Elvis contrasts a head tone with a focus in the throat.

Most of these techniques emphasize the physicality, and therefore the sensuality, of his singing. This was an aim supported by many ornamental details. The focus in the throat and mouth was often enhanced by swallowing his words (as in "That's All Right (Mama)"), by emphasizing a breathy quality (as with the snarling, syncopated baritone that sneers "I'm *through* with you" in "Just Because" [1956]), by stuttering (as in the Jerry Lee Lewis-like excited lack of control in "Baby Let's Play House" [1955]), and by adding syllables of extra vowels to words for a choppy but melismatic effect (as in "mak-a-me" for "make me" in "When It Rains, It Really Pours" [1955]). Most often, Elvis punctuated his texture with pre-Holly staccato hiccups that probably grew out of Appalachian yodeling (as suggested in the "broken heart" of "You're a Heartbreaker" and in "I'm Left, You're Right, She's Gone" [both 1955]), and were applied in various other contexts too (as in "Good Rockin' Tonight" [1954] and "I Forgot to Remember to Forget" [1955]).[10] But Elvis's early expressive ornamentation was imaginative in many other domains. "That's All Right (Mama)" features portamento slides, blue notes, and improvised syncopations; a tenor shake (a short trill) graces "Milkcow Blues Boogie" (1955) (in which Elvis also sustains a falsetto such as Robert Plant would do twenty years later) and rapid mordents figurate "I Forgot to Remember to Forget." "Harbor Lights" (an outtake from 1954) features romantically subtle dynamic swells, vibrato, and other shadings, along with mordents and appoggiaturas. "Tomorrow Night" (1955) is mostly crooned with great dynamic contrast, featuring sensitive appoggiaturas to appoggiaturas, but when the singer's questions become urgent, his retransition leads to a dynamic and syncopated outburst. "Blue Moon" (1956) is a model for John Lennon in its double-tracked falsetto melismas. Most virtuosic are the soulful improvised retransitional lead-ins borrowed from R&B (e.g., Tony Williams' lead vocal in the Platters' "The Great Pretender" [1955], at 1:41–1:54). Example 5.2 comes from the first retransition (0:53–0:57) of "Tryin' to Get to You" (1956), which concludes Elvis's dynamically shaded bridge with a great freedom from the underlying pitch and rhythmic structure (essentially gracing a descending g^2-g^1 octave) to suggest an apparently uncontrollable anguish that actually takes a great deal of vocal control to perform, even if exercised unconsciously.

Example 5.2 Elvis Presley, "Tryin' to Get to You" (C. Singleton-R. M. McCoy), *Elvis Presley* (1956): vocal retransition.

With RCA, Elvis began taking these expressive techniques, and new ones as well, to an electrified nation. His stuttering *repercussio* revoicings of sustained vowels (largely unknown since the seventeenth century) became heart-rending in "Heartbreak Hotel" and on the first-person singular pronoun in the chorus of "I Want You, I Need You, I Love You" (both 1956). In "Don't Be Cruel" (1956), "All Shook Up," and "(Let Me Be Your) Teddy Bear" (both 1957), he would continually throw away word endings in a careless manner, sometimes in a clipped style reminiscent of calypso but sultry in the baritone range, communicating his feelings more than his ideas. "Love Me" (1956) wails with crying appoggiaturas in a high range; Example 5.3, including most of that song's second bridge, shows how the word "just" (1:51–1:54) bends and then breaks up into emotive multiphonics. But Elvis's unfortunate change of style can probably be traced to the innocuous "Love Me Tender" (1956), an earnest sentimental ballad in a supported baritone, mimicked to greater melodramatic depths in "Don't" (1958) and descending even further in the post-Army "It's Now or Never" (1960) and "Surrender" (1961), both of the latter being rewritten Italian tenor airs performed with an assumptive bel canto delivery. In these and other ballads, notably the old-world (French-inspired) "Can't Help Falling in Love" (1961), subtlety of expression disappeared in favor of a lazy presumption of a captive audience. This attitude brought a Vegas quality to his rock numbers as well. "Hard Headed Woman" (1958) and "(Now and Then There's) A Fool Such as I" (1959) show that his flippancy had lost any emotive power, but was instead merely a hallmark of self-mockery. Even "(You're the) Devil in Disguise" (1963), which neatly pits his angelic tenor against a devilish baritone, pales

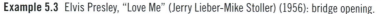

Example 5.3 Elvis Presley, "Love Me" (Jerry Lieber-Mike Stoller) (1956): bridge opening.

as a poor imitation of the former artist, partly because of the weakness of the material then being written for him—nearly all for Hollywood vehicles—but also because of a watering-down of his talent. Note how restrained his singing becomes, even in once-hot retransitional passages, as in the matter-of-fact "Return to Sender" (1962).

Elvis Presley brought the improvisational vocal ornaments of R&B and C&W artists to mainstream popular music, and most pop vocalists through the 1970s—consider John Lennon and Elton John—knew just when to embellish their lines with mordents, turns, and other such graces. But hard rock singers and the post-1970s pop singers typically avoid these and even more basic figurations (anticipations, escape tones, suspensions), based on an aesthetic whereby the more directly something is presented, without taint of artifice and often in a purely syllabic setting, the stronger is the resulting output of energy. As do most modes of presentation, rock singing exhibits sometimes polar perspectives on vitality and power. But it could still be said that many of the best vocalists of the day work in popular styles; too many (but not the best) classically trained singers have cultivated a sensually beautiful but dull homogeneity of sound, never a goal of the generally much more expressive pop or rock singer.

When a solo singer has a choral backing, the listener generally hears all of the vocal parts as representing facets of the same psyche, even when the words and the musical parts are as different as possible. This is normally true unless one or more singers are clearly intended as representing an objective, overriding narrative voice and others are not, or in some other quasi-dramatic portrayal, as when direct quotations are presented from various separate characters. As an instance of this sort of exception, the Beatles' "She's Leaving Home" (1967) is an unusual case in that McCartney's lead vocal carries the narrative voice even though the daughter's viewpoint is often expressed there; Lennon's part in the chorus, however, consists of direct quotes from the parents.[11] More often, backing vocalists simply express the ideas and emotions attributable to the lead singer in a varied way, all thereby representing related sides of the same persona. This is such a strong convention that in the Supremes' "Back in My Arms Again" (1965), even though Diana identifies backing singers Mary and Flo as friends who have offered her advice that she refuses to take, all three join together in complete agreement for the chorus, which carries Diana's story. At times, the vocal chorus simply amplifies the role of the lead singer; this happens in the Four Seasons' "Ronnie" (1964) and "Let's Hang On!" (1965), in which the other three take Frankie Valli's desperate feelings and portray them for both the love object and the listener in a more forceful, visceral manner than a single vocalist could muster. The similar united front is not quite as convincing in "C'mon Marianne" (1967), perhaps because the vocals are slightly more subdued, mixed a bit below the rhythm section.

But the parts of the single persona as represented can be at times in conflict with each other.[12] This is one factor that makes the B-52's interesting; several tracks from their *Cosmic Thing* (1989) will illustrate. Kate Pierson and Cindy Wilson focus on expressing an authentic sound, although much of it has an obvious retro cast. They clearly want to believe they *are* Sixties beach girls, and often evoke early-Beatles vocal counterpoint, as in "Roam" and "Topaz," at other times leaving mid-Beatles dissonances (such as those of "Drive My Car" [1965]) unresolved. Fred Schneider's earnestness, on the other hand, is of a violently anti-hip, fey, Pee-wee variety. His techno-edge in the face of the women's relative earthiness gives the overall vocal combo more of a *Laser Soul* effect than one of *Rubber Soul*.[13] Fred's resonating nasal cavity removes all feeling from his words; his "shake your honey buns" ("Cosmic Thing") is all neon sparkle and faux passion, a superficial irony not necessarily at the core of the songs-as-composed. His typical non-observance of tonal relevance in varied degrees of *Sprechstimme* (his pitch mocks the tune in "Love Shack") clearly separates his consciousness from that of deeper-focusing Kate and Cindy (both intent with funk in the same "Love Shack"), who frequently bear the texture's only pentatonic blue notes or offer a song's only expressive melismas. Yet the multiple consciousnesses are still different aspects of the same persona. In "Bushfire," Fred is the light but Kate and Cindy are the heat; vocal timbre and pitch selection make the difference. And Kate and Cindy are not always in agreement; there is sometimes a three-way divide, as in "Channel Z." Here, the three singers (accompanied by Kate's Yamaha DX-7, Keith Strickland's Stratocaster, Sara Lee's bass, and Charlie Drayton's drums) feel bombarded by the debris of a demented culture, shielding themselves from the emblematic static broadcast by Channel Z. All yearn for a change; the women express their optimism in the verse (0:32+), excerpted in Example 5.4a, but in different ways. Following one line in unison, Cindy's lower part continues the simple pentatonic [025] trichord (D♭–E♭–G♭), fully syncopated for an earthy, imposing sexiness; Kate's simultaneous cultivated and alert chromatic descent in a nearly straight rhythm pushes the bright major mode with its G♮, perhaps expressing more of an intellectual approach to optimism. Fred is silent here, but in the chorus (0:47+) (see Example 5.4b) his robotic interjections depict a disgust with the atmospheric static of political and social irresponsibility falling out within the broadcast area. Despite the women's optimism, G♭ has not given way to G♮ in the chorus, and so the social improvement has not come yet; Kate and Cindy are reduced to dark-age parallel fifths.

I have chosen one very individual instrumental timbre, the guitar harmonic, from among the scores of acoustic and electronic sounds commonly heard in rock music to suggest the wide range of expression available for any given sound quality. In the Beatles' "Nowhere Man" (1965), George Harrison completes his solo on a treble-dominated Stratocaster with the bright first-string natural harmonic, sounding e^3 (1:02–1:05) (three octaves above the

Example 5.4a The B-52's, "Channel Z" (Kate Pierson-Fred Schneider-Keith Strickland-Cindy Wilson), *Cosmic Thing* (1989): verse.

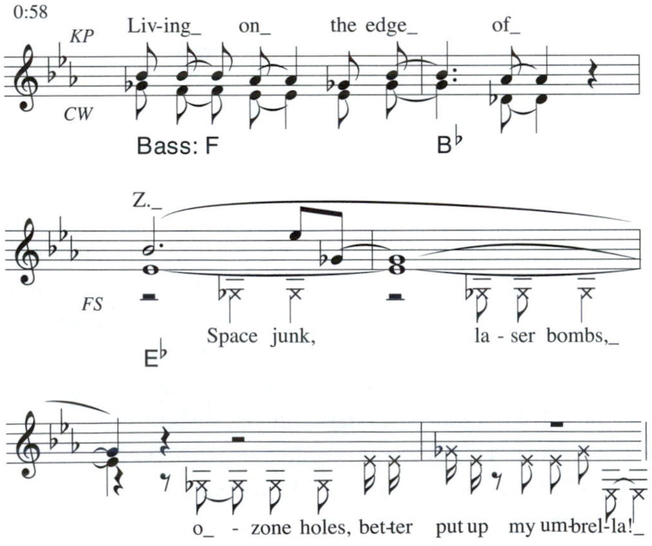

Example 5.4b The B-52's, "Channel Z" (Kate Pierson-Fred Schneider-Keith Strickland-Cindy Wilson), *Cosmic Thing* (1989): chorus.

previous note). Presaging his later use of the timbrally rich sitar and tamboura, as in the latter's retransition in "Lucy in the Sky with Diamonds" (1967) (as at 1:05–1:12), Harrison sustains the overdubbed harmonic over the arrival of the ensuing verse, which begins, "He's as blind as he can be," evoking clarity and enlightenment. Is the irony intentional? The song's highly directional harmonic pull and the straightforward $\hat{5}-\hat{4}-\hat{3}-\hat{2}-\hat{1}$ voice leading in the verse's vocal melody would also seem to signify the world-command possessed by the Nowhere Man (as argued in the first and third bridges), despite his lack of appreciation for his own talents. In other words, the guitar harmonic reflects the Nowhere Man's true but hidden, illuminated perfection in a single note, struck at a moment of form-defining emphasis. But harmonics can also suggest the opposite of such an enlightened bliss; in the introduction to Elton John's "Madman Across the Water" (1971), Davey Johnstone's fully stopped tonic A-minor acoustic-guitar chords alternate repeatedly with others comprising harmonics that sound a troubling $G^{9/\Delta 7}$. The timbral contrast, along with the wave-like tonal uncertainty, paints the brittle and transient schizophrenia glimpsed over the impressionistic play of light along a reef. Likewise, harmonics help convey an otherworldly atmosphere as the "man from Mars" plays "traveling songs" in Neil Young's "Ride My Llama" (1979). Chords built of harmonics symbolize a "walking on air" in the Grateful Dead's "Row Jimmy" (1973), and individual harmonics (one of five separate simultaneous guitar effects) illustrate the rising and exploding beads of Oasis' "Champagne Supernova" (1996). In Living Colour's "Ology" (1990), Muzz Skillings uses harmonics (some artificial) among numerous other colors (muted effects, multiple stops, tremolo, envelope effects to simulate a drawn bow, rhythms plucked at the bridge, delayed doublings, trills, pickup changes during sustained tones, etc.) in a virtuosic, post-Hendrix six-bass jam that outdoes Chris Squire's "the fish (Schindleria Praematurus)" (1972).[14] In "Ology," the bass effects create a diffuse aura that surrounds a jazzy counterpoint, which further embellishes a simple repeated ground on a chromatically descending bass, C^9–G^9/B–Gm^9/B♭–$Am\frac{9}{7}$, a theme that incongruously grafts motives from Richard Chamberlain's "Theme from Dr. Kildare (Three Stars Will Shine Tonight)" (1962) with (at 0:34+) the concert ending of McCartney's "Maybe I'm Amazed" (1976). The haze of possible references fits with the loose dissonance treatment and high-partial colors.

Harry Chapin's "Taxi" (1972) will serve as a final example of expressive uses of guitar harmonics. Over an introduction that alternates a C-major tonic with its Mixolydian neighbor ♭VII, a guitar produces repeated cycles of the unrelated harmonics d^3–a^2–f^2 so as to highlight the mist of raindrops falling outside the presumed comfort of a cab interior. (The first two verses are heard in C, but all later ones are in D, suggesting a whole-step-low tuning and the mid-course addition of a capo to produce the required tones.) The harmonics appear again, but transposed a whole-step higher (e^3–b^2–g^2, which one might call the "Roundabout" chord in deference to its appearance in that Yes track) and more fully integrated into in the A-minor bridge (beginning "Oh, I've got something inside me" [2:47]) to signal the contrast between Harry's quiet exterior and his wild but suppressed inner life (at "illuminatin' my mind" [3:03—3:09], a use poetically related to "Nowhere Man"). The same e^3–b^2–g^2 harmonics guide the retransition (4:09–4:18) to a D-major recapitulation, where the singer's wild side is once again fully suppressed. Ultimately, Harry gets what he wanted so long ago—he'd wanted to fly, and he ends the song disconnected from his earth in the e^3–b^2–g^2 harmonics that float among the rain-producing clouds, stoned, over the D-major cadence (6:07+). The unaware listener would probably be surprised to learn how frequently tone color contributes to the communication of mood and image, word-painting aside.

Rhythm, Tempo, and a Couple of Wormholes

The play of temporal relationships takes as many forms in rock music as it does in that typically studied in the academy. Displaced accents (six in the time of four and vice versa, the simple anticipation, and metric ambiguities), asymmetrical phrase rhythms, and contrasting tempos, three of a number of such techniques, will be addressed here.

The use of isolated triplets for text-painting is heard in many songs that accent six beats in the time of four, as for the gunshots in the Bobby Fuller Four's "I Fought the Law" (1966). The same figure is used for dramatic ensemble emphasis, as in Eddie Kendricks's verse-ending impassioned plea (0:45–0:50) in the Temptations' "You're My Everything" (1967), or the rein-pulling codas of the Beatles' "I Want to Hold Your Hand" (1963) and the Four Seasons' "Dawn (Go Away)" (1964). A similar emphasis results from the opposite accent shift in the Mamas and the Papas' version of "Dedicated to the One I Love" (1967), in which a twelve-bar verse (4 + 4 + 4 bars) in 6/8 is interrupted by cut-time accents (4 in the time of 6) in the second and sixth bars of the pattern.

One need not resort to the chorus of Carly Simon's "Anticipation" (1971) to find effective use of that rhythmic technique. A much more subtle and structural employment of anticipation is found in the Supremes' "You Can't Hurry Love" (1966), a second Holland-Dozier-Holland hit deserving special attention. Example 5.5 represents the essential voice leading in "You Can't Hurry Love"; indicated are all structural pitches performed by singers (Diana Ross backed by Florence Ballard and Mary Wilson) and bassist (James Jamerson). The notes on the treble staff suggest a polyphonic texture created almost entirely from Diana's solo line; rhythms are normalized to the nearest quarter note, and repeated or otherwise ornamented pitches are shown as if sustained. Notes given in parentheses are not sung but implied by the texture (in the verse) or are sung by backing singers only (in the chorus, where Diana also sometimes adjusts her line in altered repeats to sing the opening g^1 or

Example 5.5 The Supremes, "You Can't Hurry Love" (Eddie Holland-Lamont Dozier-Brian Holland) (1966): analysis.

the closing f^1); in the bridge, Diana does not sing any pitches above $b\flat^1$—the c^2–$b\flat^1$ and d^2–$b\flat^1$ motions indicated there are sung by Flo and Mary. In the conclusion of the bridge, the bass staff is used for the four-note retransition in flutes and piano (c^1–d^1–$e\flat^1$–f^1), in addition to the entire bass line. All chords are heard in root position except for the first-inversion C-minor chord, which appears once in each section.

In fact, many chords appear in each section, because—most unusually (the Beatles' "Yesterday" is another example)—the formal passages are recompositions of each other. The chorus applies a new melody to the bass line underlying the verse, and the bridge constructs yet another new melody to a rhythmic quadruple-augmentation of what had been the last two bars of the verse (progressing III–VI–II^6–V), now an eight-measure unit. (The chorus always repeats at least once; the verse and bridge do not do so until the coda. The full order of sections is Intro [0:00+]–Verse 1 [0:08+]–Chorus [0:17+]–Bridge

[0:37+]–Chorus [0:57+]–Bridge [1:17+]–Chorus [1:36+]–Intro [1:56+]–Verses 2–3, which gradually become the fade-out Chorus [1:59+].) Curiously, the bass appears throughout the stereo recording, but it has been muted out of the first verse of the mono mix—thus the parenthesized line there. This is likely because of the unsettling anticipations that are performed the same way there as in all choruses; removing the initial line allows the relatively dense rhythmic texture to unfold a bit more gradually on the hit single.

These bass anticipations, shifting some roots to jarringly early appearances, lie at the heart of the song's expression, which is manifested in time-related vocal voice-leading anomalies. Ross begins to sing anticipations at the end of the verse, where her c^1, f^1, and $b\flat^1$, in rising fourths, each predict the roots of the following chords. An unusual voice-leading effect is heard in the third bar of the chorus, where Diana's a^1 does not rise to an expected $b\flat^1$ but drops instead to an inner-voice d^1, in odd parallel fifths with the bass. Supported by a fifth below, a^1 is not bound to rise even though it usually functions as leading tone; even so, the backing singers complete the motion to $b\flat^1$. In the first four bars of the bridge, we hear that the once-aborted rise from a^1 to $b\flat^1$ is fully played out; thus, the cleaned-up voice leading in the bridge fulfills an expectation that had been withheld in the chorus. In a similar manner, the final bar of the bridge emphasizes the same dire g^1–$b\flat^1$ pair of non-chord tones, its notes sung in repeated alternation, that had brought the verse to the same dissonant conclusion. These tones resolve only with great difficulty, anticipating and suspending over the B♭ of the returning chorus as part of an accented $^6_4$ that requires two teasing measures to resolve in Mama's advice, "You can't hurry love; no, you just have to wait," thereby infecting the chorus with the slower harmonic rhythm of the bridge at the articulation of the song's title and main poetic theme.

This deep suspension goes against the grain of all of the song's anticipations; we must now consult more fully the song's lyrics, which provide the basis for all of these rhythmic and formal devices and more. In the verse, Diana is impatient to find a love; the bass suggests a romantically critical arrhythmia, and her anticipations naturally display her difficulty in waiting (she rhymes the words "waiting" and "anticipating" in a later verse). In the chorus, she remembers her Mama's advice, which restrains Diana with the heavy suspensions noted above. Told to "give it time," Diana holds in check her attempted rise to a teasing $\hat{1}$. The slow bridge draws out her heartaches; she can continue through her waiting only by remembering her Mama's advice, which memory comes with the retransitional anticipated $\hat{1}$ sung with great impatience along with some added tension from the rising c^1–d^1–$e\flat^1$–f^1 flute line. This flute line—which fills in the fourth of the V triad—is not wholly new; it completes a motion begun in the bridge by the backing singers, who used c^2 as an upper neighbor to $\hat{1}$, and then d^2 in alternation with $\hat{1}$. The flutes merely bring to fruition the complete fourth-progression anticipated by

Flo and Mary, the resulting tension perhaps also responding to memories in retrograde of Mama's advice, which in the chorus always decorates the 4-3 suspension as $e\flat^1$–d^1–c^1–d^1.

One final twist on the anticipation motive completes the song's formal puzzle. When the final verse (1:59+) is repeated, an obbligato violin sings the chorus's melody above the tune of Diana's verse in quodlibet fashion, thus preparing the way for the Chorus proper that follows (2:28).[15] As Diana sings, "It's a game of give and take"; I think Brahms, who delighted in many of these *Knupftechnik* games, would have liked this composition.[16]

Changing meters are frequent in pop songs, and the David-Bacharach hits of Dionne Warwick are frequently cited. Their "(Theme From) Valley of the Dolls" (1968) has an unusual string of accent patterns in the verse, progressing through single bars of 4/4, 3/4, 2/4, 3/4, and 5/4 in each of four phrases, all an excellent portrayal of the instability of an individual who struggles to regain her balance in the bridge, which twice follows four bars of 4/4 with four of 3/4. Many Beatle examples, such as "Good Morning Good Morning" and "All You Need Is Love" (both 1967) are celebrated as well.[17] Another song from that year, the hit by Every Mothers' Son, "Come On Down to My Boat," is less often discussed. But this is a more compelling example than the others mentioned here, because the metric accent is far more ambiguous. The meter changes often in the Warwick and Beatles numbers, but with a few hearings they can be anticipated easily; the EMS example is far quirkier. Example 5.6 represents the metric layout of the entire song's surface. The introduction has three phases of terraced instrumentation. Christopher Augustine (drums) and then Schuyler Larsen (bass) lay down the pulse as if a thoroughly solid meter is to be anticipated; they are joined by Bruce Milner (organ) and Lary Larden (lead guitar), who at 0:15 play the song's distinctive pentatonic [025] trichord, F–A♭–B♭, in unison. But the meter is already out of kilter; a quarter-note beat is added at the end of the second "phase," and three eighths are removed just as lead singer Dennis Larden enters for the verse. The verse contains two phrases (separated by double bars); each has the same total number of quarter notes, equaling that of four bars of 4/4, but each phrase offers a different reaccentuation by the entire ensemble, for a very unbalanced effect. Aside from a repeated instance of three removed eighths at the end of the first chorus, the meter in the remainder of the song is fully regular. At the hypermetrical level, however, the chorus is given an extended cadence with an added four-bar choral chord succession just before the bridge, and the chorus is heard for the only time in its prototypical four-plus-four form at 1:59, followed by a call-and-response coda and a two-bar syncopated, instrumental tag that unexpectedly concludes the song on its dominant. Apparently, the singer is attempting to entice a playful and willing young woman away from her father by offering her a compellingly pulsating rhythm (in the chorus and bridge) that she cannot muster on her own (in the verse).[18]

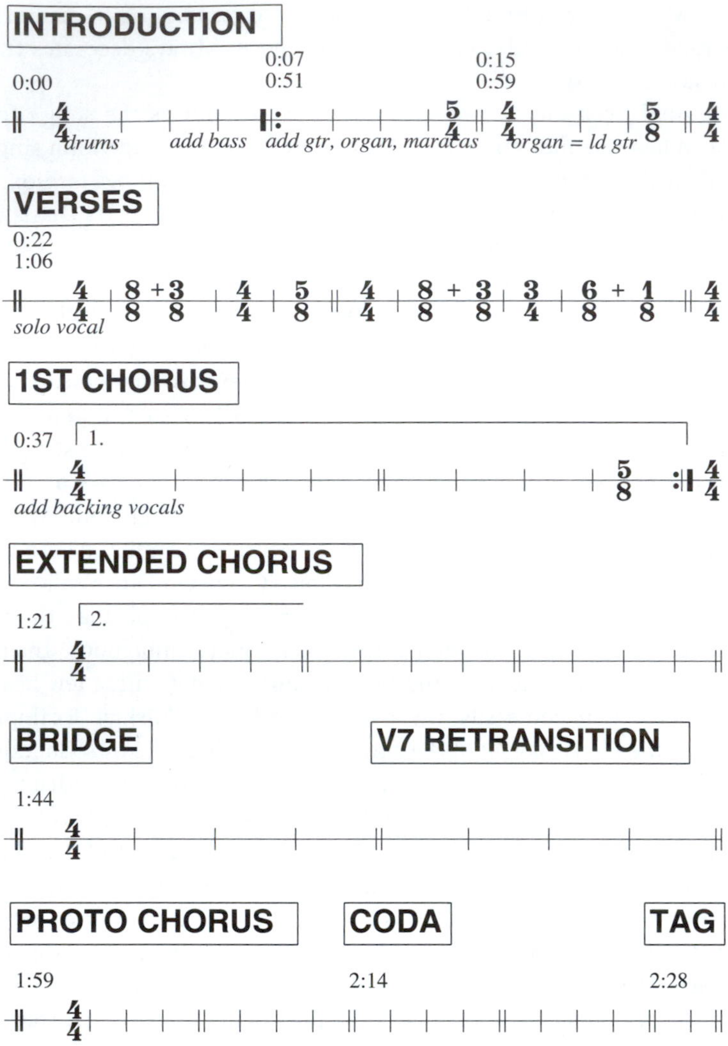

Example 5.6 Every Mothers' Son, "Come on Down to My Boat" (Wes Farrell-Jerry Goldstein) (1967): metric grid.

There is little discussion of asymmetrical phrase rhythm (essentially, metric irregularity at the hypermetric level) in pop-rock music, but this is often quite expressive. In line with the rhythmic irregularities of Robert Johnson, all sorts of folk roots provide uneven examples. One example from the Appalachian bluegrass tradition is the Grateful Dead's version of "Been All Around This World" (1981), which playfully divides the verse as 5 + 4 + 4 + 3, creating a sort of long-range rubato. Following Clyde McPhatter's "A Lover's Question"

(1958) (which builds a verse with phrases of 4 + 4 + 6 bars and a chorus with 4 + 4 + 4 + 6), Atlantic Records seemed for a time to have an unwritten law requiring such a technique; see Bobby Darin's "Beyond the Sea" (4 + 3 + 5), the Drifters' "Save the Last Dance for Me" (5 + 5 + 4 + 4), and Ben E. King's "Spanish Harlem" (8 + 7 [5+2] + 8), all from 1960. Again, the Beatles file could provide many different sorts of instructive examples, and perhaps Steely Dan's "Barrytown" (1974) would be worth a look, as its extended phrase lengths reflect an interesting added level of consciousness and commentary, as parenthetical thoughts seemingly added at the last minute. But for our one illustration of irregular phrase rhythm, let's turn to David Bowie's "Changes" (1972). Example 5.7 provides the bass line for the song's chorus, which begins with the text, "turn and face the strange changes." A post-Beatles essay in trying to comprehend one's own identity, "Changes" has the singer unable to understand his changing self through others' eyes—he changes too fast to follow his own reflection. The hard-to-follow changes are depicted in the evolving phrase rhythm and chord "changes" of the chorus, which begins simply enough as an eight-bar motion to V, until the turnaround in the first ending momentarily loses its footing on a blues-based passing IV, stretching the phrase to nine measures. This antecedent is given an even more disturbed consequent, cut short to seven bars and never reaching the dominant, interrupted by a change to triple meter at "time may change me" (reminiscent of the change to triple meter in the bridge of the Beatles' "She Said She Said" [1966], where Lennon reverts to another "time," that of his youth).

Often harder to pin down are rhythmic irregularities brought about by unexpected tempo relationships. Simple ritardandos are rare outside a more sensitive rock music, such as in retransitions to verses in Paul Simon's "Something So Right" (1973). Accelerandos—such as the one ending the introduction to the Grateful Dead's "St. Stephen" (1969)—seem even rarer. The tempo

Example 5.7 David Bowie, "Changes" (David Bowie) (1972): chorus bass line.

conversion in the Dead example reflects an integral relationship within the piece, as the bridge (1:20–2:16; timings reflect the *Aoxomoxoa* CD version) is in a slower tempo than the outer sections, all joined with a ritardando going into the bridge and an accelerando coming out. The details being of interest, we'll take a closer listen.

Example 5.8a shows the introduction to "St. Stephen" (lyrics by Robert Hunter, music by Jerry Garcia and Phil Lesh) as recorded at Pacific Recording for *Aoxomoxoa* in September 1968 (with the addition to the score of Tom Constanten's synthesizer part as performed on February 27, 1969, and heard on the *Live/Dead* LP). "St. Stephen" was one of the Dead's ten most-played songs in 1969–1970, as can be determined from 187 known set lists from that period. Lesh's 6/8 meter in the bass is stronger than the 3/4 indicated for

Example 5.8a The Grateful Dead, "St. Stephen" (Jerry Garcia-Phil Lesh-Robert Hunter), *Aoxomoxoa* (1969): introduction.

Garcia's solo guitar, but the latter is notated as such because of the recurring sixteenth-sixteenth-eighth division that comes to force the 3/4 meter in the introduction's last measure. The acceleration there is such to produce a change of tempo measuring an exact 3:4 ratio of beat divisions and 1:2 of the beats themselves (becoming quarter = 88 at the opening of the first verse [0:23]). This is tempo modulation the hard way, without a pivot function, as a gradual change of tempo (instead of the reinterpretation of beat divisions practiced in "metric modulation") creates a new half note that has the same duration value as the previous dotted quarter. The ensemble's initial metric ambiguity makes the transformation all the juicier by confusing the dominant beat divisions, and makes the resulting 4/4 all the more stable.[19]

Lesh's open bass fifths in the introduction foreshadow the texture of the slow bridge at "Lady finger dipped in moonlight" (1:20). Example 5.8b

Example 5.8b The Grateful Dead, "St. Stephen" (Jerry Garcia-Phil Lesh-Robert Hunter), *Aoxomoxoa* (1969): transition.

illustrates the transition from the end of the third verse (only the bass and vocal parts, sung by Garcia and Lesh, are notated) to that bridge. The ritardando here cuts the tempo from 90 to 72 beats per minute (bpm), a fairly simple 5:4 ratio but one not accessible through metric modulation given the beat divisions used in this passage.[20] The returning verse, reached by accelerando (see Example 5.8c), moves at 88 bpm, an exact recapitulation of the tempo of the first verse. "St. Stephen" employs several other ritards and fermatas at structural points within sections (notably at 2:38). Perhaps all of the tempo contrasts may be interpreted as the vicissitudes enjoyed and suffered by the first Christian martyr; the saint and various metaphorical images of him are portrayed as prospering and declining, up and down, gathering and spilling, and lost and regained. Stephen is troubled and perplexed, but the slow bridge brings the scarlet dawn that answers moonlight with an inspiring sunlight that banishes the confusion of darkness. Upon resumption of the faster verses, Hunter's lyrics hold the saint's questions unanswered as long as fortune (personified here as Calliope) is slow to arrive, suggesting that Stephen's fate will remain suspended as long as his tempo is different from that of the muse.

Through 1971, "St. Stephen" was performed, on average, at every fourth show. But following a five-year retirement, it was revived in a very different guise in June 1976. One soundboard tape from a concert of July 18, 1976, shows that "Stephen" had been recast with a lugubrious introductory tempo of dotted quarter = 32. Remarkably, the Dead accelerate from there to quarter = 64 for the verse, achieving exactly the same 3:4 ratio of beat divisions

Example 5.8c The Grateful Dead, "St. Stephen" (Jerry Garcia-Phil Lesh-Robert Hunter), *Aoxomoxoa* (1969): retransition to verse.

(and 1:2 beat ratio) as heard on the 1968 LP recording, even though the overall new tempo is slower than the 1968 model's by a coincidental 4:3 ratio itself (and the soundboard tape has certainly been duplicated at the correct speed and pitch, so we know these tempos are accurate). The new arrangement also alters the meter of the bridge, which adopts a shuffling 12/8 pattern. The retransitional accelerando from the 1976 bridge (at dotted quarter = 60) to the ensuing verse (at quarter = 80, a bit faster than the opening verses), demonstrates yet another 3:4 ratio, among beats, this time a ratio that could easily have been achieved with a simple pivot from the 12/8 meter, with four 12/8 eighths reinterpreted as the sixteenths that subdivide a single beat in the 4/4 verse. But again, the simple ratio is achieved the hard way. The precise tempo ratios are no fluke; an October 1971 performance relates tempos of quarter = 60 for the bridge to quarter = 80 for all surrounding verses, the same 3:4 ratio; an August 1968 performance accelerates from a bridge tempo of quarter = 72 to a verse at quarter = 96, yet another 3:4 ratio. All of these and other 3:4 ratios heard in varied live performances would seem to indicate that the odd man out is the one 5:4 ratio noted in the released studio version, which many would refer to as the "definitive" recording because of the presumed care taken in the process.

Faced with eleven different performances of "St. Stephen," I've decided that it's time to follow a Dead-inspired wormhole to a question of modern historiography, that of the definitive manifestation—the "definitive score," the "definitive performance," or the "definitive recording"—of a piece of music (these issues are also addressed elsewhere in this book by Jonathan Bernard, James Borders, Lori Burns, Jocelyn R. Neal, and Mark Spicer). Weighing words carefully, one could say that Mozart composed music but he did not write it. What he committed to paper was but an approximation of the music he heard and performed; it exists on paper merely as a road map to enable a performer to find a way through the actual music itself, which is manifest in some other space. Despite the relative detail in notation, the same should be said of a precisionistic Boulez score as it would of a permissive one by Cage. Thus, I don't understand the frequently raised argument that working with written notation of popular music taken from recordings (such as my notated examples for this essay, which as always are not my *source* but are provided to enable the reader to more easily verify my assertions for him- or herself) is somehow inherently more flawed than working with classical scores would be, because—no matter how good the score or to what purpose it is put—it is inaccurate or it is biased against certain parameters. As does any other model, the notated score can convey whatever information the skilled scribe wishes it to, whether in pitch and rhythmic notation, or in explanatory notes—as detailed as necessary—concerning articulation, dynamics, color, or any sort of subtle shading of expression.[21] But it must be remembered that no matter the level of notated detail, one is still left only with a meager representation of the actual music. Because a piece of music is a living, evolving form, the absolutist question of what constitutes a "definitive score" usually seems unanswerable and obstinate to me as well; there are frequently opposing contexts that make various "competing" versions of the same piece quite desirable, just as often as there are conditions that would cause many or most to agree on one "best" version. (And my feelings are not absolutist—of course there are inferior performances, just as there are wonderful performances marred by bad moments. But there is plenty of room for disagreement, which will often be based on matters of taste.) Varied performances of the same score—perhaps a Chopin waltz played in one decade by the composer himself (perhaps not even on piano but only in his own aural imagination), in another by de Pachmann, and in another by Rubinstein—can be different and yet equally valid, even though it is conceivable that none of them achieves the unrealizable Platonic ideal for which those living with the piece may yearn.[22] Different commercial mixes of the same rock performance can be equally appreciated, sometimes for different reasons. Consider the mono and stereo versions of the Beatles' "Help!" [1965], or take the pair of edited and full versions of Billy Joel's "The Entertainer" [1974] (the stock and promotional single edits both run at 3′05″, the actual length mentioned with irony in the lyrics of the longer LP mix). The only consideration of value to me in comparing different versions of scores, performances, or recordings is fidelity to the piece at hand. And since "the piece" cannot usually be fixed in precisely the same way for different interpreters, matters of taste usually tend to dominate such arguments, which must therefore remain inconclusive most of the time.

Probably no musical force on earth demonstrates the ideas in the preceding paragraph more thoroughly than does the Dead, almost always on tour because their music did not live in "definitive recordings" anymore than does a folksong, and the lifelong transcendence of "St. Stephen" will serve as evidence. (Segments of fifty different concert performances of "Dark Star" were once mixed together to create one new version for *Grayfolded* [1994]; how could one conceivably refer to a "definitive" version of that song?) "Stephen" had been performed in nine documented concerts (and certainly others unknown) in the three months prior to the Pacific sessions, so the band had a good working knowledge of the piece when it entered the studio. Familiarity notwithstanding, the composition was not fixed at that time but has remained vital and different in every incarnation. My references below to changes in selected aspects of "Stephen" are based on set lists in Scott et al. 1990 and studies of two studio tapings (one an outtake, the other released) from the September 1968 *Aoxomoxoa* recordings; the August 24, 1968, performance at the Shrine Auditorium, Los Angeles, heard on *Two From the Vault*; the February 27, 1969, performance at the Fillmore West, San Francisco, heard on *Live/Dead*; the October 31, 1971, performance at the Ohio Theatre, Columbus, Ohio, heard on *Dick's Picks, Vol. Two*; and soundboard tapes from other concerts at the Fillmore West (March 1, 1969), the Monterey Performing Arts

Center (June 14, 1969), the State University of New York at Binghamton (May 2, 1970), the Fillmore East, New York (April 28, 1971), the Orpheum Theater, San Francisco (July 18, 1976), and the McArthur Court of the University of Oregon (January 22, 1978).

Of course, the Grateful Dead's long, improvisatory jams on a single chord, scale, or repeated two-chord progression, let alone the atonal, free-form "space" and "drumz," were never the same from night to night. But elements of a score that would normally be fixed for other musicians were often entirely fluid for the Dead—witness the drastic changes of tempo and meter noted in connection with the 1976 revival of "Stephen." The song's intro, an accompanied guitar exposition of a definite theme, was played variously; it originally had bass support, but Lesh disappeared from this texture. Perhaps in accommodation, Bob Weir added a rhythm guitar part that became progressively richer. (Initially, he would add thirds to many chords, particularly D-major triads, and he added a suspended fourth over the bass A shown in the middle of the third system in Example 5.8a; his part later became even more involved.) Garcia's solo line itself appeared differently ($d\sharp^2$ for $d\natural^2$ in several shows, indicated above the staff at the end of the third system; $c\sharp^2$–b^1 instead of $d\natural^2$–$c\sharp^2$ in the last two guitar notes of the second system, heard in two shows; a^1–b^1–e^2 instead of b^1–e^2–e^2 in the first guitar notes of the fourth system). These are not heard as "wrong notes" as much as they are variations on a theme well established in other performances. The studio outtake (which likely precedes the released take) has a vision of the bridge that has not been repeated; during the 3/4 transition, a telephone rings and then is answered; we hear Garcia's vocal heavily filtered and its resonances distorted as through a transmission cable. This approach was abandoned, perhaps as overly idiosyncratic, but the idea of the distorted vocal became a timbral mix of orchestra bells in tremolo, two or more guitar parts (one, Jerry's distorted lead, always entering at "Sunlight splatters"), all in unison/octave doublings for an exceedingly bright color (its apparent intent reminiscent of Harrison's "Nowhere Man" Strat solo), with the bass fifths often not entering until the last few bars before the accelerando. In 1976, Keith Godchaux's countrified piano and Donna Godchaux's descant vocal in parallel sixths above Jerry's transformed the colors of the new 12/8 bridge into those of a soothing rural bliss, as opposed to the blinding acid glow that had lingered long from *Aoxomoxoa*.

But the factor that brought greatest change to "Stephen" was not intrinsic to the song itself but in its changing relation to the space around it. On *Aoxomoxoa*, "Stephen," the album opener, ends (following the words "What would be the answer to the answer man?") with a brief E-pentatonic jam. But this was merely a studio compromise; the outtake leads directly from "answer man" to the B-Mixolydian "Highlanders" passage ("high green chilly winds …," set like a march to the tune of the Beatles' "I've Just Seen a Face" [1965]), with Robert Hunter's bagpipes supported by drone fifths on the bass and Mickey Hart's snare rudiments. The end of this is then spliced to "The Eleven" (named for its 11/8 meter), which is in A major. This approximates the early concert presentation of "Stephen" (the Highlanders bagpipes replaced by Tom Constanten's organ), which in fact usually followed the decomposition of "Dark Star" (in A Mixolydian) without a break and led to a post-Highlanders B-pentatonic jam that slid after a couple of minutes into "The Eleven," all as preserved on both *Live/Dead* and *Two from the Vault.*[23] By 1970, the Highlanders section was dropped forever, and the "answer man" cadence led directly into an E-pentatonic jam that would usually evolve into a cover of Buddy Holly's "Not Fade Away" in the same key. At the same time that this ending was transforming, instrumental breaks within the song itself took on added dimension, as if replacing the Highlanders passage, gradually becoming jams with progressively varied rhythmic motives (including, more than once, a move to 6/4). These jams would eventually lead to other spaces that could open up into different songs before "Stephen" would be reprised with a late verse (the one beginning "St. Stephen will remain …"). Finally, "Stephen" was gobbled up by the great alien force, "The Other One," which was originally a suite but by 1971 one or another of its movements would routinely appear independently during second-set space explorations. By 1978, "The Other One" would open up into "Stephen," which might disappear when one of its "internal" jams led elsewhere without return. As befitting the lyrics concerning the saint's unknown destiny, there is no "definitive ending" for "Stephen." These various combinations of songs and parts of songs that may follow each other directly or may appear in the midst of jams are not medleys; every time the listener revisits "Stephen," it is through wormholes leading to a different space.

Tonal Systems

One problem complicating the analysis of rock music is that of the immediate confrontation with "noise." Because of the richly distorted colors, the wide array of vocal shadings, the dependence on heavy percussion, the limited dynamic range practicable for fully sonorous radio transmission, and the unruly competition for auditory airspace and cognitive attention in most rock performance environments short of headphone listening—aside from the obvious variety of otherwise-directed motivational interests present among the masses of rock aficionados—many lovers of rock music, and their spokespersons in various fields, seem to feel that pitch relations and other "classically marked" parameters are irrelevant in this domain. And so, as John Covach (1998, 453) points out, writers often assume that rock and art musics are somehow always radically distinct "in almost every possible way," certainly so when it comes to pitch systems.

So is Schenkerian analysis appropriate for listening to rock music? I won't extensively argue a defense of Schenkerian approaches to rock music; this is well handled in Covach 1997 and by Lori Burns in this volume. While I defer a defense of Schenkerian analysis of rock music to Burns and Covach, I would like to point out three key differences between my understanding of Schenkerian principles and those of others, critic and supporter alike. For one, I find the tension between levels of a Schenkerian graph—including tension between the surface and the foreground—rather than the product of the reductive process, to be of central interest. For me, Schenkerian analysis does not classify what is reduced "out" of a graph (whether a single note or an entire section) as less important than what remains. Instead, the process identifies the difference between ornament (which is often the "interesting" material) and the underlying structure (which is always more conventional) upon which it depends. Secondly, the structural progression I–V–I remains at the heart of the Schenkerian tonal system, whether it is articulated in any given song or not. If a song seems to be based on a I–IV–I relationship, and V does not appear at all, this does not mean that I–IV–I substitutes for I–V–I, nor does it suggest a different underlying system. My hearing of such a structure would classify it as prolongation of tonic within an incomplete I–V–I articulation of the tonal system, and therefore more static and less dynamic than a full hearing of the usual bass arpeggiation. If V does not appear, it may lie dormant, or be referred to by implication (in which case it would make sense to use V in a graph to suggest such a relationship between system and surface), or it may be irrelevant (in which case any reference to V in a graph would have to clearly show it is part of an unarticulated norm). Third, the celebrated *Urlinie* that Schenker restricts to stepwise descents to $\hat{1}$ from $\hat{8}$, $\hat{5}$, or $\hat{3}$ in his studied literature, are not the only possible background lines in other literatures, just as true of older music (as argued in Everett 2004a) as in rock (see Everett 2004b). It is in this third area that I would agree that Schenkerian analysis should often produce results different from those seen in its traditional applications, and I believe this is evident throughout my own publications from 1985 onward. However, this approach entails no "adaptation" of Schenkerian principles: the analytical procedure with rock music must proceed according to unchanging principles of counterpoint. Results may vary from those of prior repertoires depending upon the degree of modal, pentatonic, or other deviations from the abstract underlying tonal system.

From a different standpoint, I believe that every listener brings to any musical experience the sum total of a lifetime of other musical experiences, that the ideal "perfect listener" would have deep knowledge of every single musical statement ever made or ever *to* be made in any style, and that every listener should be given the freedom to categorize and conceptualize of the relationships in all of those musics in whatever ways he or she finds appropriate, significant, and satisfying. For me, a Schenkerian hearing of tonal events is useful toward these ends.[24]

But what do we mean by "tonal events"? I am referring to aspects related to tonal centricity, an achievement common to nearly all pop-rock examples. Sometimes, a tonal center is suggested by mere implication, as by the simple assertion of a sustained chord. But at the opposite extreme, it might be clarified by a concerted combination of (1) strong harmonic function (most generally, with roots descending in fifths or in fifth-dividing thirds, but still functional—if less powerful—in many other patterns) and (2) directed voice leading (expressed through straight, fluent, melodic lines, perhaps ornamented and thus deviating on the surface; leading on the foreground between chord members relating to roots on any scale degree, and at the deepest background level toward a member of the tonic triad, with greatest closure coming with the perfect authentic cadence afforded by $\hat{1}$ in the structural upper voice at the structural close). An infinite variety of tonal situations exists between these two poles. Sometimes outer-voice counterpoint governs a passage that possesses no harmonic implications whatsoever (simple neighbor and passing motions often help determine goals), and sometimes the direction is given by a normally meek single inner voice. At other times, harmonic function is strongly characterizing and yet voice leading seems extremely indirect (it may be deeply present, but richly manipulated) and thus unable to establish goals, at either immediate or long-range positions. There are as many variations along this continuum as there are styles, indeed as there are pieces and even individual passages or potential passages. It should also be stated at this time that although musicologists often think of "modal" and "tonal" processes as distinct, owing to the historically late (roughly post-1600) codification of harmonic principles in the face of already (pre-1600) sophisticated voice-leading constructs, I follow Schenkerian principles of mode mixture (e.g., allowing for not only minor, but also Phrygian, inflections of the major mode). Thus—except in the case of a purely modal practice, as with the Knack's Mixolydian "My Sharona" (1979), whereby one can discuss tonality in terms of voice leading but not of harmony—I will recognize the much more common rock techniques that mix modal elements into a tonal framework or vice-versa.

The remainder of this essay will explore in as brief a manner as possible various potential analytical approaches to tonal relations in pop-rock music. On the docket: (1) a context-establishing look at historically "normal" combinations of harmonic and voice-leading principles, including a tip of the hat to some experimental and unexpectedly rich tonicizations; (2) approaches to songs that sport tonal events but no overall tonal coherence; (3) an evaluation of systems where counterpoint is at least as crucial as harmony in governing chord succession, including emphases on non-chord tones and linear progressions; (4) a rundown on modal systems, inflection, and contrast; (5) an effort to address the tonal problem of "power-chord" rock; (6) the music of hip-hop; and (7) the recognition of a few absolutely atonal examples.

"Normal" Approaches to Harmony and Voice Leading

Probably most pop music and a substantial amount of rock music concedes fully to the norms of tonal behavior that are described by Schenker. Of the songs written and recorded by the Beatles alone, at least a third fall squarely in this category, and another third make only tangential explorations outside the system; the remaining third would hold Schenker hostage. These proportions might hold roughly for the entire pop-rock spectrum (but note that Lori Burns, in her essay here, would likely weigh the proportions more heavily against traditional Schenkerian paradigms). This judgment is in no way intended to suggest the relative value of pieces demonstrating a structure thus defined, much less to establish a guidepost on the road to canonization. Tracing the same tonal events once studied by Schenker doesn't mean that a song thus labeled is artistically comparable to the masterworks of Beethoven and Bach. It says nothing in itself about levels of complexity or the originality of their deviations from norms (which are much more the hallmarks of interesting and "great" works than are their most basic skeletons), but is merely a descriptor of organizational method. It does say, however, that the governing context of "pop" music is very systematically tonal, and it suggests that "rock" music may be somewhat less strongly expected to be so. Regular harmonically supported Schenkerian *Urlinien* appear in perhaps unexpected places, including most of Bruce Springsteen's Woody Guthrie-inspired songs (particularly throughout *Nebraska* [1982]), the verse/chorus combination of Van Halen's "Why Can't This Be Love" (1986), U2 songs such as "With or Without You" (1987), many Nirvana tracks ("On a Plain" and "Come as You Are" [both 1991] among them), and David Byrne's "Crash" (1994). Sometimes the voice leading seems exceedingly static, only to finally give way to the structural descending line, as when "the action … the motion" is finally demonstrated in Dire Straits' "Walk of Life" (1985) (1:25–1:30) or when Bob Dylan reaches into his inner-voice depths (1:09–1:20) to finally find the conviction to lay bare his tender sentiments in the cadence of "Emotionally Yours" (also 1985). Allan Moore (2001, 194) is perceptive in saying of the Sex Pistols' "Anarchy in the U. K." (1977) that "melodically, the chorus emphasizes each note of the downward scale in turn, from G through to C, a pattern so basic in its organization that its connotations could not be further from 'anarchy.'" His conclusion as to irony is spot on, but he would be even more accurate in describing the song as a simple major-mode pop tune structured as a conformist $\hat{3}$-line given fully functional harmonic and contrapuntal support. An overbearing dependence on such normal structures may be taken as an indicator of pop markers invading an otherwise rock-oriented context, as with Fastball's "The Way," "Out of My Head," "Better Than it Was," "Sooner or Later," and "Warm Fuzzy Feeling" (all 1998). Ben Folds (particularly with the well-crafted bass lines in *Rockin' the Suburbs* [2001]) also exemplifies this mixture of almost-antithetical structure and style. It is also important to recognize that an adherence to, or deviation from, Schenkerian models is not necessarily in and of itself style-determinative. A general characterization of three tracks from the Police's *Synchronicity* (1983) will illustrate: In "Synchronicity I," chord changes seem of little consequence despite a governing tonal center; a quasi-normal set of functions works in "Synchronicity II"; and "Every Breath You Take" has a fully functional set of relations supporting a $\hat{3}$-line in E minor, featuring expressive mode mixture and a conventional chromatically applied dominant harmony in the bridge. All composed by Sting, and all quite different approaches to tonal centricity; do they represent three different styles?

As suggested in the Sex Pistols example, although Schenkerian constructs are pervasive throughout the pop-rock world, they still retain enormous expressive capacity, perhaps because they are not heard universally (as they were not in Bach's choral works or Beethoven's and Brahms's songs either, a point little recognized beyond students of Schenker). For instance, Elton John's "Daniel" (1973) depends on a clearly traced $\hat{3}$-line (following an initial ascent and culminating in a flying vocal register transfer on $\hat{1}$, appropriate for the setting on a plane and using the same octave that had launched "Rocket Man" [1972]), thereby depicting the ironic manner in which a blind person (whose difficulties may be suggested by unpredictable harmonic support, as with the deceptive cadence as Daniel waves "goodbye") can see his way better than a sighted one, exactly the device governing the same but metaphorical conceit in the Beatles' "Nowhere Man" (1965). And there's the workaday, unadorned climbing down the $\hat{5}$-line in Springsteen's "Factory" (1978) heard as the perfect emblem for the ethical but dead-end monotony and depressing predictability of the blue-collar life. To further demonstrate a lack of "value" attached to the Schenkerian paradigm, I will emphasize that voice-leading closure is not always expressively useful or desirable. Springsteen's "My Hometown" (1984) ends with the futures of both the singer's community and his family unresolved, a poetic effect due in large part to the fact that the vocal part does not lead to $\hat{1}$ with tonic support, but to $\hat{5}$ instead. Similarly, Neil Young's "Powderfinger" (1979) is "left undone" on $\hat{5}$ and his "My, My, Hey Hey (Out of the Blue)" (also 1979) goes "into the black" with the final descent to $\hat{6}$. Many nineteenth-century examples defy Schenker's *Urlinien* for similar expressive purposes (as demonstrated in Everett 2004a).

Expanded journeys to chromatically derived tonal areas, i.e., the tonicization of and modulation to non-diatonic scale degrees, brings tonal richness to a substantial body of pop music. I've always found it interesting that the major-mode move from I to $\flat III^{\flat 5}$ for the bridge of the Teddy Bears' "To Know Him is to Love Him" (1958), a staple of Quarry Men and early Beatles set lists into 1962, gave Paul McCartney a device for entering the "new" world of the parallel minor through the back door for the bridges of the Beatles' "Here, There, and Everywhere" (1966) and "Two of Us" (1969). Without asserting any degree of influence from these early models, I'll note that Eric Clapton uses the same relationship in moving to the bridge, hoping time will end his pain, in "Tears in Heaven" (1992). In his brief career encapsulization of the Beach Boys, Daniel Harrison (1997) provides wonderful hearings of the chromatic modulations in "The Warmth of the Sun" (1964) and "Wonderful" (recorded 1966; released 1993). If space had allowed, I'm sure he would have also mentioned in this regard "In My Room" (1963) (which modulates to another world for the bridge), "Don't Worry Baby" (1964) (note the transcendent move from E major to F♯ major for "her" encouragement in the chorus and compare this to the Beatles' related modulation for the flashback in "Penny Lane" [1967]), "Wouldn't It Be Nice" (1966) (note how the A-major wish-fulfilling bridge "explains" the A-major introduction to a song in F), and "Caroline No" (1966) (like "God Only Knows," this starts far from tonic, but finally finds G♭ major, only to succumb to B♭ minor heartbreak in the bridge). An essay on the Supremes' hits would guide similar recognition to a number of wonderful Holland-Dozier-Holland modulations, as in "I Hear a Symphony" (1965) (where E♭ gives way to V of C in the introduction and bridge), "My World Is Empty Without You" (1966) (where the bridge's tonal center of A is reheard as a Dorian ♭VII in the return to B minor; compare "Reach Out I'll Be There"), "You Keep Me Hangin' On" (1966) (featuring an A♭-Mixolydian-Dorian verse and a B-major bridge based on a repetition of the standard ♭VII–IV–I cadence, repeating and leading to a final hearing of that IV of B [1:27–1:29] that must be reinterpreted as a pivot chord, functioning as a ♭VI upper neighbor to a cadential $^{6}_{4}$ in the returning A♭), and most majestically, "Love Is Here and Now You're Gone" (1967) (which brings an applied German sixth and a new psychedelic voice leading to hidden heartaches, supporting Ross's most expressive vocal ever).[25] The Fifth Dimension's "Up, Up and Away" (1967) is a pair of dizzying aeronautical sequences of moduations through minor thirds to areas a tritone away, occuring both in the G-major verse and in the C-major bridge, despite highly contrasting surface thematic materials in the two sections. This sort of distant pop modulation was important through the 1970s, perhaps culminating in Paul Simon's *Still Crazy After All These Years* (1975) and *One-Trick Pony* (1980), but also in much more intellectually "innocent" repertoires, as in Rod Stewart's "Tonight's the Night (Gonna Be Alright)" (the number-one record of 1976) and 10cc's "The Things We Do For Love" (1977), the latter featuring a remarkably Wagnerian relationship involving an introduction in D major that moves by way of its hexatonic pole, B♭ minor, to a verse in D♭ major (0:20–0:37), and a bridge (0:57–1:16) that rises through an ascending 6-5 sequence not to the expected V of D♭ but via a common-tone modulation to V of the introduction's D that becomes a retransition (1:16–1:40) back to D♭. It would probably surprise many students of classical music to learn that most tonal techniques of the common-practice period are demonstrated in one or another example from the pop-rock world. David Brackett (1995, xi, 4, et passim) apologizes needlessly for the relative simplicity of pop/rock music, but he makes the mistake of framing a comparison to art music through large symphonic works by Debussy, Mahler, and Stravinsky. A great deal of pop-rock literature holds up quite well in terms of complexity in comparison with the *songs* of Debussy, Mahler, and Stravinsky.

Harmonic Subversion of "Normal" Tonal Contexts

Just as the entire nineteenth century witnessed an evolution from closed tonal systems to those that were progressive, with pieces not ending where they began (as with the Mahler works to which Mark Spicer refers in Chapter 12 of this volume), pop music—and more typically rock music—reflects a great deviation from norms when it presents multiple passages that internally are tonally coherent, but which are then strung together in ways that defy a single overall tonal center. This is of course represented by the pop tune's "truck driver's modulation," whereby succeeding verses appear in successively higher keys that are unrelated to one another (discussed in some detail in Everett 1997, 117–118, and nn. 17 and 18). A related effect is heard in the Beatles' "Being for the Benefit of Mr. Kite" (1967), which swirls through a circus's three rings via keys of C minor, D minor, and E minor, before being brought back through the ringmaster's dotted-rhythm piano-banging "whistle blasts" on G triads (1:27–1:28) to C minor. Although these areas suggest a large-scale expansion of C, the parallelisms in the thematic and modulatory mechanisms are those of a progressive technique, and the piece trails off in E minor, not on III of C. Such sequential tonicizations need not be unrelated. The verse of Carly Simon's "The Right Thing to Do" (1973) creates a sense of wonder and one of recaptured ecstacy even as she adapts herself to accept whatever comes along (poetic notions clarified in the bridge lyrics), as it progresses through a remarkably long circle of fifths built on F♯, B, E, A, D, and the dominant of C, the chords variously colored (as when D major becomes D minor) so as to tonicize E minor and D major before finding C, but all voice-led to maintain a single overriding tonality. Compare Chris Montez's "Call Me" (1966).

Some songs alternate between unrelated key areas, each expanded in entire sections, creating a nontonal whole. Such is the case in Alice Cooper's "School's Out" (1972), the chorus of which is in G minor but its verse is in a Doors-like E Mixolydian; neither area subsumes the other. Similarly, Aerosmith's "Walk This Way" (1976) has verses and chorus in C but an introduction and later riffs in an unrelated E. Led Zeppelin's "Immigrant Song" (1970) is basically in F♯ Dorian, but its structural retransition (0:42–0:50) expands III by moving A–B–C, omitting a C♯ dominant that would tie all things together tonally. More interesting and (appropriately for its text) far more unstable is a song like Pink Floyd's "See Saw" (1968), where any few consecutive chords may suggest a key, but Picardy-third mixture and mid-phrase pivot and chromatic modulations occur frequently enough that no right-minded listener would look for unifying relationships between the several tonal centers. The song's fresh tangential diversions that leave behind any memory of what had come before, come to think of it, are actually beyond the ken of a right-minded listener; a bit of acid might help smooth over the confusion.

Some songs are structurally diatonic and depend on normal tonal chord progressions, and yet no single overriding tonal center can be appointed conclusively because the song's various formal sections revolve around separate tonics (perhaps in pairs suggesting the double-tonic complex of Bailey 1977) and closure is not provided by any overall directed voice leading. Pairs of relative major and minor operate this way sometimes, as in Pink Floyd's "Time" (1973), and the Beatles' "Girl" (1965) and "And I Love Her" (1964) (the last of which also undermines tonal stability with both a truck driver's modulation at the beginning of the classical-guitar solo and a Picardy-third ending on the minor "home" just as it had probably been given up for tonic in favor of its somewhat stronger relative major). Talking Heads' fa-fa-fa-fractured "Psycho Killer" (1977) alternates its allegiance between relative major and minor as easily as it moves between English and French. Similarly, single-scale systems can involve modal finals other than relative major and minor; the Moody Blues' "Story in Your Eyes" (1971) contrasts sections in A Dorian (for the negative verses) and G major (for the phoenix-invoking hopes of the chorus), but voices do not lead to anything claiming tonic status overall. The Cure's "The 13th" (1996) straddles this "relative" function with that of "Walk This Way" when it contrasts the closely related keys D♭ major and F minor without claiming one or the other as tonic. Schenkerian analysis would be useful in defining events within sections of such songs, but cannot suggest organic wholes that are clearly not the point.

Nontriadic Tones

In the realm of tonality, properties of counterpoint—dissonance treatment, passing, and neighbor relationships—are just as determinative as harmonic drive, no matter what quality the surface texture assumes in terms of numbers or independence of parts. Sometimes counterpoint is responsible for the *entirety* of tonal activity, as in single-chord pieces (typically funk-related, and with few ties to the Western tonal traditions of the past several centuries) ranging from Sly & the Family Stone's "Everyday People" (1968) through the Ohio Players' "Fire" (1974), Chic's "Le Freak" (1978), Talking Heads' "The Great Curve" (1980), Bruce Springsteen's "Born in the U.S.A." (1984), Stevie Wonder's "It's Wrong (Apartheid)" (1985), and Red Hot Chili Peppers' "Behind the Sun" (1987) to Soundgarden's "Jesus Christ Pose" (1991). In many cases, rap vocals are laid over tracks involving contrapuntal ornamentation of a single harmony; in these cases, we say that a tonal center is implied (but not defended) by assertion.

Dissonance treatment is just as crucial to most pop-rock styles as it is to the classics. Tension is created by exposed leading tones that seem to have been

Example 5.9 Stevie Wonder, "My Cherie Amour" (Stevie Wonder-Henry Cosby-Sylvia Moy) (1969): analysis.

left hanging, and relief is afforded when their resolution is finally attended. Such is a long-range ploy of Elton John's in "Goodbye Yellow Brick Road" (1973) (compare the $\hat{7}$ at 0:10 with its $\hat{8}$ at 0:21).[26] Voice leading can become quite complex and chromatic when jazzy nontriadic tones become accented dissonances, as in Stevie Wonder's "My Cherie Amour" (1969), the entirety of which is sketched in the voice-leading reduction of Example 5.9. The sketch suggests that, despite the high prevalence of accented dissonant sevenths (including those against the tonic triad), fourths, ninths, and added sixths, these are all treated as conventional appoggiaturas, suspensions, neighbors, anticipations, and chromatic and diatonic passing tones at the large-scale level, if not on the literal surface. Of singular interest here is the ♭VII–I neighboring progression in the vocalized ("la, la, la …") motto, a device already occurring in the horns' motto of "Uptight (Everything's Alright)" (1965). The ♭VII function is superficially disguised here by the addition of whole-tone-based neighboring augmented fourth and (chromatically lowered) suspended minor seventh; the whole-tone coloring appears again above a bass C♭ in the refrain, but there functions as an augmented-sixth embellishment to an applied dominant. A few years later, Wonder would invoke the entire whole-tone collection in his scales in thirds in the introduction to "You Are the Sunshine of My Life" (1973) (there coloring a dominant ninth altered with diminished fifth and minor sixth); so in terms of whole-tone colorings of altered dominants, "Cherie" seems to represent a midpoint between "Uptight" and "Sunshine." A more recent, interesting treatment of normally resolving complexes of function-clouding nontriadic tones can be found in the rolling waves of Pearl Jam's "Oceans" (1992).

Nontriadic tones, of course, don't always behave normally by resolving as would be expected in a classical work (where they may also, of course, be treated quite freely). In Steely Dan's last three albums before their two-decade hiatus, *The Royal Scam* (1976), *Aja* (1977), and *Gaucho* (1980), for example, non-resolving bop-based seventh and ninth chords far outnumber innocent triads. But some commentators would have it that such non-resolving embellishments are therefore "stable." Such a mindset reveals an underlying insensitivity to the frequent power and charm of such sonorities, which often refuse to resolve as a matter of expression. The suspended but non-resolving fourth is a frequent example: Who is unmoved by this frozen event in the introduction-ending and chorus-ending half cadence in the Mamas and the Papas' "California Dreamin'" (1966) (expressing an unresolved tension also symbolized by the singer's shivering). James Taylor's "Sweet Baby James" (1970) plays with the guitar's non-resolving fourth above V^7, but the bridge prepares the chorus with a long half-time retransition that finally resolves the dissonance. (The song ends with a signature hammer-on that inverts the dissonant preparation of a chordal third.) Eric Clapton's "Tears in Heaven" (1992) portrays the singer's declaration, "I don't *belong* here in heaven," with a non-resolving fourth over V^7, a sonic gesture with all the effect of a palms-forward not-now refusal. Is the unresolved fourth with which Bob Dylan frequently ends his vocal phrases over tonic support considered "stable" by anybody? Are the Coplandesque chords built in fourths in Bruce Hornsby's "Every Little Kiss" (1986) simply one stable chord after another?

It should be noted that a song may present nontriadic tones in a stylistic context that creates no expectation or desire for resolution. But that still does not make the embellishments stable. The understated yet unresolved tension of the "frozen" major seventh became a pervasive staple of soft rock in the 1970s, as with Carole King, Carly Simon, and Todd Rundgren. Non-resolving ornaments do not even have to be dissonant. George Harrison treated the barre-friendly added-sixth chord, which he learned from Carl Perkins—who'd learned it from Hank Williams—interchangeably with the ninth chord, or even a $^{9}_{6}$ chord, as a "fancy" way to end many an early Beatles song; of course no resolution is expected here, but the amicable tension is palpable.[27] Example 5.10 presents a reduction of Crosby, Stills & Nash's "Lady of the Island" (1969), a tune based on a barely moving, Chopin-like stream of lines above a descending bass (all performed on Graham Nash's single acoustic guitar; the treble staff outlines his vocal part). The song exhibits considerable unresolved dissonance, which even the most sensitive listener never hopes to be resolved, especially given the stubbornly poignant second scale degree that agrees with the bass only over F. The parenthesized suggested final dominant chord would "explain" the presence over the cadential II of the E♭ and the ever-sustaining B♭, but no listener would demand the structure-crunching appearance of V in this ultra-soft style. Is the V^7 with Mixolydian third and simultaneous anticipation of $\hat{1}$, with which the Beatles' "A Hard Day's Night" (1964) opens, stable because it doesn't resolve?[28] How about the complex overlay of $\hat{7}$, $\hat{6}$, $\hat{5}$, and $\flat\hat{3}$ over the I–♭VI–V^7 progression in the Cure's "Fascination Street" (1989)? Do we not notice the non-resolving nontriadic tones (♭7 over IV at 0:13, 0:36, and 0:46; ♭7 over I at 0:24) with which Aretha Franklin ends her phrases in "Baby I Love You" (1967)? Are we not struck by the unresolved $\hat{3}$ chimed over IV and then over V on the vibes in the Supremes' "Stop! in the Name of Love" (1965)? Aren't we charmed by the piano's coy added tones in Steely Dan's "I Got the News" (1977)? Frank Zappa will have the last word: Example 5.11 cites a fiercely extreme passage (beginning at 1:24) from the Mothers of Invention's "Call Any Vegetable" (1967), the highly dissonant nontriadic tones of which are influenced by Stravinsky's deliberate "wrong-note" technique, serving

Example 5.10 Crosby, Stills & Nash, "Lady of the Island" (Graham Nash), *Crosby, Stills & Nash* (1969): analysis.

Example 5.11 The Mothers of Invention, "Call Any Vegetable" (Frank Zappa), *Absolutely Free* (1967).

to trivialize the simplicity of the vocal melody in an apparent defensive self-mockery. Stable? No. Dissonance play, scale-degree status, and therefore tonal identity are only emphasized by such elisions of resolution.

Linear Progressions

Tonal identity is often achieved through chord successions that are not based on harmonic relationships, but are instead governed by contrapuntal lines. Richard Middleton (1990, 118–119) mentions the descending bass as an organizing force, and this is one of a number of approaches to having a single voice dictate the shape of a passage. As with classical forebears, much of rock music escapes the threat of staticity by way of linear progressions—the unidirectional, stepwise completions of chord intervals—that shape bass lines, inner-voice melodies, and sometimes vocal parts, providing forward impetus. The melodic lines govern their passages, usually expanding a single harmony through passing chords. In Procol Harum's "Whiter Shade of Pale" (1967), the tonic is expanded through a full-octave descent from $\hat{8}$ to $\hat{1}$ in the bass, which continues with a dominant expansion over the bass-line linear progression $\hat{5}$–$\hat{4}$–$\hat{3}$–$\hat{2}$. I^6 moves to V as the bass rises $\hat{3}$–$\hat{4}$–$\hat{5}$ in the Temptations' "My Girl" (1965) (0:28–0:36), and I moves to IV through bass descents in the opening of Percy Sledge's "When a Man Loves a Woman" (1966) and the chorus of Creedence Clearwater Revival's "Have You Ever Seen the Rain" (1970) (0:50–0:53), both built on a descending 5–6 sequence over a bass line moving $\hat{8}$–$\hat{7}$–$\hat{6}$–$\hat{5}$–$\hat{4}$. Dominant preparations may be similarly expanded, as with either the rising bass line $\hat{2}$–$\hat{3}$–$\hat{4}$ in both the Supremes' "Come See About Me" (1964) (0:34–0:40) and the Flamin' Groovies' "You Tore Me Down" (1976) (0:38–0:45), or the even more popular descent ($\hat{6}$–$\hat{5}$–$\hat{4}$) heard in the Stones' "Ruby Tuesday" (1967) (0:13–0:17), Elvis's "Burning Love" (1972) (0:33–0:42), and the Cars' "You Might Think" (1984) (0:34–0:40). We've already seen the rising linear progression, $\hat{2}$–$\hat{3}$–$\hat{4}$–$\hat{5}$, expanding V^7 in "You Can't Hurry Love" (last two bars of Example 5.5). The longest continuous bass scale in rock may be that in the bridge of the Beatles' "Lady Madonna" (1968) (0:26–0:40), actually a combination of three linear progressions, expanding II ($\hat{2}$–$\hat{1}$–$\hat{7}$–$\hat{6}$), then V($\hat{5}$–$\hat{4}$–$\hat{3}$–$\hat{2}$), and then I ($\hat{1}$–$\hat{7}$–$\hat{6}$–$\hat{5}$), all of which help rectify the mode-mixing rising scale in the last phrase of the verse ($\hat{1}$–$\hat{2}$–$\hat{3}$–$\hat{4}$–$\hat{5}$–$\flat\hat{6}$–$\flat\hat{7}$–$\hat{8}$).

This last-named mode mixture reverses the descending melodic minor that often yields the "passacaglia" bass line moving from I to V, $\hat{8}$–$\flat\hat{7}$–$\flat\hat{6}$–$\hat{5}$, unadorned in Ray Charles' "Hit the Road Jack" (1961) but the basis of the heterophonic descending progression of parallel I–♭VII–♭VI–V chords in the verses of Del Shannon's "Runaway" (1961), the Beatles' "I'll Be Back" (1964), the Lovin' Spoonful's "Summer in the City" (1966), the Beach Boys' "Good Vibrations" (1966), the Turtles' "Happy Together" (1967), Dire Straits' "Sultans of Swing" (1979), and the eponymous "Stray Cat Strut" (1982); and in the choruses of the Supremes' "Love Child" (1968) and Hall and Oates' "Maneater" (1982).[29] In the verse of Cat Stevens's "Wild World" (1971) (0:14–0:26), the I–♭VII–♭VI –V progression in A minor is a bit disguised by ornamental chords between these guideposts that fall in a descending-fifth sequence: Am–D^7–G–$C^{\Delta 7}$–F–$B^{\circ}{}^{6}_{5}$–E (the same technique is the basis of the bridge [1:20–1:35] of Smashing Pumpkins' "Cherub Rock" [1993], falling I^9–IV–$\flat VII^9$–♭III). The verse of John Lennon's "I'm Losing You" (1980) is based on the bass line $\hat{8}$–$\flat\hat{7}$–$\flat\hat{6}$–$\hat{5}$ but adds the chromatic passing tone $\hat{7}$ on the way down (beginning like the verse of Bob Dylan's "Ballad of a Thin Man" [1965]). The ostinato figure of both Cream's "Tales of Brave Ulysses" (1967) and Led Zeppelin's "Babe, I'm Gonna Leave You" (1969) adds $\hat{6}$ instead. The bass line in the verses of the Eagles' "Hotel California" (1976) (see Example 5.12) descends from $\hat{8}$ to $\hat{5}$ through a complete chromatic scale that supports a descending 5–6 sequence, which takes the listener to the dominant preparation with a tonal language quite appropriate for the Spanish mission setting. In all of these chord successions, intermediate verticalities have no harmonic function, but are instead driven by counterpoint.

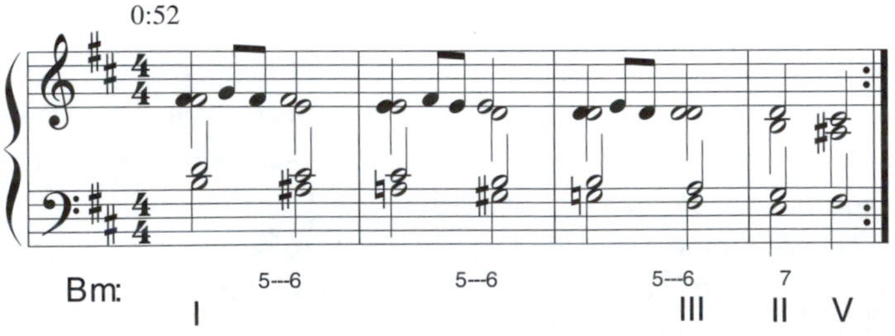

Example 5.12 The Eagles, "Hotel California" (Don Felder-Don Henley-Glenn Frey), *Hotel California* (1977): verse, analysis.

Chromatic linear descents are more often buried in inner voices, where their half-hidden pungency can still guide a structure from within. As this was once a hallmark of Beatles songs (usually in Lennon's work), Elvis Costello asked Paul McCartney why the device did not find its way into his solo compositions. They made amends together with their co-composition, "Veronica" (1989), a very catchy pop song that incorporates the descent $\hat{2}$–$\sharp\hat{1}$–$\natural\hat{1}$–$\hat{7}$ in an expansion of II that moves to V^7. In the verse's first phrase in Dionne Warwick's "(Theme from) Valley of the Dolls" (1968), the tonic is expanded when the descending interval from $\hat{8}$ to $\hat{5}$ is completely filled in with chromatic passing tones. The same full chromatic descent is heard in the verses of Bob Dylan's "Simple Twist of Fate" (1975) and "Make You Feel My Love" (1997). With one chromatic scale degree ($\flat\hat{6}$) skipped, the same descent from $\hat{1}$ reaches all the way to $\hat{3}$ through a series of ornamental chords in the verse and downbeat of the chorus (0:05–1:22) of the Dead's "Stella Blue" (1973).

Chromatic lines rising from $\hat{5}$ to $\flat\hat{7}$, all in support of V^7/IV, are fairly common after Buddy Holly's "Raining in My Heart" (1959) (0:09–0:17), as in Herman's Hermits' "There's a Kind of a Hush" (1967) (0:08–0:13), Captain and Tennille's "Love Will Keep Us Together" (1975) (0:26–0:33), and Steve Winwood's "While You See a Chance" (1981) (1:47–1:54). Otherwise, rising lines are relatively hard to come by; one astounding example occurs in Bob Weir and Gerrit Graham's structurally complex and rewarding Dead number, "Victim or the Crime" (1989). Here, IV of IV (A in the Phrygian-inflected key of B Dorian) is expanded in the bridge (1:22–1:41, beginning with the text, "these are the horns of the dilemma"); the chromatic line rises out of the underworld from $\hat{4}$ (supported by IV of IV) through $\sharp\hat{4}$–$\hat{5}$ (by IV of IV of IV)–$\sharp\hat{5}$–$\hat{6}$ to $\flat\hat{7}$ (by IV of IV) as "the wisest man is deemed insane."[30] Occasionally, the squarest pop song will use an ascending chromatic sequence, as in the rising 6-5 sequence above $\hat{3}$–$\hat{4}$–$\sharp\hat{4}$–$\hat{5}$–$\sharp\hat{5}$–$\hat{6}$ in the expectation-building expansion of IV of ♭III heard in the Cuff Links' "Tracy" (1969) (0:25–0:35). But this technique is also heard at the end of the verse in Judas Priest's rather unsquare "Fever" (1982) (0:53–1:01), where the rising 5-6 chromatic sequence between Ian Hill's bass and Rob Halford's vocal sets the text, "darkness filled my soul." Such an obviously learned technique is as rare in pop-rock music as imitative canon (and was this ever heard between Perry Como's "Round and Round" [1957] or "Catch a Falling Star" [1958] and *Revolver* [1966]?). Even the simple diatonic melodic sequence dropped out of favor as being too conventional after the time of Connie Francis's "Follow the Boys" (1963), but was revived in John Lennon's ode to Elvis Presley, Gene Vincent, and Eddie Cochran, "(Just Like) Starting Over" (1980).[31]

Other Domination of Voice Leading over Harmony

Linear progressions represent only one way that voice leading can dominate over harmonic relationships in governing the tonal direction of a passage or

Example 5.13 Wings, "Getting Closer" (Paul McCartney) (1979): analysis.

a song. Another common technique is used in choosing an accompanimental chord simply because it provides consonant support for a tone or tones in the vocal melody. Two songs by Smashing Pumpkins (both from 1993) will illustrate. In the verse of "Today" (0:35–0:57), a repeated vocal descent from $\hat{8}$ through $\hat{7}$ to $\hat{6}$ is supported with I, V, and IV, respectively; the V does not "lead" to IV, but the V is heard as back-relating while the IV ornaments the I that follows. Thus, V supports $\hat{7}$ but has no harmonic power. In "Sweet Sweet," the vocal descent $\hat{3}$–$\hat{2}$–$\hat{1}$ is supported by the chord succession I–II$^{6}_{5}$–VI; the "harmony" makes no claims whatsoever, but the melody insists that G ($\hat{1}$) is the goal. And this device is not new to alternative rock: Example 5.13 provides a voice-leading analysis of the first phrase of Wings' "Getting Closer" (1979). What is played as an E-major chord on the second bar's downbeat is simply consonant support in parallel tenths for a *descending* passing seventh scale degree within an expansion of IV, which (when followed by V of II) is subsequently understood as III of II. The long-expanded B-minor harmony does close on a true dominant at the end of the example. In demonstrating that an ear open to tonal issues demands a non-formalist approach, it must be recognized that what would look like V on the page is often something completely different.

The multitude of approaches to the harmonic value of dominant (V) harmony in Bob Dylan's *Nashville Skyline* (1969) is also instructive. The dominant acts with a vengeance in some songs, among them "Nashville Skyline Rag," "Country Pie," "One More Night" (based on a beautifully treated $\hat{5}$-line that descends following an opening arpeggiation to the primary tone), and the bridge (1:17–1:44) of "Tonight I'll Be Staying Here With You" (which moves from a wonderful mixture-enhanced expansion of a dominant preparation, IV♭–I–IV♭–I–♭II–IV–II^{7}, to a big V that then steps down, "If Not for You"-style, through nonfunctional passing root-position colors, V–"IV–III–II"–I). In "Lay Lady Lay," the opening refrain anticipates V, but this harmony is articulated only later in the verse; the nonfunctional chord succession of the refrain, I–"III"–♭VII–II^{7}, exists only for consonant support of Pete Drake's pedal steel line, which descends $\hat{8}$–$\hat{7}$–♭$\hat{7}$–$\hat{6}$, therefore contrapuntally expanding a dominant preparation. The verse finally continues to V (at 0:37–0:38), with a lyric that I hear as a description of the harmonic anticipation: "Whatever colors you have in your mind, I'll show them to you and you'll see them shine."[32] The dominant is weakened further in "Tell Me That It Isn't True," the verse of which takes V to a tonic that is ornamented by the expansion of an introductory upper neighbor II. In the bridge, II twice stands in for V (a fairly common linear substitution in jazz): In the introductory IV–III–"II"–I motion, and in the retransitional V^7/VI–VI–II–III–"II" culmination; as in Graham Nash's "Lady of the Island," the dominant is weakened to the point that the listener does not actually expect it to sound in this style, but it still haunts by its absence.[33] Finally, "Girl From the North Country" makes no suggestion of harmonic motion at all; the repeated I–III–IV–I "progression" constitutes a contrapuntal expansion of I with III acting like a modified I^6, and IV simply providing neighbors to I. In addition, the voice is often locked in octaves with the bass, reducing counterpoint to an inner-voice phenomenon within a largely heterophonic frame. This soft, V-less style often provides a wispy harmonic poetry appropriate to the lyric. In Joni Mitchell's "The Circle Game" (1970), the verse and chorus "progress" with touches of embellishing back-related V's, but there is no structural dominant to support a descending structural line, and the static upper line does not challenge with any directed descent; all goes "'round and 'round" back to $\hat{3}$ in the upper voice, a tone held captive with a never-ending promise of the future, forced always to look back "from where we came," riding only up and down alongside its upper-neighbor $\hat{4}$.

A full appreciation, a *Verstehen*, of dominant harmony—as of any other scale degree—requires that one can never take harmony literally as would a formalist; rather, one must depend instead on an awareness of a multitude of degrees of deviations from norms to be able to judge what is implied when it does not occur. Take, for example, Bob Dylan's "License to Kill" (1983). The verse includes a repeated alternation of VI and IV (0:24–0:32), which would normally amount to an expanded dominant preparation, and is particularly emphasized as such by Mark Knopfler's guitar. Instead, it moves to what would be spelled like a root-position tonic (0:32–0:34), which then moves to V (0:34–0:35) for the verse's authentic cadence. As in many other similar situations, the "I^5_3" is not tonic at all, but fills in for the cadential $^6_4$, a dominant function, even though Robbie Shakespeare plays $\hat{1}$ on the bass. What would look like I on the page is actually V to the trained ear.

Augmenting the discussion of linear progressions presented earlier, it should be noted that while some passages feature inverted passing and neighboring chords, providing the utmost in linear motion, rockers are certainly not above the ruder and more attention-demanding use of parallel root-position chords in passing and neighboring situations. For instance, passing root-position triads such as those noted earlier in "If Not For You" and "Tonight I'll Be Staying Here With You" are heard more often in ascent, as in the I–"II–III"–IV verse of the Beatles' "Here, There, and Everywhere" (1966) and the identically structured bridge of their "Sexy Sadie" (1968).[34] But much grosser is the rise through unremitting major triads, I–"II♯–III♯"–IV–V, heard in the chorus of Jim Croce's "Bad Bad Leroy Brown" (1973). Michael Jackson's "Billie Jean" (1983) is subtler, passing from I through "II" to I^6, all over a $\hat{1}$ pedal, in a Dorian context that allows for minor-colored I and II chords. Neighboring functions take many guises. One humorous example is the guitar's tag ending in Dylan's improvisatory and lighthearted "I Shall Be Free #10" (1964), which ornaments every verse-ending dominant with its upper neighbor (V–VI–V–VI–V–I); at song's end, the singer steps out of character to declare, "what's probably got you baffled more is what this thing here is for …," referring, of course, to the silly-because-it's-so-earnest neighbor pattern.

But more baffling to many listeners, apparently, is the use of IV as a neighbor to I. The root relationship between IV and I is not nearly as determinative of function as are the $\hat{6}$–$\hat{5}$ and $\hat{4}$–$\hat{3}$ neighbor resolutions that occur in upper voices. This embellishment to tonic often follows V, as in the blues pattern's V–"IV"–I conclusion, but never represents a harmonic move from V to IV. Once V gives way to the interrupting IV, the listener expects IV to melt into the I that nearly always follows directly, as found earlier in the Smashing Pumpkins' "Today." In other cases, V will actually sound like an upper neighbor to IV (still possessing no harmonic value), if the lack of an overriding voice-leading allows this to happen. Such an effect is created in the verse of the Kingsmen's "Louie Louie" (1963), the Stones' "Get Off of My Cloud" (1965), the Troggs' "Wild Thing" (1966), and many related songs, where I–IV–"V"–IV–I seems to form an arch of neighbor relations, IV to I and "V" to IV. But there is no harmonic progression implied between adjacent chords; only a contrapuntal relationship exists. Another interesting twist on IV and V functions occurs at the end of the chorus in Steve Winwood's "Slowdown Sundown" (1981) (1:02–1:03), where piano and bass agree that the governing harmony is the V of an authentic cadence, but the Hammond organ simultaneously sustains a neighboring IV chord throughout.

This brings us at last to the beloved ♭VII–IV–I chord succession, which I have elsewhere called the double-plagal cadence. A major staple of rock repertoires, particularly in the late 1960s, following the Four Tops' "Baby I Need Your Loving" (1964) and Martha and the Vandellas' "Nowhere to Run" (1965), the pattern is heard in such songs as Pink Floyd's "Remember a Day" (1968), the Stones' "Sympathy for the Devil" (1968) and "Midnight Rambler" (1969), Jefferson Airplane's "Volunteers" (1969), Led Zeppelin's "Good Times Bad Times" and "How Many More Times" (both 1969), the Stranglers' "Something Better Change" (1977), Dire Straits' "So Far Away" (1985), U2's "I Still Haven't Found What I'm Looking For" (1987), and Fastball's "Fire Escape" and "Damaged Goods" (both 1998). Following Jimi Hendrix's "Hey Joe" (1967), the pattern became extended (as noted by Timothy Koozin in Chapter 10), as in the Beatles' "A Day in the Life" (1967), the Stones' "Jumpin' Jack Flash" (1968), and Deep Purple's "Hush" (1968). But I think its tonal purpose and effect are fundamentally misunderstood by many. Allan Moore calls it "a cycle-of-fifths pattern [in] reverse direction" (1993, 55), removing all harmonic value from that pattern's "normal" descending direction. Commenting on my discussion of the extended ♭VII–IV–I pattern in the bridge of "Here Comes the Sun" (1969) (Everett 1997, 183), Henry Martin says, "The C–G–D–A progression illustrates rock's 'inversion' of the circle of fifths into what I have called a modal progression … . The Schenkerian view of it as a chain of neighbor motions is valid within its sphere, but it can be argued instead that some progressions found in the tonality of the last several decades do not fit comfortably within the original Schenkerian paradigm" (1998, 147, n. 8). There is nothing necessarily modal about the progression, no matter how far up in fourths it originates (one might similarly say that the raised fourth scale degree usually calls forth Lydian qualities, which it almost never does); the progressive flat-side accidentals are a consequence of the application of half-step upper neighbors to the thirds of the ornamented chords. Thus, the length of the "Jack Flash" progression, D♭–A♭–E♭–B♭, requires an addition of three flats to the mix. Yes, there is a systematic analogy to the circle of descending fifths, but this does not equate to a harmonic relationship; the roots simply provide consonant support for the neighbors.

I would offer two sorts of conditions that would support my contentions as to the contrapuntal nature of ♭VII–IV–I. The first condition would remove the bass roots of IV and ♭VII, so that triads are ornamented by neighboring $^{6}_{4}$'s. Such is the case in Elton John's piano part in "Candle in the Wind" (1973) and in Danny Federici's organ part during the chorus (0:48–1:00) of Bruce Springsteen's "Glory Days" (1984). Example 5.14 shows this succession first without consonant support (Example 5.14a) and then with "roots" added in the bass (Example 5.14b). (Compare the arch-shaped I–IV–♭VII–IV–I succession of the chorus [0:44–0:54] of Talking Heads' "And She Was" [1985], demonstrating the same neighbors-to-neighbors function as does the "Get Off of My Cloud" pattern, but simply with $\hat{4}$ held as a common tone.) A slightly more abstract hearing of this condition obtains in the verse (0:30–1:08) of

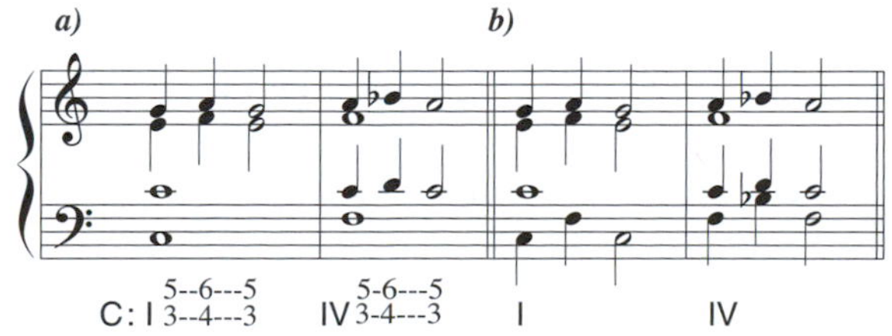

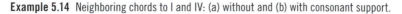

Example 5.14 Neighboring chords to I and IV: (a) without and (b) with consonant support.

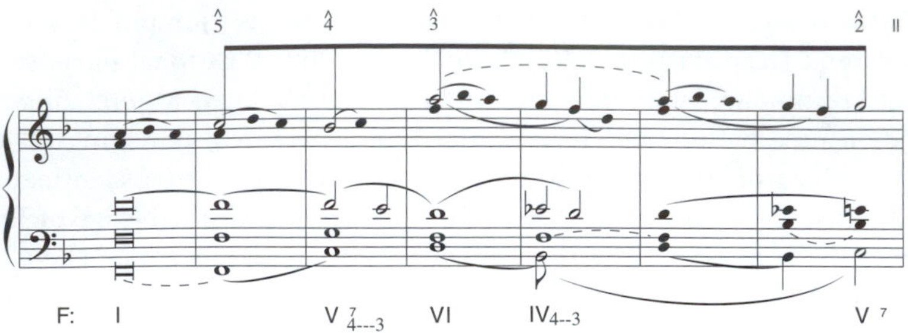

Example 5.15 Don Henley, "The Last Worthless Evening" (Don Henley) (1989): analysis.

Don Henley's "The Last Worthless Evening" (1989), sketched as Example 5.15. Here, the $IV^{4\text{-}3}$ "sounds" like ♭VII–IV because of a combined suspension and vocal neighbor; the verse's other 4-3 suspension, along with V^7, is a Henley hallmark also heard in "New Kid in Town" (1976). A second condition would substitute other discrete chords for the same functions; James Taylor's "Fire and Rain" (1970) opens with the progression C–Gm7–F–C. Would Moore and Martin argue that the root motions here are stronger than the neighbor relations in this I–♭VII–IV–I soundalike? Related substitutions appear with similar neighbor functions in the Stones' "You Can't Always Get What You Want" (1969) (whose tag, "but if you try sometime," uses a Lydian II♯ as a neighbor chord to IV in moving II♯–IV–I), Led Zeppelin's "Tangerine" (1970) (which opens with a similar but diatonic set of neighbors, II–IV–I), and the Dead's slightly more ambiguous "Here Comes Sunshine" (1973) (where ♭VII [0:28] resolves to a minor II [0:30], which moves to V [0:35–0:40] via a neighboring "I" [0:32–0:34]). Clearly, ♭VII–IV–I relies on contrapuntal neighbors, not its roots, for its identity.

I'll make reference to another of my favorite ♭VII–IV–I progressions, that heard in Carole King's "You've Got a Friend" (1971). The first chorus ends, "And I'll be there [A: $IV^{\Delta 7}$–V^{7}_{sus4}]; you've got a friend [I]." But the second chorus has a long interpolation just before the title sentiment is stated: $IV^{\Delta 7}$–V^{sus4} leads to the interruption, "Ain't it good to know that you've got a friend," set with ♭VII–IV–I. This is a major surprise, as the interrupting G♭ chord (♭VII) resolves the V^{7}_{sus4} in a deceptive way; that V7 already contains a b♭ and a d♭, and its nonharmonic fourth, a♭, resolves not to g but to g♭ to create ♭VII, which is then treated as IV of IV. Further, the drop from a♭ to g♭ is answered by a chromatic inner-voice descent that completes the idea, f–f♭–e♭–d–d♭–(c), supported by the progression, IV–IV♭–VI^7–V^9/V–V^{7}_{sus4}–(I). The ♭VII chord provides color and lines, but no harmonic function.

Modes and Mode Mixture

A good amount of pop-rock music is in a pure major mode, but probably the majority of these major-mode songs are inflected by elements from competing modes. Major modes are colored by elements of the parallel minor and vice versa in expressive ways by Carly Simon: note the Schubertian contrasts of grim minor-mode reality with major-mode dreams in "That's the Way I've Always Heard it Should Be" and "Anticipation" (both 1971), and "Legend in Your Own Time" and "You're So Vain" (both 1972). Brian Wilson uses major/minor contrasts to represent happy and sad periods in "Happy Days" (1998). But expressive mode mixture becomes far more complex. Yes's "South Side of the Sky" (1972) contrasts a major verse (0:19–2:05) with Phrygian touches (0:31–0:40) (none of the unusual shifts proving any distraction to Steve Howe's overqualified-for-Muscle Shoals funk) against a Dorian/major fantasy (3:18–3:40) ("La la la …" in parallel three-part vocalizing triads, filled with "the warmth of the sky" in Chris Squire's warm bass and Bill Bruford's bright ride cymbal), joined by instrumental Dorian/Aeolian transitions over a chromatic bass line emphasizing a composed-out arpeggiated ^{o7} chord on Rick Wakeman's concert grand (2:06–2:26, 4:17–4:37). The modal shifts work with textural contrasts to portray "the [soft] moment … lost in all the noise."

The pure (harmonic) minor mode is seldom heard in pop-rock (think of the Zombies' "She's Not There" [1964], which moves to the harmonic-minor V at structural points, but otherwise floats among Dorian, Aeolian, and Major inflections), but it is often imported from Scotch-Irish and American colonial folk sources through such traditions as learned by Sandy Denny and Joan Baez, traceable in one stylistic line to the Grateful Dead's "Jack-a-Roe" (1981).[35] The related modes, Aeolian (as in Simon and Garfunkel's "The Sounds of Silence" [1965], the Stones' "Paint It, Black" and "Mother's Little Helper" [both 1966], and the Cure's "Fascination Street" [1989]) and Dorian (the Beatles' "Don't Bother Me" [1963] and the intro and coda of Living Colour's "This Is the Life" [1990]), are well represented. The pure Phrygian and Locrian modes are probably nonexistent, but the Mixolydian is very common (as in the Beatles' "Tomorrow Never Knows" [1966], much of the Mothers' *Freak Out!* [1967], and many West Coast jams of the late 1960s, Led Zeppelin's "Whole Lotta Love" [1969], Pink Floyd's "One of These Days" [1971], Oasis' "Rock 'n' Roll Star" [1994], and Fastball's "G. O. D. (Good Old Days)" [1998], which should be compared with the Beatles' "Got to Get You Into My Life" [1966]), and there are a few Lydian examples (see the Left Banke's "Pretty Ballerina" and the Beatles' "Blue Jay Way" [both 1967]) as well. (In this volume, Lori Burns and Timothy Koozin deal extensively with the modal interpolation of ♭VII.) Most often, a nominal scale is colored by inflections from one or more of these other modes. The Beatles' "Eleanor Rigby" (1966), for instance, contrasts a Dorian verse with an Aeolian chorus; the Strawberry Alarm Clock's "Incense and Peppermints" (1967) is basically in Dorian, but is also softened by Aeolian inflections. Bruce Springsteen's "Bobby Jean" (1984) is in a major key, but has strong Lydian function as well. Major-mode songs from the Beatles' "P.S. I Love You" (1962) onward are often inflected with the inherently cross-related Aeolian

♭VI–♭VII–I cadence; examples include Gary Lewis and the Playboys' "She's Just My Style" (1966), the Stones' "Brown Sugar" (1971), Bon Jovi's "Livin' on a Prayer" (1986), and Oasis' "She's Electric" (1995). Mode mixture is so rampant and free in the music of Steely Dan that chords can have very unsettling relationships with their tonics; see "With a Gun" (1974) for a basically Aeolian song with an extensive Phrygian passage in the chorus (0:21–0:33) and later deviations toward the sharp side, some affecting the tonic triad itself. Sometimes modal convention attempts to, but cannot, fully subvert tonal function. In U2's "Heartland" (1988), for example, the verse (0:30–1:05) suggests D Aeolian, when an initial D-minor triad (over a bass G) is followed by the repeated progression, B♭–$C^{sus4\text{-}3}$, which leads not to F (the resolution suggested by such a potential $V^{4\text{-}3}$) but back to the D minor of the following verse (1:05–1:41). The eventual simple alternation of F-major and G-minor chords in the chorus (1:41–2:08)—however weakly it asserts F as tonic harmonically—fulfills the tonal expectation created in the "modal" progression and, by the way, in the direction pointed by the vocal line. To my ears, the Mixolydian, Aeolian, and Dorian cadences inflect otherwise major modes so often in rock (and less so in pop) because the lowered seventh scale degree from those modes packs a rebellious punch against the major key that the diatonic, polite, and instantly subservient dominant-supported leading tone lacks. This, I think, is probably a central factor as to why the teenagers of the 1950s unconsciously identified so strongly with rhythm and blues, which was nearly always a major-mode system with melodic inflection from either the pentatonic-minor or other modes featuring the lowered seventh scale degree.

The pentatonic-minor is probably the most common pop-rock scale other than major, but even this collection occurs quite often as a systematic melodic inflection of a governing major mode.[36] The scale is usually spelled C-E♭-F-G-B♭-C, but is alternatively C-E♭-F-A♭-B♭-C. The collections are identical in terms of intervallic content, but the lack of a half-step and the ubiquity of both minor thirds and the [025] trichord make position-finding difficult, so tonal centricity can be quite ambiguous.[37] The singer often descends through the pentatonic-minor scale in what Wilfrid Mellers (1973, 46) calls the tumbling strain—as in Carole King's "tumblin' down" in "I Feel the Earth Move" (1971). But the [025] trichord often circles aimlessly around itself—consider the vocal lines of the Kinks' "All Day and All of the Night" (1964). In the older rural blues, as with Robert Johnson, the pentatonic-minor is reserved for vocal parts and instrumental lead lines, which are nearly always supported by the major I, IV, and V triads of the major mode. (Compare George Harrison's bluesy Gretsch licks in "She Loves You" [1963] or Springsteen's Tele-Esquire licks and singing in the bridge [0:57–1:15] of "Cross My Heart" [1992].) One technique original with rock music was the heterophonic doubling in thirds and fifths of all tones of the pentatonic-minor scale so that each would be the "root" of a "major" triad (these are not functioning scale-degree roots, but rather fundamentals for Debussy-like doublings). Thus was born the parallel planing major-chord horn (or guitar) riffs of Wilson Pickett's "In the Midnight Hour" (1965), Eddie Floyd's "Knock on Wood" (1966), the "comin,' comin,' comin' around, comin' around" section (2:38–2:52) of the Dead's "Cryptical Envelopment" (1968), and the introductory riff from Creedence Clearwater Revival's "Proud Mary" (1969). The Temptations began a trend with the [025]-based major-chord succession I–♭III–IV in "(I Know) I'm Losing You" (1966) and "I Can't Get Next to You" (1969). All of these songs have a major-mode background interrupted by the pentatonic riffs and are clearly tonal, thus the appropriation of Roman numerals for "chords" that arise out of heterophonic doublings of a single line. Without the supportive major scale or very clearly directed counterpoint, tonal centricity can be hard to defend. This is a problem in some folk-based West Coast music, as in the Great Society's "Didn't Think So" (1965), and certainly in pentatonic-minor riffs with no accompanying tune, as with Red Hot Chili Peppers' "Fight Like a Brave" (1987). Allan Moore (1995, 186–187, 199) is uncomfortable in hearing ♭VII, often part of the pentatonic-minor system, as an aberrant substitute for V.[38] But as it seems to have its tonal roots in major-mode music (such as that of Buddy Holly), the ♭VII chord is often tied directly to dominant function, even when that chord is absent. The dominant, after all, has a largely contrapuntal role, in that its third, fifth, and—if present—seventh all resolve by step. So the ♭VII–I progression fulfills quite a few roles of V^7. Even Bon Jovi's dire pentatonic-minor chant, "You Give Love a Bad Name" (1986), depends on the V–I relationship.

Mixture involving the pentatonic-minor is always telling. Peter Wicke (1987, 44–46) finds Bill Haley's "Rock Around the Clock" (1955) to be rebellious. Investigation into the song's pitch content leads one to revel in the chorus's alternation of the dark, suggestive minor-pentatonic setting of "rock around the clock tonight" with the bright, innocent major-mode setting of "rock 'til broad daylight"—it's easy to see how two different sorts of rocking could have been construed. Compare the treatment of night and day in Pickett's "In the Midnight Hour"; it's not just the intrinsic dirty quality of the minor-pentatonic scale, but the contrast of its bad-boy whole-step rebellion against the squeaky-clean leading tone of the major scale, that marks the song. Pickett contains himself, marking time in the major mode of daylight, when he says he's going to wait. But when his anticipation gets the better of him, the pentatonic blue notes let go as he describes what he's going to do: "I'm gonna take you girl and hold you and do all the things I told you in the midnight hour." If the Haley number sounds so much more dated than Pickett's, I believe it's because its rockabilly melodies linger so long in that broad daylight. An opposite day/night mixture effect invokes liberation in the Lovin' Spoonful's "Summer in the City" (1966). In comparison, Chuck Berry's all-pentatonic "School Day" (1957) suggests that the anticipated world of the rock 'n' roll juke joint dominates every nook and cranny of the singer's mind; if

Example 5.16 Nirvana, "Lithium" (Kurt Cobain-Chris Novoselic-David Grohl), *Nevermind* (1991): verse.

the school day were making any impression on his consciousness, surely the major mode would be reflected somewhere, but it's not. Nirvana's "Lithium" (1991) will serve as a final illustration; see Example 5.16. Despite its anarchic power chords, this song—as do so many others of Kurt Cobain's—bows to mainstream pop; the mixture of the Beatles' "She Loves You" (1963) and "I Should Have Known Better" and "If I Fell" (both 1964) are not too distant in the background. As the verse opens, Cobain expresses unabashed happiness in the clear major mode; when Chris Novoselic's bass insists on switching to a pentatonic underpinning, rising F♮–G–A–C♮–D, the singer descends through the melodic minor scale.

The Tonal World of Power Chords

Electric amplification, as pioneered by Pete Townshend in the mid-1960s, allowed guitarists to get a tremendous amount of intensity out of playing a single pair of strings at once, especially if the interval played was as harmonically potent as the perfect fifth. Bands began to use these thirdless sonorities as "power chords," as they conveyed all of a triad's strength of mechanical perfection, often with all the position-finding scale-step identification of full chords, without the volatile, emotive coloring of a mediating third. The open fifths need not be at peak volume to have this effect. How many have noticed the vital text-supporting affects created by the open fifths played by the bass alone in the verse of the Beatles' "All I've Got to Do" and the bridge to "I Want to Hold Your Hand" (both 1963), the intro and chromatic descent (0:23–0:24) of Linda Ronstadt's "You're No Good" (1974) (on the Fender Rhodes), or the soft but harsh intro and choruses of Elvis Costello's "Alison" (1977)? (See Chapter 3 for Lori Burns's discussion of bass fifths.) And notice the pure air of emotional detachment suggested in McCartney's thirdless opening to "Yesterday" (1965); compare this with the desired effect in Living Colour's "Information Overload" (1990).

Heavy metal, new wave, punk, and grunge took power chords into new arenas, often with a reduced emphasis on tonal function. These genres are often expressed in two parts: a bass line doubled in fifths and a single vocal part. Power chord technique was often allied with modal procedure, as with the Aeolian C^5–D^5–E^5 cadence (0:25–0:29) in Black Sabbath's "Paranoid" (1971). The [025]-based post-Temptations "I–♭III–IV" pentatonic-minor riff, such as that in Deep Purple's "Smoke on the Water" (1972), G^5–$B\flat^5$–C^5, G^5–$B\flat^5$–$D\flat^5$–C^5, G^5–$B\flat^5$–C^5–$B\flat^5$–G^5 (0:00–0:50), became a mainstay, as did its half-step power-chord ornamental neighbor, repeated in the chorus (1:25–1:38) with C^5–$A\flat^5$–G^5.[39] A tonal structure often supports such superficially modal behavior, as in Blue Öyster Cult's "(Don't Fear) the Reaper" (1976). Here, dominant harmony is withheld through verses in an Aeolian repetition of I^5–$\flat VII^5$–♭VI–♭VII; this is essentially a nonharmonic, contrapuntal expansion of I with 5-6 exchange, filled in by passing motion and decked out with fifths above (and tenths in the vocal), as heard previously in Dylan's "All Along the Watchtower" (1968) and the hard-rock section of Led Zeppelin's "Stairway to Heaven" (1971). But the Chad-and-Jeremyish functional counterpoint in the chorus of "Reaper" (0:27+) includes a strong directional V (0:31–0:32) that contextualizes the structure. A similar withholding of V in the Blue Öyster Cult's "Tenderloin" (also 1976) leads power-chord fifths through a suggestive but ambiguous set of verses and choruses until V (E) finally appears at 1:49, proving A to be tonic only after the second chorus. No listener would demand a dominant in Living Colour's pentatonic-minor-based "Middle Man" (1988), but the bridge ends with a retransitional $V^{\sharp 9}$ (1:33–1:36), surely the "sign [of] something special" for which the singer, the "middle [eight?] man," the "stranger in a strange land," has been waiting. Conversely, harmonic function can be normal, but a lack of directed voice leading in the company of these parallel fifths, as in the Cars' "Just What I Needed" (1978), can create an aimless quality. These sorts of ambiguity are very similar to those caused by the breakdown of tonality through the second half of the nineteenth century, and lead to an evolutionary relationship between the "classic" pop of the 1950s through the 1970s and the sometimes quasi-atonal grunge of the 1980s and 1990s that is analogous to the sea change of tonal function over the past three centuries of art music. Much more common are tonal songs where power chords are based completely on members of the pentatonic-minor scale, as in the I^5–$\flat III^5$–$\flat VII^5$–I^5, I^5–$\flat III^5$–IV^5–I^5 settings of the doubled [025] trichord

Example 5.17 The Jimi Hendrix Experience, "Spanish Castle Magic" (Jimi Hendrix), *Axis: Bold As Love* (1968): analytical reduction.

recognition of cultural lineages that reverses the direction of Elvis's and Pat Boone's borrowings. "Elvis is Dead," in fact, rehearses the allegation that Elvis stole black music in the ironic face of praise here from cameo-guest Little Richard. "Someone Like You" has a heavy-metal lack of functional relations, Who-like rhythmic distractions from drums and bass, a totally unexpected and very white truck driver's modulation from B♭ to C♭ (portraying the meaning behind the repeated phrase, "it's never too late to change your ways"), and uses white idioms such as a rockabilly bass ostinato as a threat underneath the line "I know what to do with someone like you." A cultural emptiness is suggested by the bass ostinato's metal tritone relations in "Type," but the song's stereotype-blasting, Dylanesque sensibility is simultaneously foiled and emphasized by the highly directional tonal chorus ("this is the place where the truth is concealed"). The singer returns to his ultimate roots with the appropriation of the West African chant, "Menudi ye jewelo ogbenudo …" (1:24–1:31) sung in octaves. Tonal stylistic cues make the cultural observations absolutely vivid.

The Music of Hip-Hop

Because its lyrics are usually rapped on indefinite pitch rather than sung, the music of hip-hop is not generally considered to be as pitch-centered as are other pop-rock forms.[42] However, there is a wide variety of practices, and this portion of the essay will outline the ways in which pitch may serve a variety of functions in rap music. In its basic form, hip-hop consists of lyrics rapped in *Sprechstimme,* with pitch suggested to greater or lesser degrees in the lead vocal; this line is supported by "beats"—a rhythmic groove on drums (often electronic) and perhaps group handclaps on backbeats. (The drums are rarely tuned to each other or to the rap with any tonal impetus; the pitch suggestions in the rapped vocal come to the fore when this part is looped and heard repeatedly, as in introductory and between-verse loops often heard in the 1980s.) Additionally, there is nearly always a pitch-world that, at its most basic, may consist of split-second pitched samples of LPs scratched by a DJ, but may in more elaborate situations call for full-group arrangements with bass, guitars, and keyboards if not brass, winds, and (usually synthesized) strings. The album *Paid in Full* (1987), by Eric B & Rakim, is an effective rhythmic mix of beats, turntabling, echo, and alliterative rap. In *Raising Hell* (1986), Run and DMC often rap in a carefully worked-out hocket, trading the words of partial lines between themselves; the album's best-known track is "Walk This Way." When pitch is of little consequence, large-scale organization is achieved by lyrics divided up into stanzas (typically verses and a chorus), grand pauses that often mark the ends of sections, and sometimes contrasting equalization applied to different sections.

Tonality by assertion, rather than by functional relations, is characteristic of a lot of hip-hop. In this situation, a single chord—whether triad, seventh, or ninth chord, whether present in a sample or repeated by a live band—takes tonic status by acclamation. This is true of the major-minor seventh chords sampled in Public Enemy's "Bring the Noise" and most of their "Night of the Living Baseheads" (both 1988), and of the same sonority looped in bass, keyboard, and guitar parts in their "I Don't Wanna Be Called Yo Nigga" (1991). Band-created minor triads act as tonic in Grandmaster Flash's "The Message" (1982) and Snoop Doggy Dogg's "Gin and Juice" (1993); a $^{\flat 9}_{7}$ guitar/bass groove does so in Ice Cube's "The Nigga Ya Love to Hate" (1990), and a ♯9 chord does the same in Public Enemy's "A Letter to the New York Post" (1991).

Samples from tonal songs can run the gamut from single sonorities through looped phrases and full sections, to even entire songs given new rapped lyrics. A simple sampled melodic rising whole step, when looped and repeated as done in LL Cool J's "You Can't Dance" (1985), suggests a modal ♭$\hat{7}$–$\hat{8}$. A tonic is somewhat implied by high-register pitches that, sampled and looped, suggest ♭$\hat{7}$–$\hat{6}$–$\hat{5}$ in Public Enemy's "Terminator X to the Edge of Panic" (1988). Elements of the minor-pentatonic scale are sampled for a stronger tonal sense in LL Cool J's "I Need a Beat" (1985) and the Beastie Boys' "She's Crafty" (1986, taking the guitar riff from Led Zeppelin's "The Ocean"), and scale degrees of the major mode are heard in the sampled clarinet/bass ensemble from the Beatles' "When I'm Sixty-Four" used in the Beastie Boys' "The Sounds of Science" (1989). Tonal identity is strengthened with the addition of an electric bass; a repeated bass note supports a single repeated sampled pitch a minor tenth above in the Notorious B.I.G.'s "Hope You Niggas Sleep" (1999), and a looped gliss of C♯–C♮–B over a sustained bass F♯ suggests a tonal center of F♯ in Public Enemy's "Lost at Birth" (1991). Puff Daddy raps over a repeated minor-mode brass phrase dubbed from the *Rocky* soundtrack in "Victory" and over a looped Aeolian-mode phrase from David Bowie's "Let's Dance" in "Been Around the World" (both 1997). A major-mode phrase that dwells on minor-mode chords, taken from Bruce Hornsby's "The Way It Is," is the basis of the chorus of 2-Pac's "Changes" (1998). A two-minute a cappella performance of Samuel Barber's "Agnus Dei" is the minor-mode bed for Puff Daddy's "I'll Be Missing You" (1997), which then turns to several minutes of the Police's "Every Breath You Take" for the remainder of its underlay. The major-mode song "It's the Hard Knock Life" from the musical, *Annie*, becomes the chorus of Jay-Z's "Hard Knock Life (Ghetto Anthem)" (1998).

When a backing band exists, modes with minor-third scale degrees are preferred over their major-sounding brethren by far. The Beastie Boys' rhythm guitarist plays [025]-related power chords in both "Rhymin & Stealin" and "Fight for Your Right" (both 1986). A minor-pentatonic melody is heard in the synthesizer in Nas's "The Genesis" (1994). A bass loop of the line $\hat{8}$–$\flat\hat{7}$–$\sharp\hat{6}$–$\sharp\hat{7}$ is heard through the verse in OutKast's "ATLiens" (1996), and bass and guitar power chords repeat a I–♭VII–♭VI–♭VII riff along with reverb-soaked Led Zep-like drums in Run-DMC's "Raising Hell" (1986). Power chords in keyboard, guitar, and bass follow the minor-pentatonic scale in 50 Cent's "If I Can't." Multipart Aeolian lines from synthesizer, bass, wah guitar, electric organ, and backing vocals combine in Dr. Dre's "Let Me Ride" and "Nuthin' But a 'G' Thang" (both 1992). Full-band minor-mode phrases that could have supported the Backstreet Boys lay the groundwork instead for Eminem's "Kill You," "The Way I Am," and "The Real Slim Shady" (all 2000), and "Cleaning Out My Closet" (2002). Carlos Santana plays a minor-mode nylon-string guitar passage for Lauryn Hill's "To Zion" (1998). Mode is somewhat indeterminate in the plain fifths that double the repeated I–IV chord succession in Vanilla Ice's "Ice Ice Baby" (1990), but a major-mode texture is unimstakable in the piano/bass counterpoint of Raekwon's "Knuckleheadz" (1995).

Tonal coherence was not among the primary concerns in early rap nor, indeed, in some later rap. Grandmaster Flash's "Freedom" (1980), for instance, contrasts a bass phrase in B♭ minor with a second phrase in two trumpets moving from B♭ to C and a kazoo phrase in B major. Coolio's "Sumpin' New" (1995) similarly combines consecutive samples in different, unrelated keys. And hip-hop artists can *simultaneously* combine materials with conflicting tonal materials. In Nas's "It Ain't Hard to Tell" (1994), every part has its own pitch-class collection: the bass repeats F♯–F♮–G♯–B♭, an alto sax is looped with A–B♭–F♯, and backing vocals repeat F♯–G–D–D♭, all parts combining for a largely chromatic set with no tonal center. The Wu-Tang Clan's "Can It Be All So Simple" (1993) similarly displays different pitch collections in each part, including bass, electric piano, synthesizer, and backing vocals.

But these atonal tendencies are not characteristic of most hip-hop. Most examples are unambiguously tonal; often, even if verses are rapped, choruses are sung in a fully tonal (and usually minor-mode) syntax. This is true of

Snoop Dogg's "Gin and Juice" and "Who Am I (What's My Name)?" (both 1993), Nas's "The World Is Yours" (1994), Coolio's "Gangsta's Paradise" (1995, its sample taken from Stevie Wonder), OutKast's "Rosa Parks" (1998; the chorus is Aeolian, not minor) and "Spread" (2003), Nelly's "Hot in Herre" (2002, also Aeolian), and 50 Cent's "P.I.M.P." (2003). In 50 Cent's "In Da Club," the band supports chanted verses, all in the Aeolian mode. One phrase of the second verse of OutKast's "Ghetto Musick" (2003) approaches the style of a mellow soul ballad, but it is surrounded by rap. They sing "Roses" in E Aeolian, and "Hey Ya" (both 2003) moves from verses sung in E major to choruses sung in E minor. Whereas $\flat\hat{7}$ is an occasional neighbor to Nelly's chanted $\hat{8}$ in "Country Grammar (Hot …)" (2000), he sings the song's choruses in a major-pentatonic scale, all over an unchanging major-tonic chord. He sings "Ride Wit Me" (also 2000) completely in the major mode.

In other cases, different tonal centers are established in various sections. Public Enemy's "Night of the Living Baseheads" (1988) prolongs $I^{\flat 7}$ for much of the song, but a retransitional passage (1:53–2:10) transposes the same harmony up a semitone; the entire song thereby exemplifies a I–♭II–I structure. Their "Rebel Without a Pause" (also 1988) contrasts sections in A♭ major with others (as at 0:40-0:45) in E minor. Another harsh comparison of local tonics is made very effective in the Wu-Tang Clan's tragic "Tearz" (1993), in which an E-major sample from Wendy Rene's obscure 1964 Stax single, "After Laughter (Comes Tears)," follows verses in F minor. OutKast's "War" (2003) leads from a G-Aeolian verse and chorus through a transition (0:53–1:16) in E♭ Aeolian to a second verse in that new key. Oddly, these sections are followed by another transition and a third verse, both still in E♭ Aeolian. A song's various sections can relate organically; in Grandmaster Flash's "White Lines (Don't Don't Do It)" (1983), a "Twist and Shout"-style V^9 arpeggiation punctuates choruses for a return to tonic in succeeding verses. OutKast's "The Way You Move" (2003), however, moves from a pre-chorus that arpeggiates, in fairly determinate *Sprechstimme,* the seventh chord E♭–C–A–F, only to follow with a chorus strongly in C minor. Perhaps most like a standard tonal scheme is that of Ice Cube's "The Nigga You Love to Hate" (1990). Here, verses rapped over a funky $B^{\flat 9}_{\flat 7}$ bass/guitar groove move to a chorus in D♭ major; a minor-pentatonic retransition acts as V^7 of B♭, which then returns. Essentially, the song arpeggiates I–♭III–V^7–I in B♭. Whether tonally unified and coherent or not, these various tonal relations do emphasize their song's formal structures just as is done in more traditional pop-rock styles.

Is There Atonal Rock Music?

Other than through the few hip-hop techniques just discussed, completely atonal rock music is exceedingly rare. Occasionally, a tonal piece will be introduced by an unrelated atonal miasma, much like a Bruckner symphony though not often as aesthetically justifiable; such is the function of the wrong-note-spiked introduction to Roxy Music's "Sentimental Fool" (1975), which features a number of short whole-tone riffs in an attempt to destabilize the anticipated opening tonic. Another example, even more bizarre, is the Cure's "Strange Attraction" (1996), which opens with a sampled orchestral arpeggiation of the combinatorial [013679] hexachord, F♯–c–a–$d♯^1$–$g♯^1$–d^2; the resulting song, of course, relates to this in no way. Countless passages and whole pieces from early Pink Floyd and Soft Machine lack scale-step identity or direction-finding counterpoint in such pervasive ways as to frustrate any baseless attempts at tonal hearing—it's much better to simply float on the groove. Speaking of grooves, James Brown's "Ain't It Funky Now (Part 1)" (1969) is a remarkable Top-Forty record, probably representing the oddest pitch-world of all 1960s chart hits (it peaked at number 24 on the pop chart). Here, the bass maintains an F pedal, the rhythm guitar on the right channel simply repeats the F–G dyad, the left-channel rhythm guitar plays an ostinato involving only the A♭–B♭–D trichord, the trumpet plays from the pitch collection A–C–D–E♭–F, and the organ plays from its white-note collection, C–D–E–F–G–A–B. Extrapolating the proclivity of funk for the motion-defying concentration on a single chord, "Ain't It Funky" does away with the tonal center entirely in a timbre-based and interval-based system (note how the interval content of each of these pitch-class collections is a [usually transposed] subset of all larger collections) reminiscent of Stravinsky's late Russian style, as in the Three Pieces for String Quartet. Only electronic music (pioneered in the Beatles' musique-concrète piece, "Revolution 9" [1968]; Jerry Garcia's related "Late for Supper" and "Spidergawd" [both 1972]; and Pink Floyd's "Putney" analog sequencer in "On the Run" [1973]) defied tonal centricity with greater conviction and more powerful results before rappers such as Nas and the Wu-Tang Clan were to mimic James Brown's technique.

For me, pitch goes right down the middle of all things musical. It is hard to avoid discussing, no matter what the central musical topic might be, because pitch relations are the matter that is colorized by timbre, shaped by formal design, and measured by rhythm. Even those who agree on that basic point might disagree about just how pitches relate to each other—in the myriad tonal systems combined in the multitude of styles of rock music, the situation can be problematical. Whereas I look forward to seeing advancements in all domains of pop-rock scholarship, it is the deep understanding we can gain of pitch relationships upon which all else will hinge.

Notes

1. Since its appearance in the first edition, this chapter has been recast to such a degree as to render the original title obsolete.
2. There are, of course, conceptual forms of music, such as those investigated by John Cage and the Fluxus movement, in which pitch may be a negligible component. These experiments, however, are further from the center of the pop-rock world than they are from that of avant-garde art music.

3. Apparently, the V7 retransition does not engender the same energy level in all listeners; Richard Middleton (1990, 196) describes the long-sustained retransitional V7 of the Beatles' "Twist and Shout" (1963) [1:24–1:36] as "harmonically static"—despite the structural tension created by the arpeggiation of the dominant seventh through Lennon's falsetto and McCartney's high-pitched screams—apparently because the chord does not "change" during this period.
4. "Reach Out of the Darkness" also presents flashes of tonal interest, featuring attractive false parallel major sevenths in the motto, singer against bass, worthy of Bach; and varied suggestions of Mixolydian mode countered by the dominant major mode and by Cathy's bluesy Mama Cass Elliot-styled roulade on G$^{\sharp 9}_{7}$ in the bridge (2:06–2:10). Also intriguing is an unusual ambiguity of hypermetric accent in the "verse," whereby measures could convincingly be grouped either 4 + 3 + 3 + 3 or 3 + 3 + 3 + 4, the larger-level downbeat thus up for grabs. The latter hearing would express a resolution of incomplete three-bar asymmetrical groupings in a satisfying final four-bar symmetrical one, in line with the poetic theme of new friendship replacing a lack of caring, but this hearing is not harmonically or rhythmically dominant over the other possibility.
5. Examples from Cream are well treated in Headlam 1997.
6. Aerosmith take a different approach in "Last Child" (1976), where an extended blues form is progressively normalized: the 4 + 4 + 4 model is there stretched to 8 + 6 + 4.
7. The role of texture in the creation of thematic material is the central concern of Spicer 2004.
8. Thanks to Deborah Burton for dubbing a copy of the *Tommy* demos for me.
9. Other listeners would find later divisions as well, perhaps marking a decline [1964] and then a limited and sporadic resurgence [1969–1972] in general popularity, but these do not affect our fundamental interest here.
10. Middleton (1990, 19) finds Elvis's articulative "boogification"—a delightful term—to be a physical effect.
11. It could be argued, however, that these quotes can be taken as impersonations (as with Nick Massi's bass interjections juxtaposed against Frankie Valli's gendrically ironic falsetto in the Four Seasons' "Big Girls Don't Cry" [1962] and "Walk Like a Man" [1963]), and thus still be part of the narrator's own storytelling.
12. Sometimes this shattering can result from two double-tracked vocals by the same singer, as with the two facets of John Lennon's psyche in the Beatles' "Julia" (1968) and of Robert Smith's in the Cure's "Never Enough" (1990).
13. One might seek out Laurie Anderson's *Big Science* (1982) for an earlier appearance of such effects, which of course also have some roots in Devo (1978+). Anderson's "It Tango" comments very slyly on both *Blonde on Blonde* and *Revolver.*
14. The album's textural connection to Yes's *Fragile* is made stronger by the heavy multitracking of Corey Glover's voice in "Tag Team Partners," a corresponding reference to Jon Anderson's m.o. in "We Have Heaven."
15. For some reason—perhaps in the interest of simplicity for clearer AM-radio reception—the violin obbligato is not included in the mono mix.
16. A similar theme of anticipation ("Spend your life waiting for a moment that just don't come") is painted harmonically rather than rhythmically in the big retransition from the bridge to the chorus in Bruce Springsteen's "Badlands" (1978) (0:57–1:02).

17. Irregular meters, such as the 7/4 of Pink Floyd's "Money" (1973), cleverly enhanced by the seven different cash-register effects, one per beat, are not uncommon in rock music.
18. There is nothing metrically advanced in the other thirteen EMS songs released in their two singles and lone album (all 1967). The follow-up A-side to "My Boat," "Put Your Mind at Ease," actually has a fully regularized recomposition of the accentually displaced guitar opening of the Monkees' "Pleasant Valley Sunday" (1967), which had there artfully portrayed the difficulties of a beginning garage band attempting "Paperback Writer" (1966)-like licks.
19. Standard metric modulations are heard in the Beatles' "Lucy in the Sky With Diamonds" (1967) and "The End" (1969), and Todd Rundgren's "Cold Morning Light" (1972).
20. The material of the 3/4 transition seems to come from a passage in the Mothers' "Plastic People" (1967), also mimicked in Spirit's "Fresh Garbage" (1968).
21. Many issues concerning the art and politics of notation are thoughtfully considered in Winkler 1997. Winkler wonders how notational skills could address issues of larger scale (p. 192), but because he seems at least in part willing to put aside his transcription as soon as it's completed, he seems not to have considered what value his product might have as an adjunct tool in the analysis of the elements that combine to create the larger "unifying impulse" and in enabling a multilateral discussion of particularly complex musical issues. As I have found in my own work, the interpretation of the work has just begun with the transcription.

    Much is made of the fact that notation conveys primarily pitch and rhythmic information. Allan Moore (2001, 15) complains that in analytical presentations, "Pitch (melody and harmony) or rhythm are considered prior; texture, timbre, sound manipulation and so on are secondary." Following this argument, the next time I'm at a piano at a party and a friend asks if I'd play "Yesterday," I should sniff and respond, "I'm sorry, you'd never recognize the piece on the piano. Bring me an Epiphone Texan guitar tuned a whole step low and have a string quartet double the essential aspects of the guitar's voice leading (or really, just play whatever they like—the pitch and rhythm are secondary to the texture) and then we're in business." At the same time, of course I recognize the expressive power of what I do consider to be "secondary" musical issues, but I believe that the use of notation can enhance discussions of timbre, texture, and sound manipulation, as I've attempted to demonstrate in my essay on Paul Simon (Everett 1997, 131–141).
22. One is reminded of John Lennon's stated dissatisfaction, expressed late in his life, with how his Beatle songs—"Lucy in the Sky with Diamonds" (1967) among them—were poorly realized in the studio.
23. Regarding the "A-Mixolydian" nature of "Dark Star," see Boone 1997, particularly for the Dead's comments on p. 205, but also for the essay's larger context.
24. The "perfect listener" is my answer to those many who, since Brooks (1982, 16), have argued that music cannot be studied in isolation but that the experience of the observer must be taken into account. Short of this ideal, how could one possibly quantify the experiential history and cognitive preferences of any single listener, let alone any group of them, as the basis for the analysis of a piece of music? When we hear I–V^7–I, if we do not agree that it shares the same meaning

in "Twist and Shout" that it has in Chopin, then we cannot agree that it has the same meaning in Mozart's 40th Symphony as it has in his 41st. Everett 2004b categorizes six tonal approaches in rock music, some of which perfectly follow the Schenkerian paradigm, and others of which stray progressively, through the heavier influences of blues-based and chromatic procedures, from that domain.

25. In "Love is Here," a German sixth is applied to a cadential $^{6}_{4}$ on V of IV. The augmented-sixth chord in a tonicized area or ornamenting a chord other than V is not exceedingly rare. The one mentioned previously in "Day Tripper" is a German sixth of VI. Steely Dan's "Aja" (1977) features a French sixth (1:05) that is applied to ♭II$^{\Delta 7}$ and their "Babylon Sisters" (1980) applies a French sixth (0:28) to a IV that doesn't materialize. (For more on voice leading in Steely Dan, see Everett 2004c.) In "Along Comes Mary" (1966), the Association resolve a French sixth (0:45) to an Aeolian IV in an otherwise Dorian context. Other unconventional uses of augmented-sixth chords include the ^{ø7} sonority that resolves as an augmented sixth to IV approaching the refrain in the Beach Boys' "God Only Knows" (1966) and to IV♭ in the retransition of Billy Joel's "Everybody Loves You Now" (1971). The Beach Boys chord (heard throughout *Pet Sounds* in numerous manifestations) is transcribed in Harrison 1997, 40; I have referred to the Joel chord as the Levittown sixth in Everett 1999, Example 4.
26. Thanks to Andrew Mead for once bringing to my attention the dissonance play in this Elton John example.
27. The added-sixth chord is composed out in deep ways in Steely Dan's "Black Cow" (1977). Here, the opening tonic C-major harmony is embellished by a constant A (in bass, lyricon, and two electric guitars) that does not resolve to the G to which it's an upper neighbor until the vocal enters. The tenacity of A is rewarded in the chorus (beginning at 1:03), which brings forth the key center of A major as if an epiphany out of inebriation.
28. The "Hard Day's Night" chord (D in the bass and piano, f-a-c^{1}-g^{1} on the electric twelve-string) may have been the polychord-inspiring model for the twelve-string electric tonic chord restruck as the remainder of the ensemble moves to IV in the chorus of We Five's "You Were on My Mind" (1965), creating a non-resolving IV with ninth and major seventh ("I got troubles, *whoa-whoa*," 0:49–0:53).
29. Daniel Harrison (1997, 42–45) details the impact of linear progressions, including I–♭VII–♭VI–V, at several levels of "Good Vibrations."
30. O'Donnell 2007 shows how the chromaticism in "Victim" was inspired by Weir's hearing of Bartók's Music for Strings, Percussion and Celesta.
31. Allan Moore (2001, 37) notes the rising melodic sequence in the verse of David Bowie's "Life on Mars?" (1972). Despite the musical models that Lennon may be attempting to evoke in "Starting Over," the structure of the song's sequence is actually borrowed from the pre-chorus of the Beach Boys' "Don't Worry Baby" (1964).
32. The Smashing Pumpkins' "Soma" (1993) repeats the succession B–Em–G for nearly three minutes, suggesting B as tonic but not confirming it until its dominant finally appears as F♯^{sus4}, and then the listener is relieved by a I–V–I progression. The title of Jefferson Airplane's "D.C.B.A.-25" (1967) is simultaneously a take-off on the chemical name of a familiar substance and a cheat-sheet reduction of the song's changes; D moves to its ♭VII (C), and then B moves to its own

♭VII (A). Thus, the A chord is at first not heard as V of D, but as an applied ♭VII in a descending sequence; it gains a more potent dominant status later on in the song.

33. Suggested substitutions and elisions of functions are common in rock music, and some would be more universally understood than others. An incontrovertible instance appears in the chorus (0:37–1:14) of Aerosmith's "Home Tonight" (1976), which consists of a modified repeated phrase. The first hearing includes an applied V^7 (with 4-3 suspension) of VI that moves through an applied V of II to II^7–V; the repeated phrase manages to skip from V^7/VI directly to II, eliding through the expected functions, and continuing then to the V.
34. A Chicago-blues origin is suggested by this and other passing motions in the Allman Brothers' version of "Stormy Monday" (1971). Not only does "Stormy Monday" pass I–"II^7–III^7," but it also descends through the chromatic line of root-position seventh chords, "III^7–♭III^7"–II^7, which is somewhat of a cliché in itself, also inflecting the early bars of Wings' period piece, "Baby's Request" (1979) and the chorus of Stevie Wonder's "Whereabouts" (1985).
35. A fuller stylistic history of "Jack-a-Roe" is found in Oliver Trager's wonderful encyclopedia (1997, 211). There is, of course, a tradition of pure minor modality, blues aside, in the R&B music of Stevie Wonder and Michael Jackson; this is the heritage of the Backstreet Boys.
36. The pentatonic-*major* scale, on the other hand, such as that heard in the bass/brass break (1:06–1:23) in Stevie Wonder's "Sir Duke" (1977) and in the out-of-place chorus (0:47–0:59) in Steely Dan's "Bad Sneakers" (1975), is fairly uncommon.
37. In addition to the existence of multiple forms of the pentatonic-minor scale and other factors mentioned later in the paragraph above, one other reason that pentatonic scales lead to tonal ambiguity is their pandiatonic inclination. Unless there is a strong major-mode context underlying a given song, which is often but not always the case, the pentatonic scale is usually heard not so much as a stepwise diatonic collection (its gaps are often melodically filled in with whole-step passing tones) but as the basis of extra-triadic harmony. In other words, any of the five tones can appear against any of the other five tones without any semblance of dissonance and concomitant resolution, lacking the supportive grid of a seven-tone collection.
38. Moore also says (1995, 187) that he does not hear ♭II as a substitute for V in rock music, but this function is explicit in the Beatles' "Things We Said Today" (1964) (compare 1:04–1:09 with V and 1:11–1:16 with ♭II), and is strongly implied in the ♭II retransition of their "You're Going to Lose That Girl" (1965) (1:06–1:08). In an apparent emulation of McCartney, Alice Cooper cadences II^7–♭$II^{\Delta 7}$–I (0:14–0:21) in "Alma Mater" (1972), a very clear tritone substitution. (Rockers rarely use the major-minor ♭II^{-7} typically used by jazzers for the tritone substitution.) But even more outlandish is the use of a major-minor mediant seventh chord as a substitute for V in Stevie Wonder's "Stranger on the Shore of Love" (1985) (0:33–0:34), where the singer's line certainly implies a cadential dominant, but the $\hat{7}$–$\hat{8}$ vocal motion is supported with the exotic progression $III^{7}_{\sharp}$–I. The "real" dominant appears in the bridge's retransition (1:09–1:13).
39. [025]-based pentatonic-minor power-chord support without other counterpoint or harmonic guides to speak of can make for a much weakened, but still determinable, tonal center in such songs as the Sex Pistols' "Pretty Vacant" (1977);

Judas Priest's "Riding on the Wind," "You've Got Another Thing Comin'," and "Devil's Child" (all 1982); Guns n' Roses' "Mr. Brownstone" and "Paradise City" (both 1987); and Smashing Pumpkins' "Cherub Rock" (1993). Still tonally coherent, but a bit more destabilized than these, are Red Hot Chili Peppers' "Knock Me Down" (1989) and Soundgarden's "Mind Riot" (1991), where pentatonic-minor structures can be overshadowed by other, nondiatonic fifths that have no counterpoint above to contextualize them.

40. It bears mentioning that accent is often an important factor in determining tonal function in all contexts (but that tonal relationships are always even *more* crucial in determining metric accent), and that mere duration is never a qualifier for tonal value when harmony and counterpoint are at play.
41. Brown 1997, 161. The Glover quote comes from Charles Shaar Murray, *Crosstown Traffic: Jimi Hendrix and Post-War Pop* (New York: St. Martin's Press, 1990), 138.
42. Many musical aspects of hip-hop, including an extended analysis of Ice Cube's "The Nigga Ya Love to Hate," are well covered in Krims 2003.

References

Bailey, Robert. 1977. The Structure of the Ring and Its Evolution. *19th Century Music* 1/1 (July), 48–61.

Boone, Graeme M. 1997. Tonal and Expressive Ambiguity in "Dark Star." In *Understanding Rock*, ed. John Covach and Graeme M. Boone, 171–210. New York: Oxford University Press.

Brackett, David. 1995. *Interpreting Popular Music*. Cambridge, England: Cambridge University Press.

Brooks, William. 1982. On Being Tasteless. *Popular Music* 2, 9–18.

Brown, Matthew. 1997. "Little Wing": A Study in Musical Cognition. In *Understanding Rock*, ed. John Covach and Graeme M. Boone, 155–169. New York: Oxford University Press.

Cone, Edward T. [1960]. Analysis Today. In *Music: A View from Delft*, ed. Robert P. Morgan. Chicago: University of Chicago Press, 1989, 39–54.

Covach, John. 1997. We Won't Get Fooled Again: Rock Music and Musical Analysis. *In Theory Only* 13/1-4 (September), 119–141.

———. 1998. Popular Music, Unpopular Musicology. In *Rethinking Music*, ed. Nicholas Cook and Mark Everist, 452–470. New York: Oxford University Press.

Everett, Walter. 1997. Swallowed by a Song: Paul Simon's Crisis of Chromaticism. In *Understanding Rock*, ed. John Covach and Graeme M. Boone, 113–153. New York: Oxford University Press.

———. 1999. The Learned vs. the Vernacular in the Songs of Billy Joel. *Contemporary Music Review* 16, 105–30.

———. 2004a. Deep-Level Portrayals of Directed and Misdirected Motions in Nineteenth-Century Lyric Song. *Journal of Music Theory* 48/1 (Spring), 25-68.

———. 2004b. Making Sense of Rock's Tonal Systems. *Music Theory Online* 10/4 (December).

———. 2004c. A Royal Scam: The Abstruse and Ironic Bop-Rock Harmony of Steely Dan. *Music Theory Spectrum* 26/2, 201–235.

———. Forthcoming. *From "Blue Suede Shoes" to "Suite: Judy Blue Eyes": The Foundations of Rock*. New York: Oxford University Press.

Harrison, Daniel. 1997. After Sundown: The Beach Boys' Experimental Music. In *Understanding Rock*, ed. John Covach and Graeme M. Boone, 33–57. New York: Oxford University Press.

Headlam, Dave. 1997. Blues Transformations in the Music of Cream. In *Understanding Rock*, ed. John Covach and Graeme M. Boone, 59–92. New York: Oxford University Press.

Kramer, Jonathan D. 1988. *The Time of Music: New Meanings, New Temporalities, New Listening Strategies*. New York: Schirmer Books.

Krims, Adam. 2003. *Rap Music and the Poetics of Identity*. Cambridge, England: Cambridge University Press.

Martin, Henry. 1998. Review of *Concert Music, Rock, and Jazz since 1945: Essays and Analytical Studies*, ed. Elizabeth West Marvin and Richard Hermann. *Music Theory Spectrum* 20/1 (Spring), 141–151.

Mellers, Wilfrid. 1973. *Twilight of the Gods: The Music of the Beatles*. New York: Schirmer.

Middleton, Richard. 1990. *Studying Popular Music*. Buckingham: Open University Press.

Moore, Allan F. 1992. Patterns of Harmony. *Popular Music* 11/1, 73–106.

______. 1995. The So-called 'Flattened Seventh' in Rock. *Popular Music* 14/2, 185–201.

______. 2001. *Rock: The Primary Text, second edition* [1993]. Aldershot and Burlington: Ashgate.

O'Donnell, Shaugn. 2007. Bobby, Béla, and Borrowing in "Victim or the Crime." In *All Graceful Instruments: The Contexts of the Grateful Dead Phenomenon*, ed. Nicholas Meriwether, 38-51. Cambridge: Cambridge Scholars Press.

Scott, John W., Mike Dolgushkin, and Stu Nixon. 1990. *Deadbase IV*. Hanover, NH: Deadbase.

Spicer, Mark. 2004. (Ac)cumulative Form in Pop-Rock Music. *Twentieth-Century Music* 1/1, 29–64.

Trager, Oliver. 1997. *The American Book of the Dead: The Definitive Grateful Dead Encyclopedia*. New York: Fireside.

Wicke, Peter [1987]. *Rock Music: Culture, Aesthetics and Sociology*. Trans. Rachel Fogg. Cambridge, England: Cambridge University Press, 1990.

Winkler, Peter. 1997. Writing Ghost Notes: The Poetics and Politics of Transcription. In *Keeping Score: Music, Disciplinarity, Culture*, ed. David Schwartz, Anahid Kassabian, and Lawrence Siegel, 169–203. Charlottesville, VA: University Press of Virginia.

6
Music, Contexts, and Meaning in U2

SUSAN FAST

> The music tells you what to do and in the end that's what you gotta do. The music tells you what clothes to wear, it tells you what kind of stage you should be standing on, it tells you who should be photographing you, it tells you who should be your agent.… And so if I want to take the [sun]glasses off, I just gotta change my tune.[1]

In this comment, Bono situates musical sound at the forefront of the production of meaning in popular music, privileging it in a striking way. He takes for granted that sounds signify—a notion worrisome to many academics—and that these significations determine the appropriate contexts in which the sounds should be received. The direction of influence that Bono indicates—from music to context—is unusual and interesting to consider. In practice, the signification process is no doubt more dialectical. Certainly our reception of "the music" consists of a complex set of relationships among sounds, CD covers, radio airplay, the virtual space from which sounds have been downloaded (e.g., a featured song at the iTunes store, one of several versions available from a file-sharing program), videos, media coverage, and live concerts, not to mention our individual life circumstances at the time we consume it. Still, in the same interview Bono reiterates that his band, U2, "dress[es] in a way that is sympathetic with the music" (Light 1994, 193) and further that as the lyricist he "just tr[ies] to put into words what the other [band members] are doing with the music" (198).

Despite the self-conscious way in which Bono links U2's music to the contexts within which it is presented, it is the contexts, not the music or the connection between the two, that have received attention from writers. The music, as usual, is relegated to the background, described in general terms if at all, even in the nuanced studies of the band by John Waters and Bill Flanagan, or those by Bill Graham and Niall Stokes that catalog and annotate each album and track.[2] Here I want to begin to explore the system of significations in U2 holistically, bringing music, images, and lyrics together in an analysis that examines the band's discursive strategies from both sides of a stylistic shift that occurred with the album *Achtung Baby*. This is convenient since while there have certainly been other stylistic changes in this rich repertory (from

War to *The Unforgettable Fire*, the stylistic progression through *Achtung Baby, Zooropa*, and *Pop*, or the more recent shift back, on *All That You Can't Leave Behind* and *How to Dismantle an Atomic Bomb* to more "stripped down" rock and pop sounds, for example), the rupture that occurred with *Achtung Baby* was a particularly decisive one. Not only did the band's music change significantly, but with this album and the tour in support of it, U2 moved from a sound/text/image construction that presented their politics on the surface to one that filtered them through the distancing lens of irony. It was also with this album that their lyrics moved, generally speaking, from treating global or public themes to exploring the sphere of personal relationships more consistently and profoundly than previously, a trend that continues to the present time. The collision of these events is significant, the band turning inward at the same time that their image and, I will argue, music distanced their personal agendas from their audience, betraying anxieties about the expression of certain subjectivities in rock music (intimacy, religion, politics) that are not unique to U2.

My aim is to explore these issues through detailed analysis, treating the different musical styles as semantically rich discourses that utilize socially constructed musical codes or "conventions of practice and interpretation" (Walser 1993, 29). I take as my theoretical point of departure the excellent discussions of how popular music can function as discourse by Robert Walser, David Brackett, and Richard Middleton. I share their view that analyzing these discourses in order to learn how they achieve their effects will help us better understand their significance as cultural objects.[3] In order to contain the analysis, I have chosen two songs that represent stylistic extremes, "Sunday Bloody Sunday" (from *War*), a powerful document of the band's youthful politics, and "Zoo Station" (from *Achtung Baby*). This is a stark and artificial contrast to make, but useful, I hope, as a point of departure for the discussion of issues that arise in the band's image and music. Although my analyses of these pieces move beyond the studio versions to take into account album covers, photographs of the band, interviews, biographies, and both live and video performances, I recognize that I have still relied upon a set of sources that tend to fix the pieces in a certain way. There are, especially, many live performances of the songs that I have neither seen nor heard and so cannot comment upon, but which when considered may change the shape of these arguments, perhaps even significantly.

Context and Music I: "Sunday Bloody Sunday"

While the surface of U2's image from its inception until 1991 did not remain static, elements that lay at the core did. These include seriousness of purpose demonstrated through political and social activism, and an intensity fired by Christian morality (which encompassed the very un-rock-and-roll ethos of clean living). In their earliest days, they were known as a Christian rock band,

and biographer Eamon Dunphy (1987) recounts the tensions created in trying to reconcile playing rock music with Christian values. These characteristics were indelibly linked to the band's ethnicity—they are Irish and their concerns played out, on a general level, the powerful national tensions associated with religion and politics in their homeland. The band was (and still is) overt about its activism, especially with Greenpeace and Amnesty International (among others). They headlined a benefit tour for Amnesty in 1986, demonstrated for Greenpeace in 1992, and have encouraged fans to join both groups in the liner notes to their albums. The lyrics to their songs in the 1980s were sometimes inspired by political events. "Sunday Bloody Sunday" refers to Bloody Sunday, January 30, 1972, when British soldiers opened fire on the Irish marching in Londonderry, killing fourteen; "Bullet the Blue Sky" concerns American foreign policy toward Central America in the 1980s; "New Year's Day" was inspired by events surrounding the Solidarity movement in Poland in 1980–1981; and "Mothers of the Disappeared" refers to the Argentinean organization of that name dedicated to learning what had happened to the student opponents of the military regime of the 1970s and 1980s.[4] Bono has made brash political gestures in performance. Perhaps the two most infamous of these were his waving of a white flag during "Sunday Bloody Sunday,"[5] and making an impassioned speech about the senseless bloodshed in Northern Ireland in the film *Rattle and Hum* during a concert that was taped on the day that the IRA bombed Enniskillen, killing eleven people (Flanagan 1995, 370). During the performance of "Bullet the Blue Sky" that appears on *Rattle and Hum,* he affected his best American redneck accent during the spoken lyrics to give body and voice to the American presence in Central America. During the same performance he criticized American televangelism in a speech that culminated with the words, "The God I believe in isn't short of cash, mister."

Other powerful visual images reinforced these associations. Black-and-white photos often set the band, unsmiling, against stark backgrounds (the album cover of *The Joshua Tree* puts them in the desert, for example), and videos for songs such as "New Year's Day," "The Unforgettable Fire," and "Sunday Bloody Sunday" show the band, again shot mostly in black and white, walking through, or playing and singing in, bleak winter landscapes.[6] The photograph on the cover of the band's second album, *October,* shows band members, albeit shot in color, set against a vast, dull, grey-white sky, connecting the month not to the vibrant colors of fall, but rather the onset of winter. The first line of lyrics in the title track makes this connection explicit: "October, and the trees are stripped bare of all they wear." Black and white serves as a metaphor for simplicity, directness (honesty); color, after all, complicates things, offering range and choice. The harsh landscapes reflect a seriousness of purpose—there is no glamour or wealth displayed, no vacuous entertainment or sense of leisure; they offer a geographical metaphor for the hardship and alienation that result from a conviction to strong principles and the endurance required to maintain them. It is significant that in the photos and videos there are no "outsiders," only the band members and even, regularly, only one band member at a time (The Edge walking through the snow; Bono walking through the snow), reinforcing this idea of their alienation, their separateness.

Video from *Under a Blood Red Sky*, *The Unforgettable Fire Collection*, and *Rattle and Hum* offers Bono's moving image, arguably the most important because he is the frontman and a highly charismatic performer. He often holds his body straight, although especially by the time of *Rattle and Hum* he had the habit of bending one leg inward toward the other at the knee. This gesture weakens slightly his otherwise strong stance (the straight-held body of the male rock star is associated with power and strength), acting as a physical signifier of his vulnerability. He moves vigorously to the music, letting its energy run through him. A particularly powerful example is in *The Unforgettable Fire Collection*, when he is in the studio recording his vocal for "Pride (In the Name of Love)," throughout which he invests his whole body in each word he sings, lifting his bent arms and occasionally his legs in exaggerated gestures, his head often tilted back, the total effect suggesting ecstatic abandonment to the music. By the time of *The Joshua Tree* he had exchanged his coiffed new-wave haircut and tight pants tucked into boots for a pony tail, high-waisted pants with suspenders and vest, and bare arms that now added the idea of rural authenticity to the rest of the image. The image reflects strength, youth, a kind of vulnerable masculinity, simplicity, and deep commitment to and involvement with the music expressed through physical engagement with it.

The biography by Eamon Dunphy that covers the band from its inception through the making of *The Joshua Tree* reinforced these notions in prose, creating a narrative that glorifies band members and their high ideals. Dunphy describes Bono as "the shy, passionate man-child … so open, so exposed, sometimes strong, sometimes weak, sometimes foolish, often intuitively wise [in whom] everyone could see *themselves*, the part of themselves they were loath to expose to a brutal world" (Dunphy 1987, 253). A quote from near the end of the book is typical of the way Dunphy characterizes the band:

> Every stage of their journey has revealed a truth, about themselves or the times their music has attempted to reflect. … U2 have exited into daylight, certain now that music is a gift from God. … They belong to a generation of Irish artists which is fighting back (354–355).[7]

"Sunday Bloody Sunday" is closely identified with the image of U2 as a "political" band and with their national identity, yet the title is the only direct reference to what happened in Londonderry. The lyric does not narrate the event (the approach taken by John Lennon and Yoko Ono in their identically titled 1972 composition), but rather foregrounds its emotional impact. This is characteristic of Bono's lyric writing: what is important is the personal response evoked by the tragedy. In this case, there is the disbelief, sadness, and anger of the "I," which we tend to identify with the singer, and a "we" that might refer to three different things: the Irish people ("the trenches dug within our hearts," "how long must we sing this song"), the singer and his lover ("tonight, we can be as one"), or, in live performance, to the unity between singer (or band) and audience. Lyrically, then, the song moves through a large emotional space, touching in the process on at least two different public fronts and two or three private ones, the lines among these blurred. It is here, and in the *conflation* of public and private, that the power of the lyric resides. The same technique can be found in the lyrics to "New Year's Day," for example, in which the impressionistic description of some public event—"A crowd has gathered in black and white … Newspapers say … it's true," and so on—are set in relief to a personal relationship that somehow—we are not sure how—hinges on the public event: "And I want to be with you, be with you, night and day."

Much of the music of "Sunday Bloody Sunday" is strongly coded to contradict the lyric's message. The musical gesture heard first is on the drums alone (an instrument long associated with the military); the snare pattern is modeled on the "roll-off" of military marching bands, a cadential pattern used to keep marchers in step.[8] The instrument is close-miked and there is no reverb, so that the sound seems to be unmediated, reaching the listener directly. In 4/4 time, the snare and bass drum play *on* every beat, with the roll-off occurring as a pickup to the beat; the first guitar riff heard is also beat-oriented. It is, typically for The Edge, an arpeggiation of a triad using straight eighth notes, and the sound of the guitar is bright and big. The rhythm guitar riff emphasizes straight eighths on beats one and three of every bar while the bass articulates all beats once, sustaining through the strong beats and clipping the weak. These are all exceptionally strong and direct musical gestures. Even when syncopation is introduced (with the violin in verse three), it hardly disrupts the strong flow of the music, because it is momentary, and because this musical gesture also quickly reverts to straight eighths. (This instrument also sounds like the fiddle of Irish folk music, helping to situate the music nationally and politically.) It is not surprising that "Sunday Bloody Sunday" was taken by some to condone a continued violent solution to the political and religious turmoil in Northern Ireland, when in fact the opposite was intended.[9] Aggression is strongly encoded in the sound, so that the use of these musical gestures to convey a message of nonviolence—which is made clear in the lyric "I won't heed the battle call"—is contradictory, confusing. The sonic landscape of this song is also a rearticulation (see Middleton 1990, 8–11) of several important elements from punk: the sparseness of the texture, orientation toward the beat and lack of syncopation which drive the music forward (Laing 1985, 63, calls this the "rhythmic monad" of punk) and rawness of the guitar timbre are all derived from the punk sound (Laing 1985, 61–63), which was coded as aggressive.

The strong sound of the opening is offset when Bono enters, humming, with his mouth clearly closed. This is a personal musical gesture, the only one he makes in the song, keeping the music momentarily inside of himself before opening up for the rest of the piece, which he sings using a loud chest voice and a medium-to-high register (the melody stays above middle C). These two different uses of the voice connect the music to the private/public spheres of the lyric. The voice is not double-tracked, little or no reverb is used, and although a short countermelody is sung at the word "tonight," there is no other harmonizing of Bono's voice. So it, like the drums, appears to be unmediated, direct, honest.[10] The vocal sound is characteristic of Bono's singing until *The Unforgettable Fire*, specifically the title track of that album. The open, full sound signifies a sureness of intent, an unwavering commitment to the message, a sustained level of intensity and strength, and an emotional vulnerability. The vocal quality does not change much throughout the song, and Bono doesn't use distortion to convey extreme power or emotion. One could, in fact, characterize the general timbre of his voice as warm and hence comforting or soothing. The contour of the melody reinforces this openness. The defining melodic gesture of the verse is a rising major sixth ("and make it [go away]"), which opens up the range; the chorus begins on this high pitch in the melody and descends, eventually by a fifth. "New Year's Day" works in a similar way, the "hinge" of the melody being the rising minor seventh with which each verse begins, signaling an emotional openness right from the beginning. In a related way, the melody of "Pride (In the Name of Love)" opens up at the beginning of the chorus, which jumps up a minor seventh from the last note of the verse.

There are two further musical details in "Sunday Bloody Sunday" that are worth considering for the way in which they convey the band's ideology. The first has to do with contrapuntal movement. On the word "tonight," Bono sings a rising fifth, from C up to G, while the bass plays the tonic A against this, creating the dissonance of a minor seventh on the downbeat, which is recontextualized when the bass moves to C. This dissonance also occurs during the chorus, when with the word "Sunday," a G is sung against the A in the bass. He creates a similar pungent dissonance when twice, on the words "street" and "won," he falls to the pitch E against F in the bass; these dissonances come at the end of a phrase in each case and remain unresolved. On one hand, they serve to intensify the lyric's message, acting as musical metaphors for the dissonance of military violence. But together with Bono's desperate tone, they also tell the listener that this singer thinks there is a great deal at stake in his message, that he is completely invested in it, and that he will use extreme means to deliver it—a kind of musical analogue to the extreme physical conditions of the album covers and videos. And like those visual images, this use of dissonance is another sonic manifestation of Bono's (and by extension the band's) individuality. He introduces conflict into the contrapuntal relationship between voice and instruments not once, but consistently and at key places, and allows this conflict to remain unresolved.

The other important musical detail has to do with the harmony that occurs at the end of the chorus the first and third times it is heard. The repeated harmonic sequence, I–III–VI (A–C–F in the bass), heard throughout both verses and chorus, has been constantly reaching upward, adding to the sense of urgency in the song. But the chorus ends with a descending cadential figure that moves in the bass from F (VI) through E♭, D, and then to C, momentarily tonicizing C (the progression is ♭III–II^{7}–I in C). This modally derived progression of parallel-moving chords emphasizes the flatted third and seventh scale degrees in the first chord (E♭ and B♭, both blue notes in C), darkening the melody, but the progression ends on a C-major chord, with its brilliant Picardy-like E♮.[11] The rhetorical effect is the same as that produced over the past four centuries: a change of affect from darkness to brightness. The descending motion of this cadential figure also relaxes the tension, and during the harmonic shift the raw sound of the riff is suspended as well. Instead, Edge plays an arpeggiated pattern of electric-guitar harmonics, and the acoustic guitar is foregrounded, especially on the C-major chord. Larry Mullen keeps the beat going on the bass drum and cymbals, but there is no snare used, the military rhythmic pattern having been suspended. The cadential C-major chord lingers for a moment, before it is replaced, without any preparation, by the original Aeolian mode and the main riff of the piece.

The harmonic shift and instrumentation refocus the rhetoric of the line "Sunday Bloody Sunday" from outrage to momentary resignation and finally to the suggestion of peace brought about by the brightness of the major chord, the repose or restfulness on that chord, and the general movement away from the predominant "minor" modality to the "major." If the message of the lyric did not get through to people because of the strong way the military was encoded in the music of the verses, it should have shone through brightly during this moment when the code changes so dramatically. The band's idealism is beautifully encapsulated in this simple musical gesture.

Contexts and Music II: "Zoo Station"

On the surface, *Achtung Baby* and Zoo TV negated the image U2 had previously constructed. The German word in the album's title and the several references to "Zoo," (the Zoo TV tour, "Zoo Station," and eventually the title of the following album, *Zooropa*) allude to Berlin in 1989, the time of the city's reunification. The band traveled there in the wake of the Wall coming down in order "to seek inspiration and renewal at the celebration of the end of the world [U2] grew up in" (Flanagan 1995, 1). "Zoo" refers to Berlin's city center, which revolves around an actual zoo (the Zoologischer Garten), from which the main train station (Zoo Station) and several businesses in the area take their names. But it is difficult, at least for an English speaker for whom "zoo" also connotes craziness or chaos, not to find it particularly appropriate that this vibrant, noisy, wild urban area is known by this name.

The title of the album, *Achtung Baby*, set the new tone, weakening the force of the German imperative (attention!) through its juxtaposition with American slang. Never previously interested in elaborate stage designs or concepts for their live show, the set U2 created for Zoo TV consisted of thirty-six video screens, some of which were the largest ever built to that point (until the video wall they had built for the *Popmart* tour superseded them), foregrounding a technology that fed the audience a barrage of disconnected words and images from various media—in glorious color. (One intended effect was to satirize the information age.) Above the stage hung four Trabants—"those cheap little East German cars that U2 saw abandoned along roadsides after reunification" (Flanagan 1995, 33)—dangling from the rafters, their headlights serving as spotlights. Just before the encore, one of the video screens sported the hammer and sickle of the Soviet flag and a cartoon figure (also seen on the *Achtung Baby* CD as well as the cover of *Zooropa*) who sings a "Fanfare" from a recording called *Lenin's Favorite Songs*; these symbols of communism (like the German imperative in the album title) have been weakened in this context to the point of absurdity.[12] Bono appeared in black bug-eyed sunglasses, dyed black hair, and tight black leather, assuming a character he called "The Fly," through which he satirized the self-possessed, arrogant rock star.[13] In the film *U2 Zoo TV Live From Sydney*, The Fly appears at the beginning of the concert after the arresting opening video montage, and sonically to the strains of the climactic moment of Beethoven's "Ode to Joy" when the chorus is strained to its breaking point singing "und der Cherub steht vor Gott" (and the cherub stands before God). The Fly is elevated slowly on a moving platform, in silhouette and profile, perfectly still, a blue screen behind him (clearly intended to represent a video screen). At the beginning sounds of "Zoo Station," The Fly staggers to life. Again, the powerful images and sounds—the grandiose technology, the seriousness of particular images (some of them from the Nazi propaganda film *Triumph of the Will*), and Beethoven's music—are satirized by being put to service in the introduction of a debauched rock star.[14]

The Fly's physical gestures are slow, his body is mostly bent (at the knees, at the pelvis), and he strikes poses that seem as though he's throwing his body into spasm. Yet there is an easy flow to these movements; they are languid, limp, and sensuous in the same way as those of his main model for this character, Jim Morrison. His relationship with his body is diametrically opposed to that of his earlier persona; his bent limbs, especially the knees, signify weakness, a loss of power, a physical caving in that is associated with decadence (being drunk or stoned, or suffering from a lack of sleep, all conditions leading to a lack of physical control). In effect, he has shifted his physical balance in a radical way in order to express his character.[15] He is smoking a cigarette, which he casually tosses away before he begins to sing. During the song he poses for the cameras of adoring fans, and when he finishes singing, he checks his watch for the time in a gesture that signals his boredom with the whole scenario, gives a tired peace signal to the crowd, and turns and walks away from them.

The Fly masks Bono's eyes with sunglasses, setting up a barrier between himself and his audience; the rest of his costume encodes rock and roll (Flanagan 1995, 31, notes that the leather suit conjures up not only the image of Morrison, but that of Elvis at his 1968 comeback television special), as well as rebellious youth in general (like James Dean). These signifiers also align him with the powerful sexual attractiveness of Elvis, Morrison, and Dean, still alluring to women, who voted The Fly "sexiest male artist" in *Rolling Stone*'s 1993 readers' poll.[16] But The Fly's construction of masculinity is not vulnerable at all: he is self-assured, tough, streetwise. His former image is transformed through his feigned disinterest in his fans and in what he is doing, through indulging his ego in the camera, through his weak physical balance, and also through the presence of the cigarette, which serves as a code for transgression, especially for someone whose image was formerly built around clean Christian living.[17]

There has been a rich, polysemous analysis made of Zoo TV by journalists and band members themselves. There was a backlash against the band that occurred in the wake of *Rattle and Hum*, the album previous to *Achtung Baby*, and its accompanying quasi-documentary film of the same name made in 1988. With *Rattle and Hum*, there was criticism of what was perceived to be the band's pretense, moralizing, and self-importance. *Rolling Stone* summarized some of the response to the album as follows:

> [*Rattle and Hum*] drew the kind of flak that until now U2 had avoided. A *Rolling Stone* reader wrote in to say that the album will be remembered as "the downfall of a great band." *The New York Times* greeted the album's release with a review—headlined "When self-importance interferes with the music"—that describes the album as "a mess...." And in the *Village Voice* Tom Carson wrote, "By almost any rock and roll fan's standard, *Rattle and Hum* is an awful record. But the chasm between what it thinks it is and the half-baked, overweening reality doesn't sound attributable to pretension so much as to monumental know-nothingness." Others painted a similarly unflattering portrait of U2 as a humorless, self-satisfied band, trying to boost its own image by aligning itself with the giants of American roots music (Pond 1994, 146).

The response of the band was to radically reinvent themselves. As Brian Eno, one of the producers of *Achtung Baby*, put it: "Buzzwords on this record were *trashy, throwaway, dark, sexy and industrial* (all good) and *earnest, polite, sweet, righteous, rockist* and *linear* (all bad)" (Eno 1994, 166).

As I mentioned earlier, the band's inclinations to deal with social and political issues took a back seat to the more personal politics of intimate relationships for many of the tracks on this album. But the music, which I will discuss momentarily, and the spectacle of Zoo TV were as politically charged—if not more so—than ever. The concept of Zoo TV has been explained as a kind of meditation on the fact that "There is no more line between news, entertainment, and home shopping" on television, which was brought home to the band in a horrifying way during the first Gulf War: "Bono sits at the TV transfixed, amazed that CNN is broadcasting the war live twenty-four hours a day.… He turns on a movie, switches to the war for a while, over to MTV, back to the war" (Flanagan 1995, 18). "It's revenge," explained Bono. "Rock and roll has always been the sound of revenge and that's our revenge, to take all of this bullshit that's coming at us in this wave of information and advertising and just kind of surf[ing] it" (*Egos and Icons*, Tokyo, 1993). Artistically, the innovative use of technology in and of itself, coupled with an ironic commentary on technological overload, was a great achievement.

For Bono, who had regularly shared intensely personal feelings with his audience, a disguise seemed necessary after the onslaught of serious criticism of his image. Adam Clayton summarized it as follows:

> I think that when Bono decided to redefine himself as the Fly, as a public persona, I think he already knew he'd … become a caricature. So, rather than expose himself to that extent, he said, "Well, okay, let's give the media something that I don't particularly care about, that allows me to do certain other things but isn't me." And I think that's what happened with Zoo TV and the Fly character. … I think the real Bono is kinda harder to find now (quoted in Waters 1994, 114).

This explanation, however, tends to over-romanticize the gesture, and Bono himself has given other reasons for assuming theatrical personae: "I enjoy some of the more absurd sides of rock and roll; and I used to be shy of that, I used to kind of hide from it. I was afraid that the bullshit would kind of overtake us. And it did! But now I think it's OK. You actually find out that you like some of the bullshit. I mean, some of it's fun" (*Egos and Icons*, n.d.). He adds, "I found in amongst the trash to be a great place to develop my loftier ideas, and a great disguise as well" (quoted in Flanagan 1995, 81). Bono here follows other rock frontmen who have assumed alter egos for the purpose of exploring various facets of the human psyche—David Bowie is the prime example.

Band members have also tried to downplay any political, artistic, or otherwise "serious" intentions in developing Zoo TV, keeping with their desire to lighten things up, reasoning that from a purely practical point of view, there must be a certain amount of spectacle in order to make a stadium show work. Larry Mullen's comment is typical of what band members have said about this:

> You can't expect people to stand in a stadium and watch four people on stage perform I don't think anymore; I think those days are gone.

> You've got to have something else. And there's no doubt we're pushing the envelope. We've created monsters and tried to have a bit of fun with it. People talk about the irony and confusion, people confused about what U2 are doing. We're doing the same thing, it's just the wrapping is different (*Egos and Icons*, Winnipeg, 1997).

I chose to analyze the music to "Zoo Station" in part because it is the song with which Zoo TV opens, linking it to the show's concept and the "Fly" character, and partly because it is the first song on the album *Achtung Baby*, the first musical expression of the band's stylistic shift. There are several ways in which the music and lyrics correspond with the spectacle of Zoo TV. Perhaps the most obvious connection is the way the song, and indeed the sound of the entire album, is shaped by a use of technology new to the band. Many of the sounds are heavily processed (especially the guitar) or synthesized. There is also an affectively dark quality to the album, a product of the production—especially the foregrounding and timbre of the bass. There is a precedent for dark, technologically innovative albums such as this coming out of Hansa Studios in Berlin, where part of *Achtung Baby* was recorded. U2's producer, Brian Eno, long associated with rock's avant garde, produced David Bowie's "Berlin Trilogy" (the experimental albums *Low*, *Heroes*, and *Lodger*) there. Bowie in turn produced Iggy Pop's *Lust For Life* there, so *Achtung Baby* is associated, both musically and extra-musically, with a particular rock aesthetic. "The Berlin of the Thirties," Eno writes, "decadent, sensual, and dark—resonating against the Berlin of the Nineties—reborn, chaotic, and optimistic.... The record came to be seen as a place where incongruous strands would be allowed to weave together and where a probably disunified (but definitely European) picture would be allowed to emerge" (Eno 1994, 166).

But, in fact, it seems as though the band is unsure what to do with the technology they have found at the beginning of "Zoo Station." The piece opens with several different guitar sounds that radically mask the identity of the instrument. The eighth-note pulse is kept by a sound that reminds me of a clock ticking; this is the only sound that is rhythmically or melodically "regular." The meter of the song is 4/4, and the glissando riff that enters on the second half of the third beat overshoots the octave by a major second in its descent before sliding back up to it, the clumsiness of this gesture being magnified by its huge volume. An "explosion" sound occurs twice on beat four of every second measure, establishing a pattern that seems as though it might be maintained, but the third time it anticipates its regular entry and comes in directly after the guitar glissando, on beat two. The drums hit the pickup to one confidently, then stop, then start again. It is only when the bass enters that things finally settle into a regular groove (and if one hears the entry of the guitar glissando as marking the beginning of a series of four-bar phrases, the regular groove begins two bars early). Most of the other songs on this album also have introductions that seem to be "about" the technology itself. "Who's Gonna Ride Your Wild Horses" is probably the best example, although "The Fly," "Until the End of the World," and "Trying to Throw Your Arms Around the World" are also arresting in this respect. Unlike "Zoo Station," in the latter three examples one can recognize the sound of the guitar, yet it is heavily effects-laden, and the gestures that begin these pieces have little to do with the rest of the song. ("Zoo Station" is the exception, since the guitar glissando becomes a main riff in the tune and the part that overshoots the octave, ascending from G to A, becomes the bass riff for the verses.) In these cases, such gestures become a kind of technological assault on the listener, acting as the audio equivalent of the giant video screens of Zoo TV.

The opening of "Zoo Station" makes a powerful statement. In its deliberate use of "industrial" sounds that remind us not at all of conventional instruments, in the foregrounding of technology at the beginning of the song—indeed, in making this the opening statement of the album—there can be no mistake that U2 has embraced sound resources new to them. But the fact that it is a deliberately hesitant gesture puts it clearly in the realm of satire. Perhaps it satirizes the technology itself, or U2's new embracing of technology. Edge offered the following explanation for the change in the band's sound with *Achtung Baby*:

> We're at a point where production has gotten so slick that people don't trust it anymore.… We were starting to lose trust in the conventional sound of rock & roll—the conventional sound of the guitar, in particular—and, you know, those big reverb-laden drum sounds of the '80s or those big, beautiful, pristine vocal sounds with all this lush ambience and reverb. So we found ourselves searching for other sounds that had more life and more freshness (quoted in DeCurtis 1994a, 213).

This frame that Edge constructs around the exploration of new sounds is striking. The sounds in which he has lost trust are mediated by technology to make them sound big, open—they invite the listener into the spaces (Middleton 1990, 89), making the texture vulnerable. (It is not only U2's earlier music that has this sound—it was typical for a great deal of 1980s pop.) The way technology is used in pieces such as "Zoo Station" closes up these spaces, providing a sonic barrier between performer and audience, much as Bono's "Fly" mediates between them.[18]

The lyrics to this song play with images and ideas not heard before in U2. At one level, the lyric can be taken as a commentary on the band's new musical direction, stating and elaborating the idea "I'm ready for what's next." But further than this it explores the possibility of personal transformation through decadent means. The line "ready for the shuffle, ready for the deal" signifies willingness to take risks, to gamble; "ready to let go of the steering wheel," to throw caution to the wind; "ready for laughing gas," bizarre or "unnatural" physical transformation; and "crawling around on my hands and knees," a slightly more extreme version of The Fly's weak balance. The image of station and train brings the lyric in line with the industrial or urban sound of the music. The references to "you" and "your love" seem gratuitous in this lyric; it is about "I," not relationships. Invoking "you" seems intended here as an empty cliché—what is expected in a pop song, what the singer should deliver, but in which he has no investment. This offers a stark contrast to many of the highly personal lyrics that follow on this album. The lyrics to "Zoo Station" reflect the character of Bono's alter ego (as do, I would argue, those of the next song on the album, "Even Better Than the Real Thing").

Whereas "Sunday Bloody Sunday" moves from a close-mouthed vocal gesture to openness, "Zoo Station" does the opposite; it begins with Bono vocalizing with open throat (albeit much further back in the mix than in earlier songs), in his characteristic full-out singing style, but this quality is replaced by a vocal that has been so processed that it is difficult to recognize as Bono's. Again, it is the technology that is foregrounded, and it puts up a barrier between singer and listener. It sounds as though Bono is struggling to get through this barrier, as if it is holding him back. Although he is singing in a medium-to-low part of his range, the processing (filtering) has taken the bottom out of the sound, usurping a lot of the power of Bono's voice, emasculating it. This loss of power is also apparent in the wavering tone. Bono might be saying that "he's ready" to take on new challenges, but the sound seems to be relating a different message—one of struggle and uncertainty, just as the sounds in the instrumental introduction to the piece did. This incongruity between the lyric and its musical delivery is ironic.

"Zoo Station" is organized in verse/chorus form. The music of the verse is claustrophobic, not only because of the processing of Bono's voice, but also because the bass riff is quite static, moving only between I (A) and ♮VII (G), except for one instance, during which the harmony shifts to IV (D). During the verse, the bass becomes dynamic, creating a melodic line of its own in descending quarter notes, G–F♯–D–C–D–C–A–G–A, all on the beat, opening up the melodic space of an octave. It is during the chorus that Bono's open-throated vocalizing also returns, both musical gestures moving the song momentarily out of technology's claustrophobic grip.

Bono introduces vocal colors and techniques on this album that he has used before in only a limited way and to different effect. Two of these become guiding principles of a vocal style that match the new sound of the music and Bono's alter ego. The first is his utilization of a lower range than previously. In "Zoo Station," this is not so much exploited in the sung part, but in the lines he speaks during the chorus, and also during the middle-eight section, during which he repeats the lines "It's all right … hey baby," in a deadpan monotone, satirizing the clichéd words (the same kind of pop cliché as the "you" he invokes earlier) that have been delivered with enormous intensity countless times in other pop songs, through the inflection and range of his voice and through the absurd number of times he repeats them.

Bono first extended his vocal range downward in an appreciable way in "With Or Without You" from *The Joshua Tree*.[19] In that song, he stays below middle C for the first two-and-a-half verses, centering the melody on the mediant scale degree (F♯), but dropping an octave at the end of each stanza from A to A, the lower pitch bordering on the bottom of his range. On *Achtung Baby* this same range is used on "Even Better Than the Real Thing" and "Until the End of the World," which once again circles around the pitch F♯ below middle C, regularly dipping to the C below. He frequently uses breathy and subdued colors in his lower range, although there is a range of these, from a song like "Until the End of the World," where a full, quite brash tone is heard, to what J. D. Considine has rightly characterized as "Bono's conspiratorial whisper" in "The Fly" (Considine 1992, 729). This low and sometimes breathy singing is a remarkable change from Bono's previous use of his voice. If the earlier open-throated sound signifies emotional nakedness, youth, and unbridled idealism, the low voice belongs to an older man—or perhaps a man as opposed to a boy. It is on the one hand more relaxed, less intense (in the same way) as the earlier sound and, coupled with the lyrics that are being sung, more skeptical or distrustful, perhaps slightly cynical or ironic. There is less abandon in the voice. It is more considered, reflective, and above all, because it is not strained in any way, it signifies a kind of "cool" that the open, full-throated technique of singing does not. Bono continued to explore this rhetorical use of the low range, occasionally taking it to extremes on *Pop*, where increasingly dark and introspective lyrics seem to have pushed him into ever lower, breathier ranges. The result is that his vocals are often much less foregrounded on that album (for instance "Mofo," in which the opening verses are nearly spoken in a raspy, breathy, low voice, or the ballad "If You Wear That Velvet Dress," which begins with him speaking/singing so low in his range—E♭, an octave plus sixth below middle C—that his voice is sometimes reduced to a mumble). This connection between introspection and a low, breathy vocal range might be viewed as a quite literal construction of what Robert Walser calls musical interiority, the deeper, darker, quieter voice representing a "socially grounded experience of inner, personal 'depth'" (Walser 1997, 271). It is clearly a conscious decision on the part of the singer to develop a new kind of emotional landscape for some songs; he does not use it all the time by any means. For example, the ballad "One" on *Achtung Baby* is sung in a more balanced or "medium" range, with a full, warm sound and no breathy quality at all, as is the ballad "Stay (Far Away So Close)" from *Zooropa*.[20]

Another device that he exploits for the first time on *Achtung Baby* is what I'll call the "double voice": doubling the vocal line at the octave.[21] This is used on the chorus of "Zoo Station," and it is used throughout "Even Better Than the Real Thing," the verses of "Mysterious Ways," "Trying to Throw Your

Arms Around the World," and many other songs on *Zooropa* and *Pop*. This use of the double voice often combines the low voice with the earlier full and open sound at the octave (as in "Even Better"), or Bono uses falsetto for the high voice ("Mysterious Ways").[22] The two voices are sometimes not used simultaneously, but at separate points within the same song, to create registral and timbral contrasts. "The Fly" is an example of the octave distinction used to differentiate the voices of verse and chorus, but a different use occurs in "Until the End of the World," where prior to the third verse (following the guitar solo), Bono interjects the words "love, love," which he repeats several times, on F♯. This is an octave higher than the pitch on which he has centered the rest of the melody, introducing through this gesture a contrasting idea in the poetic text and vocal character to deliver it. Since the lyrics of this song have been interpreted as Judas speaking to Christ, the interjection might, in fact, belong to Christ.[23]

In either case, the octave separation creates two distinct kinds of discourse, because the sound and expressive characteristics of the voices are unique and each has its own semantic code. The use of octave separation, as opposed to having the voice sing harmony, is significant, because it creates voices that are simultaneously the same and different. We recognize the pitches of the octave as distinct, yet we also speak of "octave equivalence." Harmony signals a much clearer kind of difference. One way in which the double voice can be interpreted in U2's recent music is as a vehicle for irony, since the very definition of irony is that of double meaning: the literal meaning and the ironic one. As I've suggested earlier, it seems to me that the low voice is the ironic one: cool, wise, considered. Since both voices belong to Bono, the technique also complicates his identity and his position (ironic or not?) with respect to the lyric.

There are many precedents in rock music for the ways that I have interpreted both the low and double voices. Low, cool voices that have encoded irony and/or danger belong to Lou Reed, Iggy Pop, and Marianne Faithfull. And there is a rich use of double voicing in how I've described it earlier in Pink Floyd: The cool, low, ironic voice of David Gilmour contrasts with his strained voice singing an octave higher on *Wish You Were Here*'s "Welcome to the Machine," the lyrics of which are clearly ironic (the record industry mogul talking to the young artist he's recently signed), or the chorus to "Young Lust" from *The Wall*, or, in a different kind of incarnation of this technique, the children who sing an octave higher than Gilmour on "Another Brick in the Wall, Part II," also from *The Wall*.

Since octave doubling is a common technique in all types of popular music, there are also plenty of examples where its use might signal something other than irony. Metallica's "Enter Sandman" and the Police's "Bring on the Night," to choose two examples from among hundreds, are songs in which I wouldn't consider the technique to be signifying irony (just what it might signify in those songs is the subject of another essay). In fact, there are instances of the double-voice technique on *Achtung Baby* that I would not consider ironic, such as during the verses of "Mysterious Ways."

Although I have tried to argue for a strong music/context congruity in U2, I don't want to suggest that it is completely static. Zoo TV itself challenged this congruity in a profound way. As with most rock concerts, both new and older musical material was included in the show, so that the old songs were recontextualized within the Zoo TV frame. It is clear from seeing the show that there was an understanding of and sensitivity toward the problems this might create on the part of U2, and they tried to accommodate songs that did not fit the Zoo TV context in various ways. In *U2 Zoo TV Live From Sydney*, Bono signals a change out of the Fly character by taking off his bug sunglasses at the beginning of the fourth song, "Mysterious Ways" (he doesn't put the glasses back on, so presumably The Fly never returns), and the impact of this seemingly small gesture is tremendous. The audience can suddenly see the expression in his eyes, making him emotionally accessible (and vulnerable) again. The band distances themselves physically from the entire Zoo TV spectacle when they move to the "B" stage (at the end of a ramp that extended out into the audience) for a set that, except for Lou Reed's "Satellite of Love," used no theater or special lighting, foregrounding only the band and music. And although the band moved back to the main stage for "Where the Streets Have No Name" and "Pride (In the Name of Love)," the video screens were used in a much more conventional way than previously, showing the band performing, clips of the "Streets" video, and, in the case of "Pride," part of a speech by Martin Luther King (and Bono had by this time also exchanged his leather jacket for a black cloth suit jacket).

Much greater dissonance between music and context occurred in the encore, in which Bono was once again transformed, this time into an incarnation of the devil that he called Mr. MacPhisto. Two songs from *Zooropa* that correlate with the new image (the satirical "Daddy's Gonna Pay for Your Crashed Car" and the playful "Lemon") were sung, but these were followed by "With or Without You," a beautifully poignant, intense, and *serious* love song, with Bono still in his MacPhisto attire—a kitsch gold sequined suit, red shirt with front ruffle, devil horns, and pancake makeup. Bono gets rid of his devil horns right before "Lemon," but unlike the gesture of removing his Fly sunglasses earlier in the show, this does not transform him very significantly; the other visual markers of his character are too strong to negate the image. The recontextualization of the song can work, however, because Zoo TV was clearly *theater*, in which the audience was led through a narrative constructed by the visual events in combination with the running order of the songs. In this new context, the old songs are put to service in the creation of this narrative. There is real pathos to MacPhisto's melodramatic performance of "With or Without You." The strong music and lyrics transform the cocky devil's attitude, forcing him to become reflective, the repeated line "and you give yourself away" now possibly serving as a metaphor for selling one's soul instead of—or as well as—losing oneself in a personal relationship. The music/context relationship here can be radically renegotiated depending on how the song is used in performance.

At the beginning of this essay I alluded to an anxiety that I believe exists in rock music culture concerning the expression of certain kinds of subjectivity such as the idealism that U2 cultivated in their early years. John Waters writes that from the beginning, U2 "denied the pretence of rebellion and indifference, and openly expressed their interest in a different world.… A word that cropped up frequently in descriptions of U2's demeanor and outlook was 'naïve'" (Waters 1994, 48). *Rolling Stone* journalist Elysa Gardner describes U2's early music as "stress[ing] communion over segregation, compassion over blame, hope over despair" (Gardner 1994, xiv), attributes that were initially eagerly accepted by a legion of fans and the rock press, but:

> There had been some, of course, for whom the social and spiritual consciousness of the band's songs had always bordered on self-consciousness, or even self-righteousness, and for whom its over-the-top delivery had been a bit rich to the taste. But [with the success of *The Joshua Tree*], now that U2 and its music seemed to be everywhere … its image, whatever messages it was sending out took on an added dimension of grandiosity. Not helping matters was what many saw as Bono's messianic posturing during concerts (Gardner 1994, xxii).

Gardner herself, after praising the early U2, recalls a review that she wrote about *Rattle and Hum*, in which she described the album as "misguided and bombastic" (Gardner 1994, xxiii). As long as the band enjoyed only moderate commercial success, the "naïvete" and perceived moralizing were tolerated; but with worldwide acclaim there came enormous backlash. Unbridled idealism seems acceptable from an underdog, but not when it is espoused by those in a position of privilege (a common notion in rock music that needs to be problematized beyond stating it here). It seems to me remarkable, in retrospect, that U2 were embraced by a generally cynical rock press at all and that they were so commercially successful in the materialistic culture of the 1980s. But it is not surprising that they decided, in the wake of criticism, to reinvent themselves as they did, in the image of those rock personae who have aligned themselves with darker ideas and realities and who have relied on irony, parody, and/or technological innovation to deliver them (Jim Morrison, Bowie, Talking Heads, Pink Floyd, and a host of others). High ideals overtly and passionately expressed are suspicious and "naïve." Dealing with darker subject matter and approaching it with ironic distance is considered more sophisticated—an indication of wisdom and experience. I would suggest that the latter serves as a shield against vulnerability and perhaps this is why it is preferred. All that directness and openness is disconcerting, uncomfortable, dangerous, and effeminate, both for the performer who is exposing him/herself as well as the listener; it smacks of too much personal investment and the risk that one might not be in complete control. U2 could get away with it for as long as they did because their messages were coming through the medium of music, which coded their idealism in the same way that their lyrics, visual images, and actions of social consciousness did. But because listeners generally do not unpack musical codes in a conscious way—music may make you feel good, bad, moral, immoral, but what *exactly* it makes you feel and how this is accomplished should remain a mystery—it was acceptable to feel empowered by U2's music, less so to identify with the idealism of their lyrics or actions. Gardner, again, makes this clear: "Regardless of how you interpret or misinterpret the songs, it's difficult to deny the compelling intensity the group has shown in voicing them, or the exalted beauty and strength with which that intensity is relayed in U2's music" (1994, xii).

This brings me back to a point concerning the collision of U2's shift in lyric content at the time of *Achtung Baby* with the new use of technology and ironic presentation in Zoo TV. Just as Bono began to turn further inward in his lyric writing, the music and presentation distanced him from this intimate expression of subjectivity. As he became more interested in the exploration of self and self within the context of relationships—the private—the music and image became more public. It is easy to be reminded of the parallel shift that occurred with Bob Dylan in 1965, at least in terms of the music. Just as Dylan turned from writing songs that dealt with public, global concerns to what biographer Robert Shelton calls his movement toward "three aesthetic and philosophical concepts: exploration of the grotesque and the absurd in art; existentialism; dreams and hallucinations as mirrors of consciousness" (1986, 267), he moved away from that most intimate means of musical expression, the solo acoustic guitar, to embrace technology (he "went electric") and surrounded himself with a band. Through the more diverse sounds, mediated by technology and through the presence of several band members as opposed to Dylan alone, some attention could be deflected from the contemplative, private sentiments expressed in the lyrics. Despite the accompanying furor, Dylan, of course, did not drastically alter his image or stage show to accompany the change in musical style. His "acoustic persona" could accommodate what in hindsight we view as the mild transition to plugging in. But this was not the case with U2. The visual image of Bono and the rest of the band through *Rattle and Hum*, entrenched, in fact, in Dylanesque ideas of rock authenticity, would have made for unconvincing performances of the new, dark, ironic songs—another way in which the music clearly influenced the context.

Postscript, 2006

Since I wrote this essay in the late 1990s, U2 have released two studio albums (*All That You Can't Leave Behind*, 2000, and *How To Dismantle an Atomic*

Bomb, 2004) and mounted two very successful world tours, and Bono has arguably become the most audible celebrity voice in the world to speak out against extreme poverty and the fight against AIDS in Africa. In the late 1990s, Bono began to campaign against poverty, first with an organization called Jubilee 2000, dedicated to canceling the debt owed to the West by "third world" countries, then through his own organization DATA (Debt, AIDS, Trade, Africa), and most recently through the ONE campaign. He has met with most Western presidents and prime ministers, as well as American senators and congressmen, in order to convince them to drop the debt owed by African nations, and to increase the giving of aid money and antiretroviral drugs to fight AIDS in those countries. These recent political initiatives have been undertaken by Bono alone, without the rest of the band, and have made him perhaps more highly visible on the world stage of politics than has the band's music, although the two are still certainly linked. In every interview, Bono confesses to using his celebrity to advance the causes in which he is interested; and U2 played a key role in Live 8, the series of benefit concerts held in July 2005 to exert pressure on Western nations to "Make Poverty History." In 2005 in particular, Bono began to be viewed as a critical player in world politics. He was nominated for the Nobel Peace Prize and, along with Bill and Melinda Gates, named *Time* magazine's Person of the Year. This activity has once again linked U2 overtly with politics, something that was so much a part of their profile in the 1980s but seemed less apparent throughout the 1990s when they undertook their first major stylistic shift.

Once again, in the wake of a commercially and critically disappointing album (*Pop*), they decided to reinvent themselves on *All That You Can't Leave Behind*; this time, the reinvention moved in a direction opposite to that taken by the band with *Achtung Baby*. The idea with the new album was to return to rock and roll "roots," to leave behind the dance-music influences that were prevalent on *Achtung Baby*, *Zooropa*, and, especially, *Pop*, and go back to a simpler, more stripped-down style. Live shows presented the band performing on a simple set, with few frills—a far cry from the elaborate spectacles of Zoo TV and Popmart. Black-and-white photography reappeared on the album covers. Band members returned to simpler clothing.

But it was not, by any means, a straightforward return to the past. If anything, the songwriting had become more sophisticated and the lyrical content mostly an exploration of the individual psyche. Bono retained elements of his Fly character, including the shades, which he always wears, and regularly points an ironic finger in the direction of his celebrity. Politics, however, entered the live shows in a way that harkened back to the 1980s and to the second leg of the Zoo TV tour, which featured live feeds from reporters covering the war in Serbia. During the last leg of the Elevation tour, held in 2001, the band responded to the American terrorist attacks by scrolling the names of the victims on video screens as the band played the song "One." But as Bono ramped up his anti-poverty activism, politics entered 2005's Vertigo tour more profoundly. As with his long rant about the violence in Ireland during the *Rattle and Hum* tour, Bono made a lengthy spoken plea each night about extreme poverty in the world and what needed to be done to stop it. In addition, during the song "Love and Peace or Else," Bono blindfolded himself with a cloth that was imprinted with a cross, the crescent symbol of Islam, and a Star of David, and tried to bring home the message that "God is one" and is not worth killing over. The U.N. Declaration of Human Rights was scrolled on a video screen and read by a woman's voice. Interestingly, however, the first encore of this tour often included the songs "Zoo Station" and "The Fly," perhaps the two most ironic songs from the album *Achtung Baby* and strongly associated with the glossy, superficial pop world U2 explored in the 1990s. It would appear that the band, at this point, has successfully blended elements from these disparate personae. This is possible because the "ironic" stance has now been historicized, distanced from the band's current, "real" construction of itself. It can be brought out during an encore as a moment from the past, much as the songs from the band's very first album were during the Vertigo tour. We hear and view these songs as moments within a long and evolving career, no longer as current positions, but as memorials to the past.

Notes

1. Bono; see Light 1994, 199. U2 is Bono (vocals, guitar), The Edge (guitar, keyboards), Adam Clayton (bass), and Larry Mullen, Jr. (drums). I have not included representations of the music using conventional notation in this essay, believing it to be possible to follow my prose analysis without this aid. It is, however, essential for the reader to have the recordings of "Sunday Bloody Sunday" and "Zoo Station" at hand while reading. The reader unfamiliar with the band's various visual appearances (especially those of Bono discussed in some detail below) may wish to consult photographs, the greatest variety of which can be easily accessed at U2-related websites such as http://www.vaxxine.com/U2/. There, see "Pictures/Bono 1986-89" (the time period of *The Joshua Tree* and *Rattle and Hum*), and "1990-94" (for "The Fly"). I wish to thank James Deaville and Matt Link for reading this essay and providing me with valuable suggestions for improvement.
2. In a chapter ostensibly devoted to the music itself ("Composing the New Noise"), Waters even states a position—a familiar one—on the subject of discussing music in detail: "Music is a bit like laughter and libido—if you think about what it is, it disintegrates in front of your eyes" (p. 253). See chapter five of David Brackett's book for a discussion of the well-known similar sentiment expressed by Elvis Costello ("Talking about music is like dancing about architecture").
3. See especially the introductions to Walser 1993 and Brackett 1995, which argue for an analysis that takes into account the music as it signifies in relation to the contexts in which it is produced and received, and Middleton 1990, Chapter 6, which discusses the semantic analysis of popular music.
4. Stokes 1996 discusses these textual connections for "Sunday Bloody Sunday" (p. 37), "New Year's Day" (41), "Bullet the Blue Sky" (67), and "Mothers of the

Disappeared" (77). Graham 1995 discusses the connections on pp. 21, 22, 56–57, and 61, respectively. Flanagan 1995 discusses the connection between "Bullet the Blue Sky" and Central America, pp. 51–52.

5. See, for example, the performance in *U2 Live at Red Rocks: Under a Blood Red Sky*.
6. *The Unforgettable Fire* video is shot in color, but the scenes that show the band walking through the snowy field emphasize the white snow and black or gray clothing. There are no other colors used in these scenes.
7. This overly romantic view of the band was one of the reasons Dunphy's biography was not very well received by the rock press (see especially DeCurtis 1994b).
8. Thanks to percussionist Trevor Nicoll for providing me with the correct terminology.
9. Bono took to telling U2's audiences before the performance of this song that it was "not a rebel song." See the performance in *Under a Blood Red Sky*, or the 1983 interview with Much Music, in which Bono says "'Sunday Bloody Sunday' isn't a rebel song. It's not pro-violence. It's not pro-Irish. I'm sick of people flying flags. On our stage you see white flags. I find that's an important flag" (*Egos and Icons*, Toronto, 1983).
10. The musicians themselves make these rhetorical associations. Bono explained in *Musician* magazine (Graham and Stokes 1995, 31) that upon listening to an early take of the vocal for "Red Hill Mining Town," he wondered why "the singer sounded like a rich man with pound notes stuffed in his pockets when it's a song about unemployment." The answer was that the engineer had used stereo plate echo, which was subsequently taken out.
11. I wish to thank Simon Wood, a practicing rock musician as well as an academic, for helping me consider this cadential figure with language appropriate to the music. The cadence might also be thought of in terms of traditional Western theory as a tonicization of the relative major, C, which is made by dropping from an E♭ chord, through Dm7, to C. The root and fifth of the E♭ chord could be thought of as neighbors produced by mode mixture (borrowed from the parallel minor) that fall by half steps to D and A, respectively, then to C and G.
12. The show changed over the course of time, so that this segue into the encore was added after the release of *Zooropa* in 1993. The "Fanfare" sample also appears at the beginning of the song "Daddy's Gonna Pay for Your Crashed Car" on *Zooropa*, where it is identified. For a detailed description of the genesis of the show and the Zoo TV tour from someone who traveled with the band, see Flanagan 1995.
13. See Bono's explanation of the "Fly" character throughout Flanagan 1995 and Waters 1994, and in Light 1994.
14. It is unclear whether Beethoven's "Ode to Joy" is used simply because it is grandiose or in order to make a connection to the fall of the Berlin Wall, on which occasion this music was also heard. Thanks to James Deaville for pointing this out to me.
15. On creating theatrical character through shifting physical balance, see Barba 1995, especially Chapter 2.
16. The results of the poll are reprinted in *U2: The Ultimate Compendium*, 190.
17. The photograph opposite the "Zoo Station" lyrics on the inside of the booklet that accompanies *Achtung Baby* shows the band in a darkly lit pub. Adam has a

bottle in front of him, but the more striking image is of Bono exhaling cigarette smoke, which clearly signifies transgression.

18. This statement needs to be qualified, for there are songs on *Achtung Baby* in which U2's characteristic big sound is used: "Acrobat" and "Love is Blindness" are two examples.
19. He also begins the song "Drowning Man" on *War* an octave lower than the rest of the melody, and he uses his falsetto in this song as well, but it is an isolated early example of his use of these techniques.
20. After the first three albums Bono commented: "As I worked out where we wanted to be, I loosened up, and loosening up discovered other voices. I became interested in *singing*. Whereas before if it was in tune and the right time, that was enough.... I find it hard to listen to the first three records because of my singing" (Graham and Stokes 1995, 30. *Unforgettable Fire* is the fourth album). This seems a rather harsh judgment—there's much more to his singing on the first three albums than being in tune and in time—but it is true that after these albums he did find "other voices," which he began to use in specific rhetorical ways.
21. Not to be confused with how David Brackett uses this term in his essay on James Brown. There, "double-voice" refers to the twofold way in which words can signify (1995, Chapter 4).
22. The semantics of Bono's use of falsetto are complicated to work out. In the case of "Lemon," the use of falsetto for much of the lead vocal, combined with the way in which he articulates many of the words (the exaggerated vowels of the word "lemon," for example), seems to indicate irony. On the other hand, he often uses his falsetto as a clear symbol of transcendence from the mundane to the sublime, with no irony attached to it at all, in, for example, "The Unforgettable Fire," the end of "One," or the end of "Even Better Than the Real Thing," and the cover of "Can't Help Falling in Love" from the *Zoo TV Live from Sydney* performance.
23. For more on this interpretation of the lyrics, see Flanagan 1995, 52.

References

Barba, Eugenio. 1995. *The Paper Canoe: A Guide to Theatre Anthropology*, trans. Richard Fowler. New York: Routledge.

Brackett, David. 1995. *Interpreting Popular Music*. Cambridge, England: Cambridge University Press.

Considine, J. D. 1992. U2. *The Rolling Stone Album Guide*, ed. Anthony DeCurtis et al, 728–729. New York: Random House.

DeCurtis, Anthony. 1994a. Zoo World Order. *U2: The Ultimate Compendium of Interviews, Articles, Facts and Opinions from the Files of Rolling Stone*, 206–217. New York: Hyperion.

______. 1994b. U2's Forgettable Fluff [review of Dunphy]. *U2: The Ultimate Compendium of Interviews, Articles, Facts and Opinions from the Files of Rolling Stone*, 129–130. New York: Hyperion.

Dunphy, Eamon. 1987. *Unforgettable Fire: The Story of U2*. London: Penguin.

Egos and Icons: U2. 1997. (video) Much Music Special. Excerpts of interviews conducted in Toronto, 1983; Tokyo, 1993; Winnipeg, 1997; with Bono as "The Fly," n.d.

Eno, Brian. 1994. Bringing Up Baby. *U2: The Ultimate Compendium of Interviews, Articles, Facts and Opinions from the Files of Rolling Stone*, 165–170. New York: Hyperion.
Flanagan, Bill. 1995. *U2 at the End of the World*. New York: Delacorte.
Gardner, Elysa. 1994. Introduction. *U2: The Ultimate Compendium of Interviews, Articles, Facts and Opinions from the Files of Rolling Stone*, xi–xxx. New York: Hyperion.
Graham, Bill. 1995. *The Complete Guide to the Music of U2*. London: Omnibus Press.
Graham, Bill, and Niall Stokes. 1995. Interview in *Musician* no. 103 (May 1987), excerpted in no. 200 (July 1995), 30–32.
Laing, Dave. 1985. *One Chord Wonders: Power and Meaning in Punk Rock*. Milton Keynes: Open University Press.
Light, Alan. 1994. Behind the Fly. *U2: The Ultimate Compendium of Interviews, Articles, Facts and Opinions from the Files of Rolling Stone*, 191–199. New York: Hyperion.
Middleton, Richard. 1990. *Studying Popular Music*. Milton Keynes: Open University Press.
Pond, Steve. 1994. Now What? *U2: The Ultimate Compendium of Interviews, Articles, Facts and Opinions from the Files of Rolling Stone*, 144–152. New York: Hyperion.
Rattle and Hum. 1988. (video) Paramount Pictures.
Shelton, Robert. 1986. *No Direction Home: The Life and Music of Bob Dylan*. London: Penguin Books.
Stokes, Niall. 1996. *Into the Heart: The Stories Behind Every U2 Song*. London: Carleton Books.
U2. 1983. *War*. Island Records 90067.
———. 1984. *The Unforgettable Fire*. Island Records 90231.
———. 1987. *The Joshua Tree*. Island Records 90581.
———. 1988. *Rattle and Hum*. Island Records 91003 (two discs).
———. 1991. *Achtung Baby*. Island Records 10347.
———. 1993. *Zooropa*. Island Records 518047.
———. 1997. *Pop*. Island Records 524334.
———. 2000. *All That You Can't Leave Behind*. Interscope Records 3145246532.
———. 2004. *How to Dismantle an Atomic Bomb*. Interscope Records B0003613-02.
U2 Zoo TV Live from Sydney. 1994. (video) Polygram Video.
U2 Live at Red Rocks: Under a Blood Red Sky. 1983. (video) U2 at Red Rocks Associates.
The Unforgettable Fire Collection. 1985. (video) Island Visual Arts.
Walser, Robert. 1993. *Running With the Devil: Power, Gender and Madness in Heavy Metal Music*. Hanover: Wesleyan University Press.
———. 1997. Deep Jazz: Notes on Interiority, Race, and Criticism. In *Inventing the Psychological: Towards a Cultural History of Emotional Life in America*. Edited by Joel Pfister and Nancy Strong. New Haven and London: Yale University Press.
Waters, John. 1994. *Race of Angels: The Genesis of U2*. London: Fourth Estate.

Chorus

Guitar solo

Verse 3 Feel the steel butt jump
Smooth in my hand
Staring at the sea
Staring at the sand
Staring at myself
Reflected
In the eyes of the dead man on the beach
The dead man
On the beach

Chorus

Robert Smith, the band's lead singer, guitarist, and songwriter, attempted to head off the controversy by explaining that the song, originally released in 1978, was based on the central incident in Albert Camus's *L'Étranger* and that it recounts the Frenchman Meursault's seemingly gratuitous murder of an Arab. Smith's account of the source of the song's lyrics is supported by the general correspondence between events in the song and the novel's central scene; the line in the chorus "I'm the stranger"; and the use of sun, sea, and sky images that are also pervasive in Camus's text.[2]

In acknowledging Smith's explanation, ADC President Abdeen Jabara observed: "'Killing an Arab' has been and could continue to be misunderstood and/or misused by many people. There are those who may not have read Camus's 'Stranger' or not understood its connection to it. Unfortunately there are also those who would use the very title to fan ethnic or racial division in America" (Pareles 1987).

After the ADC's Chicago office launched a campaign of telephone calls to the Cure's distributor, Elektra Records, and to Warner Communications (Elektra's parent corporation), the following agreement resulted. First, Elektra would retain the song on the album but would, starting in January 1987, ship all future LPs, CDs, and cassettes of *Standing on a Beach* with a disclaimer sticker (see Figure 7.1) that clarifies the song's intended anti-racist content. They would supply retailers with stickers that were to be affixed to units already in stock, and would add a similar message to *Staring at the Sea*, a video compilation of the songs on the album, as well as to the credits of its concert film, which ends with "Killing an Arab" (ADC 1987a).

Second, Elektra would send a letter to 800 Album-Oriented Rock (AOR) stations and college radio stations across the country requesting that "effective

The song
KILLING AN ARAB
has absolutely no racist
overtones whatsoever. It is a
song which decries the
existence of all prejudice and
consequent violence. The
Cure condemn its use in
furthering anti-Arab
feeling.
60477-2

Figure 7.1 Elektra's disclaimer sticker for packages containing "Killing an Arab."

immediately, the song 'Killing an Arab' be given no further airplay at your station" because of the potential for "misuse and misinterpretation" of the song (DeCurtis 1987), which "has been, and could continue to be interpreted in such a way as to further anti-Arab sentiment and threaten the well-being of Arab-Americans" (ADC 1987a, 1). Third, the Cure would give a benefit concert and donate the proceeds to organizations aiding Lebanese, Palestinian, and American orphans.[3] Under this agreement, the song would continue to circulate but would be accompanied by the band's message that it condemned rather than advocated racially motivated violence.[4]

The Cure's willingness to meet with its critics and suggest ways to defuse the situation was laudable, displaying a level of receptiveness to criticism not often seen from a pop group.[5] Simply identifying the literary source of "Killing an Arab" does not, however, automatically exempt the song from criticisms that the work is indeed racist or that its airplay has political consequences. Recent postcolonial analyses of *L'Étranger* enable a reader to view the French narrator Meursault's killing of the Arab character within a context of racial dominance and colonialism. As Edward Said remarks, "Camus's narratives of resistance and existential confrontation, which had once seemed to be about withstanding or opposing both mortality and Nazism, can now be read as part of the debate about culture and imperialism" (Said 1993, 172). Because the song is no passive vehicle for conveying Camus's text (the lyrics portray events that are not in the novel, and the song's musical setting adds another layer of structure), it requires scrutiny on its own terms as a musical interpretation of a scene from *L'Étranger.*

After surveying the line of inquiry that has characterized scholarly interpretations of *L'Étranger,* I will examine "Killing an Arab" by exploring its musical structure and lyrics in relation to the novel's climactic scene. I will argue that through its alterations and additions to Camus's text, the song supports a reading sympathetic to the Cure's claim that it criticizes racial prejudice. Second, I will explore the tensions between an analysis of this work and its reception, which is inevitably shaped by the song's social contexts. Finally, I will discuss more generally the central issues raised in the controversy over

"Killing an Arab," namely, what it reveals about the value and limitations of critical discourse about representing racial Others in popular music, and the potential impact of such criticism on the reception of such works.

Camus's tale of a man who shoots an unarmed Arab on an Algerian beach for no apparent reason except that the sun was beating down on him and who expresses no remorse for the crime or about the death of his mother, has become a central text in Western literature since its initial publication in 1942. In a review that appeared the following year, Jean-Paul Sartre commented upon the novel's structural perfection, its portrayal of the universality of the human condition, and its unusual mode of discourse (Sartre 1943); this approach has strongly influenced several generations of critics. Camus's own remarks on *L'Étranger* also support the interpretation that Meursault's situation reflects a universal condition, one in which the narrator embodies noble ideals for which he dies:

> Meursault is not a piece of social wreckage, but a poor and naked man enamored of a sun that leaves no shadows. Far from being bereft of all feeling, he is animated by a passion that is deep because it is stubborn, a passion for the absolute and for truth.... One would therefore not be much mistaken to read *The Stranger* as the story of a man who, without any heroics, agrees to die for the truth (Camus 1955, 336–337).

Neither Sartre nor Camus focuses on the racial identity of the man Meursault shoots—indeed, in his essay Sartre refers only once to Algeria's ethnic makeup, when he remarks that "when you start reading the book you feel as if you were listening to a monotonous, nasal, Arab chant rather than reading a novel" (Sartre 1943, 40).[6]

Only recently has the issue of the ethnic identity of Meursault's victim become prominent in criticism of *L'Étranger*. In her introduction to a collection of essays that reflects on the novel fifty years after its publication, Adele King addresses whether it is appropriate to criticize Camus in relation to his attitudes about the Arab population in Algeria before its war for independence; she also asks whether *L'Étranger* condemns colonialism or whether it reveals Camus's unconscious colonial or racist attitudes (King 1992, 9–10).[7]

In interpreting the novel, it is necessary to consider Camus's staunch opposition to Algerian independence and his unquestioning acceptance of the French presence in Algeria—in short, his inability to envision Algeria *without* French colonialism—as inevitably linked to his constricted depictions of Arabs.[8] As Said notes, "Camus's writing is informed by an extraordinarily belated, in some ways incapacitated colonial sensibility, which enacts an imperial gesture within and by means of a form, the realistic novel, well past its greatest achievements in Europe" (Said 1993, 176).

Because the story draws on the tensions between French and Arabs in colonial Algeria and requires the death of a nameless Arab as its central event, it is impossible to understand Meursault as an inculpable, truth-seeking human being who is unjustly sentenced to die, an interpretation whose foundations are crumbling against current postcolonial criticism. To understand the song as presenting a universal point of view excludes the very different reading of the novel from the position of those who would not have the luxury, as Meursault does, of controlling the events of the narrative, and who would align themselves not with the narrator but with the victim of the murder.

But because of its musical setting and the alterations in the events described in the novel, it is plausible to hear the song as self-conscious and critical, as the Cure claim, even with its roots in a colonialist text.[9] My analysis focuses on four elements—musical devices used to signify the Orient, the structure of the vocal line with particular attention to scale degrees, the interaction of the instruments, and the relationship between music and lyrics—in order to suggest that the narrator undergoes a crucial change during the course of the song.

A cymbal opens the work, perhaps suggesting the repeated "cymbals of sunlight crashing on [Meursault's] forehead" (Camus 1942c, 59) just before he squeezes the trigger. This is followed by the lead guitar's introduction (see Example 7.1), which is apparently meant to evoke the mysterious world of the Arab. The lead guitar begins with a turn centered on B that visits C and A, then rests on B. A second cymbal crash in the next measure punctuates the sustained pitch, urging the melody to continue to slink up from C to D♯ and back to C. It pauses ever so slightly while tracing out the resulting augmented second, which functions as a musical symbol for the scene's exotic backdrop. The melody returns to B, repeats the turn, and then sustains the B; the lingering of the melody around the B is a further emblem of the Middle East.[10] This motive evokes the melody described in the novel that the second Arab character plays on a reed just before the murder:

> The other [Arab] was blowing through a little reed over and over again, watching us out of the corner of his eye. He kept repeating the only three notes he could get out of the instrument.
>
> The whole time there was nothing but the sun and the silence, with the low gurgling from the spring and the three notes (Camus 1942c, 55).

The bass guitar (played by Michael Dempsey) enters with the contrasting melodic line shown in Example 7.2 at a much faster tempo; it too begins on B,

Example 7.1 The Cure, "Killing an Arab" (Robert Smith), *Standing On a Beach—The Singles* (1986): guitar introduction.

Example 7.2 The Cure, "Killing an Arab" (Robert Smith), *Standing On a Beach* (1986): bass entrance.

but rather than leisurely swaying in the tritone space bounded by A and D♯, it makes a chromatic beeline for the E a fifth below B.

But just as the bass guitar reaches E, the tonic, the lead guitar returns, playing at a much faster clip than in the opening and with an improvisatory character, also suggesting Arab music.[11] At this moment the Other is not simply a mysterious, tempting, gently beckoning figure "out there," but an intruder who detracts from what was to have been a sure, satisfying descent to the tonic. The lead guitar then seizes the melody, using scale degree $\hat{4}$ (A♯) and the leading tone, $\hat{7}$ (D♯), to establish a scale used for exotic flavor in some Western music, the so-called "gypsy scale" (E–F♯–G–A♯–B–C–D♯–E).[12] Raising $\hat{4}$ doubles the number of augmented seconds in the lead guitar's music; this interval now occurs between G and A♯ as well as between C and D♯.

These four musical devices—the augmented second, emphasis on a single pitch, improvisatory style, and use of the "gypsy scale"—all help to establish an ironically inauthentic Orientalist musical backdrop rather than an actual Arab sound world, thus suggesting that we are experiencing the events through the consciousness of the Western narrator, *not* through the Arab who is also present in the scene.

In its second entrance, the "Arab music" sheds its former hesitant character. Reaching E does not seem particularly important to this melody, which moves rapidly downward in a whirl of eighth notes, touches the tonic briefly, and immediately glides back up. The relationship between the bass guitar's music that drives stepwise to the tonic and the lead guitar's music that meanders can be mapped onto the relationship between the "I," through whom we experience the incident, and the "Other," which is simultaneously a person (the Arab) and a location (the setting of the murder). The harmony throughout the song is minimal, with the primary chords being the E minor that marks the beginnings of phrases and cadence points and the strident "clash-slide" chord that punctuates each statement of "I'm alive" and "I'm dead." After the bass guitar reaches its goal of E in the intro, it provides an underlying propulsive rhythm with a simple three-note repeated figure that also employs the augmented second, E–F♮–G♯, and its subdominant variant, A–B♭–C♯, supported by the drums (played by Laurence Tolhurst).

Picking up on the bass guitar's initial B♮, Smith delivers the lyrics in a half-sung, half-chanted style with an economy of pitches. Describing the events entirely from Meursault's point of view, he sings only five pitches during the entire song: G, A, B, D, and E.[13] One to four pitches suffice for each line of text. The first, third, fifth, and seventh lines of verse 1 start on B, their melodic monotony broken by motion either a step away or a third away from B in the middle of the line, then returning to B. The stasis of Smith's vocal music reflects the narrator's stony indifference to his act of murder; the primarily syllabic setting of the vocal line and Smith's choppy delivery suggest the narrator's benumbed emotional state.

Faced with the presence of the Other, the narrator feels threatened, even though the Arab does not even confront him; he is lying on the ground, passive. The threat he poses is certainly not a physical one, but to the narrator, one that is still troubling: he calls into question the narrator's very identity. Unlike nineteenth-century depictions of the exotic, which placed the Other safely far away from and opposite to the Self, in the twentieth century, as James Clifford has observed, "the 'exotic' is uncannily close" (Clifford 1988, 13). No longer able to claim cultural superiority, dominance, and authority over the Arab, the Meursault who is portrayed in the song becomes, *to himself*, a stranger, just another "Other," surely a terrifying thought to someone who has always enjoyed a position of privilege because of his unmarked ethnic identity.

The music demonstrates the narrator's struggle against this idea when he sings the final two lines of the chorus ("I'm the stranger/Killing an Arab") to B and D♮, scale degrees $\hat{5}$ and $\natural\hat{7}$. Scale degree $\natural\hat{7}$ is not one permitted to the Arab-identified lead guitar music, marked by the characteristic *raised* $\hat{7}$, D♯, and by the resulting augmented second it forms with $\hat{6}$; by initially singing $\natural\hat{7}$, the narrator emphasizes the difference between himself and the Arab.

As the song proceeds, the distinction between the Self and the Other swiftly melts away. The five pitches Smith sings comprise the anhemitonic pentatonic scale, which is stereotypically associated with the East, and establish a second musical means by which the song reinforces its message that the identity of the Other is no longer easily distinguishable from that of the Self. That two of the narrator's central pitches, $\hat{5}$ and $\natural\hat{7}$, lie a mere semitone away from the Arab's pitches, $\hat{6}$ and $\sharp\hat{7}$, indicates the ready interchangeability of the narrator's and Arab's positions, a relationship whose potential the vocalist realizes. After the narrator discovers in the second verse that having the choice between walking away or shooting the Arab "amounts to the same/Absolutely nothing," in the last line of the second chorus he sings a pitch that is no longer solidly situated on D♮ but that has inched considerably closer to D♯.

Prior to this point, $\natural\hat{7}$ had been reserved for the narrator's music and $\sharp\hat{7}$ for the "Arab music." By this moment, however, the vocalist no longer distinguishes so clearly between the two forms of $\hat{7}$; the difference between the narrator and the Other, symbolized by the distinction between $\natural\hat{7}$ and $\sharp\hat{7}$, is no longer so conspicuous. The space between the "Arab music" and the narrator's music thus literally begins to close, as does the physical space between them. The Arab is thus no longer the "Other"; the narrator, rather, comes to resemble him in both a musical and dramatic sense.

After the second chorus, the lead guitarist starts his solo with the quasi-Arabic tune from the intro in the same manner. This time, however, he extends his solo for six additional bars before cadencing on B as before. During the lead guitar's corresponding music in the intro, the music relied on $\sharp\hat{4}$ to signify the Arab world and the augmented second that it forms with $\hat{3}$. Here, the lead guitar abandons $\sharp\hat{4}$ after the first few pitches and favors A$\natural$, which was previously the terrain of the narrator; the importance of this new version of $\hat{4}$ is underscored in the solo's tenth bar, which sustains A$\natural$ for two quarters amid a stream of otherwise continuous eighth notes. Musical boundaries between the unmarked narrator and Arab thus continue to collapse; previously exclusive musical property gets shared.

It is here that the shooting apparently takes place in the story. In the third and final verse, which begins with the words "I feel the steel butt jump/Smooth in my hand," Smith's vocal register reaches its highest point in the song, marking an increased tension, and somewhere between this point and the last three lines of the verse "Staring at myself/Reflected/In the eyes of the dead man on the beach," the murder occurs.

Finding himself in the presence of the dead Arab, the narrator recognizes him for the first time in the song as a "man," rather than as "the Arab." This change in the lyrics conspicuously departs from the scene in the novel, where the victim is repeatedly described as "the Arab" and then, after Meursault shoots him five times, "the motionless body" (Camus 1942c, 59).

A second crucial alteration to Camus's text in the song is that the narrator sees himself in the eyes of his victim: "Staring at myself/Reflected/In the eyes of the dead man on the beach." Smith's rewriting of the original scene in the final verse thus supports a reading of the song that his representation of the Arab Other can be understood as ironic and cognizant of the Orientalist politics at work. After the narrator's stable tonic pitch gets unpinned and slips down to $\natural\hat{7}$ ("Reflected in the eyes"), his melody skips over $\hat{6}$ to $\hat{5}$ ("Of the dead man on the beach"), which saves him from having to use the scale degree that he avoids throughout the song. Scale degree $\hat{6}$ had been clearly marked as the stuff of the Other, a boundary pitch of the crucial augmented second with $\sharp\hat{7}$, and he steps away from that scale degree as he attempts to distance himself from the man he has killed and in whose eyes he has momentarily seen himself. The narrator's subsequent cry of "I'm alive" and the guitar's final clash chord that follows it are defiant, as if to convince himself that his identity is indeed distinct from that of the dead man lying before him.

The piece then swiftly comes to a close. On the last line of the previous two choruses, Smith has sung B–B–B–D–B in parallel fifths with Tolhurst and Dempsey singing E–E–E–G–E below. This time, however, he exchanges melodic material with the other vocalists, singing E–E–E–G–E, clamping his vocal line down onto the tonic. The guitar's "Arab music" enters again with a four-bar version of its solo, and then exits on $\hat{5}$. The bass guitar's chromatic descent to the tonic now closes on E, this time undisturbed by the lead guitar. The brief moment in which the narrator sees himself as the Other has apparently vanished—except that the song does not end with the chromatic descent to tonic, but with the three pitches that opened the work, B–C–B–A–B, which then signaled the coming of the augmented second and hence the coming of the Arab, suggesting the inevitability of future encounters between the two.

I have proposed that "Killing an Arab" makes room for a critical reading of Western dominance over ethnic Others and can be construed to encourage listeners to grapple with issues of the loss of authority and the remaking of identity. Because of the controls imposed on the song's airplay, many potential listeners were unable to participate in debates of its meaning. Yet I doubt that a general listener would be able to discern the gradually shrinking space between the two forms of scale degree $\hat{7}$ or its symbolism; rather, the main "message" gleaned from the song is more likely to be the line "Killing an Arab," underscored by the drums. Listeners' anti-Arab biases would also make it unlikely that they would be willing to perceive the narrator's momentary feeling of kinship with the man he has just killed. When the song was first released, neo-Nazis belonging to the British National Party showed up at the Cure's concerts, attracted to "Killing an Arab" as a racist anthem (Gräfrath 2005). If the ADC had not protested the re-release of "Killing an Arab," many more instances of racist uses of the song would doubtlessly have resulted. Indeed, years after the 1986–1987 controversy faded, the continued availability of the tune has resulted in recent examples of its racist appropriation.[14]

At the time *Standing on a Beach* was released in 1986, a climate of intense hostility against Arabs prevailed in the United States. In 1985, numerous anti-Arab hate crimes occurred throughout the United States: Islamic centers were vandalized in San Francisco; Denver; Dearborn, Michigan; and Quincy, Massachusetts; a mosque was firebombed in Houston; and the ADC's West Coast regional director, Alex Odeh, was murdered by a bomb strapped to his office door (Abraham 1994). Right-wing media and popular culture in the United States frequently depict Arabs as caricatures: stealthy terrorist, rich sheik, or unshaven nomad.[15]

In such an antagonistic climate, it is not surprising that a number of American DJs introduced "Killing an Arab" with anti-Arab slurs, one reason why the Cure decided to state outright on the record packaging that they condemn its use in furthering anti-Arab feeling. ADC public-relations director Faris Bouhafa described their agreement with Elektra and the Cure as one that "eschews censorship and suppression of art in favor of using the song as a vehicle for sending a message against racism" (ADC 1987a, 8), a message that eventually reached millions when the album subsequently went gold (Azerrad 1989, 50). *Standing on a Beach* catapulted the Cure from relative obscurity as a cult band known primarily in the U.K. to international recognition with an established U.S. fan base. Their next album, *Kiss Me Kiss Me Kiss Me* (1987), reached the U.S. Top Forty (Larkin 1995, 1017).[16]

After the attacks on the World Trade Center on September 11, 2001, and subsequent renewal of anti-Arab sentiment, Smith revisited the meaning and uses of the song, stating in an interview that:

> If there's one thing I would change, it's the title.... I wrote it when I was still in school and I had no idea that anyone would ever listen to it other than my immediate school friends.
>
> One of the themes of the song is that everyone's existence is pretty much the same. Everyone lives, everyone dies, our existences are the same. It's as far from a racist song as you can write. It seems though that no one can get past the title and that's incredibly frustrating,
>
> The fact is it's based on a book that's set in France and deals with the problems of the Algerians, so it was only geographical reasons why it was an Arab and not anyone else (Robb 2001).

During the so-called global war on terrorism, Smith has limited the song's circulation. "Killing an Arab" did not appear on the Cure's *Greatest Hits* CD of 2001, the 2004 remaster of *Three Imaginary Boys* of 1979, or on the 2004 compilation box set *Join the Dots: B-Sides and Rarities, 1978–2001.* When the Cure performed the song as an encore at their performance at the Royal Albert Hall in London in April 2006, Smith changed the words to "Killing an other" (the Cure 2006), thus restricting the original lyric's circulation to a new generation of listeners while retaining the song's depiction of the senseless killing of an innocent man.

By focusing on this example of a song whose meanings have been contested and negotiated, I wish to foreground our responsibility to engage in public dialogue and discussion about works like "Killing an Arab," songs that draw upon categories of difference. Unpacking not only how racial difference operates in the lyrics and music of such songs but also how it is received by a general population allows us to underscore the rights of racially marginalized groups to exist as equals within a cultural economy, to be able to turn on the radio without finding themselves marked as objects of ridicule or violence. Acknowledging the existence of those who bear the actual burdens of such songs provides a starting point in ceasing domination through forms of cultural expression, only after which will popular music be able to realize more fully its potential to contribute to the collective social good.

Notes

This essay was presented at the 1996 meeting of the International Association for the Study of Popular Music, U.S. chapter, held at the University of Colorado–Denver. I am grateful to David Brackett, John Covach, and Anton Vishio for their helpful comments, to Michael W. Suleiman for his generous assistance with the project, and to Robert Smith for granting permissions.

1. The American-Arab Anti-Discrimination Committee (ADC) is a grassroots civil-rights organization based in Washington, D.C., that was founded to challenge "stereotyping, defamation, and discrimination ... against Arabs of American descent" (ADC 1987a, 2). More information about the ADC is available at http://www.adc.org.
2. All translations of *L'Étranger* used in this paper are Matthew Ward's (Camus 1942c).
3. The sold-out concert (with an audience of 1,800) was held on August 11, 1987, at the Ritz in New York, and raised $35,000, which was distributed to orphanages in Beirut and El-Bireh and to Catholic Charities in New York. The Cure initially offered the money to the Child Welfare League in Washington, but, according to Kim Akhtar, the Cure's New York publicist, the League's spokesperson, Joyce Johnson, wanted assurances that the rest of the money would not wind up with PLO "guerrillas." Akhtar also said that the Hale Foundation in New York declined the money because it did not want to offend its Jewish patrons (ADC 1987b).
4. ADC chose to abandon its initial attempt to convince Elektra to delete the song from future pressings of the album altogether because, according to Media Relations Director Faris Bouhafa, they "did not want to be associated with whatever the PMRC [Parents Music Resource Center, a group that monitors popular music it deems unsuitable for children] stands for. We felt that it was much more important and would be much more effective in the long run to arrive at an agreement that would, in effect, raise people's consciousness regarding discrimination against Arab-Americans and racism in general" (DeCurtis 1987). The PMRC's mission statement appears in Beahm 1993.
5. Fifteen years after the controversy, Smith remarked: "[W]e resolved it quite amicably.... I did a couple of high-profile interviews and met both sides—the Arab League of America [i.e., the American-Arab Anti-Discrimination Committee] and, I think, Jewish Homes for Children Society. We did a show for them. If anything, it had a very positive effect ... because it gave me a platform to actually talk about an issue which is never normally talked about in a rational way" (Smith 2001).

   The Cure's willingness to work with the ADC diverges from the "outsider" persona they project as the mainstay of the "Goth movement," which refers to the morbid themes in their songs and their appearance (white makeup, black clothing, heavy eyeliner, misapplied lipstick, bedroom hair); the Cure have also been disparagingly dubbed the masters of "mope rock" (Azerrad 1989, 47). Geyrhalter 1996 explores the idea that the Cure challenge traditional representations of sexuality in pop.

   In contrast to the Cure, saxophonist and composer John Zorn repeatedly brushed aside Asian-Americans' criticism of the racist and sexist elements in his CDs. For a chronology of this controversy, see Beels 1994, Lee 1994a, 1994b, Hamilton 1994, and Hisama 2004.

6. Sartre's comment resonates with the theorist Heinrich Schenker's dismissal of Arabic music as well as Japanese and Turkish songs, which he writes are like "the babbling of a child," and are "original only because of their imperfections and awkwardness" (Schenker 1910, 21).
7. King's defense of the novel against the charge of racism is insubstantial; she remarks that people who knew Camus, like his daughter, say he wasn't racist. To support a benign reading of the novel's racial politics, she notes that the non-Western contributors to *Camus's* L'Étranger: *Fifty Years On* (King 1992) do not dwell on the fact that Meursault's victim was Arab and concludes that "Meursault's recognition that he is a stranger to the Arabs, and that they are strange to him, should not strike us as more than simple honesty" (King 1992, 10). Hargreaves's essay in King's collection criticizes Sartre's and Camus's readings of *L'Étranger* in relation to the victim's ethnicity and the interethnic tensions of colonial Algeria that it employs (1992). Further comments about Camus's treatment of Arabs in his writings appear in Rigaud 1992. O'Brien's study of Camus (1970) is a watershed that considers Camus's colonial perspective in Algeria; O'Brien later abandons his critical position on colonial texts (1986).
8. Similarly limited portrayals of Arab characters also appear in Camus's *La Peste* (1947) and *L'Exil et le royaume* (1957).
9. Because my analysis of "Killing an Arab" is based on the version recorded for *Standing on a Beach*, it is not necessarily applicable for all versions of the song, which the Cure have performed differently live.
10. Locke 1998 discusses ways that Western composers of art music have represented the Middle East, and identifies the hovering of a melody around a single pitch as one feature of nineteenth-century Western conceptions of Arab music as realized in concert music (117).
11. Locke 1998 notes that while "Arab art music has long been marked by elaborate, flexible, highly decorated instrumental and vocal improvisation... and accompanied by a vast and subtle variety of accompanimental rhythms," nineteenth-century European *airs arabes* lack the sophistication in pitch and rhythm of actual Arab improvisations (116). Similarly, Smith's solo does not constitute authentic Arab music but a Western representation of it. For a discussion of representations of East Asian music in Western popular music, see Hisama 1993.
12. The "gypsy scale" or "Hungarian scale" consists of the harmonic minor scale with raised $\hat{4}$, a scale rarely present in actual Gypsy folk music or Hungarian folk music (Sárosi 1971, 27). Bellman 1998 discusses an example of this scale in Leoncavallo's 1912 opera, *Zincari* (85–86).
13. I hear the pitch sung to "I'm" in the line "I'm dead" as a bend occurring on A rather than as a true B♭.
14. On August 17, 1990, the student radio station at Kansas State University, KSDB-FM, played "Killing an Arab" in response to a listener's request. (It is surely not coincidental that this request came shortly after Saddam Hussein's invasion of Kuwait on August 2, 1990.) A listener who called the station to protest was told the song would not be taken off the air, and that the station would not apologize. After Michael W. Suleiman, University Distinguished Professor in the Department of Political Science at Kansas State, objected to the head of the School of Journalism (under whose auspices KSDB operates), several

written and verbal apologies and an on-air apology ensued, and the School of Journalism stated that the record would not be played again on KSDB. I am grateful to Professor Suleiman for sharing this information with me.

15. Suleiman 1989 discusses the political basis for Americans' negative attitudes towards Arabs. Stereotyped images of Arabs appear in the films *The Little Drummer Boy* (Viacom, 1968); *Aladdin* (Disney, 1993); and *True Lies* (20th Century Fox, 1994); protests of these films are chronicled in the *New York Times* (1991, 1993, and 1994, respectively). Shaheen 1984 analyzes images of Arabs broadcast over American television during the eight-year period from 1975 to 1983. In 1986, Toys "R" Us sold a doll manufactured by Caleco Industries named Nomad, a dark-skinned Arab wearing a burnoose whose packaging described him as a "heartless terrorist" who leads a "band of cutthroats" engaging in "terrorist assaults on innocent villagers" (Geist 1986).
16. In 1987, Smith stated: "It's just through the incredible stupidity of certain DJs that the whole thing ballooned into a controversy. If anything, the song is more well known in Europe, and it's always been understood. In America, I think we're known for making wacky videos whereas [in Europe] we've got a history as a serious group" (Coleman 1987, 144).

    Some critics might view the Cure's handling of the controversy as a play for free publicity. According to their manager Chris Parry, because the Cure wanted to avoid any suggestion that the benefit concert was intended to enhance their career, they did not publicize the date at their press conference announcing the agreement (ADC 1987a). In 1989, Smith noted that the controversy "was quite pathetic. I imagine Camus would have found it quite amusing" (Azerrad 1989, 50). Reflecting on "Killing an Arab" in 2003, Smith remarked: "[T]here's only one thing I regret in my whole life and it's the title for that song. At 17 I thought that everybody was as much into Albert Camus as I was, that everybody would understand the existential angst of Albert Camus and I'd been obsessed with this title as a writer but obviously people thought I was calling for murder, which was not the case, of course. What's nice however is that in the course of years I have managed to spread French existentialism abroad" (Smith 2003).

References

Abraham, Nabeel. 1994. Anti-Arab Racism and Violence in the United States. In *The Development of Arab-American Identity*, ed. Ernest McCarus. Ann Arbor: University of Michigan Press, 155–214.

American-Arab Anti-Discrimination Committee (ADC). 1987a. *ADC Times: The Newsletter of the American-Arab Anti-Discrimination Committee*. Victory! Rock Band, Elektra Strike Accord with ADC. 8/2 (February), 1, 8–9.

______. 1987b. *ADC Times: The Newsletter of the American-Arab Anti-Discrimination Committee*. ADC-Cure Pact Aids American, Lebanese and Palestinian Orphans. 8/6 (August–September), 4.

Azerrad, Michael. 1989. Searching for The Cure: Can the Masters of "Mope Rock" Enjoy Life at the Top? *Rolling Stone* (September 7), 47, 49–50.

Beahm, George, ed. 1993. PMRC Mission Statement. In *War of Words: the Censorship Debate*. Kansas City, MO: Andrews and McMeel, 275.

Beels, Alex. 1994. Musician John Zorn's Brutal Images of Asians Draw Fire. *Asian New Yorker* (May), 5–6.

Bellman, Jonathan. 1998. The Hungarian Gypsies and the Poetics of Exclusion. In *The Exotic in Western Music*, ed. Jonathan Bellman. Boston: Northeastern University Press, 74–103.

Camus, Albert. 1942a. *L'Étranger*. Paris: Gallimard.

______. 1942b. *The Stranger*, trans. Stuart Gilbert. New York: Knopf, 1946.

______. 1942c. *The Stranger*, trans. Matthew Ward. New York: Vintage, 1988.

______. 1947. *La Peste*. Paris: Gallimard.

______. 1955. Preface to *The Stranger*. In *Lyrical and Critical Essays*, ed. Philip Thody, trans. Ellen Conroy Kennedy. New York: Vintage (1968), 335–337.

______. 1957. *L'Exil et la royaume*. Paris: Gallimard.

Clifford, James. 1988. *The Predicament of Culture: Twentieth-Century Ethnography, Literature, and Art*. Cambridge: Harvard University Press.

Coleman, Mark. 1987. Cure Releases Double Album. *Rolling Stone* (June 4), 15, 144.

The Cure. 1986. "Killing an Arab," *Standing on a Beach*. Elektra 9604771. Previously issued on Small Wonder Records (1978) and Fiction Records (1979).

______. 1987. *Kiss Me Kiss Me Kiss Me*. Elektra 607371.

______. 2001. *Greatest Hits*. Fiction Records 62726.

______. 2004. *Join the Dots: B-Sides and Rarities, 1978–2001 (The Fiction Years)*. Elektra 78043.

______. 2004. *Three Imaginary Boys*. Rhino Records 73348. Previously issued on Fiction Records.

______. 2006. Live performance of "Killing an Arab" at the Royal Albert Hall, London (April 1), posted at http://www.pixelkid.com/goth-city/the_cure/royal_albert_hall/cd3/10_Killing_An_Arab.mp3.

______. n.d. *Songwords 1978–1989: The Cure*. London: Fiction/Omnibus.

DeCurtis, Anthony. 1987. Cure, Arab Group Reach Accord on Song. *Rolling Stone* (February 26), 30.

Geist, William E. 1986. As Insult Piles Upon Calumny, an Arab Objects. *The New York Times* (December 10), B4.

Geyrhalter, Thomas. 1996. Effeminacy, Camp and Sexual Subversion in Rock: The Cure and Suede. *Popular Music* 15/2 (May), 217–224.

Gräfrath, Arne. 2005. Far-right tendencies in the wave and gothic scene. D-A-S-H Europe, Institut für Medienpädagogik in Forschung und Praxis (June 9), http://eu.d-a-s-h.org/node/314.

Hamilton, Denise. 1994. Zorn's "Garden" Sprouts Discontent: Asian American Groups Protest His Use of S&M Images on His CD and Accuse Him of Denigrating Women. *Los Angeles Times* (August 15), F9.

Hargreaves, Alec G. 1992. History and Ethnicity in the Reception of *L'Étranger*. In *Camus's* L'Étranger: *Fifty Years On*, ed. Adele King. New York: St. Martin's, 101–112.

Hisama, Ellie M. 1993. Postcolonialism on the Make: The Music of John Mellencamp, David Bowie and John Zorn. *Popular Music* 12/2 (May), 91–104. Repr. in *Reading Pop: Approaches to Textual Analysis in Popular Music*, ed. Richard Middleton. Oxford: Oxford University Press, 2000.

______. 2004. John Zorn and the Postmodern Condition. In *Locating East Asia in Western Art Music*, ed. Yayoi Uno Everett and Frederick Lau. Middletown: Wesleyan University Press, 72–84.

King, Adele. 1992. Introduction: After Fifty Years, Still a Stranger. In *Camus's* L'Étranger: *Fifty Years On*, ed. Adele King. New York: St. Martin's, 1–16.

Larkin, Colin, ed. 1995. The Cure. In *Guinness Encyclopedia of Popular Music*, Vol. 2. London: Square One, 1016–1018.

Lee, Elisa. 1994a. Zorn's Album Art of Asian Women Sparks Controversy. *AsianWeek: The English Language Journal for the National Asian American Community* (March 4), 1, 28.

———. 1994b. Asian Activists Angered When John Zorn Cancels Meeting. *AsianWeek* (July 8).

Locke, Ralph P. 1998. Cutthroats and Casbah Dancers, Muezzins and Timeless Sands: Musical Images of the Middle East. In *The Exotic in Western Music*, ed. Jonathan Bellman. Boston: Northeastern University Press, 104–136.

The New York Times. 1991. Arab-American Group Calls a Video Racist (December 14), 47.

———. 1993. Accused of Arab Slur, "Aladdin" is Edited (July 11), 16.

———. 1994. Arab-Americans Protest "True Lies" (July 16), 11.

O'Brien, Conor Cruise. 1970. *Albert Camus of Europe and Africa*. New York: Viking.

———. 1986. The Intellectual in the Post-Colonial World: Response and Discussion [transcript of a 1985 panel discussion with O'Brien, Edward Said, and John Lukacs], *Salmagundi* 70–71 (Spring-Summer), 65–81. Repr. in *The New Salmagundi Reader*, ed. Robert Boyers and Peggy Boyers. Syracuse: Syracuse University Press (1996), 450–467.

Pareles, Jon. 1987. Rock Group Accedes to Arab Protest. *The New York Times* (January 21), C22.

Rigaud, Jan. 1992. Depiction of Arabs in *L'Étranger*. In *Camus's* L'Étranger: *Fifty Years On*, ed. Adele King. New York: St. Martin's, 183–192.

Robb, Sean K. 2001. "Oh God, not again": Robert Smith on Killing An Arab. Chartattack (October 29), http://www.chartattack.com/damn/2001/10/2907.cfm.

Said, Edward W. 1993. *Culture and Imperialism*. New York: Knopf.

Sárosi, Bálint. 1971. *Gypsy Music*, trans. Fred Macnicol. Budapest: Corvina, 1978.

Sartre, Jean-Paul. 1943. Camus' *The Outsider*. In *Literary and Philosophical Essays*, trans. Annette Michelson. London: Rider and Company (1955), 24–41.

Schenker, Heinrich. [1910] 1987. *Counterpoint: A Translation of Kontrapunkt*, Vol. 1, ed. John Rothgeb and trans. John Rothgeb and Jürgen Thym. New York: Schirmer.

Shaheen, Jack G. 1984. *The TV Arab*. Bowling Green: Bowling Green State University Popular Press.

Smith, Robert. 2001. Video interview on *Freemuse: Freedom of Musical Expression* (July 12), Part IV, http://www.freemuse.org/sw4168.asp.

———. 2003. Interview on *Tout le monde en parle* with Thierry Ardisson, transcribed and translated by Olivier Hartmann (July 12), http://ourworld.compuserve.com/homepages/ChainofFlowers/tout071203.html.

Songwords 1978–1989: The Cure. London: Fiction/Omnibus Press, n.d., 6.

Suleiman, Michael W. 1989. America and the Arabs: Negative Images and the Feasibility of Dialogue. In *Arab Americans: Continuity and Change*, ed. Baha Abu-Laban and Michael W. Suleiman. Belmont, MA: Association of Arab-American University Graduates, 251–269.

———. 1996. Correspondence with author (September 26).

———, ed. 2000. *Arabs in America: Building a New Future*. Philadelphia: Temple University Press.

8
The Imagination of Pop-Rock Criticism

NADINE HUBBS

In the theory and lore of Jungian and archetypal psychology, imagination is an important construct, understood in a singular way. Here, imagination is not only an object or activity. It entails going deeper into the imagery of some thing, and not to cure, solve, or explain it, but "to dream the dream onward," in Carl Jung's classic phrase (Moore 1990, 7). For Jung, imagination is "an authentic accomplishment of thought or reflection that does not spin aimless and groundless fantasies into the blue; that is to say, it does not merely play with its object, rather it tries to grasp the inner facts and portray them in images true to their nature. This activity is an *opus*, a work."[1]

As my title suggests, imagination will be a central theme in this essay. The particular notion of imagination to be explored here is crucially informed by writings from the quasi-mystical teachings of Jungian psychology. Jungian and post-Jungian writers have lavished considerable attention onto the concept of imagination over many years, and their approach to the subject strikes me as congruous with the musical ideals of many of my colleagues doing music theory and analysis, the primary audience to whom this essay is addressed. I hope to evoke resonances with the imaginary of Jungian and archetypal psychology and to direct these toward pop-rock music and its critical contemplation. I hope, in other words, to go deeper into the imagination of pop-rock criticism, and to suggest ways in which such criticism might take music scholars deeper into the imagination of pop-rock music and listeners' experiences with that music.

Pop-rock music is a potent cultural force whose influences extend over a wide and diverse range of listeners. Until fairly recently, critical discourse concerning rock and pop came primarily from two sources: journalistic critics, and scholars in such fields as sociology, cultural studies, and media studies. Academic music studies in the disciplines of musicology and music theory were long concerned with art music, and only in the late 1980s did they begin to forge any appreciable engagement with popular music. Musicological and music-theoretical pop-rock scholarship is a relatively young field that has grown enormously since the early 1990s. There is now a fast-expanding body of books and dissertations in the field, and institutional structures have begun—though far more slowly—to reflect the presence of pop-rock music and its scholars.

By now, too, commentators have articulated various visions for pop-rock criticism. My project in this essay will be to consider a few of these in the process of proposing my own vision for pop-rock criticism and its possibilities. Several music scholars have noted that previous academic writings on pop and rock offered little discussion of the music itself, or consideration of its place within the complex of culture, words, sounds, and images, performed and received, that often constitutes pop-rock for more sociologically oriented writers.[2] While music's significance within this complex has been neglected and even explicitly dismissed by some writers on pop music (as I'll discuss below), other scholars and fans have argued for the crucial significance of the music in pop-rock performances and receptions.[3] The musical gaps in some prior critical discourse present opportunities and challenges for music scholars concerned with pop-rock—opportunities to create a pop-rock criticism that treats the significant role of the music itself, and challenges insofar as the existing methods of music analysis have developed in connection with the rather different aims and aesthetics of Western art music, and within technically specialized, often empiricist and formalist, discourses and practices.

The situation is summarized in a passage from Ingrid Monson. She is writing on jazz discourse, but her analysis applies equally to pop-rock discourse:

> On the one hand, poststructuralist cultural theory in the humanities has had difficulty addressing nonlinguistic discourses and practices (such as music, dance, and visual images) that in some respects operate analogously to language and text but in others do not. Music theory, on the other hand, has had trouble relating structural description to aesthetics, meaning and history.[4]

Like Monson, I believe "close readings of musical works can proceed from the constant intersection of sound, structure, and social meaning" (1996, 3)—which I understand to include textual, performance, and reception factors; lyrics and visual images; and dramatic and psychological meanings. Surely the artificial and largely arbitrary division of musical experience into constituent parts (music and lyrics, musical and cultural issues, production and reception) and the subsequent isolation of such parts for purposes of scholarly and disciplinary contemplation is problematic. And a musical criticism assuming such divisions offers the reader—presumably a music lover—a discourse incongruous with the holistic musical experience, and thus a discourse that fails to engage with, let alone further cultivate, musical sensibilities. It is a discourse that fails, in Jung's terms, to portray its object "in images true to [its] nature," and thus a discourse that risks becoming superfluous.

The object of such discourse, on the other hand, stands for many of its devotees as one of life's least superfluous preoccupations. It may be impossible to overstate the real and often urgent importance of and passion for popular music among its audiences—and by "popular music" I mean to refer to the whole verbal, visual, and sociocultural encounter within which music operates fundamentally, as a powerfully embodying and subliminal force (similarly, "listening" can comprise a whole complex of activities related to perceiving, attending to, and experiencing pop-rock music, including viewing, cognizing, moving, and emoting, as well as hearing).[5] Pop-rock music and the facts of its reception, its social function and cultural stature, call for nothing less than a criticism of engagement and necessity. I envisage such a criticism as one that examines musical experience in an integrative and inclusive way—drawing in the various musical and "extramusical" dimensions of meaning in pop-rock performance, and drawing forth a discourse and approach that can embrace and engage scholars, fans, and listeners from both within and without the music academy.

If the musical dimension of pop-rock discourse is to be further advanced and expanded, we music scholars with pop-rock interests and involvements are prime candidates for leadership. The prospect offers us an opportunity to imagine and re-vision our discipline: to rethink the assumptions that have guided music-analytic efforts, to reexamine the strengths and weaknesses of existing analytic tools in the light of particular pop-rock repertories, and hence to carry forward, rework, or abandon such tools as we see fit.[6] Such a retooling could entail examining performative and sociocultural elements beside and commingling with the music, to reveal in the music's design and patternings certain potent, often subliminal significations and the play of these among the array of verbal, vocal, visual, dramatic, and other elements involved in pop-rock production and reception.[7]

Music, Discourse, and Imagination—*Not* in That Order

Imagining and re-visioning his own discipline, James Hillman has sought "to restore psychology to its widest, richest, and deepest volume so that it would resonate with soul in its descriptions as unfathomable, multiple, prior, generative, and necessary" (Hillman 1989, 26). Outlining his project of archetypal psychology, Hillman writes: "I am suggesting both a *poetic basis of mind* and a psychology that starts neither in the physiology of the brain, the structure of language, the organization of society, nor the analysis of behavior, but in the processes of imagination" (1989, 22).

With substitution of the phrase "music criticism" for "psychology," this quote becomes a statement on what strikes me as a useful approach to music criticism in general, and pop-rock criticism in particular. In saying that criticism starts "in the processes of imagination" and not in structures of the brain, language, society—nor, we might add, of notes—one does not rule out possibilities for considering such structures at some point in the critical act. And indeed consideration of such issues will be valuable for critical contemplation of certain musical experiences and texts. But placing our own "processes of imagination" prior to these other factors—and thus reversing or reconceiving the order of priorities often assumed in music analysis and theory—could lead us to talk and write about music and our musical experiences in ways more "true to their nature."

Such an ordering of critical priorities could also be an important step toward expanding our communities of musical discourse. Discourses on music, we might suppose, should hold greatest appeal for those most interested in and engaged with music (assuming they possess some contemplative inclination). But in fact, musicians and music lovers often seem at odds with much of the pedagogical and professional discourse of musical analysis. Those of us who teach music theory may notice that certain of our students who make music most adeptly, who live most intimately within music, may find our ways of analyzing and talking about music most alien or inimical. Undoubtedly there are multiple factors at work here, which surely vary among individual cases, but I am convinced that one important factor is an apparent disconnect between the nature of these students' previous musical experiences and the nature of the musical experience that technical music-theoretic discourse can suggest to them.

One scene that has brought me up short against this realization is that of students remarking to me that my way of listening to a concert or recording must be completely different from theirs—what with all the rapid reckonings of pitches and Roman numerals taking place for every moment of music I hear![8] In fact, as a music theorist (albeit one who conceives of her work in terms of music criticism), I would feel crippled were I ever to lose touch with the sort of aesthetic, intuitive, holistic listening that both my students and I value and cultivate. It is in this mode of experiencing music, in its effects—often powerful, touching the body, mind, heart, soul, and imagination—that I formulate impressions and questions on the elements, workings, and ramifications of those effects, which may eventually develop into critical discourse.[9] Gleaning structures of pitch, rhythm, and harmonic progression is one possible mode of listening (as I tell my students) and one that can be valuable as a means to certain ends, but it is neither the only one or my usual one, nor a musically or morally privileged one. And, perhaps more importantly, it is not the mode of listening to or engaging with music that brought me—or (I trust) my students—to music, much less to pursue a life in music.[10]

Beginning students' and nonspecialists' difficulties with music-analytic discourse often bespeak a perception of analysis as a project primarily dealing in labels. Of course, a label in music theory, as in any discursive domain, appears saliently as a "Label" to the extent that its meaning, its connection to the object or experience it represents, remains opaque. Conversely, among those for whom such labels are familiar currency, "labelness" has fallen away, and these terms serve to evoke, with (more or less) transparency and immediacy, vivid musical experiences. An excerpt cited by Robert Walser can underscore my point. In it a writer for the magazine *Guitar for the Practicing*

Musician takes aim at an album track—metal guitar god Yngwie Malmsteen's "Black Star"—with a rapid-fire jumble of conspicuous Music-Theoretic Labels:

> The opening guitar piece is a classical prelude (as one might expect) to the larger work. It is vaguely reminiscent of Bach's *Bourrée* in Em, with its 3/4 rhythm and use of secondary dominant chords.... The passage at the close of the guitar's exposition is similar to the effect ... [of the] spiccato ("bouncing bow") classical violin technique. It is the first of many references to classical violin mannerisms.... This is a diminished chord sequence, based on the classical relationship of C diminished: C D♯ F♯ A (chord) to B major in a Harmonic minor mode: E F♯ G A B C D♯.... The feeling of this is like in some of Paganini's violin passages.... While these speedy arpeggio flurries are somewhat reminiscent of [guitarist Ritchie] Blackmore's frenzied wide raking, they are actually quite measured and exact and require a tremendous amount of hand shifting and stretching to accomplish. The concept is more related to virtuoso violin etudes than standard guitar vocabulary.... Notice the use of Harmonic minor (Mixolydian mode) in the B major sections and the Baroque Concerto Grosso (Handel/Bach/Vivaldi) style running bass line counterpoint as well (Walser 1993, 95; 1994, 240).[11]

For music theorists trained in the classical academic tradition, this passage may provoke consternation. It invokes familiar vocabulary and points of reference but veers off in unexpected, if not incoherent, directions with them.[12] And Wolf Marshall's account may seem as rhetorically transparent as it is semantically opaque: Its frequent jargon- and name-dropping in relation to "classical music" and "music theory" are readily seen as bids for musical and intellectual authority. The passage may read this way to us as classical music theorists because it trades in an insider discourse not quite our own. But here Marshall's excerpt may also be instructive, suggesting the extent to which our discourses can be perceived similarly, among "outsiders," as nonsensical and perhaps overweening successions of jargon. It may also remind us, palpably, of the frustration a listener can feel when presented with an opaque stream of mystifying Labels parading as discourse about music—all the more if it is music he or she cares about. Ultimately, the failure of such music-discursive encounters is their failure to bridge the gap between musical discourse and musical experience.

So, in seeking to expand musical and communicative engagements in our pop-rock discourses, we might (recalling Jung) consider the extent to which these discourses present "images true to [the] nature" of music as we *experience* it. Whatever the qualities and attributes that bring people to music, we should strive to cultivate the same qualities in our discourses about music so as to appeal precisely to the musically informed sensibilities of music listeners and lovers. My proposal for critical orientation here echoes the urgings and examples of several other musical commentators. Elaine Barkin, for example, pursues a related point in citing Friedrich Schlegel's statement that the work of criticism is "superfluous unless it is itself a work of art" (Barkin 1982, 5). In music-specific terms, Kevin Korsyn exhorts that a model for music analysis "should also leave room for the imagination, so that we remain artists even in our model-building. It should integrate knowing with feeling, lest our complex modes of analysis alienate us from music" (Korsyn 1991, 6). And I believe that such integration of a perceptive knowing and feeling has much to do with why Suzanne Cusick's accounts of embodied and erotic musical engagement have struck such a deep chord in the musical-scholarly community: her discourses seem to find many of us where we live musically (see Cusick 1994a and 1994b).[13]

Compelling and resonant musical writings like these are invaluable for my purposes here. They raise the standards of engagement and attunedness and provide models for subsequent discourses; I'll return to some of this work later. But I want also to consider musical discourses that have struck sour notes with readers, as this can be equally enlightening. We might observe, for instance, that Joseph Kerman's essay on classical music analysis "How We Got Into Analysis, and How to Get Out" is at heart a complaint about musical-discursive incommensurability. Kerman's criticism of theory and analysis' failure "to confront the work of art in its proper aesthetic terms" charges the discipline with a misguided "effort to achieve the objective status of and hence the authority of scientific inquiry." It culminates illustratively in his vivid quip that "[a]rticles on music composed after 1950, in particular, appear sometimes to mimic scientific papers in the way that South American bugs and flies will mimic the dreaded carpenter wasp" (1980, 313).

Elsewhere, Simon Frith criticizes the disconnectedness and irrelevance he perceives in rock discourses emanating from "academic musicology" by juxtaposing two glaringly disparate prose passages. The first is a long and impenetrable stretch of technical jargon addressing blow-by-blow the Animals song "I'm Crying," and seemingly ascribing to it (as far as the average reader can tell) sophisticated and rarified musical techniques of the highest order—all preceded by an ascription: "Richard Middleton, musicologist." Then comes a distinctly briefer quote from the song's cowriter Alan Price, revealing from its "authentic" source the song's humbly simple, naïvely pure, and almost randomly, inevitably "natural" origins: Band members wrote it "in the back of a van" and "just threw it together" one Sunday afternoon, "just stuck it together and recorded it and by chance it was successful … you know" (Frith 1981, 12–13).

Frith's deft positioning of disjunct discourses and Kerman's canny entomological simile serve not only to criticize but to ridicule projects perceived as addressing music on incongruous terms, which thereby appear harmless and batty at best, or absurd and arrogant at worst, but alienating and superfluous in any case.[14] Their commentaries, along with those of Barkin, Korsyn, and Cusick cited earlier, can suggest some general implications for music criticism, and more particular implications for pop-rock criticism. That is, if a compelling music criticism should be commensurable with its object, resonating with the aesthetic qualities of music and thus exciting imagination, feeling, and other capacities, then a compelling pop-rock criticism should possess these musical qualities but crucially should also address its object with an eye toward pop and rock's more particular emphases. These emphases should include musical elements like texture, timbre, and groove, and dramatic elements like irony, tongue-in-cheek, and playfulness, and each of these in concert with the various verbal, visual, social, and other elements with which they are intertwined in practice and reception.[15] Central to my message here is that our critical engagements with pop-rock music should not resemble a favorite gag of one of my colleagues, who invokes a ludicrous image of incongruous critical perspective with a sniff: "Obviously you haven't read my dissertation on pitch structure and ideology in 'Why Don't We Do It in the Road'!" The joke here is directed not at the idea of taking the Beatles song seriously, but rather at the image of a tone-deaf critical consciousness that takes itself seriously at the expense of the song and its particular sensibility.[16]

Music: In the Mix?

Of course, all the preceding begs the question of whether pop-rock criticism ought to concern itself with the music at all. Many cultural critics, historians, and sociologists treating popular music have either failed or actively refused to locate much significance in the music itself—hence the strain of rock criticism in which a song's lyrics are treated as sum total of the song-as-text, as well as the more explicit, considered dismissals of music that characterize the work of some writers. Perhaps most notorious in connection with the latter position is Simon Frith, a sociologist who has argued for the importance of interpretations of the social effects of rock texts ("repressive or liberating … [c]orrupting or uplifting … [e]scapist or instructive?") over consideration of "the aesthetic question" of how they achieve their effects. In his book *Sound Effects*, Frith, who has been an influential voice in popular music studies, freely professed an ignorance of the language of musical analysis and of even simple musical description (Frith 1981, 13, 54–55).

With the 1990s' burgeoning interest and activity in pop-rock scholarship within the music-academic community, such positions came under increasing scrutiny. Music theorists and analysts in particular bring expectations, consistent with their training and disciplinary acculturation, that the music or musical experience itself should be a primary object of close and serious attention.[17] By the late nineties, the question of what constituted the right mix of musical and sociocultural considerations in pop-rock criticism had received a fair amount of comment, from popular music scholars of various affiliations and backgrounds.

Among the formulations emerging from the discussion is the one presented by Edward Macan's 1997 book on English progressive rock, *Rocking the Classics.* Macan is a performer and music academic who claims important influences from certain materialist and sociological models of popular music. He writes emphatically of the unique "affective power" of popular music for contemporary audiences, and criticizes academic analysis—what he calls "the European approach to musical analysis"—for its exclusive concentration on "the sounds themselves," and on "those elements (harmony, melody, meter, and structural organization) which the European notational system can accurately convey." Surely Macan is correct in noting, as have various pop-rock critics before him, that conventional analytic perspectives neglect some of the most crucial elements (he cites "timbral and rhythmic subtleties") of musics outside the Western art music tradition, and that this analytic framework has facilitated claims for the aesthetic superiority of this music over non-Western and popular musics (Macan 1997, viii–ix).[18]

Macan's response to the perceived limitations in scholarly perspectives on music is to seek "a new approach to musicology based on the premise that analyzing sounds should not be an end in itself." He reasons that "people do not exist for music: music exists for people." Whether or not everyone would concur with his first assertion (we may well feel at times that we exist for music), one can scarcely dispute his second; clearly music exists for people, and this is undoubtedly a useful point to keep in mind as we pursue our music-analytic endeavors. The corollary Macan infers from this is presented as if inevitable, but it hardly seems so to me: that is, since "music exists for people," so the "ultimate goal of musicology" (which subsumes analysis here) should be "to document the relationship between music and society" (Macan 1997, x).

I find in this program three flaws on which I'll comment. First, its focus on "document[ing] the relationship between music and society" skips over relationships between music and individuals, the documenting of which can often be not only a more feasible and credible undertaking, but a more fascinating and revealing one and one that, in any case, should constitute a crucial reference point for all considerations of the relationship between music and society—that is, a large group of individuals. Second, as a critic interested in cultivating the imagination of pop-rock music, I find Macan's agenda wanting in its apparent concern only with *existing* relationships between music and people: Where do fantasized, potential, even implausible relationships figure in? Some of the musical discourses I find most compelling and invaluable present ways of hearing or relating to music that might never have occurred to me: They may surprise me, shatter my old perspectives, and expand my vision, whether or not I ever adopt them for myself. By way of example here, I'll mention a trio of inventive and frankly subjective queer visions: the highly individual, often transgressive operatic musings given by Wayne Koestenbaum in *The Queen's Throat* (Koestenbaum 1993); Judith Peraino's conscious conflation of a particular opera, Purcell's *Dido and Aeneas,* with a lesbian self in her *En Travesti* essay (Peraino 1995); and Stacy Wolf's reading of *The Sound of Music* with Mary Martin as a lesbian musical (Wolf 1996). Finally, my third criticism of Macan's agenda connects with both my previous ones: Declarations of any singular and exclusive "ultimate goal" for musicology (broadly conceived) strike me as ill-attuned to the object, music, which in its depth, breadth, and richness calls for a more inclusive and imaginative treatment.

That Macan rejects "analysis for its own sake" and never "resort[s] to musical examples… [or] graphic analysis" allows him, he claims, "to address a diverse audience" of readers with backgrounds in sociology, cultural theory, history, and other nonmusical fields (Macan 1997, 4). I am entirely sympathetic with these ends and seek to address an equally broad and varied readership in my own pop-rock criticism, but I would advocate for more flexible means than those Macan demarcates. In my writing I do "resort" to musical examples, though I sometimes use them in ways that don't require notational literacy: diagrammatically, for instance, to illustrate relative degrees of activity in rhythm or melodic contours, or as side-by-side excerpts to show resemblances between some musically derivative reference and its source-model. But even in striving for accessibility it seems likely that we will need to call on some form of musical notation in our pop-rock discourse, if it is to pursue meaningful illumination of musical issues. The challenge lies in rethinking, adapting, perhaps reinventing conventional notation and modes of graphic representation for optimal transparency and illustrative effect.

Macan's proscriptive position toward "graphic analysis" and "musical analysis as it is currently constituted" seems too readily yielding to what the feminist philosopher Mary Daly once called "[t]he tyranny of methodolatry" (Daly 1985). I disagree with his assertion that analysis "does not enable one to examine music's relation to extramusical elements such as visual iconography, much less its social meaning" (Macan 1997, 4). Indeed, I think certain kinds of analyses can elucidate and inform these very issues and meanings, which are precisely some of the issues I am concerned with in my work on popular music. To assume, however, as Macan does, that analysis constitutes only discrete, authoritatively defined orthodoxies "such as Schenkerian . . . and pitch-set theory" (4) seems lacking in imagination, and does little to advance our appreciation or understanding of popular music.

It is incumbent on us as music specialists concerned with pop-rock to be more creative and pragmatic, to seek out and devise whatever means prove helpful for illuminating pop-rock musical experience, and to find ways of making our analyses more useful and broadly communicative. We need not view analytic method in terms of static and authoritative givens, staking formalist claims to empirical objectivity. In fact, Heinrich Schenker, whose approach probably constitutes the most frequently invoked emblem of this image of music theory and analysis, was preoccupied in much of his work with formulating a *psychology* of music, as Kevin Korsyn has pointed out. Schenker's focus in this work was on the musical experience, "on the subject, not the musical object—or rather, his perspective produces [an] interpenetration of subject and object" (Korsyn 1993, 116). All this is not to deny that Schenker's work has been used to formalist and objectivist ends—indeed, as Korsyn notes (114), Schenker's concern with music psychology has been largely ignored in the music-theoretic literature—or that a preponderance of modern music theory and analysis has been formalist and empiricist, but rather to suggest (in both cases) that it need not be so.

The problems of conceptualizing pop-rock texts in appropriate terms are treated insightfully by the British musicologist Allan F. Moore. In his 1993 book *Rock: The Primary Text,* Moore speaks to the necessity of considering historical, political, and sociological, as well as musicological, approaches to the music. He notes that "the importance of the sounds is too often ignored" in discourses on rock, and thus he attempts to "establish the grounds for conceptualizing and considering… [rock's musical] texts." Of this project, Moore writes:

> I shall have recourse to existing musicological concepts, although I shall further argue that the wholesale application of a conventional academic musicology is both unwarranted and unhelpful.… [S]ince the techniques of such a discipline were developed for the analysis of musical pieces from the European "classical" tradition, their application towards a music (rock) that involves very different assumptions and practices leads to unsupportable conclusions (Moore 2001, 5).

I find much in this position with which to sympathize. It seems sensible and wise to build upon the established methods of musicology and music theory where they can be useful for our work with pop-rock music. But at the same time it is important that we acknowledge, as Moore does, that "rock differs [from classical music] in its purposes, publics, and aims" (Moore 2001, 7). I do not believe that the established techniques of music analysis must necessarily yield distorted results in connection with rock music (and I would say, judging by his book, neither does Moore; *wholesale* seems a pivotal word in the passage just cited).[19] There are, for instance, a number of significant bases in common between harmonic and melodic practice in art songs and the same practice in many pop-rock songs, and although tonal syntax does not tend to carry the same weight in both styles (it is a more salient parameter in art song as compared with most pop-rock), surely some of the analytic frameworks developed in connection with the former can be meaningfully illuminating in the latter. The adoption of any critical method calls for a reckoning of the assumptions and limitations it engenders, and that we adjust, focus, and fit it, however possible and as aptly as possible, to the object at hand.

In adapting and revamping some of our musical perspectives to suit the particularities of pop-rock, several governing notions in past musicological and music-analytic work seem especially in need of reexamination. One is the notion of canonicity, which in recent years has received critical scrutiny from within traditional musicology and theory. Still, some scholars evidently assume that the expansion of music scholarship into popular realms will engender the construction of a popular-music canon, either to exist in parallel with the established canon of Western art music, or somehow to supplant it as the new Master Narrative. The rock canon thus conceived already accepts the Beatles, Bob Dylan, and "punk," as Allan Moore notes. In his book, Moore includes a broad variety of musical examples in an attempt, he admits, to subvert the growth of any rock canon. Remarking that the study of European classical music has been hampered by canonicity's effects of encouraging an "over-profusion of studies of the 'great composers'" at the expense of other, presumed-lesser composers, Moore cautions that "[p]opular music studies must not be allowed to fall into the same trap" (Moore 1993, 7).

I concur and moreover would oppose any move toward establishing a pop-rock canon on other grounds. Canonicity and related notions like monumentalism, great-man theory, and master narrative have the potential to suffocate imagination, foreclosing as they do on the range of musical topics on which scholars might focus their inquiries, as Moore suggests, but also circumscribing the modes of inquiry by which we consider even canonic music and composers. In defining authoritative terms and objects of value, of "greatness," they exert a denaturing and stultifying effect on imagination. Less authoritative but similarly stultifying is a variety of pop-rock hagiography that one encounters in some contemporary pop discourse, in which the critic's prominently performed fervent fandom and identification with the star persona leaves little room for the imagination—equally, that of author and reader.[20]

Radioheaded

Having now, at some length, considered pop-rock music criticism in relatively abstract terms, I would like to turn toward a concrete exploration of the ideas I've been discussing. In particular, I would like to go deeper into some music that has haunted my imagination, has many times transported me, transfixed, to strange and beautiful realms of Radioheadedness. Radiohead's 1997 disc *OK Computer* is a concept album that immerses the listener in images of alienated life under techno/bureau/corporate hegemony. Its atmosphere might be compared with that of Sam Phillips's brilliant 1996 sleeper *Omnipop (It's Only a Flesh Wound Lambchop)*. In both, a vivid flavor of alienation and disaffectedness (though a distinct flavor in each case) is built up by layer over the course of twelve album tracks. Throughout *OK Computer* violent embattlement—against forces of coercion at times overt, at times insidious (the latter ominously present in government and media slogans of safety and self-improvement)—alternates with a kind of dreamy resignation, evoking a state of alienation into which actual aliens figure (hovering above in "Subterranean Homesick Alien," with its odd allusion to Dylan's "Subterranean Homesick Blues") along with androids.

The album's lyrics contain periodic bursts of violent resistance to a despised and repressive presence that goes unnamed. But the lyrics, already oblique in their written form, in this recording are often intelligible only in fragments. Indeed, I find the audible effect of these songs one approaching pure musicality: They open up a monumental range of sonic and affective states, from whispers to quasi-symphonic swells, and Thom Yorke's craggy-delicate vocals present within the aural landscape as a foreground component in constant transformation of texture and color—or maybe of a merged dimension, texture-color, in which timbre, pitch, and "words" are further inextricably merged, and "words" present as vowel and consonant sounds that are molded, shifted, stretched in shadings of the texture-color.[21]

Two of the album tracks I find most affecting comprise short statements. "No Surprises" (3'48") is a major-mode song of almost naïve simplicity. Its audible effect contrasts with the neo-prog-rock grandiosity of some of the album's other tracks (most notably "Paranoid Android").[22] But the lyrics booklet reveals that this lovely music is wedded to a narrative of silent desperation and fantasies of quiet, embracing suicide. The subdued atmosphere of "No Surprises" might be compared with that created in the all-acoustic opening of "Exit Music (For a Film)," an earlier cut on the disc (see Example 8.1).

The eight-bar verse (or **A** section) of "Exit Music" presents in its pitch-rhythm structure a Baroque lament formula, performed with quiet deliberateness and restraint (see Example 8.2). We hear a B-minor ground bass proceeding by measured but inevitable chromatic descent to V, and then moving toward drawn-out resolution—on a tonic chord clouded for two beats by the voice's suspended ninth (which resolves normally, to the octave) and for a full bar by a suspended fourth, whose eventual descent to a raised (i.e., Picardy) third suggests redemption, or even transcendence, in the stanza's final moments.

INTRO	**A**	A'	**B**	A''	**C**	A''	CODA
0:00	0:23	0:55	1:26	2:12	2:50	3:21	3:52–4:24
acoust. gtr.	+ voice		(mixed mtr.) + synthetic chorus	chorus + "electric seagulls"	+ big, old synthesizer + drum set	(vc. 8va) + synthetic chorus	rep. & fade down to voice, gtr., & "gulls"

Example 8.1 Radiohead, "Exit Music (For a Film)" (Thom Yorke-Jonny Greenwood-Phil Selway-Ed O'Brien-Colin Greenwood), *OK Computer* (1997): overall "roadmap," with timings.

Wake from your sleep							
F#	F#	F#	F# E	D	C#	C# B	
/ / / /	/ / / /	/ / / /	/ / / /	/ / / /	/ / / /	/ / / /	/ / / /
Bm	F#	D / A	E / G#	Bm	F#	B^{sus4}	B
i	V	III$^{6}_{4}$	IV^{6}	i	V	I^{4} —	#3

Example 8.2 Radiohead, "Exit Music (For a Film)" (Thom Yorke-Jonny Greenwood-Phil Selway-Ed O'Brien-Colin Greenwood), *OK Computer* (1997): verse (Section **A**): basic vocal melody (without ornaments) over chords and harmonic analysis.

You can	laugh a	spine–less	laugh . . .				
D'		C#'		B		A#	
F#	E#	E	D	D	E G	F#	E' F#'
/ / / /	/ / / /	/ / / /	/ / / /	/ / / /	/ / / /	/ / / /	/ / / /
Bm	C#	F#	G	G	C	F#	F#7
i	[V]	V	VI =	[V]	♭II	V —	7

Example 8.3 Radiohead, "Exit Music (For a Film)" (Thom Yorke-Jonny Greenwood-Phil Selway-Ed O'Brien-Colin Greenwood), *OK Computer* (1997): Section **C**, setting the fifth stanza of lyrics: basic vocal melody, represented as polyphonic (dual-voiced) melody (the single line divided into its constituent voice-leading strands, with upper-octave notes marked'), over chords and harmonic analysis (brackets enclosing the symbols for applied chords, which tonicize the harmonies that follows).

The first four stanzas are set by statements of **A**, excepting stanza 3, a **B** section that gently breaks up the foregoing repetition and metric regularity, with its A-minorness and added beats (hence mixed meter). The lyrics sketch the scene of a lover addressing his beloved, as they prepare for some daring and secret escape ("pack and get dressed/before your father hears us"); the voice is intimate, attenuated (notes seem frail and evanescent), vulnerable, and the music starkly tender. Only in the final line of stanza 4 do we begin to sense imminence: a cymbal tentatively surfaces in the texture, growing more insistent as the voice declares "theres such a chill, sucha CHILL" (as spelled in the liner notes).

The cymbal leads to a full-blown drum fill that launches section **C**, which introduces marked changes of sound and sentiment (see Example 8.3). The aural landscape is charged and swelling with the addition of the drum set, and a new mien for the voice—full and expansive, and soaring over a higher plane (a sixth above that of the verse, **A**). Most striking is the presence of a new and dominating, conspicuously electronic element in the texture. It is the gothic voice of some ancient beast of a vintage synthesizer, driving out (for the first time on this track) a solid bass line that homes in on one chord root after another, while also supplying a piercing treble descant. The entrance of this voice of the beast coincides with a turn in the narrator's address, away from the beloved and toward something despised—the faceless villain that surfaces elsewhere on the album. Thus the fifth stanza is a vitriolic curse, sung with building intensity: "you can laugh/a spineless laugh/we hope your rules and wisdom choke you." Listening here, a realization dawns in me. Feeling myself subjugated to this monochrome voice of electronic authority, I recall the quality of resigned acquiescence in narrations throughout the album and recognize its foreshadowing—alongside the name of the "spineless" despot—in the album's title, *OK Computer.*

Section **C** affords me further visions of nexus, sparked by the notable difference of melodic contour and register here. Whereas previously (in sections **A** and **B** both) the vocal melody had traced a stepwise descent, that of section **C** is characterized at the surface by large leaps downward and upward. But just beyond the surface, this vocal line too can be seen as a stepwise descent, only now, proceeding on two distinct levels that descend in parallel sixths. It is, in other words, a polyphonic (or compound) melody: a single line implying two distinct voices (as illustrated in Example 8.3).

Tension builds in this melody's first five bars by virtue of the singer's continuous transiting between the upper and lower voice-leading strands, and the chain of interlocking 7-6 suspensions implied thereby—all of which participates in the harmony, a neo-Baroque power progression that presents five consecutive strong major chords in a *minor* mode. Measure 6 gives the first hint of any move toward a resolution of tensions, when the lower strand of the dual-voiced melody breaks rank via an *ascending* step, D-E (and thus also severs the chain of suspensions). What follows is unmistakably the song's dramatic climax, which shares its summit with that of the voice's soaring ascent (F♯ - A♯ - E' - F♯') into its highest registral reaches, where it will stay throughout the final verse and until song's end.

The intensity of this moment is further amplified by a sublime musical stroke: the vocal ascent F♯ - A♯ - E' - F♯' at the end of section **C**, in scaling its climactic peak, also achieves a dazzling unification of the two (implied) voices previously distinct throughout the section. For here the interlocking elements that had defined these voices' discrete identities, their separate registral terrains and stepwise voice-leading trajectories, are confounded and thus merged. The *highest* notes reached in the gesture, E' - F♯', link up (as an octave-displaced motion from F♯) with the *lower* voice-leading strand. And this musical union of two voices further resonates with the narrative's union of two souls, proclaimed immediately in the final refrain (stanza six): "now we are one/in everlasting peace." Thus we learn, following the dramatic conflict and climax, that the "Exit" foretold in the song's title has been achieved, and the two lovers are joined in eternity. From this point on their single voice, now strong and sustained, soars perpetually in the transcendent realm of the upper register.

The final (sixth) stanza recaps the song in microcosm and confirms the denouement: After beginning in the realm of the young lovers, it turns again to the sinister entity, revisiting (in the united lovers' first-person plural) the curse of the fifth stanza (section **C**): "we hope that you choke that you choke." This malediction is stated three times to close the track. Thus the symbolic point of redemption or transcendence always present in the verse, the suspended fourth resolving at long last to a Picardy third, is underlined by repetition—as is the anomaly of its coupling with such murderous sentiments, and in circumstances so dubiously redemptive or victorious.

And Finally . . . The Answer

The critical ruminations just presented leave much undone. I've said only a small fraction of what could be said about this music, and what I do say undoubtedly slights certain issues, some categorically.[23] Perhaps most obvious in the present context is the fact that my discussion of Radiohead addresses selected issues of musical and narrative-dramatic structure and experience (particularly my own) without substantively taking up the music's social function. This does not signal my subscription to any doctrine privileging "the notes" over social effects, however. Indeed, elsewhere I have written primarily about pop-rock's social effects, interrogating musical particularities only to demonstrate subsidiary points in the service of my larger sociopolitical argument (see Hubbs 1996a). In any case, the preceding critical sample is admittedly incomplete even as exemplification of my earlier metacritical argument. But it can provide several useful points for comparison and concrete connection with that more abstract discussion.

Schenkerian method informs my reading of "Exit Music" and particularly of polyphonic melody in section **C** of the song. But my discussion and diagrams invoke the latter concept in a way that assumes no prior or specialized knowledge of Schenker's techniques of voice-leading analysis. Repeated listenings to the music and lyrics together fed my imagining of the vocal line in terms of dual voices, and this imagining, and hence the critical account that it inspires, interweaves the assigned musical trait (of polyphonic melody) with the song's narrative. Such indiscrete treatment of musical qualities and narrative drama is echoed in my commingling considerations of timbre and pitch-rhythm structure, and of the individual song and its whole-album context.

Although "Exit Music" is presented as just one album cut among many on *OK Computer* (with no evident potential for single release), it sparked my critical imagination in a way unlike any of the other tracks. My avowed anti-canonic position accommodates selection of such a song as the primary object of my critical focus. In my commentary I often assert and explicate meanings in relation to the song but offer no ultimate meaning for it, and I admittedly leave off inconclusively, ascribing anomaly to the final musical and narrative gestures of "Exit Music." All told, my discussion similarly may shed little light on certain important questions attending pop-rock criticism, including the issues of perspective, authority, and valuation raised earlier in connection with canonicity and hagiography. In the face of such questions I'll turn once again to archetypal psychology, which offers a relevant observation: Our demands for unity and unifying interpretations, according to Hillman, give rise to heroic suppression of multiplicity and complexity.

Expanding on Jung's conceptions of the psyche as deeply divided and multiplicitous, Hillman advocates for a "polytheistic" psychology that can embrace conflicting impulses without "resorting to hierarchies and overarching principles to impose order."[24] I think cultivating this sort of polytheism in music criticism could help us to foster rich, textured, and musically congruous, *commensurably* complex discourse on music and our experiences with it. A polytheistic music criticism would move not in a reductive direction, narrowing our musical experiences to unitary explanations and interpretations, but rather in a generative direction, expanding and multiplying musical meanings, images, and apprehendings.

Hillman's polytheist perspective and his caveats against unifying impulses might also be brought to bear on a question taken up by all the pop-rock critics cited here: that of the relative value and priority, for pop-rock discourse, of interpretation of the music and sounds versus interpretation of the attendant sociocultural and historical facts. Simon Frith, as I've mentioned, has argued for the primacy of social effects over popular music texts and their workings (1981, 54–55). Arguing explicitly against Frith, Allan Moore enjoins us to focus our primary critical attention on the music: "[T]he sounds of rock cannot, ultimately, be divorced from their setting, [but] they must be loosely separated in the interim" (1993, 6). Outlining the argument encapsulated by his book's title (*Rock: The Primary Text*), Moore writes, "Our concern has to begin from the sounds, because *until we cognize the sounds,* until we have created an internal representation on the basis of their assimilation, *we have no musical entity to care about*" (17). Edward Macan takes issue with both Frith and Moore explicitly in staking out his own position that musicology should have an "ultimate goal" of "document[ing] the relationship between music and society" (1997, 9, 7, x).

Amid the apparent clanging and often emphatic disagreement among these writers, I am struck by their fundamental similarity. Each asserts that some particular object should constitute the primary focus of popular music criticism, and each locates that object in society, the musical text, or the relationship between the two. Each writer, in other words, purports to offer The Answer. Each one, I might add, also argues his position, and from such discussion a number of valuable and persuasive points emerge. But I find myself less than completely convinced by all these arguments and am left wondering why we might need, or should even want, to isolate and identify the single element or category of pop-rock music putatively most important and worthy of interpretive attention.

The priorities debate in pop-rock discourse concerning social effects versus musical effects invites comparison with a parallel debate, concerning timbral qualities versus pitch-rhythm structure (better known as "the notes"). I cannot but feel equally perplexed in the face of both formulations, as I'll attempt here to explain. Following a conference presentation on the Nirvana song "Lithium," Walter Everett was told by one audience member that all his talk of "notes" had been irrelevant, since the only thing of importance in Nirvana is the timbre of Kurt Cobain's guitar.[25] In later dialogue with me, Everett posed a rhetorical and illustrative question: "I wonder which performance my questioner would find closer to the heart of 'Lithium': playing its pitches and rhythms on a cheesy keyboard, or even on steel drums; or playing, say, 'Baby I'm a-Want You' on a heavily distorted Jag-stang like Cobain's?" To this question I'll add some ponderings of my own: What does it say about the significance of pitch-rhythm structure vis-à-vis timbre (and other parameters) when listeners perceive and speak of the *identity* of a particular song even when its timbral landscape (perhaps also tempo, key, and other elements) is completely changed, but its pitch-rhythm framework is retained? We might think here of Tori Amos's radical (soft, slow) cover of Nirvana's "Smells Like Teen Spirit," or Nirvana's unplugged version of David Bowie's "Man Who Sold the World," or even those instances when an artist's new release is recognized as merely "new words on an old song" by virtue of its recycling of previously used pitch-rhythm structures: chord changes, perhaps, or chorus-verse designs (such as Nirvana's much-imitated loud-soft alternations).

These rhetorical queries suggest that Nirvana's guitar timbre, though unquestionably distinctive and expressively crucial, is not the whole story of their music. Such a view finds corroboration in James Hunter's *Rolling Stone* review of Tori Amos in which he remarks retrospectively on Amos's having been "bold enough to have seized 'Smells Like Teen Spirit' as her own (on 1992's *Crucify* EP)—she recognized that grunge's uneasy blend of emotional distress and sonic kicks represented a state of mind as well as a guitar sound" (Hunter 1998, 55). Hunter's statement centrally asserts that to privilege exclusively the timbral element in Nirvana is to sell their music short. I agree and would extend the point to rock music in general. This is not to say that I cast my vote for "notes" over timbre in pop and rock music but rather that, claiming both (as well as "state of mind" and more), I reject the entire either/or proposition.

Surely much of the difficulty and controversy surrounding such questions—of timbre and/or notes, social and/or musical effects—has to do with the nature of pop-rock music as it exists for us: as a kind of experiential soup of diverse but well-mingled ingredients. In a lifetime of listening to pop and rock songs, and even in listening repetitively and obsessively to certain ones, I have never found myself playing a song this time for notes and the next time for timbre, or once through focusing on the social effects and then again for musical effects, or now for the music and again for lyrics. I don't listen, and I don't know anyone who listens to (dances to, hums along with, or otherwise experiences) pop-rock music in this way. Why, then, should its criticism proceed along such compartmentalizing lines? James Hunter muses, "What the hell is rock & roll these days, anyway? Loud guitars? Transgressive hairstyles? Samples? Electric beats? Platform shoes? At any given time, it's all or none of these things" (1998, 56). Pop-rock music, as this litany implies, is a multifarious creation, and as such can engage audiences in multidimensional, multisensory mind-body experiences. Our critical discourse could strive to reflect, even to amplify, such multidimensionality and multivalence where we find it, rather than diminish or contain it.

Warning of the limitations engendered in fixed critical focuses, Suzanne Cusick proposes a musical discourse of expansion and possibility:

> [Our] focus on texts… puts us at risk of forgetting that music… is first of all something *we do,* we human beings, as a way of explaining, replicating, and reinforcing our relationship to the world, or our imagined notions of what possible relationships might exist. I suspect for all of us the originating joy of [music] comes from assuming more varied positions than we think we're allowed in regular life, positions that enable us to say yes or no, to immerse,… to escape a system… of bewilderingly fixed categories, to wallow in the circulation of pleasures that are beyond danger and culturally defined desires (Cusick 1994, 80).

Cusick goes on to urge that "in our musics, our musicalities, our musicologies" we restore to ourselves the "originating joy" of music (80). Music in her account is first and foremost an experience, "something *we do*," and a fully human, richly imaginative experience; her pursuit of an "originating joy" seems pursuant, in musical terms, of what Jung called "the inner facts" of the object. Returning to Jung's exhortation can bring us back to the question of critical priorities: If in our discourses on pop-rock music we seek out its "inner facts" and strive to "portray them in images true to their nature," then our project will begin neither with social effects nor with the musical text, but rather, following Hillman's prescription for archetypal psychology, with *imagination*—which might dictate a high priority for social, textual, and/or other considerations, depending on the qualities or "inner facts" of the particular music-experiential instance.

Further, related ideas from Jungian and archetypal psychology can also be suggestive for pop-rock criticism, including Hillman's welcoming stance toward paradox and mutually conflicting elements and his antiliteralist program. These offer potentials for deepening and complicating our imagination of musical pleasure and pain, and their interplay—thus, of our evident need for *shadow* experiences (in the Jungian sense) in musical melancholy, tragedy, and even violence, to provide catharsis and perhaps other soul fulfillments.[26] Popular music, as the name suggests, is for people. But even more, popular music—all music—exists *only* by virtue of people's, our, desire for, imagination, and creation of it. And then it exists in rich, complex, and intimate relation to us, calling out for images and discourses that take us deeper into its mysteries—the mysteries of our passions and entanglements in it, all of which begin and end in imagination. Anything less imaginatively or less musically conceived is unequal to the task and to our object, which is after all nothing less than music.

Notes

An earlier version of this essay was presented at the meeting of the Society for Music Theory in Phoenix, November 1997. I am grateful to session attendees and colleagues for their comments and criticisms.

1. Carl G. Jung, *Psychology and Alchemy;* quoted in Moore 1992, 185.
2. See, for example, Covach 1997, 119–141; McClary and Walser 1990, 285–286; Moore 2001; and Walser 1993, xiv, 21, 28.
3. See, for example, Vermorel and Vermorel 1990, Walser 1993, and Wise 1990.
4. Monson 1996, 3. It might be more accurate to say, recasting Monson, that music theory has had trouble *seeing any need* to relate structural description to aesthetics, meaning, and history—that is, that the discipline largely has conceived and in many quarters continues to conceive itself in terms more scientific (or scientistic) than humanistic or artistic, and as such has often concerned itself with relating its structural descriptions to little or nothing beyond themselves. This situation was described some years ago in Joseph Kerman (1980), "How We Got into Analysis, and How to Get Out," which advocates ultimately not for any abolishment of music theory and analysis, but rather for analysis to move self-consciously toward cultivation of a serious and comprehensive musical *criticism,* addressing questions not only of a work's inner logic and coherence, but of aesthetic value and meaning as well.
5. See, for example, the passion and urgency of pop fandom that is invoked in the Smiths' 1987 song "Rubber Ring": "don't forget the songs/That made you cry/ And the songs that saved your life/ . . . they were the only ones who ever stood by you." For further evidence and discussion of the significance of pop-rock music for its fans, see the sources cited in note 3; with regard to music in general, see Crafts et al. 1993.
6. One essay argues that music theorists should analyze rock music for the benefits this promises their discipline: "[T]heorists should pay more attention to rock music because it is interesting, and it is interesting because as a repertory it challenges disciplinary assumptions" (Covach 1996, 133).
7. I have attempted this sort of criticism in several essays: See Hubbs 1996a, 1996b, and 2007.
8. It is relevant in this context to note that the students I refer to here were undergraduates at Wayne State University, the urban commuter institution where I was teaching when I first wrote these lines. Though it is not impossible for me to

imagine their remark coming from undergraduates at the University of Michigan, where I now teach, it seems less likely. The differences in socioeconomic and educational privilege that obtain generally between the two student bodies make for differing (i.e., especially, outsider versus insider) relations to discourses of authority. That music-theoretic description is perceived and at times contested as one such discourse is readable in this anecdotal instance as in the debates considered throughout this essay.

9. See note 4 with regard to music criticism vis-à-vis analysis.
10. For an in-depth examination of different attentional modalities available to the reader or listener and their respective pleasures and purposes, see Edward T. Cone's essay "Three Ways of Reading a Detective Story—Or a Brahms Intermezzo" (Cone 1989).
11. All ellipses are reproduced from Robert Walser's quotation of Wolf Marshall's passage in Walser 1993 and 1994.
12. From the perspective of classical music theory, the excerpt's most problematic elements include the reference to triple meter in relation to the bourrée, a duple-meter dance; apparent non sequitur references to the presence of a classical prelude "as one might expect," and to "the guitar's exposition" (within a work of unspecified form); the misspelled C-diminished chord (as enharmonic equivalent: D♯ diminished); a puzzling reference to the "classical relationship" of B-major and C-diminished chords within a key whose scale is subsequently spelled as *E minor* (harmonic form); and the ostensible misequating of harmonic minor and Mixolydian modes. But according to Walser, all of these items—with the exception of the enharmonically spelled C-diminished chord—convey solid, intelligible information to readers versed in the insider discourse around heavy metal music (e-mail to author, January 2, 2004).
13. Indeed, Cusick writes of the music she "truly 'love[s]'" that "it is about the transcendent joy of being alive, not dead, and aware of the difference" (1994a, 69).
14. Comparable in effect to Frith's passage, though more comedic than critical, is the film scene from *This is Spinal Tap* in which a band member holds forth on the lofty high-art valences of Spinal Tap's song "Lick My Love Pump."
15. A number of writers have emphasized the expressive and semiotic importance of timbre in rock and pop, including Allan Moore (2001, 44–49). Moore also underlines in particular the crucial role of the voice in popular music. I believe, with Moore, that critics of pop and rock need to cultivate a language and conceptual schema that can account closely for the qualities of voice that bear considerable aesthetic and communicative weight in this music.
16. And the joke is that of Andy Mead (with my twists and tweakings here) who is evoking, as I have always understood him, not any existing pop-rock scholarship, but the same "educated fool" archetype as is evoked in the satirical *Spinal Tap* scene cited in note 14, and in Frith's musicologist-rocker juxtaposition cited above.
17. The musical score is taken as text and object in most music-theoretic and -analytic work. The musical experience, or rather the listening experience, is treated as the object of focus in music-phenomenological work such as that of Thomas Clifton (1975) and David Lewin (1986), and in the work of such theorist-analysts as Joseph Dubiel (1996), Marion Guck (1981 and 1997), and Fred Everett Maus (1988).
18. For examinations of the incongruities, inadequacies, and inequities of conventional analysis as applied to popular and non-Western musics, see Frith 1987, Middleton 1990, Shepherd 1991, and Walser 1994.

19. On this point I concur with Covach 1997, 129 n. 21, 136.
20. See, for example, Joe Stuessy's discussion of the Beatles (1994, 119 and 141 especially). Also notable in this regard is Wilfrid Mellers's Beatles book *Twilight of the Gods,* and Simon Frith's remark that Mellers's books on Bob Dylan and the Beatles "read like fan mail" (Frith 1987, 136).
21. Several months after drafting this essay, I was surprised to discover a song from *OK Computer* appearing already in a cover version: "Exit Music (For a Film)" as recorded by Brad Mehldau for his album *Art of the Trio, Vol. 3: Songs* (Warner CD 47051, released September 1998). The choice of this song for purely instrumental treatment by jazz pianist Mehldau may attest to my claims for the purely musical qualities of *OK Computer*, and perhaps also to the particular potency I ascribe to "Exit Music."
22. Progressive (or prog) rock is a style that reached its zenith in the 1970s in the work of such bands as Emerson, Lake & Palmer; Yes; Genesis; Kansas; Pink Floyd; King Crimson; and Jethro Tull. Defining its characteristics is a central project of the essays in this volume by John Covach and Mark Spicer. Prog rock was known for "gargantuan stage shows, its fascination with epic subject matter drawn from science fiction, mythology, and fantasy literature, and above all for its attempts to combine classical music's sense of space and monumental scope with rock's raw power and energy" (Macan 1997, 3). *OK Computer* invokes a number of prog-rock characteristics and style markers, but in my view its 1990s "neo-" treatment places these somewhat in quotes, and thus sidesteps the oft-remarked pretentiousness of vintage-era prog rock. Note, for example, the postmodern ironic twists provided by the lyrics' mock-earnest recitations of hokey ad-copy fragments, or the music's subtle broken-record-player pitch wavering when the would-be poignant strings enter in "No Surprises" (ca. 1:49–2:13).
23. See Marzorati 1998 for consideration of Radiohead's *OK Computer* in relation to some sociocultural, commercial, and artistic issues not treated here. Marzorati places *OK Computer* at the center of a discussion lamenting the decline (due to digital technology and certain music industry trends) of album-oriented listening, and thus of (especially) youthful musical experiences affording "truths and recognitions … that can be gotten nowhere else [and that] cannot be gotten quickly or piecemeal" (39). Marzorati's characterizations of the album's music and apparent rock lineage echo those given by Mark Kemp in his CD review for *Rolling Stone* 765 [July 10, 1997], 117–118.
24. Thomas Moore, in Hillman 1989, 37.
25. Everett's discussion of "Lithium" was part of his unpublished paper "David Brackett, Wilson Pickett, Nirvana and Lucifer," given at the Re*pre*sent*ing Rock conference at Duke University in April 1997.
26. Used in the Jungian sense, "shadow" refers to those elements of the psyche, deemed negative, evil, or weak, that are cast off, denied, and repudiated by the conscious self and thus in need of integration, according to Jung.

References

Barkin, Elaine. 1982. In Your Own Verse: a.k.a. *An Alice Is Lost. In Theory Only* 6/4, 3–8.

Clifton, Thomas. 1975. Some Comparisons between Intuitive and Scientific Descriptions of Music. *Journal of Music Theory* 19/1, 66–110.

Cone, Edward T. 1989. Three Ways of Reading a Detective Story—Or a Brahms Intermezzo. In *Music: A View from Delft*, ed. Robert P. Morgan, 77–93. Chicago: The University of Chicago Press.

Covach, John. 1997. We Won't Get Fooled Again: Rock Music and Musical Analysis. *In Theory Only* 13/1–4, 117–141.

Crafts, Susan D., Daniel Cavicchi, Charles Keil, and the Music in Daily Life Project, compilers. 1993. *My Music*. Hanover, NH: University Press of New England.

Cusick, Suzanne G. 1994a. On A Lesbian Relationship with Music: A Serious Effort Not to Think Straight. In *Queering the Pitch: The New Gay and Lesbian Musicology*, ed. Philip Brett, Elizabeth Wood, and Gary C. Thomas, 67–83. New York: Routledge.

______. 1994b. Feminist Theory, Music Theory, and the Mind/Body Problem. *Perspectives of New Music* 32/1, 8–27.

Daly, Mary. 1985. *Beyond God the Father: Toward A Philosophy of Women's Liberation*, second ed. Boston: Beacon Press.

Dubiel, Joseph. 1996. Hearing, Remembering, Cold Storage, Purism, Evidence, and Attitude Adjustment. *Current Musicology* 60–61, 26–50.

Frith, Simon. 1981. *Sound Effects: Youth, Leisure, and the Politics of Rock'n' Roll*. New York: Pantheon.

______. 1987. Towards an Aesthetics of Popular Music. In *Music and Society: The Politics of Composition, Performance, and Reception*, ed. Richard Leppert and Susan McClary, 133–149. New York: Cambridge University Press.

Guck, Marion A. 1981. Musical Images as Musical Thoughts: The Contribution of Metaphor to Analysis. *In Theory Only* 5/5, 29–42.

______. 1997. Two Types of Metaphoric Transference. In *Music and Meaning*, ed. Jenefer Robinson, 201–212. Ithaca: Cornell University Press.

Hillman, James. 1989. *A Blue Fire: Selected Writings by James Hillman*, introduced and ed. Thomas Moore. New York: Harper & Row.

Hubbs, Nadine. 1996a. Music of the 'Fourth Gender': Morrissey and the Sexual Politics of Melodic Contour. In *Genders*, Vol. 23, *Bodies of Writing, Bodies in Performance*, ed. Thomas Foster, Carol Siegel, and Ellen E. Berry, 266–296. New York: New York University Press.

______. 1996b. A Closer Look at "Hook," & Other Comments on (Pop Music's Comments on) the Classical Canon. Paper presented at the Cross(over) Relations Conference, Rochester, NY, September 29.

______. 2007. "I Will Survive": Queer Mappings of Social Space in a Disco Anthem. *Popular Music* 26/2, 231–244.

Hunter, James. 1998. Recordings: Living it Up at the Hotel Choirgirl (review of Tori Amos, *From the Choirgirl Hotel*). *Rolling Stone* 786 (May 14), 55–56.

Kerman, Joseph. 1980. How We Got into Analysis, and How to Get Out. *Critical Inquiry* 7/2, 311–331.

Koestenbaum, Wayne. 1993. *The Queen's Throat: Opera, Homosexuality, and the Mystery of Desire*. New York: Poseidon Press.

Korsyn, Kevin. 1991. Towards A New Poetics of Musical Influence. *Music Analysis* 10/1–2, 3–72.

______. 1993. Schenker's Organicism Reexamined. *Intégral* 7, 82–118.

Lewin, David. 1986. Music Theory, Phenomenology, and Modes of Perception. *Music Perception* 3/4, 327–392.

Macan, Edward. 1997. *Rocking the Classics: English Progressive Rock and the Counterculture*. New York: Oxford University Press.

Marzorati, Gerald. 1998. How the Album Got Played Out. *New York Times* (Feb. 22): sec. 6, 36–39.

Maus, Fred Everett. 1988. Music as Drama. *Music Theory Spectrum* 10, 56–73.

McClary, Susan, and Robert Walser. [1988] 1990. Start Making Sense! Musicology Wrestles with Rock. In *On Record: Rock, Pop, and the Written Word*, ed. Simon Frith and Andrew Goodwin, 277–292. New York: Pantheon.

Mellers, Wilfrid. 1973. *Twilight of the Gods: The Music of the Beatles*. New York: Viking Press.

Middleton, Richard. 1990. *Studying Popular Music*. Philadelphia: Open University Press.

Monson, Ingrid. 1996. *Saying Something: Jazz Improvisation and Interaction*. Chicago: University of Chicago Press.

Moore, Allan F. 2001. *Rock: The Primary Text*, second ed. [1993]. Aldershot and Burlington: Ashgate.

Moore, Thomas. 1990. *Dark Eros: The Imagination of Sadism*. Dallas: Spring Publications.

———. 1992. *Care of the Soul: A Guide for Cultivating Depth and Sacredness in Everyday Life*. New York: HarperCollins.

Peraino, Judith. 1995. I Am an Opera: Identifying with Henry Purcell's *Dido and Aeneas*. In *En Travesti: Women, Gender, Subversion, Opera*, ed. Corinne E. Blackmer and Patricia J. Smith, 99–131. New York: Columbia University Press.

Phillips, Sam. 1996. *Omnipop (It's Only a Flesh Wound Lambchop)*. Virgin Records 418602.

Radiohead. 1997. *OK Computer*. Capitol Records CDP 8552292.

Shepherd, John. 1991. *Music as Social Text*. Cambridge, MA: Basil Blackwell.

Stuessy, Joe. 1994. *Rock and Roll: Its History and Stylistic Development*, second ed. Englewood Cliffs, NJ: Prentice-Hall.

Vermorel, Fred, and Judy Vermorel. [1985] 1990. Starlust. In *On Record: Rock, Pop, and the Written Word*, ed. Simon Frith and Andrew Goodwin, 481–490. New York: Pantheon.

Walser, Robert. 1993. *Running with the Devil: Power, Gender, and Madness in Heavy Metal Music*. Hanover, NH: University Press of New England.

———. 1994. Highbrow, Lowbrow, Voodoo Aesthetics. In *Microphone Fiends: Youth Music and Youth Culture*, ed. Andrew Ross and Tricia Rose, 235–249. New York: Routledge.

Wise, Sue. [1984] 1990. Sexing Elvis. In *On Record: Rock, Pop, and the Written Word*, ed. Simon Frith and Andrew Goodwin, 390–398. New York: Pantheon.

Wolf, Stacy. 1996. The Queer Pleasures of Mary Martin and Broadway: *The Sound of Music* as a Lesbian Musical. *Modern Drama* 39/1, 51–63.

9

Trapped within the Wheels

Flow and Repetition, Modernism and Tradition in Stevie Wonder's "Living for the City"

TIM HUGHES

In 1973 Stevie Wonder released one of the highlights of his career, "Living for the City," on the album *Innervisions.* Over the decades since its release, "Living for the City" has had a significant impact as a chart-topping single (reaching number 1 and number 8 on *Billboard's* R&B and pop charts, respectively), an important crossover success on album-oriented radio, a centerpiece of Wonder's live performances, the soundtrack for a controversial film scene, and most of all as a political anthem of uncommon realism, intensity, durability, and poignancy revered by fans, other musicians, and critics alike (see, for instance, The 500 Greatest 2004). It remains idiosyncratic, certainly one of the most unusual songs ever to reach the Top Ten. But it is also an interesting and instructive example of Wonder's use of repetition and flow to create a song that is at once simple and complex, natural and mannered, general and specific, and permeated with cultural memory, in a way that effectively mimics reality and makes a strong social commentary that is still applicable today. As Cintra Wilson (1996) has said, "When Spike Lee used 'Living for the City' as the soundtrack of his crack manifesto in 'Jungle Fever,' he knew what he was doing—there is no more powerful audio representation of the cruel eddies of inner-city fate."[1]

Wonder publicized the release of *Innervisions* in an unusual way, by blindfolding the guests and critics at a record-release party and leading them on a bus tour of New York City:

> They put a whole batch of us on a bus in Times Square and blindfolded us. Then they drove us around for what seemed like a long time—it was probably in the neighborhood of ten minutes, but it felt like half an hour. They pulled up in front of some place and shepherded us off the bus and into a cool, air-conditioned space.... Then they played us the record. It was an amazing thing. Totally disorienting. The music had a clarity, a lucidity, and a flat-out *power* that was greatly increased by the limitation of the visual sense; no distraction, or complete distraction, but in the

> end, it really focused the whole experience, and *not* only because the music was unforgettable, although of course it was. It was one hell of a way to experience "Living for the City" for the first time (Dave Marsh, quoted in Werner 2004, 193).

This promotion was undoubtedly designed to give the listeners a clearer sense of the "visions in my mind" that are the central theme of *Innervisions* and its title track, "Visions." But it was also clearly designed to supplement the strikingly original use in "Living for the City" of a minute-long dramatic vignette—more akin to a radio drama or a talking book than to a soul song—to tell the story of a very different bus ride to New York City and its cruel consequences and broader implications.

One of the main reasons why "Living for the City" works so well, in addition to its element of Wellesian radio theatre, is because it is a fluid combination of multiple paradoxes: Wonder fuses the collective with the individual, complexity with simplicity, and a controlled and rehearsed recording process with spontaneous flexibility. He also infuses modernist experimentation with deep cultural memory, and teaches the history of a tragic migration of millions through the story of a tragic journey by a nameless individual.

Analysis of this song not only reveals further and deeper meanings, but also suggests that it is Wonder's sophisticated use of repetition and flow that allows him to artfully yet almost imperceptibly resolve these paradoxes. Most existing discussions of repetition and flow, by authors such as John Miller Chernoff, James Snead, Christopher Small, Dick Hebdidge, Tricia Rose, and Adam Krims, have generally focused on rhythm and meter in African, African-American, and Afro-Diasporic traditions, at or near the surface of the music.[2] But, as I shall demonstrate, Wonder employs in "Living" a wide variety of repeated elements on multiple levels to create a complex, interwoven pattern of flows that effectively shapes the song, propels it forward, and generates meaning.

At 7'21", "Living for the City" is relatively long for a soul song of its era, but not unusually so. It features an extended improvisational passage, followed by its distinctive dramatic vignette and an extended closing section. (The hit single was an abridged version, omitting the vignette and the final two verses.) "Living for the City" tells the story of an anonymous, hardworking, poor black family from "hard-time Mississippi" and the son who travels to New York City, eyes wide with wonder. He is unjustly convicted of an unspecified offense, sentenced to ten years in prison, and eventually left, years later, to walk the streets. The story is told in a generalized fashion: all names are omitted, it is unclear what unintended crime the son has committed—although drug possession is implied—and the situation is of the sort that could happen to anyone in the wrong place at the wrong time. Yet despite this generality, the story directly addresses several of the thorniest and most emotional problems of its time: poverty, systematic racial discrimination, urban decay, the mass migration of black Americans from the agrarian, rural South to the industrial, urban North, and the crushing injustice of the American justice system and the power structure that it supports.[3]

The ethos of "Living for the City" emerged from the twin impulses of the civil rights movement and the political activism of 1960s and early-'70s musicians, represented in politically or socially conscious anthems by soul and funk musicians such as Curtis Mayfield (see particularly such work with the Impressions as "Keep On Pushing," "This Is My Country," and "Choice of Colors," and his solo albums, *Curtis* and *Superfly*); the Temptations (as in the Norman Whitfield-produced singles, "Cloud Nine," "Run Away Child, Running Wild," "Ball of Confusion (That's What the World Is Today)," and "Papa Was a Rolling Stone"); Marvin Gaye (in much of *What's Going On*); and the Staple Singers (as in *Be Altitude: Respect Yourself*). Wonder draws heavily on gospel, the blues, and mid-tempo soul songs—like Gaye's version of "I Heard It Through the Grapevine" and the Staple Singers' "Respect Yourself"—that are built around single, extensively repeated grooves. Despite its superficial stylistic conservatism (in comparison with some work of Mayfield and Gaye), "Living for the City" has made as much of a lasting impact as any of the political anthems of its era. This is at least partly due to Wonder's effective pairing of lyric content and musical form, using a dramatic narrative to illustrate and amplify a political message, and combining a broadly generalized subject with sharply pointed language.

The Verse (with Refrain) Sets the Groove

The first four measures of "Living for the City" quickly establish its core: the relatively simple two-measure groove that plays for nearly three-fourths of its length, evoking blues and gospel at the song's very foundation. The basis of this groove—reminiscent of the rolling blues grooves of Jimmy Reed ("Bright Lights, Big City") and the more percussive grooves of John Lee Hooker, and of the long, ecstatic closing vamps frequently used in gospel—is an electric piano part, repeated with constant slight variations on the prototypical pattern transcribed in Example 9.1. The left hand plays an unbroken pulse of quarter notes on F♯, doubled by a synthesized bass, which creates the simplest possible rhythmic flow. Meanwhile, the right hand repeatedly moves in and out of phase with this pulse: it plays on the first three downbeats, then switches to syncopated upbeats. The last upbeat of the first measure is sustained across the bar before the right hand re-synchronizes with the left, reaffirming the last three downbeats. The result is a cyclical pattern of two beats of reinforced pulse, three beats in which the pulse is opposed, and three more beats in which it is again reinforced.

This motion in and out of phase by the right-hand part occurs simultaneously in two other areas: harmony and register. When the two parts are

Example 9.1 Stevie Wonder, "Living For the City" (Stevie Wonder), *Innervisions* (1973): primary groove.

metrically in phase, the right hand plays F♯-major triads. As the two parts move into metric opposition, the right hand passes up through G♯ minor to an A-major triad, higher and further away. The A-major triad above the F♯ bass creates an F♯-minor 4/2 chord, blurring the harmony somewhat. As the two parts move back into metric phase, the right hand moves back to a stable F♯-major triad, resolving at the beginning of the repetition. Unlike a classical phrase, which generally is designed to progress strongly toward its ending, this groove progresses strongly toward *its own beginning*. As a result, it is well suited for extensive repetition and even implies infinite repetition, like a figure eight, or the Midgard Serpent swallowing its own tail. I refer to this type of groove as *autotelic* (from *auto*, meaning "self," and *telos*, meaning "goal") because it serves as its own goal.

The result is three precisely synchronized cycles: As the right hand moves up and away from the register of the left hand, it moves metrically out of phase with the left hand's quarter-note pulse and major harmony mixes with minor. As the two hands come back together, they move back in phase metrically, and major harmony is also re-established. Even as the right hand cycles in and out of focus in these three areas, however, the left hand continues to provide a sense of forward motion by continuing the simple series of F♯ quarter notes, maintaining a steady baseline against which the right-hand oscillations in meter, harmony, and register are perceptible (see Figure 9.1). Another, faster cycle occurs in the keyboard part, which pans between the left and right channels twice per beat. This creates a sound of surprising depth, as if two keyboards were employed in opposite channels in an interlocking fashion (a technique Wonder does use elsewhere on the same album in "Higher Ground"). Yet the steadiness of the spatial variation creates an expectation that it will continue in the same manner, generating a very simple type of flow purely through manipulation of the stereo mix.

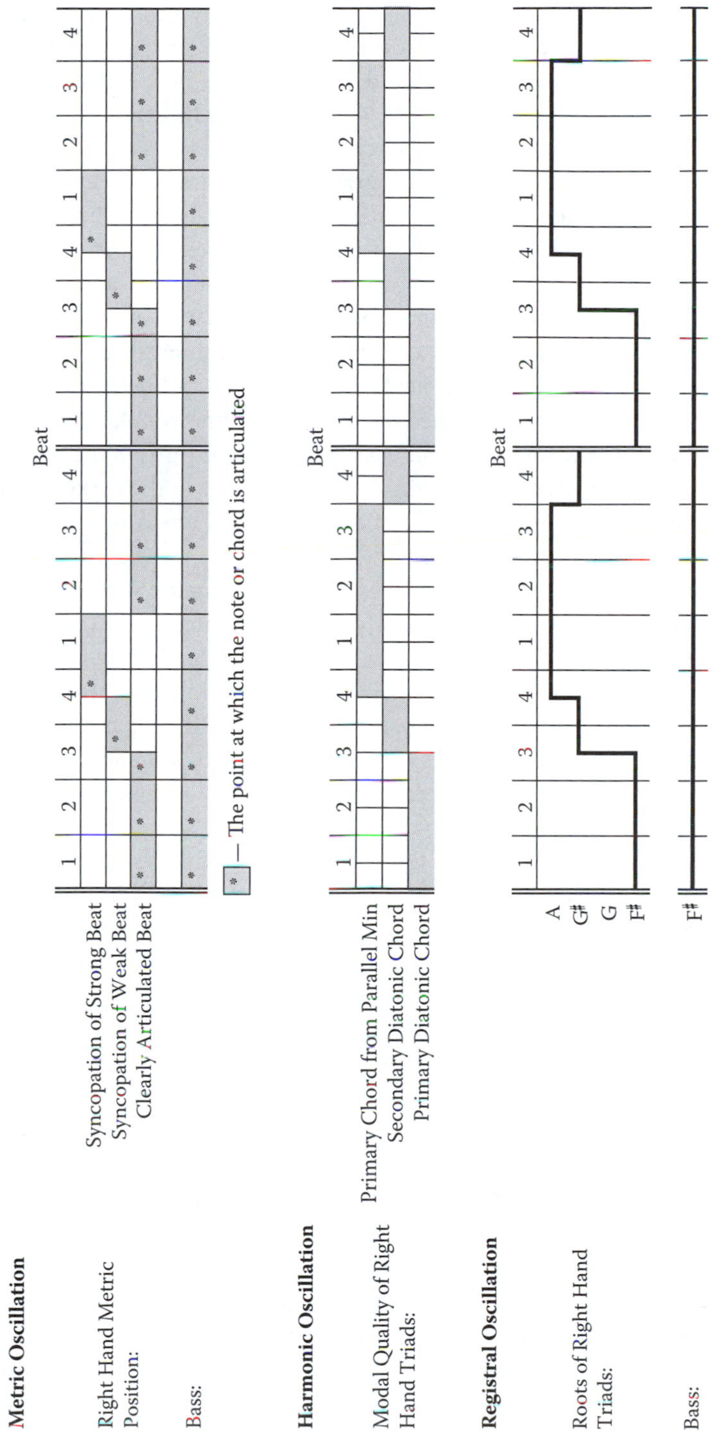

Figure 9.1 Stevie Wonder, "Living For the City" (Stevie Wonder), *Innervisions* (1973): recurring cycles in the primary groove.

The song begins with two statements of the primary groove, played on processed electric piano and synthesized bass. Wonder's lead vocal enters on the third statement, along with the bass drum, which reinforces the pulse on every beat. (Wonder recorded all the parts himself, overdubbing them one at a time, with the assistance of Robert Margouleff and Malcolm Cecil as engineers, co-producers, and synthesizer programmers.) The vocal melody works to supplement the major/minor ambiguity by drifting between major and minor thirds at the ends of each pair of lines (see the eighth bar of Example 9.2). In this excerpt, Wonder sings an arpeggiated F♯-major triad (containing an A♯) in measures 3–4, while an A-major triad is played in the keyboard part, creating a clash between simultaneous major and minor thirds above the bass F♯.[4] At the same position in the next couplet (mm. 5–8), however, his melody slides down from A♯ to A♮. Since the tune of the first couplet (mm. 1–4) reaches higher (moving up to C♯) and has a bright major third in the melody, while that of the second couplet remains lower and mixes in the darker minor third, the phrase works in the manner of a question and answer—or call and response—that complements the text.

The bulk of the text is arranged in lines corresponding to two measures in duration. Pairs of these lines share loosely rhymed endings, with the second line usually completing a sentence begun in the first (e.g., "A boy is born in hard-time Mississippi/Surrounded by four walls that ain't so pretty"). Four statements of the groove, and their corresponding pair of couplets, lead to a four-measure refrain with the words "Living just enough, just enough for the city," creating a twelve-bar verse-refrain with an **a a B** scheme, detailed in Figure 9.2.[5]

As the lyric shifts to the refrain, the accompaniment plays a cadential figure consisting of one measure each of B major and C♯ major (with the words "Living just enough, just enough") before returning once more to the groove ("for the city"). The transition to the refrain is particularly smooth because of the characteristic 6-5 suspensions sequenced in the piano and vocals, indicated in Example 9.3. As a result, the right-hand G♯-minor chord is held across the bar from the primary groove, anticipating the B-major chord and connecting the two phrases. These periodic cadential figures are not intrusive—similar figures are used in a number of related styles, particularly the blues-boogie songs of John Lee Hooker.[6]

The relation of the twelve-bar verse/refrain form to the twelve-bar blues merits some discussion here. Although it does not precisely follow the model of the twelve-bar blues in either harmony or rhyme scheme, the form is very similar. The harmonic variation—essentially omitting the motion from I to IV in the second phrase—is not unknown in the blues and is particularly common in soul and funk songs closely related to the blues. (Wonder himself used a similar strategy in "Superstition.") The **a a B** rhyme pattern is also a

Example 9.2 Stevie Wonder, "Living For the City" (Stevie Wonder), *Innervisions* (1973): verse 1.

a	Couplet 1	A boy is born in hard-time Mississippi, Surrounded by four walls that ain't so pretty.
a	Couplet 2	His parents give him love and affection, To keep him strong, moving in the right direction.
B	Refrain	Living just enough, just enough, For the city

Figure 9.2 Stevie Wonder, "Living For the City" (Stevie Wonder), *Innervisions* (1973): phrase structure of verse.

Example 9.3 Stevie Wonder, "Living For the City" (Stevie Wonder), *Innervisions* (1973): refrain. © 1973 Renewed 2001 JOBETE MUSIC CO., INC. and BLACK BULL MUSIC c/o EMI APRIL MUSIC, INC. All rights reserved. International Copyright Secured. Used by permission.

common elaboration on the typical **A A B** scheme. Because the phrase structure is the same and the harmony and rhyme schemes are so similar, it seems clear that Wonder is *invoking* the twelve-bar blues tradition—even though "Living for the City" is clearly not a twelve-bar blues song (as the chorus makes emphatically clear).

The twelve-bar phrase structure also forms a *second* repeated pattern that creates flow on a larger time-scale. The cadences cause a periodic variation in the harmony, register, timbre, and lyrics of one cycle per verse. The result

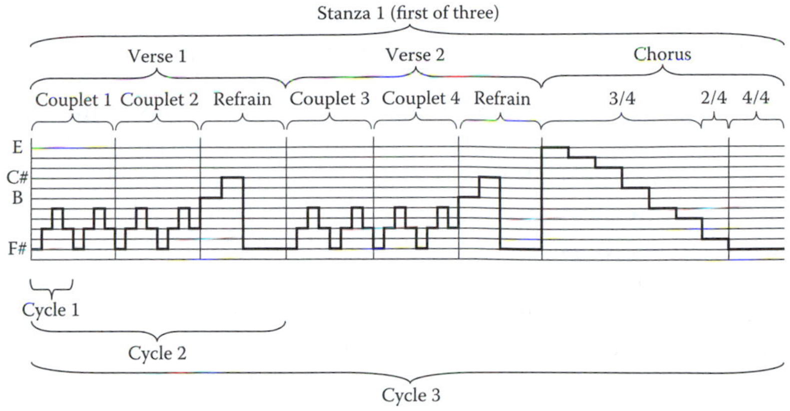

Figure 9.3 Stevie Wonder, "Living For the City" (Stevie Wonder), *Innervisions* (1973): larger-scale periodicity.

is something that might be called *compound flow*. The periodic form of the verses creates one level of flow, which contains within it the more local flow of the grooves (which contain within themselves the even more localized flows created by the basic drum patterns and the spatial shifts of the keyboard). See Figure 9.3, which shows three concentric levels of periodic form within the stanzas—which also repeat, with some variation.[7]

The steadfast simplicity, regular periodicity, and steady quarter-note pulse of the groove give these portions of "Living for the City" a very natural or familiar feel and disguise the song's complex form. This natural feel is furthered by the generalized, folksy style of the lyrics and Wonder's vocal style during the verses, which are delivered in a varied, speech-like fashion derived primarily from gospel practice.[8] The language is colloquial, including a relaxed, familiar use of slang in phrases such as "His sister's black but she is sho 'nuff pretty." This lends the song the informal character of everyday speech, in contrast to the more formal, poetic character of the songs that immediately precede and follow it on *Innervisions* ("Visions" and "Golden Lady," respectively). Wonder uses a third-person, descriptive voice throughout the song until the final verse, at which point he shifts into first person and even ends with a direct plea to "stop giving just enough for the city." By using a third-person address aimed at the listener, Wonder makes it clear that his point of view is external, like ours, until the end of the song, when he directly pleads for our help.

The Contrasting Chorus

The twelve-bar verses occur in pairs, each pair followed by a chorus that contains no text. Instead, Wonder vocalizes using the syllable "da." The result is that the verses and choruses are grouped into stanzas using an **a a B** scheme parallel to the one within each verse (see Figure 9.4).

In sharp contrast with the natural-sounding verses, the choruses are strikingly unusual. The most significant change is metric: The chorus (sketched in Example 9.4) changes from the verse's hyper-regular 4/4 meter to 3/4 for six measures, shifts to 2/4 for a single measure, and then returns to 4/4 for two final measures. The total number of beats (28) is evenly divisible by four, the tempo does not vary, and the quarter-note pulse does not cease. Therefore, the succeeding verse resumes precisely where a downbeat would occur if the metric accent had not shifted, and each nine-measure chorus is equivalent in length to seven measures in the primary 4/4 meter. Such metric variability is highly unusual in popular music, particularly in a hit single.

Wonder's use of the 3/4 meter here can be heard as creating a "deferral" of the metric pulse, similar to figures described by Mark Butler in later electronic dance music but on a larger metric level (see Butler 2006, 100–106, and also Hasty 1997). Because the length of the basic metric unit (the quarter note) does not change and the chorus ends in synchronization with the original quadruple pulse established in the primary groove, the most basic flow doesn't stop. But by shifting to 3/4, Wonder creates a series of one-beat deferrals, which is then interrupted by the shift to 2/4. By twice arriving a beat earlier than expected, the passage feels truncated, or cut against, even though the number of beats works out to a multiple of four.[9] Paradoxically, as the drummer, Wonder enhances the metric ambiguity by playing all beats evenly on snare and bass drum with ride offbeats (never confirming a downbeat until the change from 2/4 to 4/4), while simultaneously maintaining the ultra-regular quarter-note pulse. The resulting sense is a juxtaposition of disorientation with relentless forward motion.

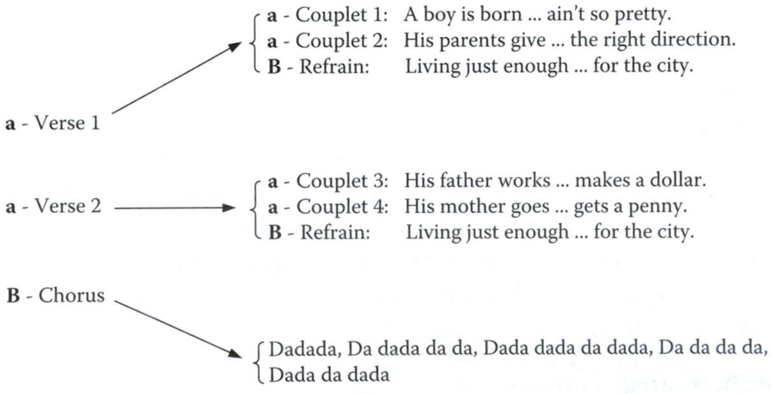

Figure 9.4 Stevie Wonder, "Living For the City" (Stevie Wonder), *Innervisions* (1973): stanzaic structure.

Example 9.4 Stevie Wonder, "Living For the City" (Stevie Wonder), *Innervisions* (1973): chorus.

The cut-against feeling is compounded by the fact that the polymetric passage doesn't work out to an *even-numbered* multiple of four (as it does in the diatonic patterns of 3 + 3 + 2 and 3 + 3 + 3 + 3 + 4 that are so common in electronic dance music), but instead is equivalent to *five* groups of four. Also, because there are two abrupt shortenings of the meter (from 4/4 to 3/4 and then to 2/4) the sense of disorientation is compounded by a sense of rushing ahead—which somehow exists simultaneously with the sense of steadiness provided by the unbroken quarter-note pulse. In other words, this passage is metrically disruptive on two higher levels (those of the meter and the hypermeter), even though it is never disrupted on the quarter-note level. The combined effect of all these metric changes, of the sensations of disorientation, forward motion, and acceleration, is much like the feeling of being carried forward by a powerful force or current.

During the chorus, the character of the vocals changes dramatically from the speech-like style found in the verse to an untexted, vocalized lament.[10] These vocals are more melodic, are sung in a legato style, and have a very different texture and spatial position. The vocal line is also doubled here by a synthesizer, further expanding its textural depth. In the verses, there is only a single vocal track, located in the center of the stereo mix. But the vocals of the first two choruses are doubled, with the two tracks mixed all the way to the left and right. The spatial/textural effect is thus a change from a single voice located directly in front of the listener to a pair of voices on either side. In other words, Wonder's vocals during the verse are directed *at* the listener, making us outside observers—we are hearing an individual's call. But in the chorus they *surround* the listener, placing us directly between a pair of lamenting voices. Although not active participants, we become a part of the responding community through this repositioning.

The harmony also changes dramatically: Here it is built on a steadily descending bass line. Such bass lines are also often associated with laments or funeral music in numerous traditions, including both European-American and African-American styles. The passage begins with an F♯-major chord in the right hand while the bass moves down to an E, creating a dominant chord with the seventh in the bass—a highly unstable chord with a strong tendency for continued descending bass motion. In the next bar, the bass moves down to a D♯, supporting the expected B-major chord in first inversion. However, the melody in this measure has an A♮, which also makes this an unstable dominant-sounding chord with a tendency to move. The A and F♯ from this chord are held over in the next bar as the bass moves down, creating a root-position D-major chord. This is followed by parallel motion in all voices to a root-position C-major triad in the fourth bar. The C-major chord is sustained as the bass moves down to B♭, again creating a dominant-sounding chord above its seventh. The bass moves down by step in measure six, but to the root of an A-major triad (rather than the expected first-inversion F♯ chord). The next two bars feature continued descending stepwise motion in the bass to G and F♯, supporting root-position major triads as the other voices move upward in contrary motion. The passage is tonally ambiguous, apparently arbitrary, and highly chromatic—a minimum of five different key signatures are briefly implied, and it includes every pitch class except F and G♯/A♭. But because the progression continually moves down through an octave, it does prolong the overall sense of F♯ as harmonic anchor. Again, Wonder combines disorientation, in this case a product of *harmonic* ambiguity, with a strong sense of forward motion, in this case a product of the stepwise descending bass line.

The combined effect of the omitted lyrics, the change in vocal character, the changing meters, the descending bass line, the progression of harmonies, and the lyrical melody is to create a strongly contrasting, lamenting chorus that creates turbulence within the steady flow of the verses as it defies conventional metric and harmonic logic. Yet because the pulse never changes, the primary groove returns after a span that is a multiple of four beats, and the bass, harmony, and vocal melody all lead to F♯ at the conclusion of the passage, the underlying continuity—the sense of flow at the most basic level—remains intact.

Second Stanza, Bridge, and Conclusion

The second stanza has only minor differences from the first, primarily in the drums and lyrics. In the second verse of the opening stanza, Wonder had added a snare-drum backbeat on beats two and four, a steady stream of lightly swung eighth notes on a closed hi-hat, and brief fills and cymbal splashes at the ends of phrases. The additions are subtle and generally reinforce the primary groove. In the second stanza, however, the drum part becomes more elaborate, more acoustically present, and (most significantly) less predictable; the crash cymbal marks downbeats in the second chorus. Of particular note, because they change the feel of the primary groove, are Wonder's occasional use of the closed/open hi-hat riffs characteristic of the nascent disco style and an addition of syncopations to the bass drum part—both of which increase the activity level of the rhythm section. An extra four bars are inserted between the verse and chorus, possibly, through such hesitation, to enhance the already-noted turbulent effect of the chorus. The lyrics also rise in intensity and anger. The second stanza concludes with one of Wonder's most memorable and aggressive lyrics: "To find a job/Is like a haystack needle/'Cause where he lives/They don't use colored people." The overall effect of all these changes in the second stanza is to steadily build intensity going into the bridge.

With the bridge as a contrasting **B** section prior to a return of opening material, Wonder has constructed "Living for the City" with a large-scale **a a B a'** form, leading to implications for both flow and drama. This scheme is quite conventional, and for good reason: The simplest possible way to use repetition to create a sense of flow is to repeat something once (**A A** or **a a**). The simplest possible way to create a sense of flow and then use rupture to add drama is to repeat something once and then depart from it (**A A B** or **a a B**). And the simplest possible way to create a sense of flow, use rupture to add drama, and then use resumption of flow to create a sense of closure (or, literally, re-cognition) is to repeat something once, depart from it, and then restate it again (typically **a a B a** or **a a B a'**).[11]

The long bridge consists of a modified third stanza and the dramatic interlude that follows. The third stanza is a long vocal improvisation of twenty-eight bars (2:46–3:53) followed by its chorus. The regular twelve-bar pattern of the verse is abandoned in the improvisation, replaced by a long stream of repeated statements of the groove. Over this, Wonder extemporizes an expressive vocal line. Accompanied by handclaps, the lead vocal interacts with a pair of backing voices, tossing the words "Living just enough for the city" back and forth almost playfully. The informal use of a wide variety of vocal effects (including squeals, growls, and contorted syllables) and the socially constructed call-and-response between the lead and backup parts in a loose, improvisational style combine to create an effect very similar to an ecstatic gospel coda vamp of the kind mentioned previously.[12] This section is nearly equivalent in duration to each of the preceding two, with a slight telescoping (the first stanza is 124 beats long, the second, 132, and the third, 140). But it is clear that this passage is designed to be of variable length in live performances, allowing for a great deal of freedom to improvise or to adjust to a particular audience.

Because Wonder played all the instruments himself, the recording is necessarily a rehearsed, tightly synchronized studio construction. Yet the free and flexible nature of this stanza is apparent even to the casual listener. While this passage could be interpreted as one in which control slips away, its highly social character just as strongly implies a communal response to the story of the individual—call-and-response again, but on a much larger time-scale than before.

After twenty-eight measures of freedom, the somehow more regular chorus (now with the drums elaborately marking their downbeats) returns, only to crossfade into the dramatic interlude (4:14–5:16). Cecil and Margouleff (1995, 6–7), the song's co-producers with Wonder, set the atmosphere:

> "Living For the City" has that beautiful little vignette in it of the drug bust, the innocent kid who comes to New York and walks across the street and finds himself arrested. That is very much like a talking book, it's a sound picture. It's like old-time radio in a way, where we used to listen to like Captain Midnight or some of the early Dragnet, or some of the early radio dramas, where they would create these sound vignettes. And it really helps sort of illustrate the story and the social consciousness that Stevie brought to his music, which I think was very, very important.

In this drama the unnamed protagonist takes a bus to New York City, which is illustrated by a voice announcing "Bus for New York City," the sound of a diesel engine revving, and a different voice saying, "Hey, bus driver, I'm gettin' on that. Hold it." Using continued combinations of sound effects and voices, a plot is loosely sketched in which the naïve protagonist (played by Wonder's brother, Calvin Hardaway) arrives ("Wow! New York! Just like I pictured it: skyscrapers and everythang ..."), is handed contraband of some sort by a stranger (Wonder's road manager, Ira Tucker Jr.) just as a police car arrives, and is then arrested, despite his protestations of innocence. He is subsequently sentenced by a judge (Wonder's lawyer Johanan Vigoda) to ten years in prison and a cell door slams, accompanied by a gruff voice (an unnamed studio janitor) ordering "C'mon. C'mon! Get in that cell, nigger!" (cast identified in Horn 2000, 139–140).

The drama serves to grab the attention of the casual listener, provides the pivot around which the perspective of the lyric turns, and vividly illustrates the point at which the hammer of injustice falls on the protagonist. It also allows Wonder to fuse the history of a mass social movement with the immediacy of an individual story. By using this drama, by making the listener an auditory observer of the events—a witness—Wonder is able to much more effectively personalize the effect of his lyrics. Yet by keeping the protagonist anonymous he keeps alive the possibility that it could be the story of anyone, and therefore more effectively represents the story of an entire migration. The interlude has an additional, interesting effect that was made more obvious by the promotional event described at the beginning of this essay: Wonder is also granting us a glimpse of the way in which he, as a blind man, experiences life—primarily through a soundscape. In essence, he has inserted a short talking book into the middle of the song. In other words, we are more directly experiencing the "visions in [his] mind."[13]

After the interlude, "Living for the City" returns to more familiar territory: a final fourth stanza (5:17+) much like the first two. There are several very significant changes, however. First, the time of the storyline has shifted to ten years later, after the protagonist's long incarceration has robbed him of youth and hope. Wonder's vocal timbre is much thicker and rougher, to signify the years of hardship endured. Additional, improvised vocal parts appear during the final verse (5:45+, recalling the ecstatic third stanza) and two additional parts harmonize the melody on the last refrain ("Living just enough, stop giving just enough for the city"). After this, a four-measure break (6:09—6:19) has the drums keep time and the rest of the music stops, except for a few stray synthesizer riffs, functioning like an extended stop-time cadence, creating anticipation of a climactic finale. Wonder plays a drum fill towards the end of this break that rebuilds momentum for a substantially altered final chorus.[14]

As coda, the concluding chorus is stated three times instead of once, and the character of the vocals is again changed. The pair of doubled, left-right voices is retained from the previous choruses, but harmonized with a third part. The additional part is louder and placed in the middle of the stereo mix (see Example 9.5, which begins midway through the second statement of the chorus). The result is a much larger sound, which unifies the single front vocal of the verses with the outer vocals of the choruses. The vocals come at the listener from all directions, immersing us in a community of lamenting voices that now includes the individual (signaled by Wonder's change to first-person voice and then by his direct exhortation to the listener). Call and response are now unified. In addition, the drum part has now become so elaborate that it tends to disrupt the flow created by the primary groove rather than supplementing it, further blurring the line between the collective and the individual previously established by the call-and-response structure.

Example 9.5 Stevie Wonder, "Living For the City" (Stevie Wonder), *Innervisions* (1973): ending. © 1973 Renewed 2001 JOBETE MUSIC CO., INC. and BLACK BULL MUSIC c/o EMI APRIL MUSIC, INC. All rights reserved. International Copyright Secured. Used by permission.

The third and last statement of the chorus ends without leaving the 3/4 meter or reaching the expected F♯ triad. Instead, the G-major triad is extended as the gospel-style vocals arpeggiate the chord in a repeated rolling pattern while singing the words "Oh no, oh no. . . ." The voices oppose each other, one singing the B above while the other sings the D below, but meet on unison G's—alternating like a pair of railroad workers hammering a spike in a tie. The final chord is drawn out, by fermata, as all instruments drop out. The lowest voice ends on a D rather than the conventional G, creating an ending that leaves the song's prevailing F♯ harmony unresolved, standing instead on an incomplete inverted triad whose root is a half-step above.

This altered ending, with its failure to return to the expected F♯ harmony, amplifies the deferred feeling already established in the choruses by the change of meters. The result is an ending that is at once both clear and ambiguous. It is clear because there are numerous stylistic clues to remove any doubt that the song is ending, and because the song's form creates a strong sense of balance at this point. But it is ambiguous because so many of the expectations created by Wonder's use of repetition remain unfulfilled: Neither the F♯ harmony, the 4/4 meter, the fundamental groove, nor even the root position voicing of the final chord return as expected. Ultimately, the flow of the song is not altered, disrupted, or cut against. It simply remains suspended, deferred, unresolved—like an unfulfilled promise. The unfulfilled promise is of course the very essence of the African-American experience of America and the source of the deadening, increasingly pervasive nihilism that Cornell West described as "the lived experience of coping with a life of horrifying meaninglessness, hopelessness, and (most important) lovelessness" (1993, 22–23). While Wonder did offer powerful images of meaning, hope, and love on the next two songs on *Innervisions*, "Golden Lady" and "Higher Ground," the bitterness and anger of "Living for the City"—amplified by its unsettling ending—provided a necessary grounding for the album in the dispiriting reality of 1973, amid the dissolution of the Civil Rights Movement.

The sense of ambiguous conclusion is heightened in the album version of "Living for the City" by a link with the subsequent song, "Golden Lady." The two are joined together by means of a short piano interlude (transcribed as Example 9.6). Before the last chord of "Living for the City" ends, a piano begins quietly arpeggiating an A-major triad. Because it was recorded on an acoustic piano with very little use of delay, the timbre is very different from the spatially shifting electric piano of the primary groove. It progresses through a series of chords, ending with a pause on the first half (dominant ninth/sus4 on D) of a deceptive cadence that concludes with the opening chord of "Golden Lady" (E♭ M^7).[15]

This piano figure doesn't seem to belong to either song. Its character is as different from "Golden Lady" as it is from "Living for the City," even though "Golden Lady" is built around a timbrally similar piano part. Its division from

Example 9.6 Stevie Wonder, Transitional figure between "Living for the City" and "Golden Lady" (Stevie Wonder), *Innervisions* (1973).

"Living for the City" is diffused because it seems to begin before that song is over. Its division from "Golden Lady" is diffused because it progresses directly to that song's opening chord. On the CD the passage is not divided into a separate track, but instead is grouped with "Golden Lady." However, no such division occurs (or is even possible other than through silence) on the original LP or cassette, since the entire first side is recorded in a single record groove or on a single spool of tape. Instead, this passage seems like a separate piece created as a joint to connect the two songs.[16]

Compound Flow Everywhere

As can be seen from the exploded diagram of the form of the entire song in Figure 9.5, there are several multiply nested levels of structure in "Living for the City." At the largest level, its form is represented as **a a B a'**. Each of the **a** sections at this level (the stanzas) has an **a a B** form and each of *those* **a** sections (the verses) likewise has an **a a B** form. Additionally, the final group of three choruses (whose form is represented in Figure 9.5 as **B B b'**) follows an

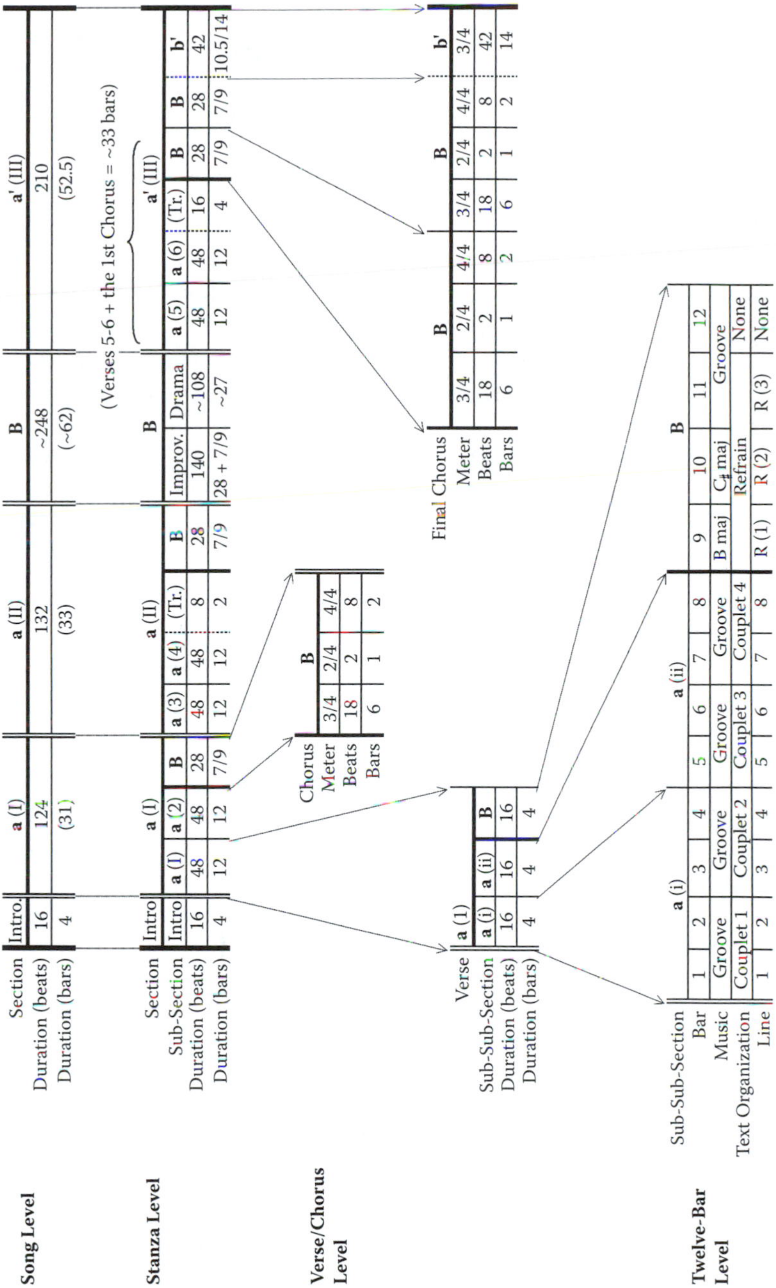

Figure 9.5 Stevie Wonder, "Living for the City" (Stevie Wonder), *Innervisions* (1973): overall form.

analogous pattern of statement, repetition, and variant, in each case creating a flow of repetition and variation. Some of the periodic flows from local to global levels are summarized here:

- The electric piano moves between the left and right channels, twice per beat.
- After the first verse, a stream of lightly swung eighth notes is played on the hi-hat.
- The groove establishes a steady pulse of one note per beat in the left-hand keyboard and bass. The bass drum initially supplements this pulse, although as the song goes on it becomes more varied.
- Beginning with verse two, the snare plays the backbeat, creating a continuous two-beat pattern.
- The primary groove establishes a regular oscillation every two measures in the harmony, register, and metric positioning of the keyboard's right-hand part.
- The rhymed couplets in the lyrics and the question-and-answer shape of the melody create a recurring four-measure pattern.
- The four-bar couplets are grouped in pairs, followed by a four-bar refrain. The pattern of two couplets followed by a cadential figure and a repetition of the groove creates the recurring twelve-bar verses.
- The verses are also paired and followed by a contrasting chorus, equivalent in length to seven measures, creating a recurring stanza 124-to-140 beats long.

Over the course of the song, the stanza is played, repeated with minor changes (other than the lyrics), followed by the contrasting bridge, and then repeated once more with much more variation including an extended ending. If considered as an **a a B a'** form, which is consistent with the use of repetition throughout the song, the **B** section is roughly twice as large as the **A** sections—an asymmetrical form. But the two parts of the **B** section are roughly equal in length, so the song can also be envisioned with an **a a B C a'** form (with the **C** referring to the mini-drama), with very balanced section lengths. This interpretation, when combined with the multilevel structure of the song, strongly suggests that it is structured like an art-music piece with compound form. But such an interpretation is misleading; it must be remembered that the song is open to both removal of entire sections and improvisatory elongation, making certain decisions about proportion elusive—and overstatement easy. In much popular music (and particularly in soul music, where groove patterns are often designed to repeat for any desired duration), recordings are not blueprints for all performances of a song as much as they are particular iterations, tailored for the practical and creative constraints, possibilities, and demands of studio recording. Live versions are a different type of iteration, tailored for different constraints, possibilities, and demands.

1974 Version

Section	Intro	a (I)			a (II)			B				(C)
Duration (beats)	16	124			124			192				Improvisational
Sub-Section	Intro	a (1)	a (2)	B	a (3)	a (4)	B	Improv.	B	B	B	
Duration (beats)	16	48	48	28	48	48	28	80	28	28	28	
Duration (bars)	4	12	12	7(9)	12	12	7(9)	20	7(9)	7(9)	7(9)	

Overall Duration: 4'35" | 6'30"

1995 Version

Section	Intro	a (I)			a (II)			B				
Duration (beats)	16	124			124			208				
Sub-Section	Intro	a (1)	a (2)	B	a (3)	a (4)	B	Improv.	B	B	B	B
Duration (beats)	16	48	48	28	48	48	28	96	28	28	28	28
Duration (bars)	4	12	12	7(9)	12	12	7(9)	24	7(9)	7(9)	7(9)	7(9)

Acceleration of Tempo →

Overall Duration: 4'27"

Figure 9.6 Stevie Wonder, "Living for the City" (Stevie Wonder): comparison of formal relations in two live performances.

It is instructive in this respect to examine the form of live versions of "Living for the City" to understand the degree of variability in Wonder's conception of the song. I'll examine here recordings of two performances (analyzed in Figure 9.6). The first version, which has been widely bootlegged, is from a concert recorded at the Rainbow Theatre in London on February 2, 1974 (Wonder 1974), while the second is from the much later live album *Natural Wonder* (Wonder 1995).

Both versions are based on the same form as the single: The mini-drama and the final fourth stanza are omitted, but the final group of choruses is still used at the end of the improvisational part of the bridge, which is variously shortened to 20 bars (1974) or 24 bars (1995) in length. The 1974 version comes to a complete stop after the third concluding chorus, followed by 6'30" of improvisation. During this section, Wonder interacts directly with the audience, leading them in singing and clapping a new melody with the words "Are you tired now?" and answering with "of living for the city." The groove changes here, primarily harmonically. A new progression develops, eliminating the first G♯-minor chord, replacing the A-major chords with B major, and replacing the second G♯-minor chord with an A-major chord, for a I–IV–♭III pattern. The bass does not stay on F♯, but instead plays the chord roots. The harmony here has clearly shifted from a simple elaboration of F♯ to a harmonization of the F♯-minor pentatonic scale with major triads (a systematic procedure classified as "Type 5" in Everett 2004, 19). The 1995 version doesn't include this long, improvised section, but it does have one other significant difference from the studio version: The tempo accelerates greatly through each of the four concluding choruses up to the ending. Clearly, proportionality of form is not essential beyond the second stanza, but is instead subject to external conditions.

It is the principle of flow, rather than proportion of form, that is the primary basis for the compound nature of "Living for the City." Its structure at all levels is based on repetition rather than progression. The result is less a compound structure than a *compound groove*: At each structural level the song has a cyclical form, designed to be repeated an indeterminate number of times. While the studio recording is a performance of striking balance and symmetry, most parts of the song—whether large-scale or local—could vary in length, to be determined by the performer. The only important exception to this is the dramatic interlude. This design explains, for instance, the symmetry-breaking two-measure and four-measure pauses before the second and third choruses, necessary to command attention and build momentum. The dramatic strategy of establishing and altering flow has overridden the dictates of sectional balance.

"Living for the City," then, is a composite of many cycles occurring on many levels—wheels within wheels within wheels. The combined effect of these many cycles is forward motion in a stream, interrupted only by the vignette. But although the stream is relatively continuous, it is a complex, patterned stream, in which occasional hesitations or changes of direction are used in a large-scale strategy to create drama and shape the listener's perceptions. The specific way that Wonder employs repetition in "Living for the City" not only has wheels spinning within wheels (just as an individual victim can feel trapped as part of an uncaring society), but it resonates deeply with longstanding African-American sacred, rhetorical, and literary traditions, in ways that are entirely consistent with its subject matter. Possibly the oldest surviving African-American musical tradition is the spiritual. Consider the **A A B A'** form of "Oh, Mary, Don't You Weep" (Dance 2002, 80):

Oh, Mary, doncha weep, doncha moan,
Oh, Mary, doncha weep, doncha moan,
Pharaoh's army got drownded,
Oh, Mary, doncha weep.

Even in this brief example, some now-familiar strategies are evident: the creation of flow through repetition, departure, and resumption; nested repetitions, here with the internal repetitions of "doncha" within the repeated full lines; and even cutting against the flow by use of an abrupt shortening of the last line.

As foundational elements of African-American religious traditions, spirituals have long been associated with religious sermons and, especially during the civil-rights movement, political speeches. Black clergymen and political activists such as C. L. Franklin, Malcolm X, Jesse Jackson, and especially Martin Luther King Jr. frequently used a more complex, multilevel strategy of repetition that created a compound flow that we can relate to Wonder's strategy in "Living for the City." Note the flow, the intensifying repetition, and the final counterstatements that refer back to the opening, creating a dramatic climb to climax and denouement, in Malcolm X's "Message to the Grass Roots," delivered on November 10, 1963:

> What you and I need to do is learn to forget our differences. When we come together, we don't come together as Baptists or Methodists. You don't catch hell because you're a Baptist, and you don't catch hell because you're a Methodist. You don't catch hell because you're a Methodist or Baptist, you don't catch hell because you're a Democrat or a Republican, you don't catch hell because you're a Mason or an Elk, and you sure don't catch hell because you're an American; because if you were an American, you wouldn't catch hell. You catch hell because you're a black man. You catch hell, all of us catch hell, for the same reason (X 2002).

Another example that demonstrates a rhetorical use of compound flow with contrast and return can be found in this excerpt from Martin Luther King Jr.'s speech, "A Testament of Hope," given at the conclusion of the march from Selma to Montgomery on March 25, 1965:

> The threat of the free exercise of the ballot by the Negro and the white masses alike resulted in the establishing of a segregated society. They segregated southern money from the poor whites; they segregated southern mores from the rich whites; they segregated southern churches from Christianity; they segregated southern minds from honest thinking, and they segregated the Negro from everything.
>
> We have come a long way since that travesty of justice was perpetrated upon the American mind. Today I want to tell the city of Selma, today I want to say to the state of Alabama, today I want to say to the people of America and the nations of the world: We are not about to turn around. We are on the move now. Yes, we are on the move and no wave of racism can stop us.
>
> We are on the move now. The burning of our churches will not deter us. We are on the move now. The bombing of our homes will not dissuade us. We are on the move now. The beating and killing of our clergymen and young people will not divert us. We are on the move now. The arrest and release of known murderers will not discourage us. We are on the move now.
>
> Like an idea whose time has come, not even the marching of mighty armies can halt us. We are moving to the land of freedom.
>
> Let us therefore continue our triumph and march to the realization of the American dream. Let us march on segregated housing, until every ghetto of social and economic depression dissolves and Negroes and whites live side by side in decent, safe and sanitary housing.

> Let us march on segregated schools until every vestige of segregated and inferior education becomes a thing of the past and Negroes and whites study side by side in the socially healing context of the classroom.
>
> Let us march on poverty, until no American parent has to skip a meal so that their children may eat, march on poverty until no starved man walks the streets of our cities and towns in search of jobs that do not exist.
>
> Let us march on ballot boxes, march on ballot boxes until race baiters disappear from the political arena. Let us march on ballot boxes until the Wallaces of our nation tremble away in silence.
>
> Let us march on ballot boxes, until we send to our city councils, state legislatures, and the United States Congress men who will not fear to do justice, love mercy, and walk humbly with their God. Let us march on ballot boxes until all over Alabama God's children will be able to walk the earth in decency and honor.
>
> For all of us today the battle is in our hands. The road ahead is not altogether a smooth one. There are no broad highways to lead us easily and inevitably to quick solutions. We must keep going (King 2002).

This, in all its evolving patterns, is compound flow. Wonder's conspicuous use of repetition in a similar, multiply compound way, therefore, evokes longstanding sacred, rhetorical, *and* musical traditions.

In summary, "Living for the City's" depth, power, resonance, and durability as a popular song and a political anthem are the products of many factors: Wonder's directly political aim, his striking use of drama, his ability to integrate conspicuous blues and gospel elements into a soul context, his overall skill as a lyricist, songwriter, and arranger, and his ability to integrate diverse elements into a seamless whole. But much of the success of the song also derives from his use of repetition to create a complex and fluid modernist form, and his ability to design a short, simple, traditional groove as an effective basis for that structure. In short, it is Wonder's use of repetition—to juxtapose the simple and the complex, the collective and the individual, and the traditional and the modern, and especially to invoke cultural themes—that allows him to create a song with such depth, power, resonance, and durability and to vividly illustrate the story of an individual trapped within the relentlessly turning wheels of society.

Notes

1. Wonder contributed all-new music for most of *Jungle Fever* (released as a soundtrack on Wonder 1991), but the original recording of "Living For the City" was chosen to accompany a particular scene in which a young black architect seeks out his brother in a crack house within an urban wasteland. By using an eighteen-year-old song, Wonder imbues the scene with cultural memory in a way that is parallel to his references to older musical, sacred, and rhetorical traditions within the song itself.

2. There are exceptions to this characterization. For instance, Garcia 2005 and Butler 2006 examine repetition in elements other than rhythm and on levels below the surface.
3. Indeed, the basic story is one that was lived by Wonder's own mother, Lula Hardaway, who migrated from rural Alabama to Saginaw in the late 1940s (Love and Brown 2002, 1–51).
4. It should be noted that a simultaneous use of major and minor thirds is conventional in soul, along with most related genres. This type of modal mixture is more typically found in the vocals or lead instruments than in rhythm parts. However, such use is not unusual and is also common in blues, gospel, rock, and jazz. One well-known example of this is Jimi Hendrix's rhythm-guitar "Purple Haze" chord, an E♭ major-minor seventh chord with added ♯9th. Vocalists and soloists in these styles—particularly the blues—frequently use forms of the pentatonic scale that include minor thirds in passages that are harmonized by major triads, setting up a clash of thirds.
5. In form designations such as **a a B**, lowercase letters indicate units with essentially the same music or the same structural function but a different text (typical of verses), and uppercase letters, those with identical texts (as with refrains and choruses). Uppercase letters may also represent sections that are not repeated.
6. Examples include Hooker's "Boogie Chillen," "Dimples," and "Boom Boom." Hooker was based in Detroit, where he sometimes worked with Motown musicians such as bassist James Jamerson, who played on "Boom Boom." "Living for the City" is similar in this respect to Led Zeppelin's "When the Levee Breaks," which also adapts a slow blues-boogie style. See also Wonder's "Higher Ground," also from *Innervisions*.
7. See Floyd 1995, 34, and Hughes 2003, 107–139 and 254–259, for studies of the relationship between differentiation (which can be represented by the individual's call, and by varied repetition) and integration (afforded by the group's response, and by return to familiar material), and the interaction between them, producing what Floyd terms the "robust collective."
8. The use of a gospel-derived vocal style in soul music is a key and possibly defining characteristic of the genre. Virtually every noteworthy soul singer of the 1960s and '70s had an extensive background in gospel before being marketed as soul artists. Particularly prominent examples include Ray Charles, Sam Cooke, Aretha Franklin, Curtis Mayfield, Otis Redding, Sam & Dave, Marvin Gaye, and Isaac Hayes.
9. See the description of the general intrusive practice of rupturing or cutting against a flow that has been generated by repeated figures with a contrasting rhythm, meter, tempo, or even timbral shift, in Rose 1994, particularly 65–74.
10. Such laments often omit lyrics, as this song does, to enhance the mournful quality of the choruses. Indeed, in Coolio and Doug Rasheed's adaptation of Wonder's "Pastime Paradise" (1976) into the funereal "Gangsta's Paradise" (1995), a chorus that had the words "We shall overcome" in the original is replaced with a textless version, helping transform a warning of dangers to come into a lament over what has been lost.
11. John Rahn uses the word "cognize" to describe perception of the intial statement and "re-cognize" to describe perception of all subsequent statements of a figure

in his phenomenology of simple repetitions—i.e., those that follow an **A A (A…)** model. I reserve the use of "re-cognition" for the *resumption* of repetition—i.e., when there is a departure from a series of repetitions and then a return, as in the last statement of **A** in an **A A B A** model. See Hughes 2003, 14–19, and Rahn 1993.

12. The explicit use of a gospel-style call-and-response is central to African-American culture, which is essentially what is called into question by the arrest and trial narrated in "Living For the City." See Werner 2004, 8, for a discussion of the preacher's call-and-response style as emulated by Mahalia Jackson, James Brown, Wilson Pickett, and Marvin Gaye, and its political ramifications.
13. The dramatic vignette was excised not only from the single edit, but also from live performances, likely due to practical difficulties. Not all performers shy away from such dramatics; see, for example, Prince's performance of "I Could Never Take the Place of Your Man" in the film version of *Sign o' the Times.*

    Interestingly, *Talking Book* is the name of the 1972 Wonder album that preceded *Innervisions*. Both titles are variations on the idea of a musical representation of an inner or hidden world, as are the titles of Wonder's earlier 1972 album, *Music of My Mind*, and his 1976 album, *Songs in the Key of Life*.
14. Wonder frequently makes effective use of stop-time effects, most notably on "Superstition." In that song a similar break occurs after the second stanza, building momentum for the **B** section (see Hughes 2003, 140–177).
15. This link with "Golden Lady" also may account for part of why "Living for the City" ends in an unsettled G major, rather than with a return to F♯. This G is followed by the piano interlude that progresses from A to a dominant that resolves deceptively but traditionally to the opening of "Golden Lady," smoothing the way very effectively. See Hughes 2003, 60–106, for a detailed analysis of "Golden Lady."
16. Often, an eight-track tape, because it divides its album into four programs instead of the LP's two sides, will offer a clue as to the identity of transitional material between songs. That of *Innervisions*, however, does not resolve the current issue: "Living for the City," "Golden Lady," and the intervening piano figure were put together on the same 8-Track program.

    There is a further possible clue, in the form of a brief rill where the grooves of a record are less tightly packed. These spaces were added to records to create a purely visual break between songs—even songs with no acoustical break—to allow the playing of a selected track. On the *Innervisions* LP, there is a small rill between "Living for the City" and "Golden Lady" that begins at the point where the final chord of "Living for the City" cuts off (and after the piano interlude has already started). It is unclear, however, whether this location was dictated by Wonder or, more likely, simply deduced by Motown's lathe operator.

References

Butler, Mark J. 2006. *Unlocking the Groove: Rhythm, Meter, and Musical Design in Electronic Dance Music*. Bloomington, IN: Indiana University Press.

Cecil, Malcolm, and Robert Margouleff. 1995. Interview. Accession No. 1996.507.1.64, WGBH Educational Foundation and BBC TV. Provided by Experience Music Project, Seattle, WA.

Chernoff, John Miller. 1979. *African Rhythm and African Sensibility: Aesthetics and Social Action in African Musical Idioms*. Chicago: University of Chicago Press.

Dance, Daryl Cumber, ed. 2002. *From My People: 400 Years of African American Folklore*. New York: W.W. Norton & Company.

Everett, Walter. 2004. Making Sense of Rock's Tonal Systems. *Music Theory Online* 10/4. http://www.societymusictheory.org/mto/issues/mto.04.10.4/toc.10.4.html.

Floyd, Samuel Jr. 1995. *The Power of Black Music: Interpreting Its History from Africa to the United States*. New York, Oxford: Oxford University Press.

Garcia, Luis-Manuel. 2005. On and On: Repetition as Process and Pleasure in Electronic Dance Music. *Music Theory Online* 11/4 (October).

Hasty, Christopher. 1997. *Meter As Rhythm*. Oxford: Oxford University Press.

Hebdidge, Dick. 1987. *Cut 'n' Mix: Culture, Identity and Caribbean Music*. London: Methuen.

Horn, Martin. 2000. *Innervisions: The Music of Stevie Wonder*. Bloomington, IN, 1st Books Library.

Hughes, Tim. 2003. Groove and Flow: Six Analytical Essays on the Music of Stevie Wonder. Ph.D. dissertation, University of Washington.

King, Martin Luther, Jr. 2002. A Testament of Hope. In *From My People: 400 Years of African American Folklore*, ed. Daryl Cumber Dance, 322–323. New York: W.W. Norton & Company.

Krims, Adam. 2000. *Rap Music and the Poetics of Identity*. In New Perspectives in Music History and Criticism, ed. Jeffrey Kallberg, Anthony Newcomb, and Ruth Solie. Cambridge: Cambridge University Press.

Lee, Spike, director. 1991. *Jungle Fever*. Feature film Prod. Spike Lee and John Kilik. 40 Acres and a Mule Filmworks.

Love, Dennis and Stacy Brown. 2002. *Blind Faith: An Authorized Biography of Lula Hardaway*. New York: Simon & Schuster.

Prince, director. 1987. *Sign O' The Times*. Feature film Prod. Robert Cavallo, Joseph Ruffalo, and Steven Fargnoli. Purple Films Company.

Rahn, John. 1993. Repetition. *Contemporary Music Review* 7, 49–57.

Rose, Tricia. 1994. *Black Noise: Rap Music and Black Culture in Contemporary America*. Hanover, NH: Wesleyan University Press.

Small, Christopher. 1987. *Music of the Common Tongue*. New York: Riverrun Press.

Snead, James A. 1981. On Repetition in Black Culture. *Black American Literature Forum* 15/4 (Winter), 146–154.

The 500 Greatest Songs of All Time. 2004. *Rolling Stone* 963 (December 9).

Werner, Craig. 2004. *Higher Ground: Stevie Wonder, Aretha Franklin, Curtis Mayfield, and the Rise and Fall of American Soul*. New York: Crown Publishers.

West, Cornell. 1993. *Race Matters*. New York: Vintage Books.

Wilson, Cintra. 1996. Stevie Wonder: "Innervisions" (Tamla, 1973). Salon (June 17). http://www.salon.com/weekly/wonder960617.html.

Wonder, Stevie. 1992. *Talking Book*. Motown 37463-0319-2.

______. 1973. *Innervisions*. Motown 37463-0326-2.

______. 1974. *Live USA*. Imtrat GMBH imt 900.006.

______. 1991. *Jungle Fever*. Motown 37463-6291-2.

______. 1995. *Natural Wonder*. Motown 530 546-2.

X, Malcolm. 2002. Message to the Grass Roots. In *Malcolm X Speaks: Selected Speeches and Statements*, ed. George Breitman. Reprinted in *From My People: 400 Years of African American Folklore*, ed. Daryl Cumber Dance, 325. New York: W.W. Norton & Company.

10

Fumbling Towards Ecstasy

Voice Leading, Tonal Structure, and the Theme of Self-Realization in the Music of Sarah McLachlan

TIMOTHY KOOZIN

The songs of Sarah McLachlan are finely wrought and immensely popular, combining captivating vocal and electronic sounds, poignant lyrics, visceral rhythms, and a broad range of stylistic elements. Her songs deal with themes of inner contemplation and the personal struggle toward self-actualization. This study explores four songs that span her creative output, showing how McLachlan's distinctive approach to voice leading helps depict narratives of an inner journey towards self-realization. In songs from Sarah McLachlan's third studio album, *Fumbling Towards Ecstasy*, this inner journey is represented in voice-leading figures that migrate through shifting harmonic contexts and become superimposed upon each other through extended chords and chromaticism. A hierarchical approach in the analysis shows how linear/modal chord patterns nested within larger tonal frameworks form open musical structures that become an artistic statement themselves, integral to the representation of McLachlan's powerful narratives.

"Building a Mystery"

Sarah McLachlan describes "Building a Mystery" (*Surfacing*, 1997) as her most simple and straightforward song. While apparently simple, it employs elegant relationships in harmony, voice leading, and formal structure to characterize the ambiguous relationship between the singer and the mystery figure described in the lyrics. According to McLachlan, this Grammy-winning song began as "a guitar riff, a four-chord pattern."[1] She and co-writer Pierre Marchand developed the song starting with the chords of the chorus (see Example 10.1a), fashioning the essential elements of the song in about half an hour. While McLachlan's music defies strict categorization, processes of harmonic patterning in her music identify it with the idiom of rock music. Chord motions by descending perfect fourth and parallel shifts by step frequently occur in rock songs. Harmonic patterns in descending perfect fourths reverse the usual "functional" progression by descending fifth typical of common-practice harmony, working instead as groups of stepwise-descending neighbor tones

Example 10.1 Sarah McLachlan, "Building a Mystery" (Sarah McLachlan-Pierre Marchand), *Surfacing* (1997). Copyright © 1997 Sony/ATV Songs LLC, Tyde Music and Pierre J. Marchand. All rights on behalf of Sony/ATV Songs LLC and Tyde Music administered by Sony/ATV Music Publishing, 8 Music Square West, Nashville, TN 37203. International copyright secured. All rights reserved.

(as can be traced among the chorus's three upper voices in Example 10.1a).[2] Motion toward the subdominant in this song is expanded through a cycle of descending fourths. Dotted slurs on the graph in Example 10.1a show how the cycle of fourths continues on a larger level, spanning verse, bridge, and chorus.

The four-chord pattern of the verse and chorus, which McLachlan characterized in one interview (McLachlan 1997) as "bonehead simple," is not entirely simple to describe from the standpoint of functional tonality. The tonal polarity of D major is diffused through the competing modal/linear pattern around B minor. Example 10.1 combines two contrasting views. Example 10.1a shows how the modal rock linear pattern of i–♮VII–i is expanded in this song.[3] The A-major chord ending each section acts as a modal neighbor to B minor each time the verse or chorus repeats. The pre-chorus passage elongates the stepwise approach to B minor through G and A major. McLachlan makes her chord pattern a great deal more interesting by placing the D chord just before the phrase ending on A major in the verse and chorus. This suggestion of D-major tonality near the end of the phrase destabilizes the priority of B minor as a modal "tonic."

The tonal orbit of D major is mapped in Example 10.1b. The tonal influence of D is internal to each phrase, but it is never solidly confirmed. While the A-major chord unquestionably appears at "turnaround" points, articulating the phrase in the manner of a half cadence, there is ambiguity as to whether it functions as a linear/modal agent of B minor (as ♮VII) or as a functional dominant in D. A hierarchical analysis provides a means to acknowledge the dual role of the A chord. At a local level it can be interpreted as a linear/modal chord elaborating B minor, as diagrammed in Example 10.1a. At a higher level, as shown in Example 10.1b, its prolongational role as functional dominant becomes clear.

The voice-leading structure and the outer form provide a musical counterpart to the narrative of the lyrics. Blues inflection with F♮ against B minor in the verse accompanies the singer's description of the dark charismatic figure who has captured her attention. She pokes fun at his dark side. He is a predatory egotist, a "vampire."[4] His mannerisms are contrived to keep others at a safe distance. Harmonically stuck in the circular pattern on B minor, the character reveals little about himself, "holding out and holding in." She ironically compares him to a faithless Christ figure who carefully doles out his mysterious revelations. The use of religious and mystical imagery in this ironic context seems to point towards a longing for faith—not for the arcane mysteries of this man's invention, but for a deeper truth.

The singer, by contrast, is not afraid to reveal her feelings. We learn of her affection for him during the harmonically directed pre-chorus. The descending melodic figure derived from the opening is higher and major in inflection, with A major supported by its dominant, E major. Functional harmonic progression and major inflection accompany the singer's expression of empowerment. She is attracted to this man, but clearly in charge. Through the singer's affectionate critique, the man's superficialities—the barriers he builds to avoid intimacy—are rendered mere illusion.

Verse 1	You come out at night. That's when the energy comes and the dark side's light and the vampires roam. You strut your rasta wear and your suicide poem and a cross from a faith that died before Jesus came. You're building a mystery.
Verse 2	You live in a church, where you sleep with voodoo dolls and you won't give up the search for the ghosts in the halls. You wear sandals in the snow and a smile that won't wash away. Can you look out the window without your shadow getting in the way?
Pre-Chorus	Oh you're so beautiful, with an edge and a charm, but so careful when I'm in your arms.
Chorus	'Cause you're working, building a mystery, holding out and holding in. Yeah you're working, building a mystery and choosing so carefully.

(Lyrics from "Building a Mystery" by Sarah McLachlan and Pierre J. Marchand used with permission of Hal Leonard Corporation and Studio Nomade Music.)

The dissonant blues inflection on F♮ in the verse is shown with a flagged note in the graph. Another flagged note is the "added sixth" on E accompanying the G-major chord. The flagged notes form an inner-voice descent to the D-major chord, which initiates a large-scale descending structural line from an upper-voice F♯. The approach to $\hat{2}$ in each section by way of both blues and major inflection is an important element of large-scale continuity. This is dramatized at the end of the piece. With the harmonically open pattern completed, the song simply stops on the word "mystery." Lacking a conclusive descent to $\hat{1}$, the structural line underscores the unresolved dynamics of the lovers' relationship.

"Building a Mystery" provides a concise example of McLachlan's distinctive approach to harmony and voice leading. The modal/linear patterning around B minor and the subdued tonal focus on D major form a structural opposition that is never resolved. McLachlan's reference to the functional tonality of D major is covert and inconclusive; the A-major chord always leads away from D, never toward it. The linear focus on B minor is strongly asserted through phrase rhythm while the tonal influence of D major is underplayed. At the ending, McLachlan shows her predilection for avoiding the finality of any candidate for a concluding tonic. Choosing to leave the mystery unresolved, the piece ends on A major—a kind of half cadence left hanging.

"Ben's Song"

In "Ben's Song" from McLachlan's first album, *Touch* (1988), ephemeral shifts in and out of a dreamlike state of romantic longing are depicted through McLachlan's distinctive approach to voice leading and harmony. The song is like a Celtic ballad, combining rich modal colorations with romantic imagery of an idealized lost love.

Verse 1 On the hills of fire, the darkest hour,
I was dreaming of my true love's pyre.
Who will bring a light to stoke the fire?
Fear not for you're still breathing.

Chorus On a windless day,
I saw the life blood drained away.
A cold wind blows on a windless day.

Verse 2 Hear the cry for new life the mourning's flame,
You were the brightest light that burned too soon in vain.
Who will bring you back from where there's no return?
Fear not for you're just dreaming.

Chorus On a winter's day,
I saw the life blood drained away.
A cold wind blows on a windless day.

(Lyrics from "Ben's Song" by Sarah McLachlan used with permission of Hal Leonard Corporation.)

This song shows McLachlan's ability to use the pure tones of her highest vocal range in an almost instrumental way. The melody begins with a high flute-like sound; it takes a moment before one can identify it as a human voice. After beginning on nearly the highest note in the song, the melody makes a graceful, ornamented descent. As in many McLachlan songs, tonal orientation is understated at local and large-scale levels, with cycles of fourths employed in the verse to project a modal/linear framework. The chord changes in descending perfect fourths provide a context for the D-major-denying Mixolydian modal inflection created by C♮'s. After the opening wordless vocalization, the first verse extends the descending melodic structural line. As shown in Example 10.2, the octave descent into McLachlan's rich lower vocal register accentuates the Mixolydian C♮ coloration while grouping the recurring three-chord harmonic pattern into broader eight-measure units (marked by double bars and dotted barlines).[5]

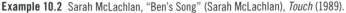

Example 10.2 Sarah McLachlan, "Ben's Song" (Sarah McLachlan), *Touch* (1989).

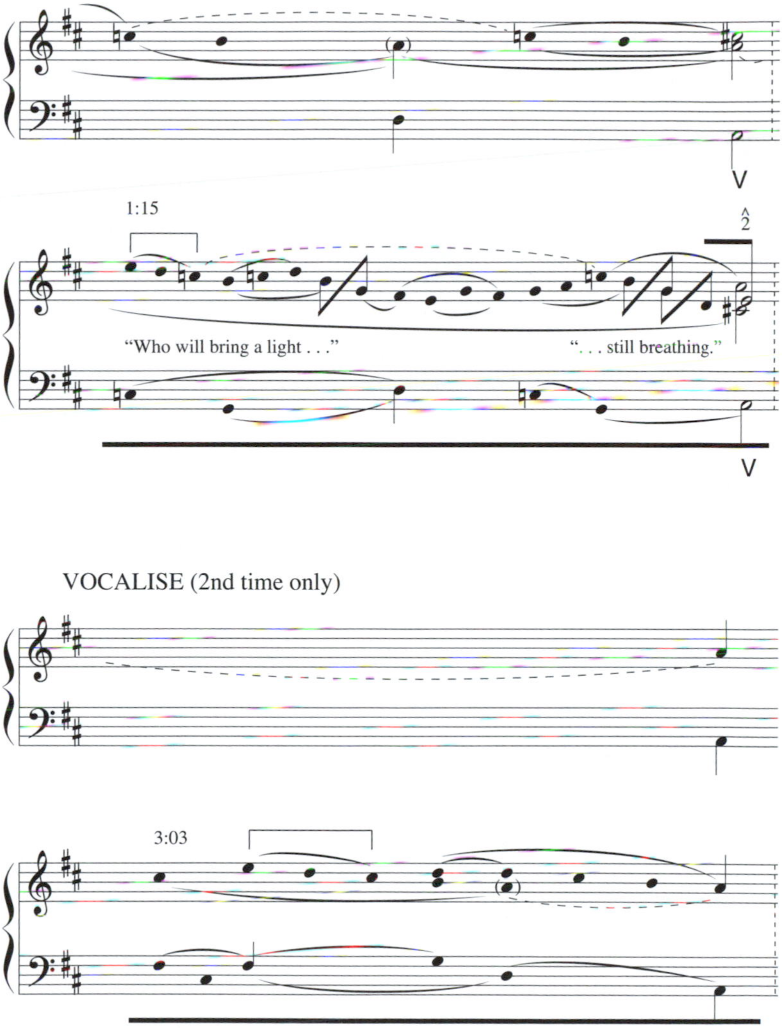

Example 10.2 (*Continued*)

Example 10.2 (*Continued*)

Voice-leading patterns in "Ben's Song" enhance the narrative depicted in the lyrics. Mixolydian inflections are associated with a dream world in which a lover is consumed by fire, while emergences of clear tonal orientations provide a link to the world outside of the dream. The singer imagines a funeral pyre for a lost lover, but at the arrival of the functional A-major dominant chord, the dream fades. We learn that the lover is "still breathing." Arrival of the dominant serves to clarify large-scale tonal structure while highlighting the meaning of the text, linking the underpinnings of tonality with the apparent reality that the lover is not actually dead. The second verse brings back the dream of mourning: "You were the brightest light that burned too soon in vain." The dominant chord at the close of the verse again brings consolation that the loss is not real, but something experienced "just dreaming."

Example 10.3 distills harmonic patterning and characterizes the modal inflections throughout "Ben's Song." The A-major chord ending the verse provides for the tonal orientation of D major without ever resolving directly to the tonic. It also provides a connecting link for the modal excursion on F♯ minor in the chorus. The passage presents a static, disorienting image of the

Example 10.3 Sarah McLachlan, "Ben's Song" (Sarah McLachlan), *Touch* (1989). © Copyright 1990 Songs of Universal, Inc. and Nettoverboard Publishing, Ltd. All Rights Controlled and administered by Songs of Universal, Inc. All rights reserved. Used by permission.

day the lover died: "A cold wind blows on a windless day." After a return of the verse, the linear elaboration of F♯ minor is enlarged through a wordless vocalise and an elongation of the chorus.

The modal chord pattern on F♯ minor and C♯ minor dislocates the listener from the overall D-major context. It continues to the end, as if to suggest that the dream is a persistent image that will not be dispelled. As shown with brackets above the staves in Example 10.2, a descending melodic motive derived from the verse is transformed, creating a haunting effect in the modal context of the passage. The harmonically open ending allows for an interesting large-scale chromatic linear motion. The goal note in the melody of the verse is A, supported with dominant harmony. The modal shift on F♯ minor supports G♯ as a ninth in the final chord. The large-scale projection of A in the melody, and its denial in the melodic shift to G♯ at the end, forms an unresolved tension in the song's overall structure. McLachlan underscores this tension in a final vocal gesture, sliding back and forth between F♯ and G♯ in a sigh of mournful reverie as the final chords sound.

The ultimate denial of the D-major tonality underscores the tragic theme of lost love in the lyrics. So persistent are the images of mourning, with their attendant modal harmonies, that it is possible to view the song as an image of a dream within a dream. The unresolved conclusion suggests that the consuming fire of lost love may represent something real; perhaps it is the denials of death in the song that are only wishful.

"Elsewhere"

In, *Fumbling Towards Ecstasy* (1993), voice leading processes depict in musical terms a personal journey toward self-actualization.[6] The lyrics explore fears and self-deceptions that diminish our inner peace and our capacity to love. As the songs chart a course through this inner landscape, voice-leading figures migrate through changing harmonic contexts and are superimposed upon those contexts through use of ninths, elevenths, and other extensions. The album's most introspective song is entitled "Elsewhere." The singer's inner journey of self-realization is spatialized: Her solitude is "the space where I can breathe"; her life experience, "a distance I have wandered." The first verse is a harmonically closed linear elaboration of E minor, depicting her solitude with solo voice and quiet accompaniment. The feeling here is one of calm stability, as the singer reflects on experiences gathered in reaching out to others and reaching within. In this piece, we again see the linear elaboration of a minor chord in an opening gesture as a foil for the subdued global reference to a major tonal center. With E minor heard at beginnings and endings of four iterations of the two-bar pattern, the dominant function of the D^9 chord is less pronounced than its linear association as ♮VII.

Verse	I love the time and in between, the calm inside me in the space where I can breathe. I believe there is a distance I have wandered to touch upon the years of reaching out and reaching in,
Transition	holding out, holding in.
Chorus	I believe this is heaven to no one else but me and I'll defend it as long as I can be left here to linger in silence. If I choose to would you try to understand?

(Lyrics from "Elsewhere" by Sarah McLachlan used with permission of Hal Leonard Corporation.)

A transition extends the verse from eight to ten measures. At this crucial turning point in the song, the voice leading in thirds previously elaborating E minor is now projected over a new bass line outlining functional harmony in G major. The destabilization of once-steady four-bar phrases, along with the shift from a modal/linear elaboration of E minor to a clear tonal projection of G major, coincides with the singer's emergence from her contemplative inner world, her time of "holding out, holding in."[7]

In the chorus the singer moves from introspection to a more outward stance. Still protective of her inner world, describing it as "heaven to no one else but me," the singer nonetheless desires intimacy and trust. The singer's emergence from her silent world entails risk and sacrifice. We come to understand that her reaching out to another is a profound gesture, a gift. The chorus ends with a question: Will the other accept her silence and "try to understand?" The singer's progression from solitude toward interaction in the chorus is set with an open harmonic structure that prolongs A minor—supertonic to the expanded III of the verse's E minor—and moves to D major at the end. As shown in Example 10.4, this implies a tonal ii-V progression in G major, but there is no direct resolution of the questioning V. Instead, the D-major chord once more forms a linear ♮VII, moving back to E minor.

In the following verses, the singer asserts her self-identity within archetypal relationships with lover and parent. Her acknowledgment of love and desire in the second verse builds to a climactic moment at the transition. At the shift to functional G-major harmony on the words, "I believe," the singer overcomes her resistance and accepts the love of another. The third verse is a more subdued flashback to the singer as quiet child rebelling against a mother's authority. Again the transition provides a crisis point. She addresses her mother directly, breaking away from parental influence to find her own way:

Example 10.4 Sarah McLachlan, "Elsewhere" (Sarah McLachlan), *Fumbling Towards Ecstacy* (1993). Copyright © 1993 Sony/ATV Songs LLC and Tyde Music. All Rights administered by Sony/ATV Music Publishing, 8 Music Square West, Nashville, TN 37203. International copyright secured. All rights reserved.

Mother can't you see I've got
to live my life the way I feel is right for me,
might not be right for you
but it's right for me,
I believe.

Tonally directed chord progressions are positioned carefully in "Elsewhere" so that their influence is minimized at phrase beginnings and endings. Inflection of major tonality is used to highlight points in the song's narrative in a controlled and careful way, so that it does not overpower the modal coloration and linear framework of the song. The transitional passage on A minor and D major that ends the chorus becomes a vamp that ends the song. The ambiguity as to whether these chords function in G major or as modal agents of E minor becomes a moot point. The transition simply repeats, becoming a pattern that eventually fades out. Through repetition, the "transition" becomes tonally self-contained, projecting a standard Dorian rock chord pattern, i^7 – IV (if, that is, A were now heard as tonic). The emergence of a newly independent tonal locus from a pattern previously tied to another key area is an expressive device in the song, and may be interpreted as an arrival at a new "place" in musical terms, just as the singer asserts herself through spatialization of her own inner "place" of the mind.

"Circle"

The final chords of "Elsewhere" derive from an unresolved dominant of G, which provides harmonic linkage to the next song on the album, "Circle." This upbeat rhythm-and-blues song outwardly takes the form of a frank discussion between lovers. The song opens upon a scenario where "There are two of us talking in circles and one of us who wants to leave." Recalling the inner world of solitude described in the previous song, "Elsewhere," the action of "Circle" occurs within a place of the mind, "a world created for only us." It gradually becomes evident that the singer is not having dialogue with a lover to decide whether or not to end an unhealthy relationship, but is rather expressing a schizophrenic anxiety as she explores this question in her own mind. The layering of instruments depicts the singer's conflicting feelings of attraction and resistance, as the seductive rhythm and vocals are projected against an ominous background of sustained, descending chromatic lines in the guitar and synthesizer. A grainy vocal utterance that punctuates the start of the song also dramatizes the dualistic conflict expressed in the lyrics. A bit of gasping laughter carefully edited for rhythmic effect, it is both sensual and strangely unnatural.

Verse There are two of us talking in circles
and one of us who wants to leave,
in a world created for only us,

an empty cage that has no key.
Don't you know you're working with flesh and blood,
carving out of jealousy?
Crawling into each other,
it's smothering every little part of me.

Chorus — What kind of love is this that keeps me hanging on
despite everything it's doing to me?
What is this love that keeps me coming back for more
when it will only end in misery?

(Lyrics from "Circle" by Sarah McLachlan used with permission of Hal Leonard Corporation.)

In "Circle" the singer expresses her anxiety outwardly in the chorus. As the melody moves higher, it is as if she is able to step out of the confines of the relationship to reflect on its consequences. In contrast to the harmonically closed modal elaboration of G minor in the verse, the chorus moves from the major subdominant on C to B♭, establishing the relative major key with its subdominant, E♭. The second verse expands on the idea of confining relationships, as the singer observes that others around her seem to be similarly trapped: "Oh my brother, my sister, my mother, you're losing your identity." This recalls the progression through reflection on self, lover, and mother in the previous song. Encouraging others toward self-realization seems to provide the key to the singer's own inner anxiety, but the chorus repeats and the circular argument is continued.

Voice-leading patterns in "Circle" are similar to those noted in "Elsewhere." In both songs, tonic and subdominant ninth chords are elaborated with figuration in descending thirds. In "Circle," the song's chromatic voice leading artfully depicts the circular theme in the lyrics; as the singer sinks further into a descending spiral, the melody embellishes a repeating chromatic figure in descending thirds (see the slurred motions in the treble staff of Example 10.5a). This repeated figure passes through an embellishing diminished-seventh chord. Sounding rather out of place against the song's funk rhythms, the diminished chord creates a kind of stylistic dislocation, suggesting that the composer is appropriating, rather than expressing, rhythm-and-blues style. The descending motive in thirds is supported with tonic harmony in the verse but superimposed over the subdominant in the chorus. Extended harmonies including the seventh, thirteenth, and added sixth enable the descending figure to migrate through shifting harmonic contexts, its character being enriched with every turn.

The idea of harmonic juxtaposition is expanded in the guitar solo. As the chorus ends on B♭, an A♭ chord is superimposed, surprisingly, over its sustaining root in the bass forming an eleventh chord. A sonority not heard before here in this song (its manifestations elsewhere, as in Stevie Wonder's "Uptight" and throughout the Beatles' *Revolver*, are mentioned in Walter

a) Harmonic Reduction

b) Opening Phrase

Example 10.5 Sarah McLachlan, "Circle" (Sarah McLachlan), *Fumbling Towards Ecstacy* (1993).

Everett's essay in this volume), the dissonant shift aptly coincides with the final word of the chorus, "misery." The guitar solo also provides an important link to the large-scale voice leading. As shown in Example 10.5a, the motive descending in thirds to B♭ continues downward through A♭ to G during the guitar solo. A dotted line in the graph shows how this extends the motion by descending thirds, completing a linear motion that circles back to the opening of the piece. Through this connection, the descending melodic framework of the song can be viewed as circular in nature on local and large-scale levels.

Sarah McLachlan (1994, 2) has described the writing of *Fumbling Toward Ecstasy* as "a kind of therapy" in which she confronted her innermost fears and concerns by articulating them in her music. Why are listeners so drawn to these highly personal inner dramas? Susan Sontag writes that through artworks we find emotional release for collective fears of self-alienation and loss of feeling that are deeply rooted in Western culture. Our spiritual need to be transformed through suffering and passion stems from a romantic "tradition of introspection" that can be traced back to the writings of Paul and Augustine (Sontag 1966, 41–43). The artist transforms suffering into art. We look to works of art in order to "test ourselves for strength of feeling." Artworks become meaningful to a culture as people recount themselves in the narratives they express (Lyotard 1989, 23). As we identify with McLachlan's inner journey, we give attention our own inner mysteries. Through the effective use of metaphor in music and text, McLachlan's life experience resonates with our own.

Sarah McLachlan's unique approach to voice leading helps communicate her powerful stories of self-actualization. While major tonality operates as a global force in the songs, the polarity of the major triad is subdued at local levels. Linear/modal chord patterns inherent to the rock style project fields of local color and stability that challenge the priority of the tonic chord. As voice-leading patterns migrate through shifting tonal fields, they become part of the symbology that represents the narrative depicted in the lyrics. Open forms lacking final resolution imply a narrative in progress that travels beyond the boundaries of the song. In this way, the musical form itself signifies the unresolved mysteries we each face in our personal struggles toward self-realization.

Notes

1. Video interview with Sarah McLachlan included on the enhanced *Surfacing* CD (1997). McLachlan received two Grammy awards in 1998: Best Female Pop Vocal Performance for "Building a Mystery" and Best Pop Instrumental Performance for "Last Dance."
2. Examples of songs employing harmonic cycles of descending fourths would include the Jimi Hendrix rendition of "Hey Joe," the Rolling Stones' "Jumpin' Jack Flash" (chorus), and the Beatles' "Hey Jude" (final section). Both the descending-fourth cycle and the stepwise "shift" progression are identified as rock-based progressions in Mark Spicer's chapter on Genesis.

3. The chord is modal because its root is drawn from the seventh scale degree of the Mixolydian (or some other competing) mode, and it is of linear derivation because its root functions as a complete neighbor to the tonic. Moore 1995 provides an analytical approach to the ♭VII in rock; for a perspective on the ♭VII in jazz, see Potter 1989.
4. The F♮ against B forms the interval of a tritone, the infamous "Diabolus in musica." Although this chromatic inflection is common in blues and blues-rock styles (witness, for instance, its chilling character in John Lennon's "Cold Turkey"), it is interesting to note here the use of this "dangerous" interval to introduce the vampire character.
5. So pervasive is Mixolydian inflection that a key signature of one sharp is used in the published transcription. I prefer to represent the global influence of D major in graphing the song, as I believe it shapes the whole piece even as it is refuted at the song's ending. This study is based on aural analysis of recordings and differs in many details from the reduced settings found in the Hal Leonard edition. Selections from the *Touch, Solace,* and *Fumbling Towards Ecstasy* albums are included in the 1994 songbook, *Sarah McLachlan.*
6. For another analytical perspective on music from *Fumbling Towards Ecstasy,* see Burns 2000–2001. Burns relates McLachlan's voice leading to the theme of erotic dominance in the song, "Possession." Her discussion of voice leading and modal ambiguity in the song parallels some of my observations here. See also Burns 2005.
7. The balanced opposition of "holding out and holding in" must appeal to McLachlan. The phrase occurs at pivotal points in both "Building a Mystery" and "Elsewhere," set with dominant harmony in each case. The double meaning of "holding out," in the sense of extending an offering as opposed to "holding out" as concealing something, seems to parallel the double meaning of the chord, as it shifts between a linear/modal context (as ♮VII) and a functional context (as V) in both songs.

References

Burns, Lori. 2000–2001. Sarah McLachlan's "Possession" (1993): Representations of Dominance and Subordination in Lyrics, Music, and Images. *Studies in Music at the University of Western Ontario,* 19–20.

______. 2005. Meaning in a Popular Song: The Representation of Masochistic Desire in Sarah McLachlan's "Ice." In *Engaging Music: Essays in Musical Analysis.* Edited by Deborah Stein, 136–148. New York: Oxford University Press.

Lyotard, Jean-François. 1989. *The Postmodern Condition: A Report on Knowledge,* trans. Geoff Bennington and Brian Massumi. Minneapolis: University of Minnesota Press.

McLachlan, Sarah. 1988. *Touch.* Arista 8594.

______. 1992. *Solace.* Arista 18631.

______. 1993. *Fumbling Towards Ecstasy.* Arista 18725.

______. 1994. *Sarah McLachlan* songbook. Milwaukee: Hal Leonard.

______. 1995. *The Freedom Sessions.* Multimedia-enhanced CD. Arista 18784.

______. 1996. *Rarities, B-Sides and Other Stuff.* Multimedia-enhanced CD. Arista 30105.

______. 1997. *Surfacing.* Multimedia-enhanced CD, including video interview. Arista 07822-18970.

Moore, Allan. 1995. The So-Called "Flattened Seventh" in Rock. *Popular Music* 14/2, 185–201.
Potter, Gary M. 1989. The Unique Role of ♭VII7 in Bebop Harmony. *Jazz Forschung* 21, 35–47.
Ramsey, Ian T. 1972. Models and Mystery. In *Essays on Metaphor,* ed. Warren Shibles, 163–168. Whitewater, Wisconsin: The Language Press.
Sontag, Susan. 1966. The Artist as Exemplary Sufferer. In *Against Interpretation*, 39–48. New York: Farrar, Straus and Giroux.

11
Country-Pop Formulae and Craft
Shania Twain's Crossover Appeal

JOCELYN R. NEAL

In 2002, country-pop superstar Shania Twain released her fourth major album, the third of her collaborations with husband and producer, Robert John "Mutt" Lange.[1] The optimistically titled *Up!* satisfied hungry fans for whom five years had passed without a new Twain release. Music critics generally lauded the album, while fans of more traditional and honky-tonk-infused country bemoaned the continued reign of the pop-crossover diva. But through an unexpected marketing strategy, the album also challenged complacent notions of musical style and the very concept of what comprised a "song": the album was released in three color-coded versions, each with an ostensibly different stylistic version of the same lineup of nineteen songs. The red disc featured pop-rock mixes, the green, country-pop, and the blue, world music. All three were a thorough repackaging of the same vocals. Ironically, across all these stylistic treatments of the songs, what remained most salient were the songs' hooks: the attention-getting musical devices and elements of form and structure that captured and held the listener's focus.

This essay explores the songwriting strategies and compositional techniques through which those hooks emerge. The analyses of these songs' formal structures, particularly in the domains of harmonic stability, meter, and sonic texture, reveal a performative signature for Shania Twain's recordings and suggest how those songwriting techniques have contributed to her commercial success. Comparisons of Twain's musical output to the broader country-pop scene reveal what makes her work distinctive within a style plagued by accusations of bland homogeneity. Finally, Twain and Lange's music is contextualized in relation to pop music beyond country's borders. This exploration offers a new perspective on the concept of crossover success, where songwriting techniques and musical-structural elements are as central to the identity of a style as is fan reception and acceptance in different radio and marketing formats.

The Country Music Landscape

Shania Twain's rise to fame in the country music industry is an oft-told story, typically beginning with her eponymous debut on Mercury Records in 1993.[2] As her career unfolded, it did so in the context of an ever-changing country music genre, which shaped how her musical style was received by the listening audience. By the midpoint of the 1980s, mainstream commercial country had reached saturation point with pop-crossover "countrypolitan." That style had been spurred on by John Travolta's appearance in *Urban Cowboy* (1980), a phenomenon that turned country bars and country musicians into the latest national trend. Johnny Lee's theme song from the movie, "Lookin' for Love," ushered in the era where number-one hits on *Billboard*'s "Hot Country Singles" charts were also hugely successful on the "Hot 100" pop charts. Synthesizer-infused accompaniments with everything from handclaps to horns graced the biggest hits, including Dolly Parton's "9 to 5" (number 1 on both pop and country charts), while the era's general style is best epitomized by Dolly Parton and Kenny Rogers's duet, "Islands in the Stream," written by the Bee Gees, which charted at number 1 in both pop and country. Alabama offered up twenty number-one country hits in this crossover country-pop style between 1980 and 1986, eight of which also appeared on the pop charts; Janie Fricke, Ronnie Milsap, and Crystal Gayle among others also contributed. Even Willie Nelson abandoned his outlaw persona and progressive country sound during those years for forays into Latin pop with Julio Iglesias ("To All the Girls I've Loved Before," number 1 country and number 5 pop) and other such experiments, while both he and Kenny Rogers turned their careers toward acting in made-for-TV movies and other films.

Dolly Parton and Sylvester Stallone's sequined, glitzy country-singing characters in *Rhinestone* (1984) found themselves at the tail end of the crossover fad, much to the vast relief of traditionalist fans. A new crop of artists arrived on the scene in the mid-'80s to shepherd country music back into the nostalgic spaces of its musical past, and in so doing, set country on a stylistic path that diverged from pop. George Strait brought fiddle-oriented Texas Swing back into the airwaves with a string of twelve number-one country hits between 1985 and 1989, but unlike the country songs from earlier in the decade, none of Strait's hits made an appearance on the pop "Hot 100." During the same years, Dwight Yoakam resurrected the sounds of Bakersfield; Reba McEntire's Oklahoma-cowgirl, barrel-racing past was center-stage; Randy Travis relied on traditional honky-tonk twang; and the Judds, with their blues-infused vocals, sang about a rural idealism that resonated with the country audience. The Highwaymen, featuring Willie Nelson, Waylon Jennings, Kris Kristofferson, and Johnny Cash, resurrected outlaw personas with a cover of an old shuffle-beat Ned Miller tune from the early 1960s, "From a Jack to a King." By the end of the decade, mainstream country had left behind most of its pop-crossover stylings and retrenched itself in a thoroughly neo-traditionalist movement.

When Garth Brooks' first album debuted in 1989, it launched a career that paid tribute to neo-traditional country styles thriving in the hands of George Strait and Keith Whitley, while embracing the rock-based entertainment ideals of Journey, Foreigner, and others of his musical influences. He thus began a massive transformation of the country music industry as a whole, paving the way for Twain and Lange's collaborations. Brooks boldly reinstated pop instrumentation on country radio (the audible strings on "The Dance" are often cited as a radical decision), rebelled against his record label's management, and promised his fans spectacular concert effects that rivaled anything in the pop-rock touring scene.[3]

During the same years that Brooks was reshaping the genre musically, political and economic climates in America were shifting. The confluence of these factors led to a meteoric rise in the popularity of country music.[4] Sales figures released by the Recording Industry Association of America reported that country music accounted for less than 8 percent of all music sales when Garth Brooks' debut album appeared; four years later, country music claimed almost 19 percent of all music sales (see Figure 11.1). Explanations for the dramatic shift include the March 1, 1991, introduction of Nielsen SoundScan technology into the data-collection process (correcting systematic flaws by which country music sales had likely been previously underreported) and the inherent problems in genre classification, but the change was stylistically significant nonetheless.

By 1993, rock music had lost market share, country was enjoying an unprecedented popularity, and in that setting, one of rock's most celebrated producers took an interest in country music. Mutt Lange contacted Twain after hearing her lackluster debut album, and around the time of their December 1993 wedding, the two made plans to collaborate professionally.[5] Lange produced Twain's second album, *The Woman In Me*, as a meticulous treatment of country tradition combined with pop sensibilities, all twelve tracks co-written by the two. The results were eight songs on the *Billboard* "Hot Country Singles" chart in 1995–1997, four of which reached the top position.[6]

Newcomers in this country music boom period were not always welcomed by Nashville with open arms, yet Twain succeeded in establishing herself as

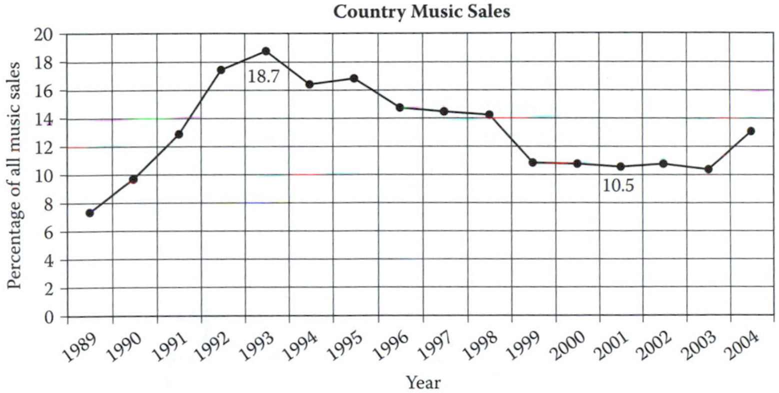

Figure 11.1 RIAA Consumer Profile Data: Country music as a percentage of all music sales, 1989–2004. [Data extracted from Annual Consumer Profile reports, Recording Industry Association of America, http://www.riaa.com/news/marketingdata/default.asp, accessed July 10, 2006.]

a central presence in the scene, partly through the album's music and partly through her, and Lange's, construction of her image. The Canadian-born Twain had packaged her first album with photographs of a lone wolf in the snow, the singer bundled in a fringed parka and a woven jacket and jewelry that evoked her stepfather's Native-American Indian heritage (born Eilleen Regina Edwards, she changed her name early in her career to "Shania," which fans have long believed to be an Ojibwa word meaning "I'm on my way"), an incongruous and ultimately confusing collection of images for an early 1990s country album.[7] But for 1995's *The Woman In Me*, Twain, like her music, was wrapped in the most iconic elements of country's stereotyped identity: denim, leather chaps, a cowboy hat, and, on the inside cover, a big-haired, red-headed artist with a Palomino (see Figure 11.2). Her red-tinged, curl-tussled hairdo matched the album-cover photography popular with many female country singers of the time including Reba McEntire, Faith Hill, and Jo Dee Messina, while the horse evoked the inside cover shot from Garth Brooks' biggest seller, at sixteen million copies, *No Fences*.[8] In other words, Twain's new image was entirely centric to the country music scene at the time, and connected strongly with the genre's most prominent figure. In 1997, Twain and Lange followed with their second collaboration, *Come On Over*, which sold over twenty million copies and placed eleven songs on the *Billboard* "Hot Country Singles" chart—an incredible feat.[9] As opposed to the situation with her first collaboration with Lange, Twain's country identity was by now firmly established, freeing her to offer unabashedly pop musical hooks and an overtly sultry image as well.

By the end of the decade, Twain was the undisputed queen of country pop, even though her success was underscored by charges of a lack of authenticity, a watering-down of the musical essence that comprised country music, a disregard for tradition, and an overt act of selling out. Meanwhile, country's market share had slipped to just over 10 percent of all music sold, with the country audience

Figure 11.2 Horses on inside cover-art for Garth Brooks, *No Fences* (1990) and Shania Twain, *The Woman In Me* (1995).

seemingly tiring of country-pop sounds. Music sales overall had fallen from an all-time high of $14.6 billion in 1999 to nearly $2 billion less by 2002, and consumers were annoyed by climbing retail prices for CDs. A musical-roots revival took hold in country music, spurred by the novel bluegrass, acoustic, blues, folk, and roots soundtrack to *O Brother, Where Art Thou?,* which sold eight-million-plus copies and led to a burgeoning interest in bluegrass. Thus, when Shania Twain released her fourth album (and third collaborative effort with Lange), *Up!*, in 2002, the three simultaneously available versions of its songs were both a musical experiment with and an expression of artistic creativity, yet they also represented a calculated marketing strategy for both a vastly different musical landscape and a more demanding audience than had existed a decade earlier.

The domestic release of *Up!* handed buyers the green (country-pop mix) and red (pop-rock) disks in one package, with an insert advertising the blue (world-music) disk. The international release, available to U.S. buyers via import, contained the red and blue disks. The cover art for each version featured Twain undressed to her white underwear, waiting for the listener to figuratively dress her (and her music) in any of the three styles (see Figures 11.3a and 3b). What was radical about this album was that the three

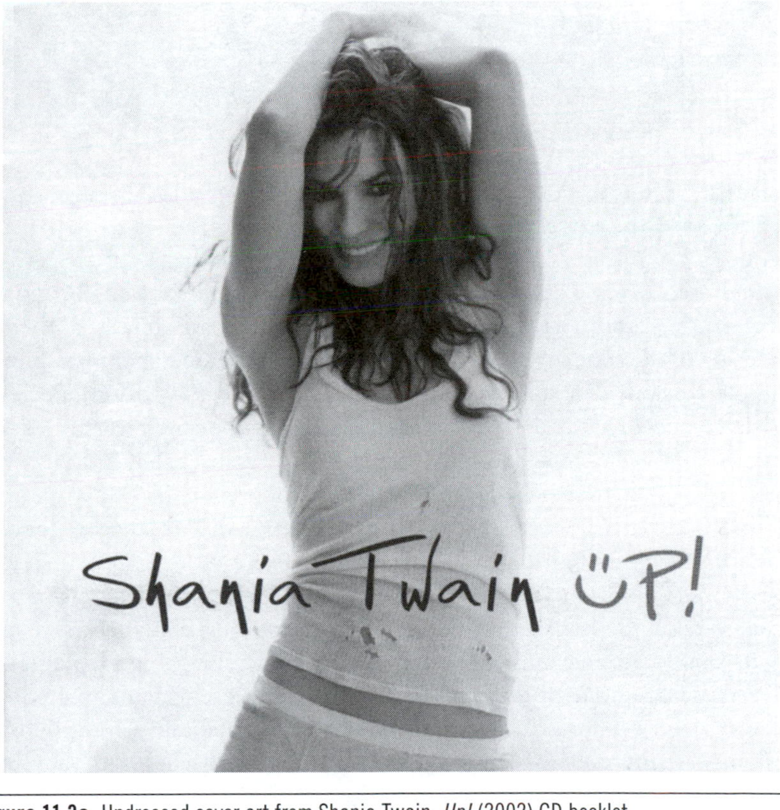

Figure 11.3a Undressed cover art from Shania Twain, *Up!* (2002) CD booklet.

Figure 11.3b Three dressed, color-coded CDs of Shania Twain, *Up!* (2002), Top: [green] country-pop mix; Bottom Left: [blue] international mix; Bottom Right: [red] pop-rock mix.

versions were released simultaneously, with no primacy of an "original." According to Twain, each version was conceived as an equally authentic rendering of the song.[10] There was nothing unprecedented about producing multiple versions of a song: popular artists had a long tradition of releasing shortened or extended versions, dance mixes, explicit versus edited versions, and even "international" remixes, as Twain herself did with the album *Come On Over.* Analysts frequently study versions of a tune distinguished as "live," whether formally released or distributed on concert bootlegs. In these situations, analysts and writers either grant primacy to an "original," typically the studio version of the song, or else situate a particular version in an intended mode of consumption (i.e., dance vs. listening, or small-club live audience). But *Up!* offered something ideologically different, where none of those distinctions were present. Fans treated the red and green versions as essentially interchangeable, and while the blue versions were more sonically remote and less frequently acquired, they, too, were accepted.

Ironically, from an analytical perspective, Twain's multiple CDs highlight aspects of each song that do not change from one version to the next, but instead become its structural and performative essence. The rhythmic and metric structure, the placement of unexpected sonic events, and in almost all cases the harmonic structure remain constant, even as texture, timbre, and groove vary. Certainly, analysts of popular music are rightly interested in timbre and texture, along with the processes by which those aspects of a recording are controlled; with regard to Twain's music, interested writers have even shared with their readers "inside" knowledge as to the equipment, studio techniques, and recording processes (down to the placement of the microphones) that Lange used in the studio.[11] But Twain's three sets of recordings for this album allow wide variation in those domains, while the multiple versions of the songs remain essentially the same in the fans' reception. Thus, it is to the areas of rhythm, meter, and harmony—musical structure and compositional strategy—that the following analyses look to explore the unique identity of Twain's music, an essence proven adaptable to multiple styles.

The Craft of Composition

Throughout their collaboration, Twain and Lange faced a difficult musical negotiation between the traditional musical transparency that was a hallmark of country, and the demands for innovation coming from a contemporary, pop-influenced audience. Their songwriting had to adhere to the accepted conventions of country music, at least sufficiently to gain acceptance. Those accepted conventions, implicitly defined by the country fan base, include an *apparent* narrative simplicity, transparency and adherence to past traditions in the music, and a recognizable similarity, however defined, to the rest of contemporaneous country. At the same time, Twain's music had to be differentiated as unique within the larger body of country-pop recordings in order for her to hold sway as a solo artist. The challenge her music faced was both to belong and to stand out from the crowd, and the craftsmanship displayed in their songwriting accomplished both of these goals. In particular, three compositional approaches feature prominently: the first is that of modulation, handled deftly and in a variety of guises. The second encompasses irregularities and asymmetries in phrase structure and hypermeter. The third is the use of carefully placed, unexpected sonic disruptions in the recordings. In combination, these structural devices comprise Twain's musical signature.

Modulation as Sonic Renewal

One of the enduring clichés about country music is its primitive harmonic language: "Three chords and the truth" are touted as the only ingredients necessary for a country song.[12] In the work of contemporary songwriters, nothing could be further from the truth, but what is accurate is that country music still adheres to functional tonality; its songs are in a readily perceptible key and behave accordingly. Twain's adventurous harmonic palette certainly violates any three-chord assumptions, but it is specifically her frequent use of modulations, not only to expand the harmonic vocabulary in the midst of a song but also to redefine the tonal relationships among those chords, that most distinguishes her music from that of her contemporaries. As in other styles of popular music, there are a variety of modulatory techniques present in her songs: an arranger's (truck-driver's) modulation, a modulation to relative major/minor keys, an inversion of the tonic-dominant relationship, and a common-tone modulation. The prevalence of these techniques in Twain's work, and their relative scarcity in other commercial country music from that era, contribute to the identity of Twain's sound.

The arranger's modulation, frequently called a truck-driver's modulation, is generally regarded as a structurally insignificant event in popular music, although its presence often enhances the dramatic narrative and sense of excitement in a recording.[13] In the history of country music, it gained popularity during the Nashville Sound era of the 1960s and '70s, when professional studio arrangers polished each country recording to a well-orchestrated final sheen. The technique involves a direct modulation upwards by either a half-step or whole-step, usually prior to the final chorus, and may serve to brighten or intensify the final section of the song. Arrangers frequently employ chains of these modulations as a stock technique, particularly in strophic songs where the endless succession of verses demands some musical interest be added through the arranging process (hence, the term). Loretta Lynn's autobiographical "Coal Miner's Daughter" (1969) is a prime example: over the course of six verses, the song employs the technique twice, with verses one and two in D Major, verses three and four in E♭, and verses five and six in E.

Despite the ubiquitous presence of these modulations in mainstream Nashville recordings from the 1960s and '70s, they faded almost entirely from the scene in the subsequent decade. Suddenly, with Shania Twain and Mutt Lange together, they were back: fully one-third of the songs on *The Woman In Me*, *Come On Over*, and *Up!* feature the technique, frequently in successive chained occurrences. One obvious result is that Twain's vocal range is displayed more ambitiously throughout the song: "high notes" get higher and the sense of arrival is intensified through the overall ascent in pitch. But another effect of this technique is to help bridge the requirements of country's musical transparency on the one hand and the need to capture and refresh the pop-listener's attention on the other.

The magic of these simple modulations is perhaps best explained by listeners who lack a formal vocabulary for describing the harmonic-structural event. Non-musician undergraduates, asked to describe these instances of modulation, recount something changing, something different happening, yet at the same time, all the readily identifiable elements of the song—melody, chord progression, rhythms, text—appear unaltered.[14] The effect of sameness juxtaposed with intangible change is often intensified by the particular chord progression and voice leading at the moment of modulation. Although the tonal center moves up and the melody is consequently transposed up in pitch-space, the chord that is audibly disjunct from the prevailing diatonic progression is frequently voiced lower in pitch-space than the preceding chord, thereby masking the tonal ascent with a surface-level descent.

Twain's ballad "From This Moment On" features two of these modulations, taking the song from G Major through A to its conclusion in B. The song is built on Standard Song form, an **AABA** pattern with partial reprise, whose title and hook line appear at the beginning and end of each **A** section.[15] The first modulation (see Example 11.1) occurs between the bridge and the third verse. From the half cadence at the end of the bridge, the vocal and bass lines descend. In retrospect, the chord progression across the modulation could be heard as a V reinterpreted as IV, resulting in a motion from IV to I—a motion common in many formal positionings but not in a retransition such as this, where the dramatic narrative calls for a V–I return that is initially promised, but then foiled by the modulation. Furthermore, the presence of pitch-class A in both vocal line and (briefly) bass line foreshadows the new harmonic space with a plagal common-tone connection.

The two modulations in this song refresh the listener's experience without disturbing the continuity of the song's salient musical elements; in other words, they produce a renewal without disruption that thereby adheres to the formula of the contemporary country wedding-ballad without breeding musical complacency.

Twain's chained arranger's modulations also appear in "It Only Hurts When I Breathe," which moves from D♭ Major through E♭ to F, and "In My Car (I'll Be the Driver)," where verses and choruses alternate between D and E Major, and the last verse of the song moves progressively from D Major to E, setting up a final chorus in F♯. "If You Wanna Touch Her, Ask!" maximizes the tonal exploitation of this technique with three chained occurrences. Opening in C Major, the song rises through D and E, finally to arrive at F♯

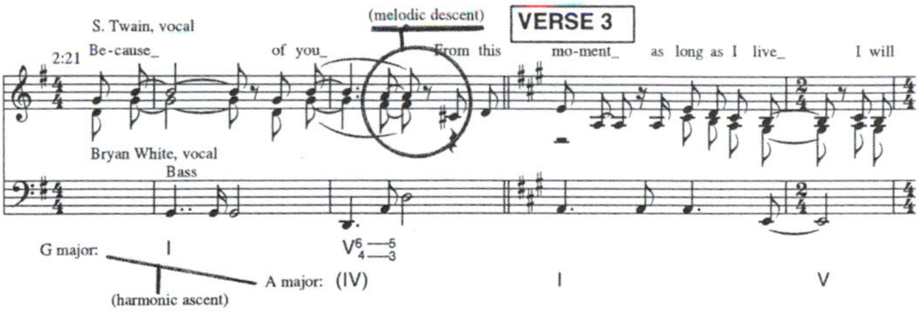

Example 11.1 Shania Twain, "From This Moment On" (Shania Twain-Robert John "Mutt" Lange), *Come On Over* (1997): first modulation.

Major, so the last chorus (see Example 11.2b) is sung a full tritone above its initial presentation (Example 11.2a).

Of the 47 songs on Twain and Lange's complete albums, 30 exhibit some type of harmonic modulation. Nine of these have what are most easily described as a shift between relative major and minor keys, alternating for different sections of the song. "What a Way to Wanna Be," for instance, sets verses in B minor and the chorus in D Major. Other songs use a common-tone approach to modulation by third, such as "Rock This Country," with its move from G Major to B♭ Major. Employing a still different modulatory approach, several of Twain's biggest hits redefine tonal identity by exploiting an inverse relationship whereby the original key's I–V progression is reinterpreted as IV–I in a new key. "Up!," the first track on the album of the same name, features a verse in C Major and a chorus in F Major, arrived at by just this method. A summary of the song's sections in Figure 11.4 shows that a secondary chorus is also set in C.[16] What is most striking about the modulations in "Up!" is their re-contextualization of a single chord. In an unusual tonal move (albeit

Example 11.2 Shania Twain, "If You Wanna Touch Her, Ask!" (Shania Twain-Robert John "Mutt" Lange), *Come On Over* (1997): beginnings of a) first and b) last choruses, indicating the transposition up a tritone via three successive stepwise modulations.

Time	*Section*	*Key*	*Effect*
0:00	INTRO	F	
0:13	VERSE 1	C	
0:29	VERSE 2	C	*expanded dominant for chorus in F*
0:42	CHORUS	F	*arrival, tonic, stability, but ends on V*
0:57	VERSE 3	C	*"V" from chorus becomes local "I"*
1:11	CHORUS	F	
1:26	2ndary CHORUS	C	*unexpected reinterpretation*
1:56	VERSE 4	C	
2:12	CHORUS	F	
2:27	CHORUS EXT.	F	
2:38	2ndary CHORUS	C	*song ends in C*

Figure 11.4 Shania Twain, "Up!" (Shania Twain-Robert John "Mutt" Lange), *Up!* (2002): form and principal key areas. The boxed sections are sketched in Examples 11.3a and 11.3b.

one that is commonplace in contemporary dance-pop), the chorus ends on V, which sounds convincingly like a dominant chord and a potential turnaround (see the end of the second staff in Example 11.3a). The subsequent verse begins immediately in the *key* of V, reiterating the same harmony that the listener just heard, but now contextualizes it as tonic.

As the song continues, the chorus appears again in F Major, followed by a secondary chorus at 1:26 (see Example 11.3b). The first chord of this new section, however, is an F-Major triad, instantly recognized by the listener as tonic of the chorus from just a few seconds earlier (circled on Example 11.3b).

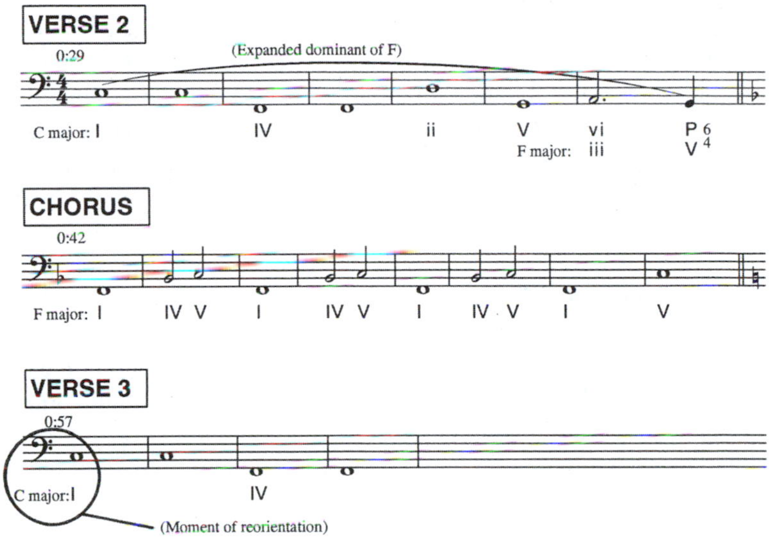

Example 11.3a Shania Twain, "Up!" (Shania Twain-Robert John "Mutt" Lange), *Up!* (2002): modulations between verse 2, chorus, and verse 3.

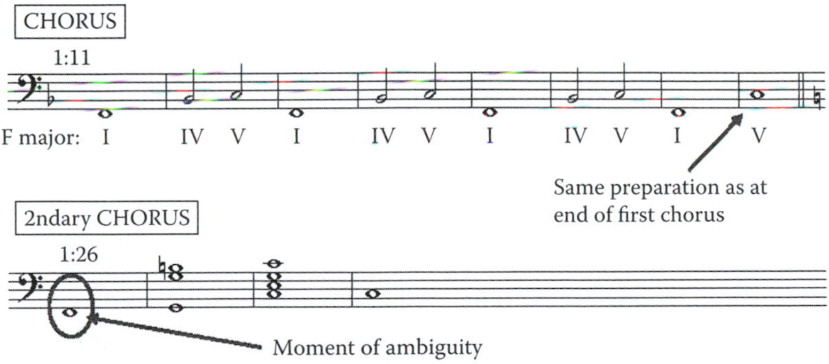

Example 11.3b Shania Twain, "Up!" (Shania Twain-Robert John "Mutt" Lange), *Up!* (2002): secondary chorus, with ambiguous harmonic opening.

Whereas up to this point all song sections have begun with a clear statement of tonic, a moment of ambiguity is offered here: Has the song modulated again or not? The final harmonic twist in "Up!" occurs at its end. Until that point, the essential chorus has appeared in F Major, and it is a matter of simple harmonic reduction to view the verses and secondary sections as expansions of the dominant (C) in relation to the chorus's tonal center. However, the song ends with a restatement of the secondary chorus, convincingly and satisfyingly in C Major.

One might pursue a harmonic analysis of "Up!" that interprets it as all related to one key, or perhaps in a dual tonality. But such an analytic exercise would get no closer to understanding the effect of this modulatory technique in Twain and Lange's songwriting craft or its role in this song's audience appeal. Instead, the technique as employed in "Up!" and several other Twain recordings centers on the moments of transition, when a listener's tonal frame of reference is reoriented with regard to sustaining harmonies. The harmonic vocabulary remains audibly the same, but the relationships among the chords change, all while preserving an implicit foundation of functional tonality.

In certain instances, these harmonic techniques support narrative interpretations of the songs. The smash hit "Man! I Feel Like a Woman" became one of Twain's signature songs almost overnight when released on *Come On Over.* The song's text plays with gendered lyrics and offers a lighthearted subversion of gender roles ("man's shirt, short skirts" are the wardrobe choices for the girls' night out), culminating in the song's title as a celebration of feminine (not necessarily feminist) liberation. With its modulations between F and B♭ Major, the harmonic structure also inverts the listener's expectations of tonic-dominant relationships with each transition from key to key.

Although Twain's approach to harmonic structure was not entirely unique within the country-pop scene, it set her music apart from the vast majority of the field. For instance, although Mindy McCready's image and country-pop musical stylings mirrored Twain's in many ways, these harmonic elements were not part of her music's vocabulary, nor did her music sustain its audience's interest over as many years. McCready's debut album, *Ten Thousand Angels*, was released just a year after Twain's *The Woman In Me*. McCready's album included the number-one country single, "Guys Do It All the Time," along with "A Girl's Gotta Do (What a Girl's Gotta Do)," all produced by the capable ears of David Malloy and Norro Wilson. The lite-girl-power themes in the poetic texts matched the trend set by Twain and others. McCready's publicity photographs showed the same styles of midriff-baring pantsuits and lace tops that featured prominently in Twain's publicity shots, her vocal sound was similar to Twain's, and "Guys Do It All the Time" was even set over the same rhythmic groove as many of Twain's biggest hits. Unlike Twain's, McCready's career trajectory found short-lived commercial success, a result of many different factors.[17] But in spite of the superficial similarities in their recordings, the fact that McCready's album features only one song with a single, trivial arranger's modulation, and none of the other structural features that this essay highlights in Twain's work, simply confirms one significant incongruity between the musical products of Twain and those of most country-pop divas such as McCready.

Even more removed from the musical styles of country-pop, Garth Brooks' 1997 album, *Sevens*, further emphasizes distinctions between musical styles at the level of harmonic structure and stability of key. While Brooks' album is clearly distinct from Twain's brand of country-pop in its poetic themes, instrumentation, vocal timbre, and historical references, it is also different in its treatment of harmonic structure. None of the songs on the album modulate, nor do they exhibit the other compositional traits central to Twain's sound that will be discussed shortly.

The only artist in the country-pop scene whose commercial draw rivaled Shania Twain's was Faith Hill, and indeed, when subjected to the same music-analytic examination, Hill's music reveals the same structural approaches as are found in Twain's recordings. When Hill returned to the recording studio in 1998 after a few years off, it was readily apparent that country was changing; her music would have to compete in a country-pop marketplace dominated by Shania Twain's slick instrumentation, songwriting, and production values. Hill's first two country-pop albums, 1998's *Faith* and 1999's *Breathe*, mastered the style and catapulted her to the forefront of the scene, partly by presenting similar poetic themes, constructed pop image, instrumentation, and production values as those that had shaped Twain's career. But beneath those more superficial elements, Hill's songs exhibit the same structural approaches and compositional techniques that characterize Twain's.[18]

The quintessential illustration of these elements is Hill's recording of "The Way You Love Me," from *Breathe*. The song opens in C Major, but at the end of the pre-chorus (see Example 11.4a), a stepwise ascent takes it to D. The chorus begins in D, but at its end (see Example 11.4b), a similar stepwise ascent lifts it into E just in time for the next verse. Rather than launching a limitless climb through pitch-space, the song quickly executes a third-related direct modulation back to C (see Example 11.4c), where the next verse begins the process again. The stepwise ascents (circled on Example 11.4) are highlighted by the linear bass motion through scale degrees $\hat{5}$ and $\hat{6}$, while Hill's voice rises audibly from phrase to phrase. The returns from E Major to C are sudden and brief, and occur when Hill is not singing. The resulting song structure, then, functions like a harmonic barbershop pole. The spiraling ascent is readily perceptible to the listener; the moments when the structural key area returns to C Major, however, are easily missed. As a result, the song generates the effect of endless rising, soaring on the optimism of a newfound love, yet never entirely abandoning safe musical (harmonic) grounding.

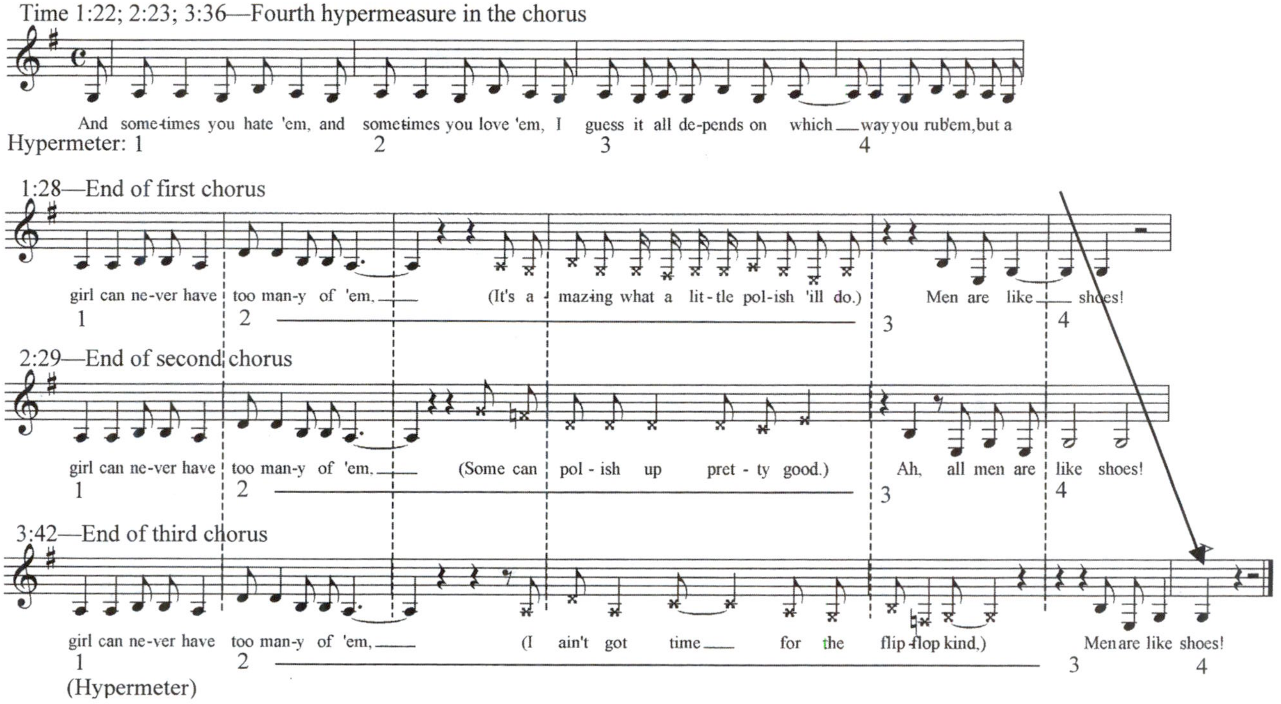

Example 11.5 Shania Twain, "Shoes" (Shania Twain-R. J. Lang-Tammy Hyler-Kim Tribble), *Music From and Inspired By Desperate Housewives* (2005): fourth and fifth hypermeasures of the chorus, indicating the spoken insertions and different metric treatment of the fifth hypermeasure in each successive iteration of the chorus.

version was done specifically for a television soundtrack. When the producers of the ABC Network television show *Desperate Housewives* decided to release an album, *Music From and Inspired By Desperate Housewives,* they contracted with several female artists whose images corresponded to the show's popular, lite feminist ideology, including Martina McBride, Sara Evans, Liz Phair, the Indigo Girls, and of course, Shania Twain.[22]

Despite the fact that the television show, the album, and a majority of the artists working on it had nothing to do with country music per se, the project turned out to be a catalyst as a virtual link for Twain's fans between her as a modern artist and country's more traditional past. Several of the tracks created for the album were cover versions of well-known songs from earlier generations, including country classics "One's On the Way" (made famous in 1971 by Loretta Lynn) and "Harper Valley P.T.A." (1968's signature song for Jeannie C. Riley). Thus, when the studio leaked the news that Shania Twain was participating with a song called "Shoes," fan sites, blogs, and chat rooms lit up with speculation that Twain's "Shoes" was the cover of a song Patsy Cline had recorded in 1960, written by the venerable team of Harlan Howard and Velma Smith.[23] Indeed, Patsy Cline's song draws on the metaphor of shoes for love—those that fit, those that don't, those that are worn out and discarded—but there the similarity between the two songs ends. With every blog post and chat-room conversation, fans attempted to weave Shania into the revered history of country's legendary female stars with speculation about the cover and the presumed Twain-Cline musical connection. Here was an instance where the potential for intertextuality—a shared song title within a genre that thrives on tradition and tribute—was seized by eager fans as an extramusical means of confirming or intensifying Twain's "belonging" in the country scene.

The original version of Twain's song, which turned out not to be a Cline cover, was a product of three A-list Nashville songwriters whose résumés include a long run of commercially successful cuts: Joey Scott, Tammy Hyler, and Kim Tribble. A fledgling artist named Brittany Roe had cut the song on her debut album *Is It Hot in Here?* in 2004, and released it as a single to radio, but it never received noticeable airplay, nor did it make an appearance on *Billboard*'s Top-Sixty "Hot Country Singles and Tracks" chart. When the *Desperate Housewives* producers picked it for the album, Twain and Lange insisted on rewriting it before they would perform it. Of course, the act of recomposition entitled them to a share of copyright royalties for the song. But it also transformed the song structurally into a signature Twain/Lange piece. The poetic content was reworked to create more internal rhymes and alliteration; the song's form was modified to include more distinct sections; and most substantially, the hypermetric patterns and phrase rhythm of the song were altered to alleviate the regular, predictable squareness of Roe's version.

In addition to the phrase-rhythm and hypermetric tricks already noted, Twain and Lange frequently combine regular hypermetric structures with

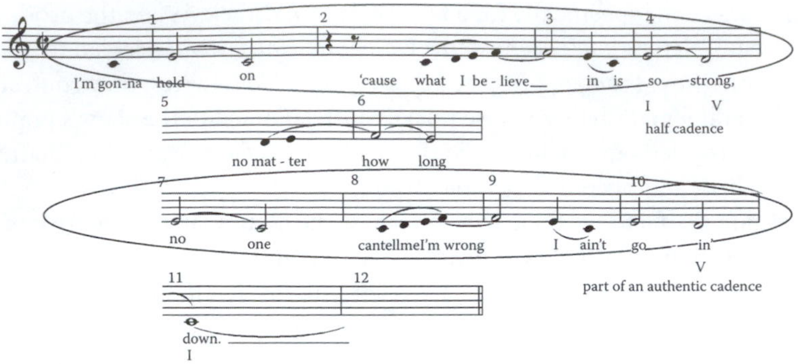

Example 11.6 Shania Twain, "I Ain't Goin' Down" (Shania Twain-Robert John "Mutt" Lange), *Up!* (2002): melodic outline of the opening twelve bars, which offer multiple interpretations of phrase structure and hypermeter.

highly irregular metric patterns of musical and poetic rhyme, all without altering the basic, danceable pulse of the music. The twelve bars that comprise the chorus for "I Ain't Goin' Down" (outlined in Example 11.6) are recorded with Twain's vocals, a bare percussion track, a few synthesizer chords, and some mandolin fills. One could conceivably parse these twelve bars as three hypermeasures, each a prototypical four bars. However, repetition and placement of rhythmic motives and textual rhymes undermines such an interpretation. "Strong"/"long"/"wrong" do not occur in regularly spaced positions within the twelve bars, nor do the rhythmically parallel and assonance-related motives of "hold on"/"so strong"/"how long"/"go-in'." Furthermore, for the listener, the musical parallelism of measures 1–4 and 7–10 is easily heard, but is contraindicated by the different roles of the dominant harmonies at the ends of those sections.

With the contributions of a bass line and Twain's vocal inflections, the most satisfactory hypermetric interpretation of this opening is a division into 3 + 3 + 4 + 2 bars, but the most significant point of this analytic exercise is that the compositional craft of Twain and Lange relies heavily on the apparent structural regularity (in this instance, a twelve-bar section) with internal complications and asymmetries. They are meeting the requisite simplicity of country-pop's musical style head-on, but still imbuing their music with unique structural twists and turns that belie its apparent accessibility.

Two associations with related patterns are relevant here. First, the asymmetric parsing of a twelve- or sixteen-bar unit of music into three-bar or three-beat groupings occurs frequently in the physical motion of line-dance choreography, a fan activity for which Twain's music is frequently appropriated. In these situations, the basic dance patterns with various types of hemiola and phrase-rhythmic asymmetries counteract the threat of monotony that generally characterizes line dancing, and the experiential relationship

Example 11.7 Shania Twain, "I'm Holdin' On to Love (To Save My Life)" (Shania Twain-Robert John "Mutt" Lange), *Come On Over* (1997): opening of chorus. Vertical alignment shows hypermetric relationships; circled numbers indicate those of truncated measures.

between song and dance becomes far more interesting.[24] Second, the presence of closely-spaced internal rhymes, both poetic and musical, in syncopated or asymmetric placement, mirror the performance practices in hip-hop that infiltrated most pop music genres in the 1990s and help modernize the sound of the songs.

One more representative example of their hypermetric style is worth considering. In "I'm Holdin' On to Love (To Save My Life)," the verse's musical structure adheres entirely to the prototypical sixteen-bar section. After that square set-up, the chorus shifts into an implied triple hypermeter, further shaped by the presence of periodic measures truncated in half (see Example 11.7). The rhythmic activity in this chorus is characterized by unexpected hypermetric shifts (particularly with the measures notated in 2/4), syncopations, and relative periods of rhythmic stasis in the vocal line. The result is a chorus that pushes, pulls, and tugs on the listener's attention. These musical effects are intensified by the location of this chorus in the midst of an otherwise symmetric and regular set of musical patterns in the song.

Sonic Disruptions

A final compositional technique that Twain and Lange use frequently on their recordings after 1995 is again a balance between regularity and disruption. The regularity, in this case, is found in the domain of the waveform of the actual recording, or essentially in the sonic consistency over the span of the song. Contemporary country radio asks that songs have a fairly consistent sonic profile from beginning to end: Marketing data confirm that most listeners want the sound waves coming out of their car speakers to be constant in intensity so as to support but not disturb or jar the listener.[25] Lange's mastery of the studio process has produced record after record that meets just that criterion, carefully layering and then mixing with plenty of compression and other post-processing aimed at producing a static product. This consistency and homogeneity keeps listeners from reaching for their radio dials, but it also runs the risk of letting their attention wander mid-song. The antidote for this potential complacency comes in the form of sonic disruptions.

In more than one-third of the songs that Twain and Lange have produced, they have inserted some sort of incongruous sound effect at a time-point approximately two-thirds to three-quarters of the way through the song, literally a wake-up call to listeners. These effects are not subtle events, and they are markedly distinct within the sonic fabric of each recording. The timing of these events in relation to the song's duration is consistent across Twain's repertory (see Figure 11.5) and contributes to their effectiveness. Two clusters of disruption placements appear on the graph: one near the Golden Mean (roughly 62 percent of the total duration) and one three-quarters of the way through the songs' durations. In both placements, the majority of the song has already played, and at least one iteration of the chorus or hook has been presented. The sonic events, therefore, refresh the listener for the final sections of the song, and reconnect the audience with the hook.

The specific nature of these sonic events varies from song to song. In some instances, it is a moment of near silence; in others, it is an amplified, electronic instrument playing solo for a brief moment. The best representation of these events' effect is a visual graph of the waveforms of the recordings, displayed here for two songs (see Figure 11.6). In "In My Car (I'll Be the Driver)," an amplified fiddle ascends a frantic scale while the rest of the band drops out; in "Honey I'm Home," the band stops for a brief moment under Twain's vocals, then re-enters on a weak beat with a syncopated crash (usually emphasized in her live concerts with pyrotechnics that erupt at that instant). The location of each stop–time event in the waveform is marked with an oval on Figure 11.6, although the marked change of decibel level makes their locations readily apparent.

It is significant that these sound effects do not always occur in the same structural places within the songs' forms. Eight of them occur at the beginning

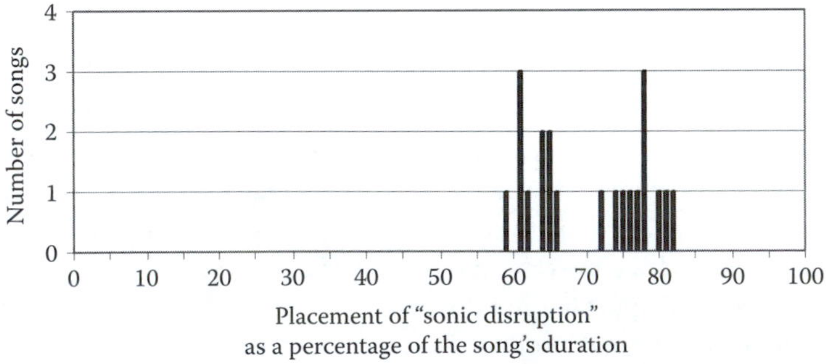

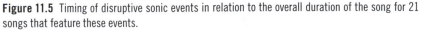

Figure 11.5 Timing of disruptive sonic events in relation to the overall duration of the song for 21 songs that feature these events.

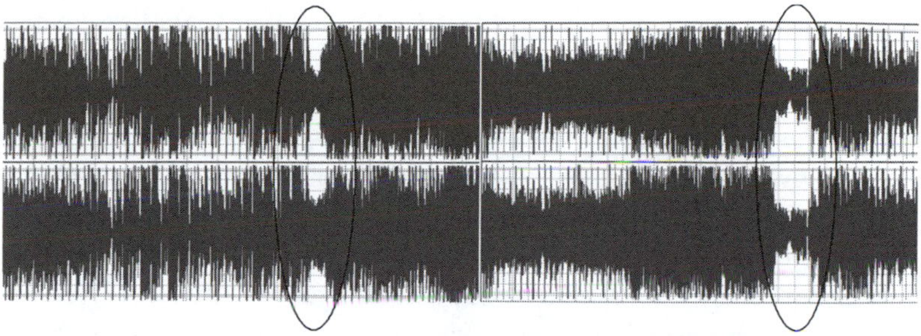

Figure 11.6 Shania Twain, "In My Car (I'll Be the Driver)" (Shania Twain-Robert John "Mutt" Lange), *Up!* (2002) (left), and Shania Twain, "Honey, I'm Home" (Shania Twain-Robert John "Mutt" Lange), *Come On Over* (1997): (right): thirty-second segments of the recordings' waveforms (shown in stereo), with the visually obvious sonic disruptions at 2:28–2:29 (left) and 2:48–2:50 (right).

of a song's third chorus in a verse–chorus form ("Black Eyes, Blue Tears"), but in the rest of the cases, events are equally likely to occur at the end of a second chorus before an instrumental interlude, at the end of the third chorus, in the middle of a bridge, or before an extended vocal vamp and play-out ("Waiter! Bring Me Water!"). In Twain and Lange's songwriting craft, the technique serves its purpose within the time-span of the song regardless of the particular formal model on which the song is built.

Crossing Over, Going Home

The compositional techniques and structural features discussed in these analyses contribute significantly to Shania Twain's signature country-pop sound. Even as these structural features distinguish her sound within the larger fields of country-pop and country in general, they also connect it to musical projects outside of country music in a type of stylistic crossover via the songwriting process itself. The connection between Twain and, in these instances, pop and pop-metal, reflects Mutt Lange's work with other artists. A few brief examples here highlight how Twain's country-pop harmonic vocabulary and use of carefully timed sonic disruptions in particular are essentially shared with those other musical styles, but more importantly, function as a Twain/Lange marker.

As rock fans know, Mutt Lange's career in popular music predates Twain's by several decades with a résumé that includes AC/DC, Foreigner, the Cars, and Def Leppard, among others. After making a name for himself with the pop-metal of Def Leppard in the mid-1980s, Lange shifted gears stylistically and helped craft movie-theme rock ballads for Bryan Adams. During the beginning of Twain's career, Lange's compositions appeared, albeit infrequently, on mainstream country artists' albums along with albums of established rockers including Heart and Huey Lewis & the News. At the height of Twain's success, Lange worked as a producer on only a handful of other projects, but it was during this era that he produced an album for the Corrs, an Irish pop-rock band of siblings with a Celtic-folk flair that offers an excellent point of comparison for Lange's studio production with artists other than Twain. Although Lange's musical projects span a far wider scope than what can be discussed here, a few representative examples will illustrate the way certain songwriting techniques have crossed over from these resident styles into Twain's country-pop.

As we have noted, Shania Twain's harmonic language is predominantly that of functional tonality, as should be expected in country music. However, as the analyses in this essay highlight, her music takes advantage of progressive tonality in the form of modulations, many of which are not simply stepwise ascents but instead may reorient the song's entire tonal system and reorganize its harmonic language from one section to the next. Her songs also feature an occasional falling-fourths progression, ♭VII–IV–I, and frequently treat the submediant as a functional tonic substitute, avoiding I with progressions that cycle through connections such as vi–IV–V–vi.

In the context of commercial country songwriting from the 1990s, Twain's harmonic vocabulary is adventurous and provocative, to say the least. But viewed as an outgrowth of Lange's work with Def Leppard in metal songs like "Gods of War," it appears tempered and toned down. "Gods of War," one of the songs that Lange co-wrote with the group, features sharp disjunctions of harmonic center. The key aspects of the song's tonal structure for purposes of this discussion are the abrupt discontinuities between song sections, so any cohesive tonal interpretation of the song in its entirety is left to other analyses. Example 11.8 sketches the overall tonal vocabulary for a verse through the end of a chorus, with the sections appearing progressively as a passage in C♯ minor, an ostinato moving from F Major to G, a B–to–E progression elaborated with falling fourths, and a D–to–G progression that slides back to E minor. The seeds of all the elements previously noted in Shania Twain's harmonic vocabulary are present in some form in this sketched excerpt: rising

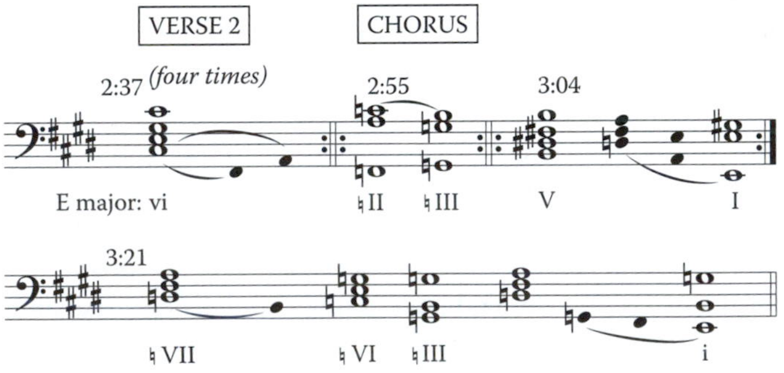

Example 11.8 Def Leppard, "Gods of War" (Steve Clark-Phil Collen-Joe Elliott-Mutt Lange-Rick Savage), *Hysteria* (1987): sketch of harmonic vocabulary, verse through chorus.

seconds, modulation by common-tone and third relation, tonic-dominant inversions, and play between relative major and minor.

Irish siblings Andrea, Jim, Caroline, and Sharon Corr have been favorites of the folk-infused pop scene since the early 1990s. In 2000, Mutt Lange produced the Corrs' *In Blue,* co-writing three of the tracks and handing listeners an album that fared reasonably well on the *Billboard* pop charts, peaking there at number 21. What is remarkable about the compositional structure of the songs on *In Blue* is how closely they match the musical elements of Shania Twain's repertory discussed here. The opening track and hit single, "Breathless" (co-written by Lange), features a chorus with three-bar hypermeasures and a tonic-subdominant modulation. The second Lange composition on the album, "All the Love In the World," appears with the same finger-picked guitar motives and textural padding via strings that launch "When You Kiss Me," and matches the vocal timbres that Lange used on Twain's *Come On Over.* More noticeable is the harmonic structure that features modulations between an A-Major verse, a C-Major pre-chorus, and a D-Major chorus. At the end of the song, an additional arranger's modulation takes the chorus into E. Unsurprisingly, the third of Lange's co-written tracks, "Irresistible," is also the most harmonically adventurous on the album, opening in F♯ minor, then moving to A Major and finally to F Major for the chorus. Carefully placed sonic disruptions enliven several tracks on the album as well. While all fifteen songs on *In Blue* exhibit certain of these commonalities, the compositional strategies that have been the focus of this essay are most apparent in Lange's three contributions, adding weight to the idea that these structural approaches are part of his songwriting signature.

With no historical or social context of country music surrounding them, the Corrs' recordings are unburdened by the musical identities and traditions that define country music. In this setting, Lange's compositional techniques are merely the language of contemporary pop. However, in Shania Twain's recordings, context and audience reception bring the musical ideology of country into the discussion. As illustrated in these analyses, Twain's music carries the structural signatures of Mutt Lange's pop stylings. These aspects are one way in which Twain's music distinguishes itself from the rest of country-pop. Furthermore, these analyses point to specific stylistic borrowings from pop-music traditions removed from country music.

Given our identification of pop constructions in Twain's recordings, along with the clear distinctions we have drawn between Twain's songs and those of other country-pop artists, one might wonder how this music fits into the country genre at all. Indeed, plenty of listeners (and readers) might take issue with any legitimate claim of Shania Twain as "country." Are we simply left with her management's marketing decisions and her success on the country charts? It is here that analysis of Twain's recordings leaves off, and analysis of the cultural reception of her music might begin. The blog sites that once speculated about

Twain covering a Patsy Cline song, the country dance traditions that have adopted Twain's grooves as foundations for core line-dance steps, and the affinities of young, female country listeners for the social themes found in her lyrics might illuminate the connections and tensions between Shania Twain as an artist and country as a genre. There are also a few overlooked musical nuggets on her albums that tie her to the lineage of country's styles, like "I Ain't No Quitter," whose shuffle-boogie beat, rockabilly guitars, Texas-swing fiddling, and honky-tonk lyrics convinced some listeners that Twain had a country heart after all.[26] But what these musical analyses have attempted to contribute is an interpretation of Twain and Lange's songwriting craft within the context of country-pop. The compositional strategies explored here are not alone sufficient to construct a hit country-pop song, but they do appear to be an essential part of the songwriting strategy that has sold well over 60 million records for Shania Twain. There exists a delicate balance between the apparent musical transparency and traditional nostalgia of country music and the musical seduction of a well-crafted pop hook; the art and craft of song-writing is the means of achieving that balance.

Notes

1. See References for a list of relevant recordings.
2. Prior to signing with Mercury, Twain recorded a set of pop tunes for Limelight Records in 1989, only one of which found commercial success, as a dance-club remix.
3. Bruce Feiler (1998) offers a compelling account of Brooks' career, his effect on country radio, and his radical reinvention of country music in *Dreaming Out Loud*; see especially pp. 112–113 with regard to "The Dance."
4. The economic downturn of the early 1990s is often cited as one reason why country music, with its down-home rhetoric and celebration of working-class life, enjoyed a resurgence of popularity; the election in 1992 of a southerner to the White House is considered by some analysts as indicative of this overall trend.
5. Mutt Lange has rarely consented to interviews; one of the most revealing pieces focusing on Twain and Lange's relationship is Handelman 1999.
6. "Hot Country Singles" number-one hits from *The Woman In Me* were "Any Man of Mine," "You Win My Love," "No One Needs to Know," and "(If You're Not In It For Love) I'm Outta Here!" Although the album entered The *Billboard* 200 in March 1995, only the first of these singles reached number one before 1996, bringing the album to its sales peak many months after release.
7. Robin Eggar (2005, 145) suggests that the closest translation of her name might be "money," not "I'm on my way," and that the latter is simply part of the artist's legend.
8. This particular photographic and fashion style appeared on the covers of Reba McEntire's *Read My Mind*, Faith Hill's *It Matters to Me*, and Jo Dee Messina's *Jo Dee Messina*.
9. RIAA certification lists the album at twenty times platinum; Twain claims substantially higher sales figures in her website's own publicity (http://www.shaniatwain.com).

10. A small white card inserted in the CD case quotes Twain, "Sometimes I even put my CD player on 'random' so I can listen to [the three versions] all mixed together.... I hope you enjoy the different flavors...."
11. Daley 2004 is particularly insightful from this perspective.
12. Among the countless uses of that phrase are Laurence Leamer's 1997 book, *Three Chords and the Truth: Hope, Heartbreak, and Changing Fortunes in Nashville*; Sara Evans' first album from the same year, *Three Chords and the Truth*; and the title track off that album, co-written by Evans, Ron Harbin, and Aimee Mayo, all three considered among the top writers in Nashville. The phrase is usually attributed to country songwriting legend Harlan Howard (and is proudly displayed with his name in the Country Music Hall of Fame and Museum); rock fans may recognize it from its insertion into U2's live 1987 cover of "All Along the Watchtower."
13. Discussions of these modulations abound; see, for instance, references to what are variously called arranger's modulations (Josefs 1995, 94–97), truck driver's modulations (Everett 1997, 117–118 and especially p. 151 n. 18), and pump-up modulations (Ricci 2000, 130–132). Sayrs 2003 discusses other terminology for the effect; see especially her n. 11.
14. These characterizations emerged in discussions among undergraduate students, all non-musicians, enrolled in my "History of Country Music" course at The University of North Carolina at Chapel Hill in the years 2000–2005.
15. Covach 2006, 100–101, defines "partial reprise" as occurring "when only part of the AABA structure is repeated" in subsequent hearings.
16. Twain's song forms frequently include short sections of music that supplement the conventional verse–chorus–bridge options. As a result, her songs are often built from many more units than is conventional in country songwriting, but each unit is itself brief. These multiple sections of songs fragment the listening experience into shorter segments and allow wider sonic diversity over the course of a single song. In "Up!," two chorus-like units appear: each is harmonically closed, each recurs with its own set of lyrics, and each anchors the narrative in a point of reflection. The second of the two is identified as a secondary chorus in this analysis.
17. McCready's name has been prominently displayed in the media in recent years for escapades that have nothing to do with her music, and in as fickle an industry as country-pop, these aspects of her public persona carry as much sway as her musical output in regard to career success.
18. Of course, such musical-stylistic similarities between Hill's and Twain's work will not surprise fans who remember that Dann Huff, co-producer of Hill's 1998 and 1999 albums, had played guitar and several other instruments on both *The Woman In Me* and *Come On Over.*
19. Tracing the musical connections of Mutt Lange's quotations would be an entire project unto itself; through reference and quotation, he has woven new and old cultural signifiers together in ways that both pay tribute and appropriate. For instance, the opening instrumental part in "You're Still the One" invokes the title theme from the 1982 Oscar-winning soundtrack, *Chariots of Fire*, composed by Vangelis, whose work in the electronic-music studio was considered pioneering.
20. See Neal 2000, 133, for a transcription of the harmonic and hypermetric structure, and a discussion of the expansions, in "Man! I Feel Like a Woman."

21. The fifty-one songs are twelve from *The Woman In Me*, sixteen from *Come On Over*, nineteen from *Up!*, three new songs on the *Greatest Hits* album, and one on the *Desperate Housewives* CD.
22. The brazen behavior of the television show's characters resonated with the sisterhood of female country singers, who have celebrated a feminist stance in their songs since the earliest recordings of country music. See Keel 2004 for an excellent overview of feminist themes within the genre. The inclusion of Sara Evans and Martina McBride on the soundtrack acknowledged their voices as being among the more outspoken of contemporary female country singers, notably for McBride's "Independence Day" (1994). The soundtrack included covers of two of the most radical artists from the 1960s: Loretta Lynn, whose lyrics for songs like "Don't Come Home a Drinkin' (With Lovin' On Your Mind)" are often cited as representative of the feminist streak in 1960s country, and Jeannie C. Riley, whose recording of songwriter Tom T. Hall's "Harper Valley P. T. A." questions sexual double-standards within a small-town community. No discussion of feminist ideology in country music should omit mention of Dolly Parton, whose earliest hits included "Just Because I'm a Woman" (1968), another reconsideration of social double-standards, and whose business acumen in a predominantly male industry has garnered her as much attention.
23. See, for instance, the Pulse Music Board's thread on "Shania Twain—Shoes": http://pulsemusic.proboards48.com/index.cgi?board=country&action=display&thread=1123524474&page=1#1123790871 [accessed October 10, 2006].
24. See Neal 1998 for further discussion of asymmetric phrase patterns in line dancing and their relationship to musical phrase rhythm.
25. This goal is right in line with the preference among all AM broadcasts and most other commercial radio formats for heavily compressed pop music that maintains a consistent decibel level at all times.
26. Chuck Taylor's *Billboard* review of "I Ain't No Quitter" announced, "Shania Twain goes for broke on the third new track from *Greatest Hits* with a song that tries so hard to be country, you suspect that Twain means it" (Taylor 2005, 46).

References

Brooks, Garth. 1990. *No Fences*. Capitol 98366.

______, Garth. 1997. *Sevens*. Capitol 56599.

Covach, John. 2006. *What's That Sound? An Introduction to Rock and Its History*. New York: W.W. Norton.

Daley, Dan. 2004. "Recording Shania Twain's *Up! Sound On Sound* (August). http://www.soundonsound.com/sos/aug04/articles/bobbullock.htm [accessed May 18, 2005].

Eggar, Robin. 2005. *Shania Twain: The Biography*. New York: CMT Pocket Books.

Evans, Sara. 1997. *Three Chords and the Truth*. RCA 66995.

Everett, Walter. 1997. Swallowed by a Song: Paul Simon's Crisis of Chromaticism. In *Understanding Rock*, ed. John Covach and Graeme M. Boone, 113–153. New York: Oxford University Press.

Feiler, Bruce. 1998. *Dreaming Out Loud: Garth Brooks, Wynonna Judd, Wade Hayes, and the Changing Face of Nashville*. New York: Avon Books.

Handelman, David. 1999. She's Still the One. *Redbook* 194/1 (December), 114 ff.

Hill, Faith. 1995. *It Matters to Me*. Warner Brothers 45872.
______. 1998. *Faith*. Warner Brothers 46790.
______. 1999. *Breathe*. Warner Brothers 47373.
Josefs, Jai. 1996. *Writing Music for Hit Songs: Including New Songs From the '90s*. New York: Schirmer Books.
Keel, Beverly. 2004. Between Riot Grrrl and Quiet Girl: The New Women's Movement in Country Music. In *A Boy Named Sue: Gender and Country Music*. Edited by Kristine McCusker and Diane Pecknold, 155–177. Jackson: University of Mississippi Press.
Leamer, Laurence. 1997. *Three Chords and the Truth: Hope, Heartbreak, and Changing Fortunes in Nashville*. New York: HarperCollins.
McCready, Mindy. 1996. *Ten Thousand Angels*. BNA 66806.
McEntire, Reba. 1994. *Read My Mind*. MCA 10994.
Messina, Jo Dee. 1996. *Jo Dee Messina*. Curb 77820.
Neal, Jocelyn R. 1998. The Metric Makings of a Country Hit. In *Reading Country Music: Steel Guitars, Opry Stars, and Honky-Tonk Bars*. Edited by Cecelia Tichi, 322–337. Durham, NC: Duke University Press.
______. 2000. Songwriter's Signature, Artist's Imprint: The Metric Structure of a Country Song. *Country Music Annual* 1, 112–140.
Ricci, Adam. 2000. A "Hard Habit to Break": The Integration of Harmonic Cycles and Voice-Leading Structure in Two Songs by Chicago. *Indiana Theory Review* 21, 129–146.
Roe, Brittany. 2004. *Is It Hot In Here?* Labeless Nashville LBE 1002.
Sayrs, Elizabeth. 2003. Narrative, Metaphor, and Conceptual Blending in "The Hanging Tree." *Music Theory Online* 9/1 (March). http://mto.societymusictheory.org.
Taylor, Chuck. 2005. Review of "I Ain't No Quitter." *Billboard* 117/21 (May 21), 46.
Twain, Shania. 1993. *Shania Twain* [Produced by Harold Shedd and Norro Wilson]. Mercury 514422.
______. 1995. *The Woman In Me* [Produced by Robert John "Mutt" Lange]. Mercury 522886.
______. 1997. *Come On Over* [Produced by Robert John "Mutt" Lange]. Mercury 536003.
______. 1999. *Come On Over: International Version* [Produced by Robert John "Mutt" Lange]. Mercury 170123.
______. 2002. *Up!* [Produced by Robert John "Mutt" Lange]. Universal 170314.
______. 2004. *Greatest Hits* [Produced by Robert John "Mutt" Lange]. Mercury B000307202.
Various artists. 2005. *Music From and Inspired By "Desperate Housewives"* [Audio CD soundtrack]. Hollywood Records 7-2061-62499-20.

12

Large-Scale Strategy and Compositional Design in the Early Music of Genesis

MARK SPICER

The title of this chapter might remind some readers of an article by Andrew Mead that appeared in *Perspectives of New Music* more than two decades ago (Mead 1985), in which the author used sophisticated set-theoretic analytical techniques to dig beneath the surface of Arnold Schoenberg's music, disclosing a "large-scale strategy" at work within several of the twelve-tone compositions. Mead had the advantage of writing for a scholarly community already well convinced of Schoenberg's genius. I suspect the idea of placing the music of the British rock group Genesis in the same league as Schoenberg would be greeted with considerable skepticism—if not downright horror—by many musicologists, and this is certainly not my intent in the present essay. (Alas, it will probably require some drastic revolutions in taste before such early-Genesis classics as "The Return of the Giant Hogweed" are admitted into the canon of twentieth-century masterworks.) But I do hope to show that despite being several musical worlds removed from Schoenberg, Genesis' music is rich, diverse, and equally worthy of our analytical attention.

One of the most influential and long-lasting of the so-called "progressive rock" bands that emerged in Britain around 1970 in the wake of the Beatles, Genesis is probably better known to most pop-rock fans as the supergroup who made frequent appearances on the *Billboard* charts during the 1980s and early 1990s, with a string of consecutive Top-Five singles in 1986–1987 including "Invisible Touch" (which reached number 1), "Throwing it All Away," "Land of Confusion," "Tonight, Tonight, Tonight," and "In Too Deep."[1] Yet before they were to master the art of composing the four-minute pop song, the early Genesis—along with Yes; King Crimson; Emerson, Lake & Palmer; Jethro Tull; and other compatriots in British prog—were famous for crafting rock pieces of much greater scope and complexity, compositions in which the multiple shifts of texture, affect, and tonality echo those typically found in a nineteenth-century symphonic poem. Most progressive rock was not intended to be immediately catchy or danceable (or even commercially successful, though legions of fans ultimately proved otherwise); on the contrary, prog was "serious" music intended for serious listeners. Indeed, as John Covach (1997, 4) has noted, "there was the perception [among progressive rock fans] that these musicians were attempting to shape a new kind of classical music—a body of music that would . . . be listened to (and perhaps even studied) . . . for years to come."[2]

The "serious" study of progressive rock offers at the very least a twofold challenge to the analyst. On the one hand, these big pieces share with their classical counterparts a concern for long-range coherence—both thematic and harmonic—and therefore lend themselves well to a formalist approach. With a little bending of our traditional analytical tools, we can probe the "music itself" for motivic connections and harmonic relationships, both on the surface and at deeper levels of the musical structure—much as we might, say, a symphonic piece by Liszt or Mahler.[3] On the other hand, formalist analysis alone does not adequately address the issue of stylistic eclecticism in progressive rock, an issue that so often plays a crucial role in the composition of its large-scale pieces. To understand better why progressive rock is shaped as it is we must also approach the music from an intertextual standpoint, looking beyond the individual pieces themselves to the multiple musical traditions from which they spring and to the specific other works with which they may be in dialogue.[4] I will attempt to reconcile these two analytical approaches—formalist and intertextual—in this study of Genesis' early music.

Table 12.1 shows a chronology of Genesis albums released through 1975, when frontman and founding member Peter Gabriel left the group to embark on what has become a highly successful solo career of his own. The majority of my analysis in this chapter will focus on the 1972 track that Genesis aficionados often tout as the group's masterpiece: the 23-minute epic "Supper's Ready" from the album *Foxtrot*. This album (and the European tour that supported it) represented a major turning point in Genesis' career, as Gabriel's penchant for mime and onstage theatrics—complete with elaborate changes of costume to parallel the narrative of the songs—began to give their concerts a distinctive style that set them apart from other progressive rock groups.[5] The cover of *Genesis Live* (recorded in February 1973, during the *Foxtrot* tour) offers us a glimpse of Genesis performing "Supper's Ready" during this remarkable period. Gabriel stands center-stage decked out in one of his many costumes (that of "Magog"), while the remaining band members—guitarist Steve Hackett, bassist Mike Rutherford, drummer Phil Collins, and keyboardist Tony Banks—are removed from the spotlight, seemingly absorbed in their role of providing a musical accompaniment to Gabriel's one-man opera. (Hackett and Rutherford are both seen performing sitting down, in a manner more characteristic of classical than rock guitarists.)[6]

Although their frontman's new-found flamboyance was undoubtedly a key factor in Genesis' sudden rise to stardom, Peter Gabriel—looking back on this period—has insisted that "whatever else was going on in the visual department, our central interest was always . . . the writing, the composition of the music."

Table 12.1 Chronology of early Genesis albums: British releases (year of American release given if different from that of original British album).

From Genesis to Revelation	March 1969 [1974]
Trespass	October 1970
Nursery Cryme	November 1971
Foxtrot	October 1972
Genesis Live	June 1973 [1974]
Selling England By the Pound	October 1973
The Lamb Lies Down on Broadway	November 1974

He goes on to confirm that "'Supper's Ready' … was extremely important for the band, … a sort of centerpiece for our ambitions in terms of writing, and [our] most adventurous piece to date."[7] Cast almost entirely in the first person, the seven interconnected tableaux of "Supper's Ready" (see Figure 12.1) chronicle a young Englishman's twisted vision of the apocalypse: the classic conflict of good against evil as seen through a decidedly British lens.[8] Interspersed within the lyrics in Figure 12.1 are program notes (in square brackets) written by Gabriel himself as an aid to understanding the story, taken from a handbill customarily distributed to audience members at Genesis concerts (1972–1973). Gabriel's intentions here were perhaps merely practical rather than historical, yet one cannot ignore the strong echoes of nineteenth-century program music. One is reminded, for example, of the program written by Berlioz to be distributed at performances of his *Fantastic Symphony* (1830).[9]

I. "Lover's Leap"
[In which two lovers are lost in each other's eyes, and found again transformed in the bodies of another male and female.]

Walking across the sitting room, I turn the television off.
Sitting beside you, I look into your eyes.
As the sound of motor cars fades in the night time,
I swear I saw your face change, it didn't seem quite right.
    … And it's hello babe, with your guardian eyes so blue,
    Hey my baby, don't you know our love is true?

Coming closer with our eyes, a distance falls around our bodies.
Out in the garden, the moon seems very bright.

Figure 12.1 Lyrics to "Supper's Ready" interspersed with program notes by Peter Gabriel. Words and Music by Tony Banks, Phil Collins, Peter Gabriel, Steve Hackett, and Mike Rutherford.

Six saintly shrouded men move across the lawn slowly,
The seventh walks in front with a cross held high in hand.
    … And it's hey babe, your supper's waiting for you,
    Hey my baby, don't you know our love is true?

I've been so far from here,
Far from your warm arms.
It's good to feel you again.
It's been a long time. Hasn't it?

II. "The Guaranteed Eternal Sanctuary Man"
[The lovers come across a town dominated by two characters: one a benevolent farmer and the other a head of a highly disciplined scientific religion. The latter likes to be known as "The Guaranteed Eternal Sanctuary Man" and claims to contain a secret new ingredient capable of fighting fire. This is a falsehood, an untruth, a whopper and a taradiddle; or to put it in clearer terms, a lie.]

I know a farmer who looks after the farm,
With water clear, he cares for all his harvest.
I know a fireman who looks after the fire.

You, can't you see he's fooled you all?
Yes, he's here again, can't you see he's fooled you all?
    Share his peace,
    Sign the lease.
He's a supersonic scientist,
He's the Guaranteed Eternal Sanctuary Man.
Look, look into my mouth he cries.
And all the children lost down many paths,
I bet my life, you'll walk inside
Hand in hand,
gland in gland,
With a spoonful of miracle,
He's the Guaranteed Eternal Sanctuary Man.
    We will rock you, rock you little snake,
    We will keep you snug and warm.

III. "Ikhnaton and Istacon and Their Band of Merry Men"
[Who the lovers see clad in greys and purples, awaiting to be summoned out of the ground. At the G.E.S.M.'s command they put forth from the bowels of the earth, to attack all those without an up-to-date "Eternal Life Licence", which were obtainable at the head office of the G.E.S.M.'s religion.]

Figure 12.1 *(Continued)*

Wearing feelings on our faces while our faces took a rest,
We walked across the fields to see the children of the West,
But we saw a host of dark skinned warriors
standing still below the ground,
  Waiting for battle.
The fight's begun, they've been released.
Killing foe for peace . . . bang, bang, bang . . . bang, bang, bang . . .
And they're giving me a wonderful potion,
'Cos I cannot contain my emotion.
And even though I'm feeling good,
Something tells me I'd better activate my prayer capsule.
Today's a day to celebrate, the foe have met their fate.
The order for rejoicing and dancing has come from our warlord.

IV. "How Dare I Be So Beautiful?"
[In which our intrepid heroes investigate the aftermath of the battle and discover a solitary figure, obsessed by his own image. They witness an unusual transmutation, and are pulled into their own reflections in the water.]

Wandering in the chaos the battle has left,
We climb up the mountain of human flesh
To a plateau of green grass, and green trees full of life.
A young figure sits still by her pool,
He's been stamped "Human Bacon" by some butchery tool.
  (He is you)
Social Security took care of this lad,
We watch in reverence as Narcissus is turned into a flower.
  A flower?

V. "Willow Farm"
[Climbing out of the pool, they are once again in a different existence. They're right in the middle of a myriad of bright colours, filled with all manner of objects, plants, animals, and humans. Life flows freely and everything is mindlessly busy. At random, a whistle blows and every single thing is instantly changed into another.]

If you go down to Willow Farm,
to look for butterflies, flutterbyes, gutterflies
Open your eyes, it's full of surprise, everyone lies,
like the focks [*sic*] on the rocks,
and the musical box.

Figure 12.1 *(Continued)*

Oh, there's Mum & Dad, and good and bad,
and everyone's happy to be here.

There's Winston Churchill dressed in drag,
He used to be a British flag, plastic bag. What a drag.
The frog was a prince, the prince was a brick, the brick was an egg,
and the egg was a bird.
    Hadn't you heard?
Yes, we're happy as fish, and gorgeous as geese,
    and wonderfully clean in the morning.
We've got everything, we're growing everything,
    We've got some in,
    We've got some out,
We've got some wild things floating about. …
Everyone, we're changing everyone,
    You name them all,
    We've had them here,
And the real stars are still to appear.

ALL CHANGE!

Feel your body melt:
Mum to mud to mad to dad
Dad diddley office, Dad diddley office,
    You're all full of ball.
Dad to dam to dum to mum
Mum diddley washing, Mum diddley washing,
    You're all full of ball.
Let me hear your lies, we're living this up to our eyes.
Ooee-ooee-ooee-oowaa
Momma I want you now.

And as you listen to my voice
To look for hidden doors, tidy floors, more applause.
You've been here all the time,
Like it or not, like what you got,
You're under the soil,
Yes deep in the soil.
So we'll end with a whistle and end with a bang
and all of us fit in our places.

Figure 12.1 *(Continued)*

VI. "Apocalypse in 9/8 (Co-Starring the Delicious Talents of Gabble Ratchet)"

[At one whistle the lovers become seeds in the soil, where they recognise other seeds to be people from the world in which they had originated. While they wait for Spring, they are returned to their old world to see the Apocalypse of St John in full progress. The seven trumpeteers cause a sensation, the fox keeps throwing sixes, and Pythagoras (a Greek extra) is deliriously happy as he manages to put exactly the right amount of milk and honey on his corn flakes.]

With the guards of Magog, swarming around,
The Pied Piper takes his children underground.
The Dragon's coming out of the sea,
With the shimmering silver head of wisdom looking at me.
He brings down the fire from the skies,
You can tell he's doing well by the look in human eyes.
You'd better not compromise.
   It won't be easy.

666 is no longer alone,
He's getting out the marrow in your back bone.
And the seven trumpets blowing sweet rock and roll,
Gonna blow right down inside your soul.
Pythagoras with the looking-glass, reflecting the full moon,
In blood, he's writing the lyrics of a brand new tune.

And it's hey babe, with your guardian eyes so blue.
Hey my baby, don't you know our love is true?
I've been so far from here,
Far from your loving arms,
Now I'm back again, and baby it's going to work out fine.

VII. "As Sure as Eggs is Eggs (Aching Men's Feet)"
[Above all else an egg is an egg. "And did those feet ..." making ends meet.]

Can't you feel our souls ignite,
Shedding ever changing colours, in the darkness of the fading night?
Like the river joins the ocean, as the germ in a seed grows,
We have finally been freed to get back home.

There's an angel standing in the sun, and he's crying with a loud voice,
"This is the supper of the mighty one".
Lord of Lord's,
King of King's,
Has returned to lead his children home,
To take them to the new Jerusalem.

[Jerusalem=place of peace.]

Figure 12.1 *(Continued)*

Before proceeding with my analysis of "Supper's Ready," it is necessary to make a few preliminary points about the nature of the musical examples. Genesis—like most rock groups—did not notate any of their compositions, preferring instead to use the recording studio as their canvas. Many rock analysts are content to dispense with written scores altogether, and I certainly agree that some of rock's most interesting features (timbre, for example) are rendered neutral by conventional notation. Yet it is difficult to discuss other equally important details of this music (harmony, for example) without the aid of some kind of graphic representation.[10] The musical examples in this chapter represent my own transcriptions of passages from the 1972 studio version of "Supper's Ready," which I consider the *Urtext* for this piece.[11] I have rendered some excerpts more or less in full, while others have been condensed or otherwise simplified; I have also limited myself to three staves, so instruments are at times intentionally omitted for the sake of clarity. (Phil Collins's drums have been given especially short shrift.) My goal has been to reproduce the vocal line as accurately as practical, while condensing other parts into a manageable short score. Measure numbers are provided for ease of reference within an individual tableau. I have used Roman numerals, figured-bass symbols, and (in one instance) pitch-class set names where I felt they were pertinent to my discussion of the harmonic language of a particular section.

The plan for presenting my analysis is this: First, I will examine "Supper's Ready," section by section, commenting on surface aspects of the compositional design and suggesting intertextual references to other styles or to specific other works; second, I will briefly consider the large-scale strategy, suggesting ways in which melodic and harmonic ideas introduced during the opening measures of "Supper's Ready"—in the manner of a *Grundgestalt*—continue to shape the music of subsequent sections as the piece unfolds.[12]

I. "Lover's Leap"

Like most of the individual sections of "Supper's Ready," "Lover's Leap" exhibits a self-contained miniature form of its own (see Example 12.1): An eight-bar verse in classical period form—a four-bar antecedent phrase followed by a four-bar modulating consequent—is answered by a four-bar refrain.[13] The piece begins without introduction, the vocal and accompanying instruments all entering together on the downbeat, grabbing the listener's attention at once. Peter Gabriel's voice is overdubbed during the verses so as to sound both at pitch and an octave higher; not only is this a neat effect (called the "double voice" by Susan Fast in Chapter 6 of this volume), but it gives the singer's persona a "split personality" in accordance with the message in the lyrics. Gabriel reveals the autobiographical source of the supernatural events described in the opening tableau, based on an experience with his wife, Jill:

> I really felt that I was writing about myself in a lot of ways. The first sequence was about a scene that happened between me and Jill. … It was one night at Jill's parents house in Kensington, when everyone had gone to bed. … We just stared at each other, and strange things began to happen. We *saw other faces in each other,* and … I was very frightened, in fact. … The curtain flew open, though there was no wind, and the room became ice cold. And I did feel that I saw figures [on the lawn] outside, figures in white cloaks (Gallo 1980, 49 [emphasis mine]).

Dominating the accompaniment is a continuous sixteenth-note arpeggiated figure played by two acoustic twelve-string guitars (only the lower part is transcribed here), a favorite instrumental texture in early Genesis.[14] The "organic" nature of this accompaniment—in which a distinctive shape is established in the first measure and then maintained on a bar-by-bar basis

Example 12.1 Genesis, "Lover's Leap" (Tony Banks-Michael Rutherford-Peter Gabriel-Steve Hackett-Phil Collins), *Foxtrot* (1972): opening tableau.

Example 12.1 *(Continued)*

as the harmony changes—is reminiscent of classical instrumental writing, recalling in particular the vivid piano accompaniments of many nineteenth-century Lieder.[15]

Yet similarities with nineteenth-century compositional practice are not confined to the realm of texture; from a harmonic standpoint, "Lover's Leap" also features several of the characteristic quirks normally identified with composers of that era. The verse alone, for example, exhibits:

- A beginning reminiscent of Schumann's *Dichterliebe* cycle in its tonal ambiguity: A short cadential progression (mm. 1–2) in E major is truncated before the arrival of the anticipated tonic in measure 3, instead moving abruptly to the tonal level of the dominant (mm. 3–4).
- Modal mixture: Several sonorities have been "borrowed" from the parallel minor into their respective major keys, including the half-diminished supertonic in measure 1, the minor tonic in measure 3, and the minor subdominant in measure 7.

- A modulation to the distant key of B♭ major (♯IV) in measures 6–8, musically portraying the accompanying lyric, "I swear I saw your face change."[16]

What makes this convincing imitation of nineteenth-century style all the more remarkable is the fact that none of the members of Genesis had ever received any formal training in harmony or voice leading.[17] Like the Beatles before them, Genesis possessed an uncanny natural ability to mimic and assimilate musical styles from outside of the pop-rock domain and transform them into something fresh and unique. We shall encounter further examples of this ability in the later sections of "Supper's Ready."

II. "The Guaranteed Eternal Sanctuary Man"

With the onset of the second tableau, we are drawn into a markedly different musical world; its opening is given as Example 12.2. Perhaps the most notable difference in texture between "Sanctuary Man" and the preceding music is the presence of the drums, which up until this point have remained tacet.[18] Now the drums and bass work in tandem to create a driving ostinato that provides the harmonic and rhythmic foundation for the first seven measures. Steve Hackett's electric guitar (not shown in the example) sidesteps its more usual role of lead instrument in this section and is instead limited to sliding figures that help paint an atmospheric background for Tony Banks's fanfare-like organ part (notated in simplified form on the middle staff).

In stark contrast to the nineteenth-century harmony of "Lover's Leap," the chord vocabulary of "Sanctuary Man" falls squarely in the tradition of post-1960s rock. First and foremost, the harmonic language of this section should be understood as *modal* rather than tonal in the sense of common-practice function: Despite the key of A major, G♮—the lowered-seventh scale degree—is clearly given primacy over the leading-tone G♯, resulting in a predominantly Mixolydian environment. Notice also that there is no V–I progression to establish A major as the tonal center; in fact, dominant harmony is absent from this section altogether. We must remember that in mode-based rock, root motion by descending *fourth* often supersedes traditional root motion by descending fifth, yielding more of a contrapuntal than a harmonic value to chord succession and progression. This is especially apparent here in the cadential passage (m. 10), which employs the common Mixolydian progression ♭VII–IV–(I) as opposed to a more stereotypically tonal II–V–I.[19]

Two other notable paradigms of rock harmony are featured in "Sanctuary Man." First, the opening bass ostinato establishes A as the tonal center by virtue of its constant repetition, and creates an extended tonic pedal point for the oscillating progression I–♮VII–I. By the late 1970s, textures dominated by pedal points such as this had become a well-worn hallmark of progressive rock as they had of funk, and were already making frequent appearances in more commercial styles such as stadium rock and synth-pop.[20] Despite the cliché, Genesis remain in my opinion the masters of the "pedal-point groove." What experienced listener can forget, for example, the giant crescendo that precedes the entrance of the vocal in "Watcher of the Skies" (1972), or the sheer power of the booming bass pedals in "Back in NYC" (1974)?[21]

A second harmonic paradigm appears after the pedal point is broken, with the rising progression II–III–♮III–IV (mm. 8–9).[22] Such stepwise passing of root-position chords is infrequent in classical tonality because of the characteristic stability of the perfect consonances measured above the bass; when it does occur there it is usually in limited and isolated contexts, such as in the carefully voice-led deceptive progression V–VI. In rock harmony, on the other hand, it is relatively common to pass by step through root-position chords

Example 12.2 Genesis, "The Guaranteed Eternal Sanctuary Man" (Tony Banks-Michael Rutherford-Peter Gabriel-Steve Hackett-Phil Collins), *Foxtrot* (1972): second tableau.

Example 12.2 *(Continued)*

(e.g., the cadential progression ♭VI–♭VII–I, used at the climax of the sixth tableau). Yet what betrays even more clearly this progression's rock derivation as opposed to any possible classical origins is its voice leading. As I have shown in Example 12.2, not only do we have a succession of root-position triads, but also a succession of exposed parallel fifths. These fifths are not surprising, since Tony Banks originally came up with the "Sanctuary Man" progression via barre chords on the guitar (see Gallo 1980, 15–16).

III. "Ikhnaton and Istacon and Their Band of Merry Men"

IV. "How Dare I Be So Beautiful?"

The preceding analysis has demonstrated that the first and second tableaux are markedly different from one another in compositional design, especially from the standpoint of harmonic procedure. This also holds true when we compare the third and fourth tableaux, both excerpted in Example 12.3. The majority of the battle sequence in "Ikhnaton and Istacon" (Example 12.3a; Ikhnaton was an Egyptian Pharaoh who ruled from 1379 to 1362 B.C.) is accompanied by what is often described in rock parlance as a "one-chord jam": in this case, a single D-major chord reiterated over and over again, with the third above the bass ornamented by its upper-neighbor fourth every other measure, a highly idiomatic guitar figure. To compensate for this lack of harmonic motion, the surface rhythm in the third tableau is very active. A militaristic snare-drum figure in constant sixteenth notes suggests the chaos of battle, ultimately

Example 12.3 Genesis, "Supper's Ready" (Tony Banks-Michael Rutherford-Peter Gabriel-Steve Hackett-Phil Collins), *Foxtrot* (1972): harmonic/rhythmic undercurrents in the third and fourth tableaux:

a) III. "Ikhnaton and Istacon and Their Band of Merry Men."

b) IV. "How Dare I Be So Beautiful?"

providing the rhythmic platform for a blistering Steve Hackett electric guitar solo (7:23+). This solo represents the only stereotypically "rock-sounding" electric guitar in the entire work.

The character of the fourth tableau could not be more different. For one, the rhythm section—which had been so prominent in "Ikhnaton and Istacon"—is now entirely absent. The accompaniment in "How Dare I Be So Beautiful?" consists solely of a series of rhythmically free sustained piano chords (given in Example 12.3b), above which Peter Gabriel sings in a declamatory style suggestive of recitative.[23] As I have shown in my Roman-numeral analysis, the two pairs of underlying harmonies alternate between major-seventh and half-diminished chords. Although I have interpreted these chords in G major, the presence of C♯ in the half-diminished chord of the second pair renders this tonality ambiguous, suggesting instead a strong pull towards its dominant area. Once again, the musical language seems to make reference to a stylistic practice outside of the usual confines of rock and pop. The harmonic and rhythmic fluidity here reminds me of the impressionistic writing of Debussy, where seventh chords (especially half-diminished and dominant-sevenths) are often used coloristically for their sheer sonic value, irrespective of any definite functional implication.[24]

V. "Willow Farm"

For those Genesis fans lucky enough to have seen "Supper's Ready" performed live in 1972 or 1973, one of the most memorable moments was no doubt Peter Gabriel's sudden appearance in a bright orange flower mask (pictured on the back cover of Gallo 1980) to begin the fifth tableau, "Willow Farm" (see Example 12.4). Tony Banks sheds light on the origins of what is probably the most bizarre of all the sections of "Supper's Ready":

> I thought . . . why don't we do something really stupid and go straight into "Willow Farm." Just bang . . . stop the song and instantly go into it. This was a little song that Peter had, lyrics and everything. And once we all got used to the idea and slotted "Willow Farm" in, it gave us great momentum to write the rest of the thing (Gallo 1980, 51).

"Willow Farm" is cast in a large ternary form (the reprise of its Part 1 is not shown in Example 12.4). Following Banks's suggestion, Part 1 begins *attacca* after the half cadence that closes the fourth tableau. A descending Phrygian bass guitar figure (note the use of $\flat\hat{2}$) plunges us into a loping 12/8 musical landscape that is about as far removed as one could imagine from the ethereal calm of the music immediately preceding.[25] In addition to the obvious differences in meter and rhythm, the governing tonality is A♭ minor, which—with its dependence on seven flats—is a highly unusual key in classical music (although it did make several appearances in the nineteenth century), let alone rock.

The harmonic language again suggests a nineteenth-century chromatic style, although this time the voice leading is hardly impeccable (e.g., the overt and stylistically irrelevant parallel fifths and octaves in mm. 2–4). Certain features are reminiscent of the "freer" approach to harmony characteristic of later nineteenth-century composers, most notably Liszt. It would be difficult to explain, for example, the "function" of the D-major-seventh chord as it resolves locally into an apparent cadential $^6_4$ in measure 13. Given the harmonic syntax of this passage, we would expect the chord of measure 12 to behave as a normal V $^4_2$ and resolve to a first-inversion tonic; instead, the bass rises and upper voices move freely to ♯IV in measure 13. One might then expect the resulting chord to act as a first-inversion dominant or root-position diminished-seventh despite its major-seventh color. It is a chord, in short, that functions as an applied dominant or leading-tone seventh of V; while the bass complies, the upper voices refuse to resolve normally. Despite the oddball surface harmonies in this passage, there does seem to be an inner logic governing the overall harmonic design. One might hear the German augmented-sixth chord of measure 14 as having been prepared by the VI chord of measure 9, embellished first in the bass by a local chromatic descent from F♭ via E♭ to D♮ (mm. 9–10), and then by an expansion of this bass motive articulated on the downbeats of every other measure (F♭ in m. 9, E♭ in m. 11, D♮ in m. 13), with

Example 12.4 Genesis, "Willow Farm" (Tony Banks-Michael Rutherford-Peter Gabriel-Steve Hackett-Phil Collins), *Foxtrot* (1972): fifth tableau.

Example 12.4 (*Continued*)

the vocal part moving in accented parallel fifths above. The overall effect of measures 9–14, then, is a large expanded German augmented-sixth sonority that appears in its full form in measure 14 and ultimately resolves to the dominant a bar later.

According to the program notes, after Part 1 "a whistle blows and every single thing is instantly changed into another." With the onset of Part 2, this is depicted musically in an obvious fashion: the 12/8 meter becomes 4/4, the prevailing pulse of triplet eighth notes gives way to constant duple eighths, the organ is replaced with a piano, and the tonality moves to the parallel A♭ major.[26] Adding to the humor, Gabriel's voice has been sped up (as if on helium) and panned in the mix so as to bounce back and forth between the speakers on the lyric "mum to mud to mad to dad."[27] Overall, the style of the middle section of "Willow Farm" alludes to the pitter-patter quality of early twentieth-century British music hall songs, providing yet another example of Genesis' remarkable stylistic eclecticism.

VI. "Apocalypse in 9/8"

VII. "As Sure as Eggs is Eggs (Aching Men's Feet)"

We have come now to the climactic sixth tableau, in which we are made to witness "the Apocalypse of St John in full progress."[28] The music in this section is perhaps the most complex of all of "Supper's Ready," and so for the sake of practicality I have chosen to highlight just a few of the key passages. As its title informs us, the sixth tableau is cast entirely in a 9/8 meter; furthermore, the meter is subdivided into constant eighth notes, grouped most of the time as 2 + 2 + 2 + 3. These pulsing eighth notes—and their accompanying repeated harmonies—at the beginning of the "Apocalypse in 9/8" (15:38+) have long reminded me of the famous incessant "Augurs of Spring" chord in Stravinsky's *The Rite of Spring* (1912). As I began to analyze this passage more closely, however, I soon realized that the resemblances between the two pieces were more than superficial.

As I have shown in Example 12.5a, the second of the two harmonies in the repeated passage at the beginning of "Apocalypse" is a complex six-note sonority, pitch-class set 6-Z25. When we compare this sonority to the "Augurs of Spring" chord, set 7-32 (Example 12.5b), we find that the smaller is a transposed subset of the larger superset; in addition, a comparison of the bass notes of the two chords reveals that they map directly onto one another.[29] Putting set theory aside momentarily, what this means for our purposes here is that—with the exception of just one additional note in the "Augurs of Spring" chord—these two harmonies sound essentially the same.

Yet the striking similarities do not end here. At the heart of the "Apocalypse in 9/8" is an extended organ solo over an ostinato played by the bass and guitar. This ostinato figure consists of just three pitches—E, F♯, and B—all three of which were contained in the preceding larger chord 6-Z25. Likewise in *The Rite of Spring,* an ostinato figure consisting of three pitches—B♭, D♭, and E♭—is pervasive throughout the entirety of the "Dances of the Young Girls" section, and again these three pitches were all contained in the larger "Augurs of Spring" chord that had sounded immediately before. I should remind the reader that by making these comparisons, I am not insisting that Genesis consciously modeled the "Apocalypse in 9/8" on Stravinsky—in fact, I would be highly surprised if this were the case.[30] Rather, I merely wish to provide further evidence of Genesis' sheer stylistic diversity; by evoking Stravinsky, we are able to learn more about how this section of the piece is put together.

The beginning of the aforementioned organ solo is transcribed as Example 12.6a. Again, Tony Banks offers us insights as to how this music was composed:

> The organ solo started off as a very tongue-in-cheek thing, I thought I'd play like Keith Emerson to see what it sounds like. There were little phrases in there that were supposed to be almost humorous in a way. The other idea on that was to just keep the notes simple, and I said [to Mike Rutherford], "If you can keep just to the three notes E, F sharp and B then I can do any chord I want on top of it." I could go major, minor, all sorts of things. It was great fun actually as I could go for the real dramatic stuff like a C major chord on top of that, which sounds very tense and that was how it was developed. I was very satisfied with the result of that.[31]

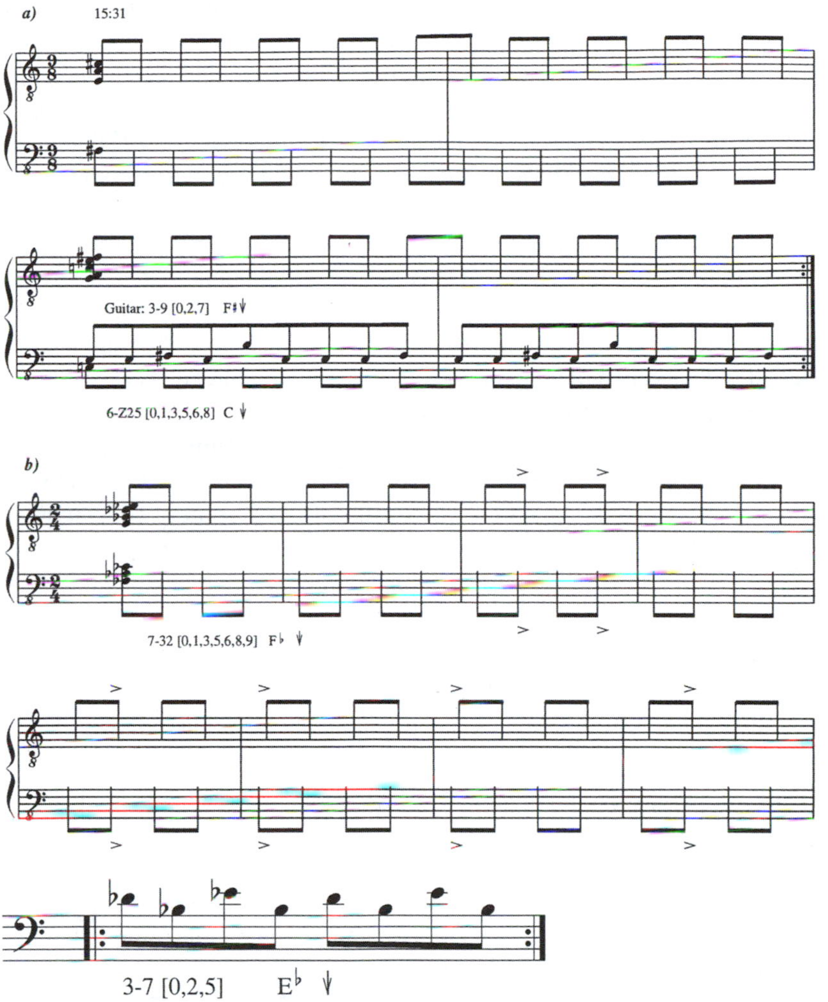

Example 12.5 A comparison of compositional strategies in Genesis and Stravinsky:
a) Genesis, "Apocalypse in 9/8" (Tony Banks-Michael Rutherford-Peter Gabriel-Steve Hackett-Phil Collins), *Foxtrot* (1972).
b) "Augurs of Spring," *Le Sacre du Printemps* (Igor Stravinsky) (1912).

Though originally intended to be just "tongue-in-cheek," Banks creates in this section what must rank as one of the finest keyboard solos in all of progressive rock. The overall character of the solo is established in the opening measures: continuous elaborate passagework dominated by constant sixteenth notes, reminiscent of the high-Baroque instrumental style of *Fortspinnung*.[32]

As in "Sanctuary Man," the tonal center is achieved during this section by virtue of the constant repetition of E as a tonic pedal point in the bass/guitar ostinato. As Banks has informed us, the limited pitch material of the ostinato accompaniment allowed him to take great liberties in the harmonic structure of his solo above ("I could go major, minor, all sorts of things"). Indeed, this harmonic freedom can be heard from the very onset of the solo: He begins squarely in E major, then quickly introduces A♯ ($\sharp\hat{4}$), invoking a Lydian quality. The modality continues to fluctuate two bars later with the introduction of G♮ ($\natural\hat{3}$) and D♮ ($\natural\hat{7}$), effecting a brief excursion into the Dorian mode.

The organ solo continues for over two-and-a-half minutes, culminating in a melodic sequence that rises to a spectacular climax on a high C♮.[33] At this point the vocal makes an impassioned return ("666 is no longer alone"), and here—for the first time in "Supper's Ready"—we are bathed in the massive orchestral timbre of a Mellotron chordal accompaniment, an effect that seems to have been consciously saved for this climactic moment, shown in Example 12.6b.[34] Following this passage, the tonality quickly modulates from E major to B♭ major, signaling a brief yet triumphant reprise of the refrain of the first tableau (20:11+). This "Lover's Leap" refrain is densely orchestrated, complete with tubular bells, snare-drum rolls, and electric-guitar tremolos.

Example 12.6a. Genesis, "Apocalypse in 9/8" (Tony Banks-Michael Rutherford-Peter Gabriel-Steve Hackett-Phil Collins), *Foxtrot* (1972): sixth tableau, from the beginning of the organ solo.

Example 12.6b. Genesis, "Apocalypse in 9/8" (Tony Banks-Michael Rutherford-Peter Gabriel- Steve Hackett-Phil Collins), *Foxtrot* (1972): Sixth tableau, from the Mellotron / vocal entrance.

An immediate segue (20:47) takes us into the seventh and final tableau, where we are presented with nothing less than a full-fledged recapitulation—what Nors Josephson (1992, 84) describes as a "Lisztian, symphonic apotheosis"—of the A-major "Sanctuary Man" theme from the second tableau. In live performances, Peter Gabriel would typically sing this final section of "Supper's Ready" suspended like an angel above the stage, expressing visually the idea that the ordeal is over and that good has ultimately prevailed over evil. It is no accident that Gabriel's lyrics for "As Sure as Eggs is Eggs (Aching Men's Feet)" contain the most explicit intertextual reference of the entire piece: a recasting of William Blake's famous poem about building a "new Jerusalem" on English soil, as immortalized in C. Hubert H. Parry's rousing World War I hymn, "Jerusalem" (1916).[35] One can hardly imagine a more fitting conclusion for this decidedly British retelling of the story of the apocalypse.

The Large-Scale View

Having examined surface aspects of the compositional design, section by section, I shall now turn as promised to a discussion of the large-scale strategy of "Supper's Ready." On the most basic of levels, Genesis and nineteenth-century composers of multi-movement programmatic pieces shared a similar dilemma: How does one maintain both a sense of variety and a sense of direction throughout the course of such a massive work? Concerning the issue of maintaining variety, Macan (1997, 43) suggests that the early progressive rockers achieved this primarily through "systematic juxtapositions" of "electronic and acoustic" sections in their music. Genesis employs such a technique throughout "Supper's Ready," as sections dominated by electric instruments and drums are followed by quieter, more contemplative sections in which the rhythm section is entirely absent (consider, for example, the stark "electric/acoustic" juxtaposition of the third and fourth tableaux). Concerning the issue of maintaining a sense of direction, Macan goes on to suggest that the early progressive rockers achieved this largely "by drawing on nineteenth-century symphonic music's fondness for building up tension until a shattering climax is reached, abruptly tapering off, then starting the whole process anew" (1997, 44). Again, we encounter Genesis employing such a strategy in several places during "Supper's Ready." Consider the close of the second tableau (Example 12.2), where the majestic "Sanctuary Man" theme abruptly breaks off on the subdominant—avoiding a cadence altogether—at the second ending (5:29), followed quickly by a quiet reprise of the verse melody of "Lover's Leap" that in turn initiates a gradual build-up towards the bombastic entrance of the third tableau.

Certainly each of these compositional techniques is an effective means of achieving both variety and continuity; to be sure, these are techniques that are likely to be perceived by most listeners as they experience the work, whether they are musically educated or not. Likewise, one does not need to know much about nineteenth-century musical forms to be aware of the cyclic thematic design of "Supper's Ready," made obvious by the full recapitulation of the "Sanctuary Man" theme in the final tableau.[36] But what about those melodic and harmonic ideas that might affect deeper levels of the musical structure, levels that would not be so obvious in a cursory hearing? To begin to answer this question, let us return to Example 12.1 in order to examine the opening measures of the piece in greater detail.

In my earlier discussion of "Lover's Leap," I mentioned that its harmonic language has more in common with nineteenth-century practice than with the conventions of post-1960s rock. Indeed, a "nineteenth-century sound" is immediately suggested by the harmony of measure 1: an F♯ half-diminished seventh—a transposed "Tristan chord"—borrowed into E major from the parallel E minor. As it turns out, this Tristan chord is consciously brought back at crucial moments throughout the piece, almost in the manner of a Wagnerian *leitmotif*.[37] To catalog just a few of its structural appearances, the harmony (1) is isolated as the sustained organ chord that initiates the brief echo of "Lover's Leap" at the close of the second tableau (Example 12.2), (2) is the second chord in the first pair of oscillating harmonies underpinning the fourth tableau (Example 12.3b), and (3) comprises the upper four pitches of the aforementioned 6-Z25 chord at the opening of the "Apocalypse in 9/8" (Example 12.5a). While a thorough analysis of the large-scale ramifications of this Tristan chord on the composition of "Supper's Ready" lies beyond the scope of this present essay, it should suffice to say that its reappearance in altered guises from section to section contributes markedly to the overall coherence of the work, and suggests a considerable degree of sophistication—at least a strong ear for unity—on the part of Genesis as composers.[38]

Both the initial Tristan chord and other melodic ideas introduced during the opening measures are composed-out in subsequent sections of "Supper's Ready." The chromatic inner voice in measures 2–3 of the accompaniment (E–D♯–D♮), for example, is recast both in the small and in the large as the descending chromatic bass motive (F♭–E♭–D♮) in measures 9–13 of "Willow Farm" (see Example 12.4 and its accompanying discussion). And although the melodic correspondence is not exact, I hear strong resonances of the pitch content of the opening vocal melody (mm. 1–4) in the first few measures of the organ solo in the "Apocalypse in 9/8" (Example 12.6a). In short, one could argue that the first four measures of the piece serve as a kind of *Grundgestalt*, providing a source of basic materials to which the music of subsequent sections makes constant reference.

A discussion of the large-scale strategy of "Supper's Ready" would not be complete without considering its overall key scheme. Most eighteenth- and nineteenth-century tonal pieces—even those in multiple movements—are harmonically closed, i.e., they begin and end in the same key. But like turn-of-the-century symphonic works (as with Mahler) and many other progressive rock works, "Supper's Ready" exhibits an *open* key scheme: It begins (albeit loosely) in E major and ends in A major. One might be tempted to interpret these framing keys as exhibiting a large-scale dominant-to-tonic relationship. Accordingly, the "Apocalypse in 9/8" could be viewed as a gigantic prolongation of the dominant that prepares for the arrival of A major as the home tonic in the final tableau.

An alternate interpretation, however, would be to hear these keys as manifesting a large-scale tonic-to-*subdominant* relationship, one which is played out on a number of levels as the piece unfolds. In my earlier discussion of the harmonic design of the "Sanctuary Man" theme, I mentioned that rock harmony is often driven by root motion in *fourths* rather than fifths, giving primacy to the subdominant-tonic axis over the traditional dominant-tonic relationship.

With this in mind, one could make a case such that the first tableau struggles to establish the tonic key of E major (undermined by a swerve to the tritone-related key of B♭ major), and that the second, third, and fourth tableaux are cast in tonalities that systematically move further away from the home tonic around a circle of fourths: A major, D major, and G major, respectively. After a digression to A♭ (enharmonically III) in the fifth tableau—breaking the series of fourth-related keys—the tonic E is regained as an extended pedal point for the "Apocalypse in 9/8," and it is only at the end of the climactic Mellotron-soaked passage (19:30; see Example 12.6b) that we arrive triumphantly for the first time on a root-position tonic chord. Following this plan, when Christ finally does "return to lead his children home" in the seventh tableau, he is actually leading them to the sanctuary of the subdominant.

Unlike many nineteenth-century composers, Genesis did not leave us with a wealth of sketches that might help us to unravel their compositional process as they put this huge piece together. Despite the lack of such evidence, the preceding analysis has sought to demonstrate that Genesis was indeed concerned with achieving motivic and harmonic coherence at deeper levels of the musical structure, similar to what we would expect of large-scale pieces by their nineteenth-century predecessors. At the same time, the elaborate web of intertextual references in "Supper's Ready" paints an overall picture of stunning stylistic diversity that surely Liszt or Mahler would have appreciated.

I would like to conclude on a personal note. Writing a "serious" essay about Genesis for this book has been especially significant for me. As I was growing up in the late 1970s and 1980s—and playing in as many rock and pop bands as I did orchestras—this group was one of the main reasons why I came to love music and to love thinking about music. This essay was originally given as a talk as part of an entire mini-conference on progressive rock, where the audience was primarily professional musicologists and music theorists. Judging by their enthusiastic response, I am sure that there are several others within our discipline who also care a great deal about this music, those whose formative years were similarly shaped by both a classical and a rock aesthetic. I hope then that my analytical methodology in this chapter may prove fruitful, and encourage others to draw upon the rich and varied body of work that is progressive rock for their own analyses. In any event, analyzing Genesis represents for me a homecoming of sorts, and as such I shall let Peter Gabriel have the last words: "Now I'm back again, and . . . it's gonna work out fine."

Notes

An earlier version of this essay was presented to the "Cross(over) Relations" conference, held at the Eastman School of Music in September 1996.

1. "Progressive rock" is the label adopted almost universally now by rock historians to refer to a style of popular music that has also been described variously as

"art rock," "symphonic rock," and "classical rock." Continuing the trend toward stylistic eclecticism spearheaded by the mid-1960s British-invasion groups (and popularized especially by the Beatles on their later albums), the progressive rockers attempted to synthesize rock and pop with traditional elements of Western art music. There has been a considerable resurgence of interest in progressive rock among popular music scholars in the past decade or so. (See for example Covach 1997; Holm-Hudson 2002; Josephson 1992; Macan 1992 and 1997; Martin 1998; Moore 2001, 64–118; and Stump 1997). The most comprehensive account of the history and reception of the genre to date is Macan 1997, a book-length study noteworthy for the author's attempts to address progressive rock from both a musicological and sociological perspective.

2. This enthusiasm was certainly not shared by many rock critics at the time. Genesis and other progressive rock groups were often branded as elitist, and their music—with its penchant for large-scale forms and frequent excursions into complex meters and non-tertian harmony—as entirely divorced from the "true" spirit of rock, which, according to the critics, should be grounded in the simple harmonies and dance rhythms of rhythm and blues. *Rolling Stone* and *Creem* have been particularly scathing in their criticisms of progressive rock over the years. For example, the neo-Marxist critic Lester Bangs accuses Emerson, Lake & Palmer (ELP) of no less than "the insidious befoulment of all that was gutter pure in rock" (Bangs 1974, 44; quoted in Macan 1997, 169).

   Although most well-known progressive rockers enjoyed considerable album sales and ever-increasing concert audiences in the first half of the 1970s, their decision to avoid, for the most part, writing and releasing *singles* greatly limited their radio exposure and hence their mainstream commercial success. For example, it took almost a decade—and only after these three groups had each consciously decided to work within smaller and more commercial forms—for ELP, Yes, and Genesis to crack the Top Twenty in their native Britain: ELP with their rock arrangement of Aaron Copland's "Fanfare for the Common Man" (which peaked at number 2 in July 1977); Yes with "Wonderous Stories" (number 7, October 1977); and Genesis with "Follow You Follow Me" (number 7, April 1978).

3. For models of a rigorous approach to rock analysis, see the work of Walter Everett (most recently 1997, 1999, 2000, 2001, and 2004a). Though he does not deal directly with progressive rock, Everett uses Schenkerian analytical techniques to examine the musical structure of songs by Paul Simon, the Beatles, Billy Joel, and Steely Dan.
4. Drawing on ideas in literary criticism, the central premise behind musical intertextuality is that compositions acquire a richness of meaning through their relationship to a potentially infinite universe of prior works (see Hatten 1985). For models of an intertextual approach to rock analysis, see Covach 1990 and 1995; see also Lacasse 2000.
5. Genesis had already attracted quite a cult following in Britain, but in 1972 they quickly found themselves major stars on the Continent, especially in Italy. Genesis biographer Armando Gallo (1980, 40) has aptly diagnosed this phenomenon, noting that "the Italians had never really identified with the twelve-bar syndrome of rock 'n' roll, and young fans and musicians who had grown up within Italy's strong classical and operatic traditions suddenly responded en masse to the English 'progressive' scene."

6. Hackett and Collins had joined the band for *Nursery Cryme,* following the 1970 departures of founding-member guitarist Anthony Phillips and drummer John Mayhew. For many fans this resulting quintet—Banks, Collins, Gabriel, Hackett, Rutherford—is fondly remembered as the consummate Genesis lineup. After Peter Gabriel left the group in 1975, Phil Collins added the role of lead singer to his job as drummer; likewise, Mike Rutherford assumed the dual role of guitarist/bassist in the studio when Steve Hackett left to pursue a solo career in 1977. Genesis has continued to record as a trio through their 1991 album *We Can't Dance*, with the American session musicians Daryl Stuermer (guitar) and Chester Thompson (drums) regularly augmenting the group for their live performances. In 1996, Collins—who enjoyed even greater success as a solo artist during the 1980s and 1990s—officially left the group, and was replaced by singer Ray Wilson for the 1997 album *Calling All Stations*. Although reaching as high as number 2 in the U.K., *Stations* was met with disappointing sales in the U.S. and elsewhere, and consequently, as of this writing (July 2006), Genesis has yet to release another album of new material. Rumors of an impending reunion of the classic 1970s quintet continue to circulate voraciously among Genesis fans, despite the December 2005 statement to the contrary on the group's official website, http://www.genesis-music.com. This seems all the more unlikely, at least in the immediate future, now that the 1980s lineup of Banks, Collins, and Rutherford have announced that they will be reuniting, without Gabriel and Hackett, for a 2007 world tour.
7. As with most of Genesis' large-scale pieces, the composing of "Supper's Ready" was a group effort. Banks, Collins, Gabriel, Hackett, and Rutherford are listed jointly as composers, although the individual contributions of each band member varied widely. The Gabriel quote is transcribed from an interview in the 1990 BBC film *Genesis: A History* (available on video). I highly recommend this film to the reader who wants a more detailed account of the group's early history, including fascinating concert clips.
8. As Macan (1997, 1) has noted, one of the most memorable features of British progressive rock was "its fascination with epic subject matter drawn from science fiction, mythology, and fantasy literature"—not unlike the subject matter of many nineteenth-century operas. Indeed, during the course of "Supper's Ready" we encounter several mythical and historical characters, including Narcissus, Pythagoras, The Pied Piper, and even "Winston Churchill dressed in drag." Gabriel's lyrics to "Supper's Ready" are given in Figure 12.1 as they appear on the inner sleeve to *Foxtrot.*
9. Regarding the *Fantastic Symphony* program, see Cone 1971. Although he was later to change his mind, Berlioz originally felt that the program was "indispensable for a complete understanding of the dramatic outline of the work" (Cone's translation, p. 21).
10. For a useful discussion of the pros and cons of using transcriptions in popular music analysis, see Brackett 2000, 27–29. Walter Everett also addresses this question in Chapter 5 of this volume.
11. Like most progressive rock groups, Genesis usually made an effort to reproduce the studio version as faithfully as possible in live performance. There was little room for improvisation; for example, Tony Banks always played his keyboard solos note-for-note off the record, as if each were an extended "melody" whose

original structure was essential to the work's integrity. This performance aesthetic is in stark contrast to that of a rock group like the Grateful Dead, who used the "original," studio-produced, versions of many of their songs as foils for extensive and elaborate improvisations that changed from one concert to the next, often rendering their sources almost unrecognizable (see Boone 1997 and Walter Everett's essay in this volume). Also in this book, John Covach finds the concert reproduction of fixed parts to be a prog hallmark when practiced by jazz-rockers. Certain effects—the overdubbing of Peter Gabriel's voice at the octave during "Lover's Leap," for example—were difficult or impossible to reproduce live and would be left out, often diluting the richness and meaning of the original, as in the loss of the "split personality" cited in my discussion of this passage below. All this I think points toward considering the original studio version as the standard against which subsequent live performances should be measured.

A live recording of "Supper's Ready" has long been available as side three of the 1977 double live album *Seconds Out*, recorded in Paris during the *Wind and Wuthering* tour with Phil Collins on lead vocals. While Collins does an admirable job, his rendition for me simply does not measure up to the nuances of Gabriel's impassioned delivery on the *Foxtrot* version. With the 1998 release of the CD boxed set, *Genesis Archive: 1967–75*, Genesis fans at long last had access to a 1973 live recording of "Supper's Ready" with Gabriel at the helm.

12. I should make it clear from the outset that in making such comparisons, I am not necessarily suggesting that Genesis themselves were conscious of all the multiple intertextual references that I hear in their music (many of which, coincidentally enough, are to nineteenth-century techniques). I am adopting an intertextual approach simply because I believe it is the best way of showing how this multivalent music is shaped. The issue of "intentionality" in musical influence is a thorny one that space does not permit me to treat adequately here; for a detailed study that explores this issue in relation to nineteenth-century music, see Korsyn 1991.

    The concept of a *Grundgestalt* ("basic shape") lies at the heart of Arnold Schoenberg's theory of musical coherence. Schoenberg likened a composition's *Grundgestalt* to a "musical seed": a distinctive melodic, harmonic, and/or rhythmic motive from which the entire *Gedanke* ("idea") of the work evolves. References to the concept are scattered throughout his theoretical writings; for the most thorough explication of his theory, including an excellent commentary by Patricia Carpenter and Severine Neff, see Schoenberg 1995.
13. Following a brief instrumental retransition, not shown in Example 12.1, this verse/refrain pattern is repeated.
14. Compare, for example, the opening section to "The Musical Box" (*Nursery Cryme*).
15. I am reminded especially of Schubert's organic piano accompaniments for his songs, for example, the "babbling brook" arpeggiated figure pervasive throughout "Wohin?" (*Die schöne Müllerin,* 1823).
16. As has been said of Schumann, one might say that "Supper's Ready" "begins with an ending" (Agawu 1991, 51–79). As I will show later, the initial F♯ half-diminished seventh chord is referred to at crucial moments throughout "Supper's Ready." I have respelled the new key at m. 7 enharmonically, as B♭ major, to avoid the notational inconvenience of a key signature of ten sharps.

Although the modulation in mm. 6–7 looks abrupt on paper, the accompanying voice leading could not be smoother: D♯ and F♯ are retained as common tones (E♭ and G♭), while the bass moves by semitone from B to B♭. The smoothness of this modulation is also due in part to the clever correspondence between the bass motives that punctuate both the antecedent and consequent phrases (marked ß and ß1 in Example 12.1). Notice that ß and ß1 share identical rhythm and contour, and, while their initial pitches are different, both motives arrive deliberately on the enharmonically equivalent pitches A♯ and B♭, respectively.

17. Aside from obvious features of instrumentation (e.g., the use of an electric bass), I would argue that the only elements sounding truly out of place in an otherwise very "nineteenth-century sounding" musical landscape are the speech-like syncopations in the vocal melody, which seem more typical of a rock singing style than a classical one. Regarding the musical backgrounds of group members, see Gallo 1980, *passim*. Tony Banks had received some formal training on the violin and piano as a boy, but was self-taught in composition and much preferred playing the piano by ear to working from notation (pp. 123–125).
18. It is evident from the lyrics that the "Guaranteed Eternal Sanctuary Man," "a fireman who looks after the fire," is meant to represent Satan himself. The second tableau follows an extended folk-like instrumental transition, lasting more than two minutes, continually dominated by the opening arpeggiated twelve-string guitar texture.
19. Many of rock's harmonic idioms owe an allegiance to blues traditions. The progression ♭VII–IV–I, for example, can be understood as a variant of the progression V–IV–I that closes a typical twelve-bar blues, with ♮VII substituting for V. For a more extended discussion of modal harmony in rock music—and the use of the lowered seventh in particular—see Moore 1995 and Everett 2004b. This volume's essays by Lori Burns and Walter Everett also address modal harmonic and contrapuntal procedures in rock music.
20. One could cite hundreds of examples, but two standouts are Van Halen's "Jump" and Frankie Goes to Hollywood's "Relax" (both 1984).
21. The term "groove" has long been used by pop and rock musicians to describe the repetitive rhythmic foundation upon which a song was built. In an attempt to formalize the term for purposes of music analysis, I have elsewhere defined groove as "the tapestry of riffs—usually played by the drums, bass, rhythm guitar and/or keyboard in some combination—that work together to create the distinctive rhythmic/harmonic backdrop which identifies a song" (Spicer 2004, 30).
22. Although the harmonic language of "Sanctuary Man" is unmistakably in the rock tradition, its form is not unlike that of a classical "sentence": A four-bar basic idea (mm. 1–4) is immediately followed by a varied and shortened repetition of the basic idea (mm. 5–7), which together comprise the harmonically static and tonic-prolonging "presentation." A harmonically active and condensed "continuation" follows (mm. 8–10), culminating in an elided plagal cadence at the repeat. For useful summaries of the distinguishing formal characteristics of the classical period and sentence, see Schmalfeldt 1991 and Caplin 1998, 35–58.
23. Accordingly, the stripped-down accompaniment—with its rhythmically free sustained chords—suggests the role of a continuo. The eerie effect of the piano chords is the result of a series of "volume fade-ins," achieved in the studio by

running the piano signal through a volume/tone control pedal so as to allow the removal of all attack points. I am grateful to the unidentified respondent who called my attention to this technique during the question/answer session following my paper delivery at the Eastman School of Music's "Cross(over) Relations" conference in 1996. This device was likely first used by George Harrison to manipulate the electric-guitar sound on a handful of his Beatles songs (e.g., "Yes It Is" and "I Need You") from February 1965 onward.

24. Compare, for example, the nonfunctional, oscillating half-diminished and dominant-seventh chords over a sustained bass A♯ (B♭) in the famous opening section of Debussy's *Prelude to "The Afternoon of a Faun"* (1892–1894).
25. In the film *Genesis: A History,* Gabriel informs us that his intention in "Willow Farm" was "to explore this unreal world of English subconscious." Indeed, his lyrics are loaded with cryptic allusions and wordplay in the tradition of English absurdist humor, continuing a precedent made popular by John Lennon in his later work with the Beatles. One is immediately reminded, for example, of the Lewis Carroll-inspired surrealism in "I Am the Walrus."
26. The use of the parallel major for the contrasting middle section was of course a favorite key scheme of nineteenth-century composers for their large-scale ternary pieces in minor keys. See, for example, the funeral march from Beethoven's Op. 26 piano sonata, one well-known piece in A♭ minor.
27. Although he had the "tricks" of the recording studio available in this case, Gabriel was famous for his ability to adjust his vocal timbre and adopt different musical personae as the narratives of given songs demanded. In Part 1 of "Willow Farm," for example, he progresses from a talkative style reminiscent of Noël Coward all the way to a full-blown scream.
28. The entrance of the sixth tableau immediately follows a second instrumental interlude (14:16–15:37), featuring a folk-like A-Dorian melody played by Gabriel on the flute and accompanied quietly by acoustic guitar and organ.
29. The set nomenclature follows the standard form as established in Forte 1973. Of course, even a rudimentary explanation of set theory lies well beyond the scope of the present essay, but it ought to be noted here that the set names refer to particular collections differentiated by interval content. The integers bracketed underneath Examples 12.5a and 12.5b label all constituent pitch classes as distant from some particular reference point (the supersets measured down from C in Example 12.5a and down from F♭ in Example 12.5b).
30. To my knowledge, none of the members of Genesis have specifically confirmed the influence of Stravinsky on their music. Yet Stravinsky clearly did have a profound impact on other British progressive rock bands. For example, Yes opened their concerts during the *Close to the Edge* tour (July 1972–May 1973) with a recording of the finale to *The Firebird* (1910), which as a result is heard as the opening track on their live album *Yessongs* (1973).
31. From a Banks interview by Alan Hewitt that originally appeared in *The Waiting Room* magazine (1994), the text of which is available online at http://www.genesis-path.net/art-tonyWR; see also Hewitt 2000, 34. Banks goes on in the interview to describe how the organ solo crystallized during an extended jam session in the studio involving a trio consisting of himself, Phil Collins, and Mike Rutherford. Interestingly, this foreshadows what was to become Genesis' preferred method for composing new pieces beginning with the 1978 album *… And Then There Were Three …*, when the group was in fact reduced to just these three members.

32. Although the virtuosic passagework here was perhaps simply a result of trying to "play like Keith Emerson," such a *Fortspinnung* approach to crafting keyboard solos quickly became a hallmark of Banks's style. Compare, for example, the extended synthesizer solo in the middle section of "In the Cage" (1974).
33. A sense of mounting intensity is conveyed during the organ solo not only by the organ itself, but also by the ever-increasing complexity of Phil Collins's drumming, which engages in a rhythmic dialogue with the solo part that unfolds freely against the rigid 9/8 pulse of the ostinato. The drumming here suggests the complex polyrhythmic style of free jazz, a style that Collins was able to explore more fully in his work with the British fusion group Brand X during the late 1970s and 1980s.
34. A forerunner to modern samplers, the Mellotron uses a standard keyboard to engage selected banks of magnetic tapes, of actual sustaining orchestral instruments, voices, or effects, in between pinch rollers and an elongated capstan rod that pulls the tapes across heads: one tape, one head, and one pinch roller for each key. As each tape is only a few feet long, sounds can be sustained only for about ten seconds before a spring resets the tape with a snap. Mellotrons were notorious for malfunctioning on the road, as one might imagine, but they were the only practical way for early-1970s prog groups to simulate the sound of a full choir or orchestra in their live performances. For a detailed discussion of the Mellotron and the myriad other keyboard instruments used in prog, see Vail 2000.
35. Parry's "Jerusalem" is perhaps the most famous and beloved of all Anglican hymns. In concert, Peter Gabriel made the reference to the hymn even more explicit through the bizarre story he told as a lead-in to "Supper's Ready," which culminated in his whistling an odd, jazzy reinvention of the tune he called "Jerusalem Boogie." (One can hear Gabriel's story on the live version of "Supper's Ready" available on *Genesis Archive: 1967–75.)* Certainly Banks, Gabriel, and Rutherford would have known it from their boyhood years spent at the exclusive Charterhouse school, where they would have often been made to sing the hymn at morning assembly. ELP even went so far as to record a full-blown arrangement of "Jerusalem" for the opening track of their 1973 album, *Brain Salad Surgery*. For a discussion of the profound influence that Anglican church music seems to have had on many of the early progressive rockers, see Macan 1992, especially pp. 102–103.
36. Macan (1997) and others have tended to view full recapitulations of earlier themes in progressive rock pieces as evidence of a kind of "sonata form." There is great danger, however, in mapping large-scale classical tonal forms too literally onto this repertoire: for instance, one might get the thematic scheme to line up loosely with the classical model, but then the harmonic scheme has no bearing at all. See, for example, Macan's "sonata-form" reading of Yes's "Close to the Edge" (pp. 95–105).
37. The "Tristan chord" reference is to the opening harmony of Richard Wagner's opera *Tristan und Isolde* (1859), which sounds enharmonically like a half-diminished seventh. As Forte (1995, 340 n. 4) has noted, "in post-Wagnerian European music ... the often-quoted chord assumes the attributes of an erotic symbol." Although the resemblance to the Tristan chord is not as powerful when the

harmony is transposed and revoiced, as in this case, the fact that Genesis have chosen to *open* "Supper's Ready" with an unstable half-diminished seventh, coupled with their subsequent treatment of the harmony as a *leitmotif*, makes the connection with Wagner especially potent and appropriate.

38. For an attempt at such a large-scale view, see Josephson 1992, 84–85, in which the author reads the overall tonal plan of "Supper's Ready" against the half-diminished seventh backdrop of an "A-C-E-F# harmonic matrix."

References

Agawu, V. Kofi. 1991. *Playing With Signs: A Semiotic Interpretation of Classic Music*. Princeton: Princeton University Press.

Bangs, Lester. 1974. Blood Feast of Reddy Kilowatt! Emerson, Lake and Palmer Without Insulation. *Creem* 5/10 (March), 40–44, 76–78.

Boone, Graeme M. 1997. Tonal and Expressive Ambiguity in "Dark Star." In *Understanding Rock: Essays in Musical Analysis*, ed. John Covach and Graeme M. Boone, 171–210. New York: Oxford University Press.

Brackett, David. 2000. *Interpreting Popular Music*. Reprinted. Berkeley: University of California Press.

Caplin, William E. 1998. *Classical Form: A Theory of Formal Functions for the Instrumental Music of Haydn, Mozart, and Beethoven*. New York: Oxford University Press.

Cone, Edward T. 1971. The Symphony and the Program. In the Norton Critical Score of Hector Berlioz's *Fantastic Symphony*, 18–35. New York: Norton.

Covach, John. 1990. The Rutles and the Use of Specific Models in Musical Satire. *Indiana Theory Review* 11, 119–144.

———. 1995. Stylistic Competencies, Musical Humor, and "This is Spinal Tap." In *Concert Music, Rock and Jazz Since 1945*, ed. Elizabeth West Marvin and Richard Hermann, 402–424. Rochester: University of Rochester Press.

———. 1997. Progressive Rock, "Close to the Edge," and the Boundaries of Style. In *Understanding Rock: Essays in Musical Analysis*, ed. John Covach and Graeme M. Boone, 3–31. New York: Oxford University Press.

Everett, Walter. 1997. Swallowed by a Song: Paul Simon's Crisis of Chromaticism. In *Understanding Rock: Essays in Musical Analysis*, ed. John Covach and Graeme M. Boone, 113–153. New York and Oxford: Oxford University Press.

———. 1999. *The Beatles as Musicians:* Revolver *through the* Anthology. New York: Oxford University Press.

———. 2000. The Learned vs. the Vernacular in the Songs of Billy Joel. *Contemporary Music Review* 18/4, 105–130.

———. 2001. *The Beatles as Musicians: The Quarry Men through* Rubber Soul. New York: Oxford University Press.

———. 2004a. A Royal Scam: The Abstruse and Ironic Bop-Rock Harmony of Steely Dan. *Music Theory Spectrum* 26/2 (Fall), 201–235.

———. 2004b. Making Sense of Rock's Tonal Systems. *Music Theory Online* 10/4 (December).

Forte, Allen. 1973. *The Structure of Atonal Music*. New Haven: Yale University Press.

———. 1995. *The American Popular Ballad of the Golden Era: 1924–1950*. Princeton: Princeton University Press.

Gallo, Armando. 1980. *Genesis: I Know What I Like.* Los Angeles: D.I.Y. Press.

Genesis: A History. 1990. Best of British Films and Television Ltd. and Hit and Run Music Productions, in Association with NBD Pictures and Ripple Productions (Polygram Music Video 082 769-3; released in the United States in 1991).

Hatten, Robert. 1985. The Place of Intertextuality in Music Studies. *American Journal of Semiotics* 3/4, 69–82.

Hewitt, Alan. 2000. *Opening the Musical Box: A Genesis Chronicle.* London: Firefly.

Holm-Hudson, Kevin, ed. 2002. *Progressive Rock Reconsidered.* New York and London: Routledge.

Josephson, Nors S. 1992. Bach Meets Liszt: Traditional Formal Structures and Performance Practices in Progressive Rock. *The Musical Quarterly* 76/1 (Spring), 67–92.

Korsyn, Kevin. 1991. Towards a New Poetics of Musical Influence. *music analysis* 10/1-2 (March-July), 3–72.

Lacasse, Serge. 2000. Intertextuality and Hypertextuality in Recorded Popular Music. In *The Musical Work: Reality or Invention?*, ed. Michael Talbot, 35–58. Liverpool: Liverpool University Press.

Macan, Edward. 1992. "The Spirit of Albion" in Twentieth-Century Popular Music: Vaughan Williams, Holst, and the Progressive Rock Movement. *The Music Review* 53/2 (May), 100–125.

———. 1997. *Rocking the Classics: English Progressive Rock and the Counterculture.* New York and London: Oxford University Press.

Martin, Bill. 1998. *Listening to the Future: The Time of Progressive Rock, 1968–1978.* Chicago: Open Court.

Mead, Andrew. 1985. Large-Scale Strategy in Arnold Schoenberg's Twelve-Tone Music. *Perspectives of New Music* 24/1 (Fall–Winter), 120–157.

Moore, Allan F. 1995. The So-Called "Flattened Seventh" in Rock. *Popular Music* 14/2, 185–201.

———. 2001. *Rock: The Primary Text*, second ed. [1993]. Aldershot and Burlington: Ashgate.

Schmalfeldt, Janet. 1991. Towards a Reconciliation of Schenkerian Concepts with Traditional and Recent Theories of Form. *music analysis* 10/3 (October), 233–287.

Schoenberg, Arnold. 1995. *Musikalische Gedanke und die Logik, Technik und Kunst seiner Darstellung.* Edited and translated by Patricia Carpenter and Severine Neff as *The Musical Idea and the Logic, Technique, and Art of Its Presentation.* New York: Columbia University Press.

Spicer, Mark. 2004. (Ac)cumulative Form in Pop-Rock Music. *twentieth-century music* 1/1 (March), 29–64.

Stump, Paul. 1997. *The Music's All That Matters: A History of Progressive Rock.* London: Quartet Books.

Vail, Mark. 2000. *Vintage Synthesizers: Pioneering Designers, Groundbreaking Instruments, Collecting Tips, Mutants of Technology*, second ed. San Francisco: Miller Freeman.

13

Rock and Roll Rhapsody

Pop Epics of the 1970s

ALBIN ZAK

A hallmark of progressive rock of the 1970s was its tendency to use extended musical forms more characteristic of classical works than pop songs, notably in such tableaux as Genesis' "Supper's Ready" and *The Lamb Lies Down on Broadway,* and Yes's "South Side of the Sky" and "Close to the Edge." Some groups, particularly Emerson, Lake & Palmer, went so far as to adapt actual classical pieces to their own instrumentation (see Macan 1997). But while expanding narrative design beyond pop conventions is widely acknowledged as one of the genre's defining aims, it is also the case that progressive rock shared this ambition with many of its contemporary peers. Indeed, most genres in the 1970s indulged, at one time or another, in some sort of grandiosity. Consider a quick list of representative tracks: Led Zeppelin's "Stairway to Heaven," Bruce Springsteen's "New York City Serenade," Queen's "Bohemian Rhapsody," Lynyrd Skynyrd's "Free Bird," Patti Smith's "Birdland," David Bowie's "Station to Station," Stevie Wonder's "Ordinary Pain," Parliament's "Aqua Boogie (A Psychoalphadiscobetabioaquadoloop)," Steely Dan's "Deacon Blues," and Billy Joel's "Scenes from an Italian Restaurant." The range of styles and aesthetic stances that this list represents illustrates how widespread was the impulse to expand the pop song's conventional frame, and to take an episodic approach to writing rock songs and producing records. On the one hand, developments in technology and media common to all rock genres helped to foster this fascination. The late-1960s rise of FM radio, the focus on albums rather than singles, and a fascination with novel record production techniques all contributed to a climate where long-form pop flourished. But there was also clearly an aesthetic intent peculiar to the time. For all of these surrounding factors continued in the 1980s as the pendulum swung back to, if not a strict three-minute format, at least to more traditional song forms and tightly packaged singles. While the most obvious attribute of rock's epic tendency is length, many longer songs are simply the result of extended instrumental sections or extra verses. This essay, on the other hand, explores a range of examples outside the progressive rock genre whose unusual formal structures both betoken a particular artistic ambition and exemplify some of those artists' strategies.

Early History

Among the sources of long-form rock tracks are the narrative urban folk ballad and the improvised live jam, traces of which are common in both American and British psychedelic styles of the later 1960s. In the case of the ballad, the longer song length results simply from an extended series of strophes, as in Bob Dylan's "Sad Eyed Lady of the Lowlands." Jams, too, are often based on strophic structures—as in Jimi Hendrix's extended blues jam, "Voodoo Chile"—but may also employ a drone over which improvisation unfolds, as in the Doors' "The End." Drones may also take the form of chord sequences that repeat endlessly while the rest of the track's elements unfold in a continuous progression—see Van Morrison's "Madame George." While none of these techniques suggests any through-composed formal conception at the structural level, their increasing frequency of appearance through the later 1960s—along with an expanded diversity of verbal and timbral resources—signaled a developing conception of pop music's expressive possibilities. Other signs are to be found in such thematic concept albums as the Kinks' *Village Green Preservation Society* and in collections of songs joined loosely together by narrator (the Small Faces' "Happiness Stan" cycle) or segue (the Beatles' *Abbey Road*, side 2). Leading musicians increasingly asserted that their records were about ideas, poetic imagery, and musical exploration. Fans and critics concurred. As rock records became more complex, rock criticism came into its own. If Elvis Presley, Chuck Berry, and Little Richard remained mythical figures in rock's genesis story, it was such artists as Dylan, the psychedelic Beatles, the Velvet Underground, and the Band that gave critics their subjects for probing, if often remarkably idiosyncratic, criticism.[1] The marketplace, too, embraced rock's growing complexity. Dylan's "Like a Rolling Stone" (1965) shattered Top-Forty time limits with its six-minute length as it rose to number 2 on the *Billboard* chart. But the more natural home for long tracks was the FM radio format, which treated album cuts like singles. As FM grew into a market force to rival AM Top Forty, its predilection for albums exerted an influential cultural force as well.

One of the first Top-Forty rock hits to employ a complex, unconventional song structure was the Beach Boys' "Good Vibrations" (1966). Interestingly, however, the song is not particularly long. It goes through its multiple sections—changing keys, texture, and groove along the way—in a fairly compact three minutes and thirty-five seconds. The time frame, however, is deceptive owing to the large amount of musical information and the surprise arrivals of new ideas following the first two verse / chorus segments. The track could easily end at this point; fading away on the sustained dominant chord, it (like many early Beatles singles) would come in at just two minutes, having made a pithy statement and lodged a powerful hook in the listener's ear and mind. Instead, the track continues with two brief sections of new music ("I don't know where but she sends me there" [2:01+], and then "Gotta keep those loving good vibrations" [2:21+]), each in a different key and groove.[2] Finally, the chorus returns (2:57+), but in a different key from its first two appearances and quickly yielding to a coda (3:13+) that introduces still more new material.

If Brian Wilson managed to rein in his fertile imagination within radio time limits, Crosby, Stills & Nash's "Suite: Judy Blue Eyes" (1969) gobbled the radio time usually allotted for two songs as it strung together four contrasting sections, evoking the wordplay of its title. Among the longest Top-Forty hits of the late 1960s, the track's length (7'22") exceeded even those of the Beatles' "Hey Jude" (7'11") and Richard Harris's "MacArthur Park" (7'20").[3] But the dimensions of "Hey Jude" resulted simply from its long coda. And "MacArthur Park" is a commingling of Hollywood film and Broadway musical stylings. "Suite: Judy Blue Eyes" placed in the public soundscape a *rock* track whose unfolding narrative changes melodies, chord sequences, groove, and tempo, culminating in a final flourish set in a new key and sung in Spanish. Indeed, the single most unifying element is the group's signature vocal texture, which provides in each of the sections a distinctive sonic hook. But the track also has an overarching tonal connectivity that gives the verbally nonsensical "doo doo doo doo doo" finale a satisfying feeling of arrival. The track's first three sections are in E with persistent inflections of D♮, and while the flatted seventh is a common, blues-derived occurrence in many rock songs, implying no specific harmonic function, here it ends up doing a certain amount of duty as a dominant preparation. For as the final section kicks in with its repeated I–ii–IV–V phrase in A, its arrival is reinforced by a retrospective sense of tonal direction arching back to the track's opening.

Albums, of course, made the best homes for ambitious musical statements, and sprawling album tracks proliferated in the late 1960s as artists took advantage of the opportunity to stretch their performances. Only two of the eight tracks on Van Morrison's *Astral Weeks* are under four minutes—four exceed six minutes. Isaac Hayes's *Hot Buttered Soul*, only four tracks altogether, contains a cover of "By the Time I Get to Phoenix" that lasts nearly twenty minutes. The Velvet Underground's "Sister Ray" blasts away for more than seventeen minutes. Because Top-Forty radio was never really happy with tracks that went on for too long, record companies struck a compromise. Album tracks were sometimes shortened to make radio-friendly single versions, as with the Doors' "Light My Fire" mix losing the long instrumental solos of the album version, or Isaac Hayes's cover of "Walk on By," a hit at about one-third the length of the album cut.[4] Conversely, FM-radio often played entire sides of LPs, even entire LPs. In addition, double-, triple-, and even quadruple-albums began to appear. By the end of a decade that had begun with the industry's primary focus on three-minute singles, it was clear that much pop music had grown restless with the conventional limits.

Hard Rock and Glam

Among hard rockers, no band had a more pronounced affinity for epic tracks than Led Zeppelin. Their improvisational prowess in live performance, their attraction to mythic imagery and topics (the stuff of literary epics), and their skilled studio craft led easily to elaborate record making. Zeppelin epics are scattered throughout their albums and include the signature "Stairway to Heaven," "Dazed and Confused," "Kashmir," "The Rain Song," and "Achilles Last Stand." Zeppelin's long-form tracks take various shapes, sometimes resulting from extended blues workouts ("You Shook Me"), sometimes interpolating contrasting middle sections to form large **A B A** structures ("Dazed and Confused"), sometimes moving progressively through a process of continuous change ("Stairway to Heaven"). In each case, the expanded dimensions allow time for musical ideas to spin forth, and narrative space for contrasting sections to interact. The interaction includes stylistic interplay. From their first album, Zeppelin worked from a composite style palette where blues, folk song, high-energy rock, and psychedelic textures rubbed shoulders—both across the span of the album and within individual tracks—providing a diversity of resources and associations that helped to fuel their extended dramatic narratives.

Consider "Dazed and Confused," whose woozy chromatic blues appears after a couple of minutes to collapse into disoriented fragments floating in a sonic dreamscape. The guitar glissandi, articulated with a violin bow, are drenched in reverb, inhabiting their own sonic world. The voice responds from a different ambient place with moaned echoes of each guitar utterance. The rhythm recedes to light background scatterings. In this **B** section's second part (announced by the hi-hat at 3:28), things snap into a sharper focus. The guitar fragments are replaced by sustained melodic lines, and a furious rhythmic energy erupts from the drums, the cymbals sizzling incessantly. Still, however, the voice continues its moaned, then shouted, vocalise. Finally, after a three-minute diversion, the opening material returns and then, in the coda's final flourish, we hear a residual effect of the track's musical journey as the opening riff from the **B** section returns with a difference. Instead of announcing a dreamy fragmentation, it now introduces a driving push to the final cadence. As John Bonham pounds out an elongated bolero rhythm, and Robert Plant's once-dreamy moans change to a rhythmic suggestion of sexual fulfillment, the contrast with the earlier music is clear. And in its foreshortening and fusion of the two kinds of **B**-section music, the coda leaves an impression in the track's final moments that some sort of transformation has occurred.

Susan Fast has written that, for Zeppelin fans, the music's "transformative power … is paramount" (Fast 2001, 58). In many Led Zeppelin tracks, the transformative emotional and spiritual experiences reported by fans is mirrored in specific musical transformations. Zeppelin epics often consist of several contrasting sections strung together whose very juxtaposition seems to effect transformation. The "Dazed and Confused" coda is a brief example, but a better one is a track like "In the Light," from *Physical Graffiti*. The track's three main narrative components are presented in an **A B C A′ B′ C′** plan, sharing some common features that also bear some element of contrast: (1) Sections **A** (1:43–2:44) and **C** (4:09–4:58) have in common a repeated rising gesture, one in the minor mode with chromatic additions intoned by a synthetic bass sound, the second in the major mode, entirely diatonic and played by a clearly ringing electric guitar. (2) Before the rising bass line enters in the first **A** section, a synthesized pipe-like sound holds a pulseless drone over which Mixolydian fragments approximate the effect of an Indian raga in its alap phase of presentation. One of the repeated fragments (C♯–D–E) will become key in the **C** section's rising gesture; in this new context, however, it is given a sharp rhythmic articulation. (3) Sonically, the **A** and **C** sections also have in common a buzzy keyboard sound, but in the **A** section the sound's envelope has slow attacks (creating the pipe-like effect), while in the **C** section the attacks are quick and sharp, effectively turning the pipes into a clavinet.

Sandwiched between the **A** and **C** sections, the **B** section (2:45–4:09) is a typical blues-derived Zeppelin stomp. Here, too, there is a central instrumental gesture—two related ones, in fact, both *descending* (see Example 13.1). They share with the **A** section the minor mode with chromatic additions, and with the **C** section, the sound of the electric guitar.

With this three-part scheme of contrast and development as a backdrop, the vocal protagonist moves between two different roles, finally achieving a kind of transcendence. In the opening, the voice's electronic processing makes it barely recognizable as human. The lyrics, too, are vaguely mystical—

Example 13.1 Led Zeppelin, "In the Light" (Jimmy Page-Robert Plant-John Paul Jones), *Physical* Graffiti (1975): **B** Section's two descending gestures.

Example 13.2 Led Zeppelin, "In the Light" (Jimmy Page-Robert Plant-John Paul Jones), *Physical* Graffiti (1975): **C** Section's guitar riff.

"In the light you will find the road"—like an oracle's promise. As the track moves to the **B** section, the voice changes; it comes closer to the listener and loses its electronic affectation as Plant sings with a passion both empathic (in word) and at times menacing (in tone), expressing an all-too-human emotional ambivalence. In the first **C** section, the voice drops out altogether as the music shifts to the anthemic rising diatonic guitar riff (see Example 13.2). **A′** and **B′** are shorter than their previous counterparts, but otherwise largely reprise the earlier material, the voice moving from electronic spirit to human character once again. The transformative effect becomes apparent immediately upon the arrival of **C′**. Once again, we hear the butt-splice juxtaposition of heavy rock (now with a second, overdubbed, electric guitar) to solo clavinet, but now the human voice continues singing. And what it sings is the oracle's words "in the light." The spirit has become human, but devoid now of any implied menace. As the shouts ("light, light, light") continue sporadically over the repeating four-bar A-major phrase, and the lead guitars make their joyful, soaring noise, the final section delivers a resounding expression of hippie transcendence achieved through musical transformation.

Combining elements of hard rock with glam, cabaret, and campy melodrama, Queen's "Bohemian Rhapsody," from the album *A Night at the Opera*, is one of the best known of all rock epics. The track appeared sixteen years after its 1975 release in the film *Wayne's World*, and was adopted after Freddie Mercury's 1991 death as an AIDS fundraising tool. But its central place in the public pop mind was owed initially to its success as a number-two hit single, a surprising contradiction of prevailing record company marketing wisdom. Expressions of grandiosity in pop are often characterized as operatic: Roy Orbison, with his extended range and dramatic vocal style, was referred to in the press as the "Caruso" of rock (Amburn 1990, 97). The Who's *Tommy* was called a "rock opera." The absurdity of this stock characterization is part of the point invoked by Queen in the album's title, a self-aware acknowledgement that they are about to go over the top. Indeed, "Bohemian Rhapsody," at 5′55″, is not even the longest track on the record.

The recording begins with processed, stylized voices setting an existential scene ("Is this the real life?/Is this just fantasy?") in rich vocal harmonies and exaggerated dynamics—a sort of electronic chorus accompanied sparsely by piano. The song's protagonist, an "easy come easy go" fatalist, emerges from the processed texture with a human voice and a sad tale of violence and waste that, in the second verse ("Too late, my time has come … ," 1:55+) becomes eerily prescient of Mercury's own future fate.

The music now has a folk-like diatonic directness and an intimate vocal presence suggesting an introspective ballad. Following an expansive Brian May guitar solo (2:35–3:03), however, the music takes an entirely unexpected turn as the band drops out, the tempo quickens, and the chorus returns to stage a mock trial for the protagonist in a manically camp pop buffa style laced with odd references to Scaramouch, Galileo, Figaro, Bismallah, and Beelzebub. The music, too, is a mock version of classical harmonic complexity, moving from a chromatically inflected opening ("I see a little silhouetto of a man") to a dizzying harmonic swirl delivered in the vocal style and antiphonal textures of a psychedelic eighteenth-century oratorio. This, of course, climaxes with the famous "head-banger" guitar solo (4:07+) and the protagonist's defiance that yank the track into yet another stylistic place followed, finally, by a return to the slower tempo and original key of the track's opening. The protagonist affirms once more, and this time like a poignant farewell, that "nothing really matters." The track is a spectacular piece of virtuoso pop composition, equal parts kitsch attitude and serious craft. Its stylistic sprawl engages promiscuously with apparently unrelated musical sensibilities, yet forges them into a satisfyingly eclectic mélange.

While "Bohemian Rhapsody" has a sense of departure and return, David Bowie's "Station to Station" is a progressive narrative that mirrors the suggestion of travel between distinct places—either geographically, as suggested by the train sounds that open the track; or psychically, as the protagonist lurches from one self-reflexive position to another; or between places in disembodied aural space among the stations on a radio's dial, as the track seems to lead us through several songs strung end-to-end. The track's first instrumental section (i.e., following the train sounds) articulates a persistent half-step riff—C♯–C over a bass note A (1:13)—that is joined eventually by a stomping groove and a periodic VI–VII–I harmonic/rhythmic interruption that carves repeated five-bar phrases (Example 13.3). The voice enters finally at 3:18, causing a disruption of its own as groove, key, and riff are all instantly displaced by a brief foray into a surreal calypso that marks "the return of the thin white duke." The sudden shift in texture and harmonic style are a jolt, as though the listener is passing through a doorway between musical worlds. There is, however, one bit of consistency, for the duke's visit lasts but five bars, just like all the previous phrases. Then we are plunged back into the previous music, which repeats its five-bar sequence, now with an overlay of lyric imagery, through ten iterations—about a minute and a half of gathering intensity reflected in the increased urgency of Bowie's singing. Finally (at 4:50) the duke's music returns and is itself repeated several times to conclude this section of the track.

Example 13.3 David Bowie, "Station to Station" (David Bowie), *Station to Station* (1976): opening riff featuring half-step.

To this point, which brings us up to a little over five minutes, we've had a pretty odd song incorporating a jarring musical juxtaposition. But idiosyncrasy is certainly not unusual for the ever-experimental 1970s Bowie, passing here through his "plastic soul" phase on the way to his avant-pop Berlin trilogy during a time of heavy cocaine use and a displaced existence in Los Angeles. If the train sounds were to be nipped off the front of the track, it could be a radio single. But this first half of the song has really only set the scene for the glam rave-up that follows, itself a three-part series of musical ideas. The first two—ten (5:20) and eleven (5:40) bars, respectively—are heard only once each, serving, on one hand, as an introduction to the track's final section, which will go on for four minutes. But Bowie also invents a clever disguise here, for what sounds like a new song beginning turns out to be a transition from the track's first half to its second. The transitional conceit is hidden in the metric proportion, as the first ten bars ("Once there were mountains")—otherwise entirely different from the preceding music—retain the five-bar phrase lengths of the opening section. Having changed all other aspects of the music, Bowie finally begins to move away from five-bar phrases beginning in measure 11 with a two-bar interruption ("Wonder who, wonder who, wonder when" [5:40]) followed by a thrice-repeated three-bar phrase that leads to the final section. Each new idea in this series emerges seamlessly, like a stream of consciousness narrative dictating its own logic. And part of the logic is the unfolding style pageant that, from a standpoint of personal interpretation, invokes ABBA, Queen, and T. Rex all fashioned in the image of Bowie.

The Singer/Songwriter (and the Punk)

Rock epics are often born of a set of lyrics that resist containment in conventional song forms. Stephen Stills' lyrics for "Suite: Judy Blue Eyes" were drawn from what he calls a "long narrative poem" written to exorcise the emotional pain of his breakup with Judy Collins. It was the form and meter of the poem that dictated some of the musical decisions in the song (Rogan 1998, 8). While the folk-derived diatonic and strophic qualities generally characteristic of the 1970s singer/songwriter genre seem rather spartan compared to the musical extravagance of Led Zeppelin or Queen, the genre's emphasis on lyric imagery can lead to surprising twists in a song's musical narrative. For as the music meets the lyrics' dramatic requirements, it may assume a flexibility of form akin to a film score.

One of the wordiest of early 1970s songwriters was Bruce Springsteen, whose first album, *Greetings from Asbury Park*, gained him the dubious "new Dylan" accolade. As Ken Emerson wrote in *Rolling Stone*, the songs "sounded like 'Subterranean Homesick Blues' played at 78, a typical five-minute track bursting with more words than this review" (Emerson 1974, 49). With his second album, *The Wild, the Innocent & the E Street Shuffle*, Springsteen put his wordplay to use in generating epic tracks filled with image-laden stories of street characters real and imagined, and musical settings whose contours belie their relatively limited musical resources. Of the album's seven tracks, four top seven minutes in length. Springsteen told an interviewer at the time that, unhappy with the folkie associations of his first album, he had sought to capture the feel and style of his live show developed in the bars of New Jersey—songs based on simple harmonic frames that nevertheless built up to extended narratives whose forms appeared conventional yet, in following an episodic narrative rhythm, were in fact whimsically irregular (see Rockwell 1975, 10). In Emerson's characterization, the "songs dart and swoop from tempo to tempo and from genre to genre, from hell-bent-for-leather rock to luscious schmaltz to what is almost recitative" (Emerson 1974, 50).

"Incident on 57th Street," for example, initially presents a typical verse/pre-chorus/chorus design, but because the flow of the story governs the form, the song ends up feeling less sectional than my description suggests. Several factors account for this. First, the initial statement is an extended one; the first verse (which is in two sections of eighteen [9 + 9] and fourteen bars, respectively) and pre-chorus last one minute and forty-five seconds—long enough to leave precise metric proportions obscure in the listener's memory. In addition, the metric phrase scheme of the verse and pre-chorus is prose-like in its irregularity:

Verse 1, section 1 (0:28+)—18 (as 9 + 9) bars
Verse 1, section 2 (1:07+)—14 (as 4 + 4 + 6) bars
Pre-chorus (1:38+)—17 (as 6 + 11) bars.

Following the chorus (Spanish Johnny's reassuring "Goodnight, it's alright Jane" [2:15–2:49]), the second verse begins as though adhering to a conventional strophic design, remarkable only insofar as the two nine-bar phrases are shortened to eight, each simply removing the pauses in the vocal line. The verse's second section, however, is omitted as the song moves straight to the pre-chorus. But the second pre-chorus is deceptive, because Springsteen follows it not with another chorus but with a third verse whose first section is elongated by eight bars, as the story demands. The verse's second section ("Those romantic young boys" [4:42–5:06]) is once again included, but it is different from its initial appearance in both length and chord sequence; indeed, its focus on the subdominant is the only thing it has in common with the first verse. It feels more like a new section of music, and in fact it functions as one since it replaces the pre-chorus, which is not heard again. Instead, the third verse is followed by the song's first and only refrain (5:07+) in the form of the previously withheld chorus. Using the chorus this way changes its conventional function, for it does not allow the chorus to be taken for granted. Instead of a regular recurrence anchoring the song's progression with a sure sense of repetition occurring at prescribed intervals, this chorus only makes itself known as such after more than five minutes of track time. It then repeats with ever more urgency for over two minutes, Johnny's whispered promise of a meeting on "Lover's Lane" rising to ecstatic cries capped by a guitar solo (6:48–7:20), and then recedes to the solo piano coda. In its postponement, the chorus seems to have gathered an extra degree of energy that now spills forth to serve as the track's climactic conclusion.

"Incident on 57th Street" is followed by a transitional passage leading directly into "Rosalita (Come Out Tonight)," one of the finest examples of recorded bar-band rock I know of. This sort of loose-grooved, rough, and spontaneous-sounding performance is thrilling in live shows, but notoriously difficult to capture effectively in the studio.[5] Again, the structure is deceptively simple, and again the unexpected diversions and asymmetries are indicated by the story's flow, which reaches its apex in a shouted chant (6:32+), its energy—and Springsteen's ardor—no longer containable in melody. At the track's end, some fifteen minutes into the album side, we finally get a break. Then follows the album's final song, the nearly ten-minute-long "New York City Serenade." The track's introduction begins with a solo piano film noir emulation, courtesy of David Sancious, that sets a scene by turns mysterious (strummed piano-harp chords), melodramatic (mock classical gestures), and world-weary (blues-inflected gestures). The texture then settles into a lovely atmosphere of piano and acoustic guitar intoning a I–vi–ii–IV chord sequence again and again, while congas sketch an airy groove. The introduction creates both a mood and a sense of casual pace as the musicians take their time getting into the flow. Finally, just when many pop singles would be ending—at around two-and-a-half minutes—the vocal and then the bass enter. What ensues is a soulful rumination filled with allusions to a romantic cityscape peopled with shadowy characters—"Billy," "Diamond Jackie," "Fish Lady," "Junk Man"—sketched in cryptic strokes as the harmonic mantra repeats, lifting the track finally to yet another of the album's ecstatic moments.

As in Van Morrison's "Madame George," the repeating harmonic series serves as an extended drone over which Springsteen's textures, made up of both composed and improvised events, wax and wane in a sonic choreography that mirrors the singer's expressive mood. Although the overall feeling is of a continuous narrative unfolding, the track does have section breaks in the form of three shifts to the relative minor that approximate the feeling of a bridge. While most of the track is a play of shifting textures over the four-chord series, the breaks also give it an articulated shape of irregular design. The four primary sections have differing lengths of sixteen, thirty-six, sixteen, and sixty-four bars; that is, we never know if or when a bridge section will interrupt the flow. And when they do surprise us, the bridge sections vary in sonic texture, tempo, harmonic rhythm, and length, while their lyrics move from narrative description ("Jackie's heels are stacked") to call-and-response chant ("She won't take the train") to introspection ("Save your notes"). Once again, Springsteen and the E Street Band manage to create from a limited set of resources an expansive and free-flowing narrative. In his 1975 *Rolling Stone* feature on Springsteen, John Rockwell wrote, "One of the astonishing things about his music is the way he recycles stylistic bits and pieces from so many rock, pop, R&B, and even Broadway artists of the past 20 years—from Elvis to Dylan to the Drifters to Van Morrison to Leonard Bernstein and his *West Side Story*" (Rockwell 1975, 9). "New York Serenade" exactly embodies Rockwell's assertion and, as such, it is infused with the same eclectic attitude as our Zeppelin, Bowie, and Queen tracks.

Springsteen's flirtation with epic rock would continue for one more album. Garnering far wider notice than his relatively poor-selling first two efforts, *Born to Run* landed Springsteen on the covers of both *Newsweek* and *Time* in the same week in October 1975. In his *Rolling Stone* review, Greil Marcus pronounced the "sound" itself to be "epic" and "full of grandeur," invoking Phil Spector yet to be most truly "compared only to the music of Bob Dylan & the Hawks made onstage in 1965 and '66"—that is, comparable to some of rock's legendary figures and performances. The album, much more rocking than the first two, is capped by the nine-and-a-half minute "Jungleland," Springsteen's own "Bohemian Rhapsody." "Jungleland" is more composed than the earlier tracks, with more elaborate string arrangements, unison instrumental gestures, and architectonic key areas. Even the saxophone solo was worked out in the studio note by note (see Springsteen 2005). "Jungleland" has a more stilted feel than the tracks on the previous album, its more stylized character probably the result of too little improvisation, too much fretful overworking. Whatever the case, Springsteen would move away from epic songs following *Born to Run*. He would still think big; it might be argued that all Springsteen albums are concept albums. But the individual songs would be to the point. If his fifth album, *The River*, was a sprawling double-LP affair, its songs, in and of themselves, were not; the album's hit single, Springsteen's first Top-Ten hit, was the early 1960s throwback "Hungry Heart." The singer/songwriter genre, however, continued to produce ambitious efforts into the early 1980s, notably on records from Rickie Lee Jones (*Pirates*: "Living It Up," "Traces of the Western Slope") and Dire Straits (led by Mark Knopfler), whose *Love Over Gold* has only five tracks, including the nearly fifteen-minute-long "Telegraph Road."

Aside from its loose connection to the extended strophic ballad, the epic impulse among singer/songwriters seems a bit surprising, for its artifice-laden methods would seem to run counter to the sensibilities of a "direct, confessional troubadour," the genre's conventionally authentic, if problematic, image (Maslin 1980, 340). Seemingly even more oxymoronic, however, is the notion of the monumental punk statement. Punk defined itself, in part, as a reaction against all that had become excessive in rock. Punk songs were meant to be short, direct, to the point. And largely, they were. Patti Smith's epic cover of "Gloria," or her own "Birdland," are exceptions that conflate punk attitude and avant garde artiness. But if punk's songs were compact, its aesthetic and political statements were another matter, particularly in Britain. The Clash were punk's Beatles, Dylan, and Rolling Stones all in one. That is, when it came to hooks, they had fine pop sensibilities; their lyrics were both evocative and poetic; and they were a superb live rock band. If the Sex Pistols defined British punk's public snottiness and anarchic rebellion, the Clash were its musical soul and substance. It is worth noting, then, that in articulating and solidifying their premier punk position, the Clash, on two occasions, gathered their gem-like pop songs into mammoth collections worthy of the prog "dinosaurs" that punk had sought to overthrow, with the double-LP *London Calling* and the triple-LP *Sandinista*. Clearly, the punks of the 1970s, like the singer/songwriters, the bar bands, the Southern rockers, the glams, the funksters, the hard rockers, and the pop rockers, had a taste for the grandiose.

Brevity, of course, does not limit a pop song's expressive scope. Indeed, it is often key to a song's impact, as what remains unsaid resonates between the lines and in the listener's imagination. This old truth reasserted itself in the 1980s, when all genres of pop music, as if recovering from an extended bout of profligacy, turned again to concision. David Bowie joined with disco producer Nile Rodgers to make *Let's Dance*, which spun off three Top-Twenty singles; Springsteen made *Born in the U.S.A*, which yielded seven Top-Ten singles; Led Zeppelin was replaced as hard rock hit-maker by the likes of Def Leppard, produced by multi-platinum pop wizard Mutt Lange; Queen had their biggest hit in the U.S. with the neo-rockabilly number-one shuffle "Crazy Little Thing Called Love"; Dire Straits' *Brothers in Arms* generated three Top-Twenty pop singles; and the second British invasion, dominated by synth pop, peppered the charts with pithy tracks such as the Eurhythmics' "Sweet Dreams (Are Made of This)." Even elements of prog and art-rock embraced the resurgent single-mania. Yes, now with South African guitarist Trevor Rabin and producer Trevor Horn on board (the latter, fresh from his mega-hit production of Frankie Goes to Hollywood's "Relax"), released "Owner of a Lonely Heart" and had their only Top-Ten hit, reaching number 1. Former Yes guitarist Steve Howe joined former members of Emerson, Lake & Palmer (Carl Palmer) and King Crimson (John Wetton) to form Asia ("Heat of the Moment"). Genesis guitarist Mike Rutherford formed the band Mike + the Mechanics ("All I

Need Is a Miracle"), while two other former Genesis members—Peter Gabriel and, most dramatically, Phil Collins—became reliable pop hit-makers. From the ranks of the pop-rock singer/songwriters, Billy Joel followed his most thoughtful and complex album, *The Nylon Curtain*, with *An Innocent Man*, a paean to his musical roots in 45-rpm singles.

Overall, however, the shift in the 1980s was not an exercise in nostalgia. New sounds and styles of performance and recording mingled with residue from new wave, punk, disco, and prog in a pop nouveau that spread around the world. Emblematic of the change was the deadpan Human League anti-epic "Don't You Want Me," which topped the charts in 1982. Pop music of many stripes—the Police, the Eurhythmics, Cyndi Lauper, Michael Jackson, Culture Club, Lionel Richie, Madonna, Whitney Houston, John Cougar (Mellencamp), Huey Lewis and the News, Men at Work—was catchy, danceable, and single-oriented. The remaining bastion for long tracks was the dance mix (a mid-1980s retail staple as well as dance club fixture), which provided an outlet both for such extended hip-hop tracks as Grandmaster Flash and the Furious Five's "The Message" and for twelve-inch remixes of pop hits in all genres. In the case of the latter, however, the compositional control was ceded largely to remix engineers and producers who had their way with artists' recorded tracks, aiming to raise the record to a higher level of danceability while slicing, dicing, and overdubbing their way to an altogether different version from the original. While twelve-inch singles did not expand a song's essential lyric, they did often create sonic narratives of some intricacy and scope.[6]

Rock epics embody an aesthetic ambition that had been growing since the late 1950s. Just before his death in 1959, Buddy Holly was recording with orchestra, sketching home demos in his Greenwich Village apartment with his own tape recorder, and making a list of lofty aspirations: "making a jazz album, a Cajun album, even an album of classical pieces," as well as a duo album with Ray Charles (Norman 1996, 236). Roy Orbison's work of the early 1960s—songwriting, singing, and recording—exhibits a complex musical sensibility that had been shaped over years. Jerry Leiber, Mike Stoller, Phil Spector, and Brian Wilson were assiduous and innovative in the details of their craft, driving progressive developments in pop record production. And the Beatles gave all rock musicians an example of sustained artistic growth that spanned their entire career. If rock and roll had sprung to life from the energy and spirit of amateurs, it fairly quickly assumed the trappings of professionalism. The 1970s saw the young idiom probing boundaries. Having participated in the heady business of creating a new musical language that happily borrowed from all others, rockers explored the possibilities it held forth. Moreover, record-making as composition was by now a settled issue. This conception of sound recording, key to rock's development, engaged a cinematic sensibility among recordists foretold early on in Sam Phillips's recollection of the first Elvis Presley sessions: "To me every one of those sessions was like I was filming *Gone with the Wind*" (Guralnick 1994, 132). The epics of the 1970s opened an expressive space that artists continue to explore. In that space emerges, from time to time, pieces like Radiohead's "Paranoid Android" and DJ Shadow's "What Does Your Soul Look Like Parts 1–4." If rock and roll was born of miniatures, epic rock showed that the idiom, using its conventional resources in fresh ways, could also work effectively on large canvases of opulent spectacle.

Notes

1. A survey of critical responses to rock's big ideas is beyond the scope of this essay. It is sufficient to note that critics often shared some consensus about what kind of grandiosity was acceptable. Led Zeppelin, for instance, were subject to general opprobrium, while Bruce Springsteen was celebrated as the "rock and roll future" (Jon Landau, *Real Paper*, May 22, 1974), his music so "stately … that it might be the prelude to a rock and roll version of *The Iliad*" (Greil Marcus, *Rolling Stone*, October 9, 1975).
2. Key overview: Verses 1 (0:00–0:25) and 2 (0:51–1:15)—E♭ minor; Choruses 1 (0:25–0:50) and 2 (1:16–1:41)—G♭ ending in B♭; Transition (1:41–2:01)—B♭; Continuation 1 (2:01–2:13)—E♭; Continuation 2 (2:14–2:57)—F; Chorus 3 (2:57–3:09)—B♭; Coda (3:10+)—G♭, A♭, B♭, A♭.
3. The long, album version of "Suite: Judy Blue Eyes" would have found its natural home on the FM dial, which, by 1969, played a significant role in breaking hit records. The single version was edited down to 4'35" retaining, however, the track's multiple-section form, albeit in a somewhat crude adaptation.
4. In a private communication of August 18, 2006, Walter Everett points out that "Light My Fire" actually had three mixes: the full LP mix, the 2'52" edit that appeared on both stock 45 copies and promotional singles for Top-Forty radio, and an FM edit that had some, but not all, of the organ/guitar solos.
5. For an in-depth examination of the issue, see Stokes 1977.
6. If artists had turned from epic *songs*, critics were still impressed by remixers' epic *tracks*. Jim Miller, writing in *Newsweek*, characterized Arthur Baker's remix of Springsteen's "Dancing in the Dark" (from *Born in the U.S.A.*) as "a rock and roll symphony in the spirit of 'Born to Run.'" Dave Marsh called it "a monumental achievement, making a great record even greater" (Marsh 1987, 234; Miller is cited in Marsh 1987, 233).

References

Amburn, Ellis. 1990. *Dark Star: The Roy Orbison Story*. New York: Carol.

Emerson, Ken. 1974. Springsteen Goes Gritty and Serious. *Rolling Stone* (January 31), 49–50.

Fast, Susan. 2001. *In the Houses of the Holy: Led Zeppelin and the Power of Rock Music*. New York: Oxford University Press.

Guralnick,. Peter. 1994. *Last Train to Memphis: The Rise of Elvis Presley*. Boston: Little, Brown.

Macan, Edward. 1997. *Rocking the Classics: English Progressive Rock and the Counterculture*. New York: Oxford University Press.

Marsh, Dave. 1987. *Glory Days: Bruce Springsteen in the 1980s*. New York: Pantheon.

Maslin, Janet. 1980. Singer/Songwriters. In *The Rolling Stone Illustrated History of Rock and Roll*, ed. Jim Miller, 339–346. New York: Rolling Stone Press.
Norman, Philip. 1996. *Rave On*. New York: Simon and Schuster.
Rockwell, John. 1975. New Dylan from New Jersey? It Might as Well Be Springsteen. *Rolling Stone* (October 9), 9–10, 20.
Rogan, Johnny. 1998. *The Complete Guide to the Music of Crosby, Stills, Nash and Young*. London: Omnibus.
Springsteen, Bruce. 2005. *Wings for Wheels: The Making of Born to Run*. DVD included in the boxed set, *Bruce Springsteen Born to Run (30th Anniversary Edition)*. Columbia 82796 94175 2.
Stokes, Geoffrey. 1977. *Star Making Machinery: Inside the Business of Rock and Roll*. New York: Random House.

Disc References

Asia. 1982. "Heat of the Moment," *Asia*. Geffen 2008.
Beach Boys. 1966. "Good Vibrations." Capitol 5676.
The Beatles. 1968. "Hey Jude." Apple 2276.
———. 1969. *Abbey Road*. Apple SO 383.
Bowie, David. 1976. "Station to Station," *Station to Station*. RCA APL1-1327.
———. 1983. *Let's Dance*. EMI America SO 17093.
The Clash. 1979. *London Calling*. Epic 36328.
———. 1980. *Sandinista!* Epic ETX 37037.
Crosby, Stills & Nash. 1969. "Suite: Judy Blue Eyes," *Crosby, Stills & Nash*. Atlantic SD 8229.
Dire Straits. 1982. "Telegraph Road," *Love Over Gold*. Warner Bros. 23728.
———. 1985. *Brothers In Arms*. Warner Bros. 1-25264.
DJ Shadow. 1994. *What Does Your Soul Look Like*. Mo Wax MW 027.
The Doors. 1967. "Light My Fire," "The End," *The Doors*. Elektra 74007.
Dylan, Bob. 1965. "Like a Rolling Stone," *Highway 61 Revisited*. Columbia CS 9189.
———. 1966. "Sad Eyed Lady of the Lowlands," *Blonde on Blonde*. Columbia C2S 841.
The Eurhythmics. 1983. "Sweet Dreams (Are Made of This)," *Sweet Dreams Are Made of This*. RCA AFL1-4681.
Frankie Goes to Hollywood. 1984. "Relax." ZTT-Island ZTAS1.
Genesis. 1972. "Supper's Ready," *Foxtrot*. Atco 7818482.
———. 1974. *The Lamb Lies Down on Broadway*. Atco SD-2401.
Grandmaster Flash and the Furious Five. 1982. "The Message" (12" single). Sugar Hill 584.
Hayes, Isaac. 1969. "By the Time I Get to Phoenix," "Walk on By," *Hot Buttered Soul*. Enterprise ENS-1001.
Hendrix, Jimi. 1968. "Voodoo Chile," *Electric Ladyland*. Reprise 2RS 6307.
Human League. 1981. "Don't You Want Me," *Dare!* A&M 4892.
Joel, Billy. 1977. "Scenes From an Italian Restaurant," *The Stranger*. Columbia 34987.
———. 1982. *The Nylon Curtain*. Columbia TC 38200.
———. 1983. *An Innocent Man*. Columbia HC 48837.
Jones, Rickie Lee. 1981. "Living It Up," "Traces of the Western Slopes," *Pirates*. Warner Bros. BSK 3432
The Kinks. 1969. *The Kinks Are the Village Green Preservation Society*. Reprise 6237.

Led Zeppelin. 1969. "Dazed and Confused," "You Shook Me," *Led Zeppelin*. Atlantic 8216.
———. 1971. "Stairway to Heaven," *Led Zeppelin IV.* Atlantic 7208.
———. 1973. "The Rain Song," *Houses of the Holy*. Atlantic 7255.
———. 1975. "Kashmir," "In the Light," *Physical Graffiti*. Swan Song 2-200.
———. 1976. "Achilles Last Stand," *Presence*. Swan Song 8416.
Lynyrd Skynyrd. 1973. "Free Bird," *Lynyrd Skynyrd (pronounced leh-nerd-skin-nerd)*. MCA 363.
Mike + the Mechanics. 1985. "All I Need Is a Miracle," *Mike + the Mechanics*. Atlantic 81287.
Morrison, Van. 1968. "Madame George," *Astral Weeks*. Warner Bros. 1768.
Parliament. 1979. "Aqua Boogie (A Psychoalphadiscobetabioaquadoloop)," *Motor-Booty Affair*. Casablanca NBP-7125.
Queen. 1975. "Bohemian Rhapsody," *A Night at the Opera*. Elektra 1053.
———. 1980. "Crazy Little Thing Called Love," *The Game*. Elektra 513.
Radiohead. 1997. "Paranoid Android," *OK Computer*. Capitol CDP 8 55229 2.
Small Faces. 1968. "Happiness Stan," *Ogdens' Nut Gone Flake*. Immediate 52008.
Smith, Patti. 1975. "Birdland," "Gloria," *Horses*. Arista 4066.
Springsteen, Bruce. 1973. *Greetings from Asbury Park*. Columbia JC 31903.
———. 1973. "Incident on 57th Street," "Rosalita," "New York Serenade," *The Wild, the Innocent and the E Street Shuffle*. Columbia JC 32363.
———. 1975. "Jungleland," *Born to Run*. Columbia JC 33795.
———. 1980. "Hungry Heart," *The River*. Columbia PC2 36854.
———. 1984. *Born in the U. S. A.* Columbia QC 38653.
Steely Dan. 1977. "Deacon Blues," *Aja*. ABC 1006.
Velvet Underground. 1968. "Sister Ray," *White Light/White Heat*. Verve V6-5046.
Wonder, Stevie.1976. "Ordinary Pain," *Songs in the Key of Life*. Tamla T13-340C2.
Yes. 1971. "South Side of the Sky," *Fragile*. Atlantic 7211.
———. 1972. "Close to the Edge," *Close to the Edge*. Atlantic 19133.
———. 1983. "Owner of a Lonely Heart," *90125*. Atco 7901251.

Contributors

Jonathan W. Bernard is Professor of Music Theory at the School of Music, University of Washington. His articles on the music of Varèse, Bartók, Carter, Messiaen, Ligeti, Zappa, Feldman, minimalism, the history of theory, and the history of twentieth-century compositional practice have appeared in numerous scholarly journals and anthologies. His books include *The Music of Edgard Varèse* (Yale University Press, 1987), *Elliott Carter: Collected Essays and Lectures, 1937–1995* (University of Rochester Press, 1998), and, most recently, *Joël-François Durand in the Mirror Land* (University of Washington Press, 2005).

James Borders is Professor of Music (Musicology) at the University of Michigan, Ann Arbor, specializing in the history of plainchant and medieval liturgy. His musical training began as a choirboy in the pre-Vatican II Catholic Church—the first music he learned to read was chant notation. Growing up in Chicago in the 1950s and early '60s led him to expand his musical horizons quickly. Disappointed by rock music and having turned his attention to jazz and R&B, he bought *Absolutely Free* from the cut-out bin at a neighborhood record store, not long after its release. Then, thanks to Zappa's recorded remarks (heard on the radio), he discovered the music of Varèse, Webern, and Stravinsky. A music nerd in elementary and high school, he later earned an undergraduate degree in theory and composition from DePaul University and a Ph.D. in musicology from the University of Chicago.

Lori Burns is Professor of Music and Associate Dean for Research of the Faculty of Arts at the University of Ottawa. Her work on Bach has been published in *Music Theory Spectrum*, the *Journal of Music Theory*, and by Pendragon Press (*Bach's Modal Chorales*, 1995). More recently she has written on popular music subjects, including articles in *Understanding Rock* (Oxford, 1997), *repercussions* (1999), *Engaging Music: Essays in Music Analysis*, (Oxford, 2005), and *Music Theory Online* (2004 and 2005), as well as reviews in *Popular Music*, *Notes*, and the *Canadian University Music Review*. Her book on popular music, *Disruptive Divas: Critical and Analytical Essays on Feminism, Identity, and Popular Music* (Routledge Press, 2002) won the Pauline Alderman Award from the International Alliance for Women in Music in 2005. The research for the paper included in this volume was supported by a grant from the Social Sciences and Humanities Research Council of Canada.

John Covach is Professor of Music at the University of Rochester and Professor of Theory at the Eastman School of Music. He has published dozens of articles on topics dealing with popular music, twelve-tone music, and the philosophy and aesthetics of music. He is the author of *What's That Sound? An Introduction to Rock Music* (Norton, 2006) and has co-edited *Understanding Rock* (Oxford University Press, 1997), *American Rock and the Classical Tradition*, and *Traditions, Institutions, and American Popular Music* (the latter two both 2000 issues of *Contemporary Music Review*). As a guitarist, Covach has performed widely on electric and classical guitar in both the United States and Europe and recorded with the progressive rock band Land of Chocolate. He is the host of Radio Rock, a weekly radio show broadcast on WRUR-FM in Rochester, New York.

Walter Everett is Professor of Music and Chair of the Department of Music Theory at the University of Michigan. He is the author of the two-volume book, *The Beatles as Musicians* (Oxford University Press, 1999 and 2001), and is currently writing another entitled *From "Blue Suede Shoes" to "Suite: Judy Blue Eyes": The Foundations of Rock* (Oxford, forthcoming), made possible by a fellowship with the National Endowment for the Humanities. He has written scholarly essays on many aspects of song analysis ranging historically from Mozart's opera to Beck and Radiohead, as well as on other topics, in nine book chapters and a wide range of music periodicals. Everett will serve as co-chair for the 2008 Mannes Institute in Jazz and Popular Music studies.

Susan Fast is Associate Professor of Music at McMaster University. Her work focuses on constructions of identity in popular music performance. She is author of the book, *In the Houses of the Holy: Led Zeppelin and the Power of Rock Music* (Oxford, 2001), a collection of essays that explores the body in performance, gender and sexuality, cultural appropriation/hybridity, and ritual/mythology in rock music. Her publications also include articles on Live Aid and cultural memory, constructions of authenticity in U2, and Tina Turner's gendered and racialized identity in the 1960s. Her current project, funded by the Social Sciences and Humanities Research Council of Canada, investigates normative genre boundaries in mainstream popular music.

Ellie M. Hisama is Professor of Music at Columbia University and a former Director of the Institute for Studies in American Music at Brooklyn College. She is the author of *Gendering Musical Modernism: The Music of Ruth Crawford, Marion Bauer, and Miriam Gideon* (Cambridge University Press, 2001) and co-editor of *Critical Minded: New Approaches to Hip Hop Studies* (Institute for Studies in American Music, 2005) and *Ruth Crawford Seeger's Worlds: Innovation and Tradition in Twentieth-Century American Music* (University of Rochester Press, 2007). She is currently writing a book on popular music, Asian Americans, and activism.

Nadine Hubbs is a musicologist, critic, and cultural historian with interests in classical and popular music. She has published on topics including musical queer codes in disco, sex-gender rhetoric in the songs of British pop star Morrissey, and lesbian-gay involvements in classical music and opera, and is currently writing on country music and class identity. Her book *The Queer Composition of America's Sound: Gay Modernists, American Music, and National Identity* (California, 2004) has been recognized by the Philip Brett Award of the American Musicological Society, Irving Lowens Award of the Society for American Music, and John Boswell Prize of the American Historical Association's Committee on Lesbian and Gay History. She is Associate Professor of Women's Studies and Music (Theory) at the University of Michigan.

Tim Hughes teaches popular music harmony, popular song analysis, African-American music, and traditional harmony at the University of Surrey, in Guildford. He has previously taught at The University of Washington, The University of the Incarnate Word, Saint Mary's University, and San Antonio College, and he is a former chair of the Society for Music Theory's popular music interest group. Hughes was also the Multimedia Editor for *The Jimi Hendrix Gallery*, *The Next Rock Record*, and *The History of Recorded Sound* at Experience Music Project in Seattle, where the work of his teams received numerous industry-wide awards. He received his Ph.D. from the University of Washington in 2003. His research interests include R&B, soul, funk, punk, hip-hop, and blues-rock, the music of Stevie Wonder, the use of repetition and grooves, and the analysis of popular music. He also still tries to find time to play guitar, sing, and write songs.

Timothy Koozin is Associate Professor and coordinator of Music Theory at the University of Houston, where he teaches courses in music theory, analysis, and music technology. He was an active studio musician in Los Angeles for several years before completing his Ph.D. in Music Theory at the University of Cincinnati. Koozin's writings appear in *Perspectives of New Music*, *Contemporary Music Review*, *Music Theory Online*, *College Music Symposium*, *Notes*, and *Computers in Music Research*. Known internationally as a specialist in music instructional technology, he is author of several multimedia software applications, including *The Music for Ear Training CD-ROM* (Schirmer, 2004). He is also editor of the electronic journal, *Music Theory Online*.

Jocelyn R. Neal is Assistant Professor at The University of North Carolina Chapel Hill. Her articles on early country music, narrative and songwriting in country music, and the relationship of music and dance have appeared in numerous collections and journals including *Music Theory Spectrum*. Neal regularly teaches classes and guest-lectures on rock music, country music, and the analysis of popular music, and she is the recipient of a fellowship from the Institute for the Arts and Humanities for a fieldwork project on racial identity and country music. She serves on the editorial board for *Southern Cultures* and is currently completing a book on the music of Jimmie Rodgers.

Mark Spicer is Associate Professor and Director of Undergraduate Studies in Music at Hunter College and the Graduate Center, City University of New York. He specializes in the reception history and analysis of popular music, especially British pop and rock since the 1960s, and his writings on this subject have appeared, or are forthcoming, in *Contemporary Music Review*, *Music Theory Online*, *twentieth-century music*, and other scholarly journals, as well as three essay collections (including *Rockology*, which he is currently co-editing, with John Covach, for the University of Michigan Press). He also maintains an active parallel career as a professional keyboardist and vocalist, and continues to take the stage most weekends with his own "electric R&B" group, The Bernadettes.

Albin Zak is Chair of the Music Department at the University at Albany (SUNY). He holds degrees in composition and performance from the New England Conservatory and a Ph.D. in musicology from the City University of New York. His research specialties are popular music studies (especially post-1945 repertories) and the history of sound recording. He is the author of *The Poetics of Rock: Cutting Tracks, Making Records* (California, 2001) and editor of *The Velvet Underground Companion: Four Decades of Commentary* (Schirmer, 1997). He is currently working on a book entitled *"I Don't Sound Like Nobody": Remaking Music in 1950s America* (University of Michigan Press). He is active as a songwriter, performer, and record producer. His most recent album of songs is entitled *An Average Day* (Insatiable Records).

Index of Names and Titles

C

E

M

Q

R

T

X

Y